"Johann Peter Murmann's book is a major contribution to our understanding of the inter-relations between technological change and industry evolution. This comparative study of the emergence of the synthetic dye industry wonderfully illustrates how differences in public policy, university traditions, and industry context affect both technical as well as industrial change. Murmann's book will have a major impact on coevolutionary theory as well as industrial policy. It is a book for researchers as well as for policy makers."

Professor **MICHAEL TUSHMAN**, Paul R. Lawrence, Class of 1942 Professor, Harvard Business School

● ● ●

"Murmann's admirable book provides the most persuasive account, to date, for Germany's early leadership and long dominance of the synthetic dye industry after the momentous, serendipitous scientific discovery by a young Englishman in 1856. It is an account that employs a sharply focused, coevolutionary lens upon the differing historical experiences of Germany, the UK and the United States. The book calls attention to the ways in which the earlier development paths of the German states had equipped them, much more effectively than their potential competitors, to exploit the specialized research tools of synthetic organic chemistry, upon which commercial success was to become heavily dependent."

NATHAN ROSENBERG, Professor of Economics (Emeritus), Stanford University

● ● ●

"Johann Peter Murmann's book shows convincingly that competitive advantage, especially in the knowledge-intensive industries, is firmly rooted in national institutions. Blending quantitative analysis and case study evidence over a period of decades, he makes a major contribution to the fields of strategic management, organizational theory, and technological innovation."

MAURO F. GUILLEN, Dr. Felix Sandman Professor of International Management, The Wharton School, University of Pennsylvania

● ● ●

Knowledge and Competitive Advantage

Entrepreneurs, managers, and policy makers must make decisions about a future that is inherently uncertain. Since the only rational guide for the future is the past, analysis of previous episodes in industrial development can shape informed decisions about what the future will hold. Historical scholarship that seeks to uncover systematically the causal processes transforming industries is thus of vital importance to the executives and managers shaping business policy today. With this in mind, Johann Peter Murmann compares the development of the synthetic dye industry in Great Britain, Germany, and the United States through the lenses of evolutionary theory. The rise of this industry constitutes an important chapter in business, economic, and technological history because synthetic dyes, invented in 1856, were the first scientific discovery quickly to give rise to a new industry. Just as with contemporary high-tech industries, the synthetic dye business faced considerable uncertainty that led to many surprises for the agents involved. After the discovery of synthetic dyes, British firms led the industry for the first eight years, but German firms came to dominate the industry for decades. American firms, in contrast, played only a minor role in this important development. Murmann identifies differences in educational institutions and patent laws as the key reasons for German leadership in the industry. Successful firms developed strong ties to the centers of organic chemistry knowledge. As Murmann demonstrates, a complex coevolutionary process linking firms, technology, and national institutions resulted in very different degrees of industrial success among the dye firms in the three countries.

Johann Peter Murmann is Assistant Professor of Management and Organizations at the Kellogg School of Management, Northwestern University. He is on the editorial board of the Journal of International Business Studies and is the editor of Evolutionary Theories in the Social Sciences.

Cambridge Studies in the Emergence of Global Enterprise

Editors

Louis Galambos, The Johns Hopkins University
Geoffrey Jones, Harvard Business School

Other books in the series

National Cultures and International Competition: The Experience of Schering AG, 1851–1950, by Christopher Kobrak, ESCP-EAP, European School of Management

The World's Newest Profession: A History of Management Consulting, by Christopher McKenna (forthcoming)

Knowledge and Competitive Advantage

*The Coevolution of Firms,
Technology, and
National Institutions*

Johann Peter Murmann   Northwestern University

CAMBRIDGE
UNIVERSITY PRESS

PUBLISHED BY THE PRESS SYNDICATE OF THE UNIVERSITY OF CAMBRIDGE
The Pitt Building, Trumpington Street, Cambridge, United Kingdom

CAMBRIDGE UNIVERSITY PRESS
The Edinburgh Building, Cambridge CB2 2RU, UK
40 West 20th Street, New York, NY 10011-4211, USA
477 Williamstown Road, Port Melbourne, VIC 3207, Australia
Ruiz de Alarcón 13, 28014 Madrid, Spain
Dock House, The Waterfront, Cape Town 8001, South Africa

http://www.cambridge.org

First published 2003

Printed in the United States of America

Typeface Garamond 10/12 pt.   *System* LATEX 2$_\varepsilon$ [TB]

A catalog record for this book is available from the British Library.

Library of Congress Cataloging in Publication Data
Murmann, Johann Peter, 1967–
   Knowledge and competitive advantage : the coevolution of firms, technology, and
national institutions / Johann Peter Murmann.
      p.   cm. – (Cambridge studies in the emergence of global enterprise)
   Includes bibliographical references.
   ISBN 0-521-81329-8 (hc.)
   1. Dye industry – Germany – History.   2. Dye industry – Technological
innovations – Germany – History.   3. Dye industry – Great Britain – History.
4. Dye industry – United States – History.   5. Competition, International – Case studies.
6. Comparative advantage (International trade) – Case studies.   I. Title.   II. Series.
HD9660.D843G35   2003
338.4'76672 – dc21   2003043048

ISBN 0 521 81329 8 hardback

For the one who knows my gratitude

Contents

Series Editors' Preface

By blending historical evidence with evolutionary economic theory, Johann Peter Murmann enhances our understanding of economic change and helps us see why firms and nations prosper or fall under the pressure of competitive capitalism. Central to this process in the Second Industrial Revolution was the ability to apply scientific knowledge to industrial processes in the electrical and chemical industries. Murmann surveys with great care the early development of one of those industries, synthetic dyes – an often-told story, but now placed in a new and exciting comparative context. Great Britain had the early lead in dyestuffs, but Germany parlayed a powerful scientific establishment and aggressive entrepreneurial firms into a successful challenge. Favored by its unique research institutions and patent laws, the German industry was able to lobby the government to strengthen its position even more. Coevolution of firms and national institutions was at the heart of a process that had important ramifications for the political economy of Europe and the United States in the nineteenth and twentieth centuries. Firms maintaining strong links to the relevant scientific networks prospered; their competitors gave way.

Murmann's dynamic model of this process should be of great interest to economic and business historians, economists, and scholars analyzing business management and strategy in the modern era. We are pleased to publish this innovative study as the second volume in our series, *Cambridge Studies in the Emergence of Global Enterprise*.

Louis Galambos, Johns Hopkins University

Geoffrey Jones, Harvard Business School

Author's Preface

Synthetic dyes represent the first time when a scientific discovery quickly gave rise to a new industry. In 1856, the nineteen-year-old William Henry Perkin serendipitously invented the first synthetic dye and successfully commercialized his discovery. Perkin, along with entrepreneurs from Britain and France, dominated the synthetic dye industry for the next eight years. Contrary to contemporary predictions, however, these firms were not able to sustain their leadership position in the new industry. By 1870, Germany had about 50 percent of the global synthetic dye market; Britain fell to second place. By 1900, Germany's worldwide share climbed to as high as 85 percent, where it stayed with relatively minor fluctuations until World War I. In the 1860s, American firms tried to be successful participants in the U.S. market, but they could not compete with German and Swiss firms before World War I and remained relatively small players or went out of business.

Adam Smith (1776) and David Ricardo (1817) and more recently Michael Porter (1990) and David Mowery and Richard Nelson (1999) are prominent examples of a wide array of social scientists who have tried to identify the factors that lead nations and firms to prosper. This book follows that tradition. In tracing the development of one industry within the context of three countries – Great Britain, Germany, and the United States – during the period from 1857 to 1914, I attempt to make a contribution toward formulating a much-needed dynamic theory of industrial leadership.

Frequently, enterprise, technological, and economic developments are examined in separate studies. In this book I bring together these different literatures and investigate an important chapter in business, economic, and technological history. I argue that a complex evolutionary process led to very different degrees of industrial success by dye firms in Britain, Germany, and the United States. Based on the empirical findings, this monograph articulates a dynamic model of competitive advantage that has at its center coevolutionary processes linking firms and national institutions.

The study identifies differences in educational institutions and patent laws as the key reason for the long-lasting German leadership position in this industry. When the German synthetic dye industry had pulled ahead of its foreign competitors, its superior performance allowed it to lobby government agencies to enhance educational institutions and patent regulations, creating a cumulative spiral of competitive advantage. To observe in greater detail how national institutions help or hurt the competitive position of domestic firms, I also analyze the performance of individual firms, examining the development of two synthetic dye companies (one successful and one unsuccessful venture) in each of the three countries. At the level of the individual firm, a key finding is what the winners in all three countries shared in common: In contrast to the losers, they had strong ties to the centers of knowledge about organic chemistry.

Many activities compete for our scarce attention. Because not everyone will have the time to read this book from beginning to end, I have designed Chapter 1 to provide a summary of the entire monograph. The sections in the introductory chapter that present an outline of evolutionary theory are a bit technical for the general reader, but the empirical analysis presented in Chapters 2 through 4 will be readily accessible to a wide scholarly audience. Readers who are most interested in the national industry level of analysis can skip Chapter 4, which presents detailed case studies of six individual firms. In contrast, this chapter will be most valuable for management scholars and business historians who look for thick descriptions of how firms actually develop over time. Those who are mainly interested in my articulation of coevolutionary theory of industrial development may want to jump directly to Chapter 5, where I spell out in detail how the national synthetic dye industries of Britain, Germany, and the United States coevolved with dye technology and national institutions. My hope is that Chapter 1 or Chapter 5 will stimulate many a reader to work through the rich empirical study of the synthetic dye industry between 1857 and 1914 that I present in Chapters 2 through 4. Enjoy!

Some of the ideas and empirical facts presented in this book have been published previously in articles and book chapters. Part of the demographic data on national firm populations appeared in the *Journal of Evolutionary Economics* (Murmann and Homburg, 2001). Some facets of the evolution of synthetic dye technology were described in a section of a chapter on the institutional foundations of entrepreneurship published in the edited volume *The Entrepreneurial Dynamic: Origins of Entrepreneurship and its Role in Industry Evolution* (Murmann and Tushman, 2001). A less detailed comparison of the British and German educational systems from 1857 to 1914 was published in a section of a chapter in the edited book *Chemicals and Long-Term Economic Growth* (Murmann and Landau, 1998). More information on these and other of my publications can be found at http://johann-peter.murmann.name.

Acknowledgments

What started out as a dissertation project at Columbia University now lies in your hands as a substantially revised, expanded, and more sharply articulated book. Although only my name appears on the cover, I want to acknowledge here that many people aided me in the course of analyzing the synthetic dye industry, which served as my laboratory for understanding a bit better the role of organizations in the economy. I would like to thank all of you who helped me to tell the beginning of what I believe to be an important investigation of how one of the first science-based industries developed. In particular, I would like to express my gratitude to the people who were most directly involved in the creation of this study.

As anyone who is familiar with his work will readily discern, **Richard Nelson** has left the greatest mark on this book. My study undoubtedly is much better because of his advice and encouragement. He was a superb counselor in writing a book that crosses terrains of literatures that were previously separated by disciplinary boundaries. Thanks, Dick!

Charles Tilly thought that I had a very promising book manuscript when he saw an early version of my study. Tirelessly and with breathtaking speed, he made extremely helpful suggestions on how to reorganize the early manuscript and gave useful comments on new draft after new draft. He also shared with me much wisdom about how to go about publishing a book. Chuck, merci beaucoup!

I arrived in graduate school with a plan to study social sciences broadly, but with a particular focus on psychology. This focus on psychology quickly was pushed into the background of my attention when I began to immerse myself in the literature on technological innovation as I was taking in the second semester **Michael Tushman's** organization theory Ph.D. seminar. Together with Phil Anderson, Elaine Romanelli, and Lori Rosenkopf, earlier doctoral students in the Columbia management department, Mike had done important work on the impact of technological change on the fate of firms and industries. In the middle of the term, Mike invited me to work with him on a paper that would clear up a few loose ends in the literature on dominant designs and the technology cycle. For the paper we eventually published, *Dominant Designs, Technology Cycles and Organizational Outcomes* (Tushman and Murmann, 1998), I read many historians of technology and became convinced that detailed knowledge of how individual technologies and industries developed was necessary if one wanted to build reliable generalizations. Mike, many thanks for getting me started on this. Take this book as a follow-up on the term paper. There are still some "loose ends" but not the same ones as ten years ago!

Chance favors the prepared mind. I was very fortunate that an innocuous reference led me to **Ernst Homburg**, whose knowledge of the early synthetic dye industry is unparalleled. The sophistication of the empirical analysis I offer in these pages owes a great deal to the computer databases Ernst and I put together on all the synthetic dye firms that existed between 1857 and 1914. As will become apparent throughout the text, when I refer to our correspondence, he helped me at every turn to get the history of the dye industry right. Thank you, Ernst. Now that the book is done, I look forward to analyzing with you in more detail the synthetic dye industry database we created. I am sure that when we publish the entire database on the Internet, it will be a treasure for other scholars.

It is a particular honor and delightful experience when a distinguished senior scholar with whom you have never interacted personally responds to your request for comments on a manuscript with, "I want to publish your study in my series at Cambridge University Press!" **Louis Galambos** helped nourish the infant manuscript into a grown-up book. I thank him in particular for helping me figure out how to write the concluding chapter in a way that it will be valuable for all three groups of scholars for whom this book is primarily written: management scholars and organization theorists, business and economic historians, and evolutionary economists. I also express my gratitude to **Geoffrey Jones**, who coedits with Lou Galambos the series in which this book appears. He was an enthusiastic supporter of the early manuscript and the need to subject it to substantially more work. Two original anonymous reviewers for Cambridge University Press did me the honor of pointing out how I could remove the shortcomings of an earlier manuscript. They pushed me to better situate my work in the literature on comparative business and economic history and to articulate more forcefully my theoretical arguments and the empirical support I found for them in the synthetic dye industry. A final anonymous reviewer prompted me to articulate more clearly the purpose of Chapter 3 in the overall architecture of the book and helped ensure that my claims in that chapter did not go beyond the data I could marshal for them.

Fellow comparativist **Mauro Guillén** went far beyond the call of duty in making superb comments on generations of drafts.

My arrival at Northwestern University in 1997 brought me in close physical proximity to **Art Stinchcombe** and **Joel Mokyr**. Art did me the great service of reading the manuscript with superb care, pointing out little tautologies here and there that needed to be fixed. His sharp and experienced eyes uncovered many opportunities to improve the manuscript. As you will find in Chapter 5, Art may have unwittingly sparked in my mind a key idea for making coevolutionary arguments work in the social sciences. It took a year for Joel and me to realize that we were both working on developing evolutionary models for the development of technology and industry.

Joel's comments on the manuscript and my conversations with him in the past years – especially when I visited him on the West Coast at the Center for Advanced Studies in the Behavioral Sciences during January 2002 – have been enormously beneficial in articulating the details of my coevolutionary theory.

Many colleagues did me the honor of reading at least parts of the generations of manuscripts that I circulated. **Howard Aldrich, Robert Aunger, Thomas Brenner, Guido Buensdorf, Bruce Carruthers, Frank Dobbin, Giovanni Dosi, Leonard Duddley, David Hull, Neil Fligstein, Martin Fransman, Jeff Furman, Gerald Hage, Rogers Hollingsworth, Paul Ingram, Gregory Jackson, Margaret Jacob, Mark Kennedy, Bill Kingston, Steven Klepper, Bruce Kogut, Ryon Lancaster, Arie Lewin, Ken Lipartito, Jim March, Stan Metcalfe, Keith Murnighan, Willie Ocasio, Nathan Rosenberg, F. M. Scherer, Andy Spicer, Max Voegler, Isabell Welpe, Ulrich Witt, Hagen Worch,** and **Ed Zajac** all helped improve the book. Besides commenting on an early manuscript, Jeff Furman convinced me that a timeline of the major events in the industry would come in very handy for the reader.

The "macro" colleagues in my department – **Bob Dewar, Bob Duncan, Ranjay Gulati, Paul Hirsch, Willie Ocasio, Mike Radnor, Huggy Rao, Alva Taylor, Brian Uzzi, Marc Ventresca,** and **Ed Zajac** – not only provided me with a sympathetic ear for my historical studies in our regular seminars on work in progress but also helped me figure out how to explain the importance of my study to an audience of organizational theorists. I have benefited from the collective brainpower that has been assembled in our department. Being surrounded as well by psychologists and social psychologists – **Jeanne Brett, Adam Galinky, Deb Gruenfeld, Vicki Medvec, Dave Messick, Keith Murnighan, Kathy Phillips,** and **Leigh Thompson** – has increased my awareness of the cognitive and social psychological influences on individual decision making.

I am grateful also to the two other members who, besides Richard Nelson, Charles Tilly, and Michael Tushman, served on my dissertation committee. **Jerry Davis** and **Rita McGrath** helped me think more clearly about an early version of this study.

I wish to express my gratitude to a few others who contributed significantly to the making of this study. I was fortunate to meet **Ralph Landau**, one of the successful American entrepreneurs in the chemical industry after World War II. On retirement from business, Ralph embarked on a second career as a prolific scholar. For almost four years I collaborated with this Renaissance man of the twentieth century on the book *Chemicals and Long-Term Economic Growth* (Murmann and Landau, 1998). Ralph shared with me his vast knowledge of the chemical industry, opened doors at synthetic dye firms, helped organize funding for this project, and invited me to many a lunch at 2 Park Avenue in midtown New York City, where we discussed the fine points in the development of the chemical industry. **Anthony Travis** was the first historian of the dye industry I met at a meeting of the Society for the History of Technology in Lowell Massachusetts almost a decade ago. He pointed me to many valuable sources of information for this study. **Kathy Steen**, whom I also met at that meeting, was an invaluable help in giving me sources on the American dye industry and sharing with me her fine dissertation on the U.S. synthetic organic chemicals industry, 1910–30. At the early stage of this project **Peter Morris** and **Robert Bud** of the Science Museum in London pointed me to the literature on the chemical industry.

Writing is, on one level, a deeply mysterious process. **Joy Glazener** was so kind as to read over the different generations of the manuscript to bring it closer to what Mr. Fowler would accept as the King's English. **Tom Wyse** and **Jean Schulz** helped in earlier versions to eliminate all the little mistakes that would distract the eye of the reader. At the beginning of the project, **Richard Tilly** commented on my study proposal, giving me confidence that I had the basic facts under control.

I received financial support from many institutions. I thank **Columbia Business School** for providing me with a four-year scholarship for their doctoral program. A travel grant from the **Chazen Institute** at Columbia Business School in 1994 got this project off the ground. The **Stanford Institute for Economic Policy Research** at **Stanford University** funded me for over a year to write a study of the development of the British and German chemical industries since 1850. The **Pine Tree Charitable Trust** gave me very generous support to collect data on the synthetic dye industry and complete my dissertation. The support of the **Kellogg School of Management** at **Northwestern University** allowed me to write this book when I was not teaching MBA students how to analyze and run organizations. I thank in particular Deans **Dipak Jain**, **Don Jakob**, **David Besanko**, and **Bob Magee** for their support. A sabbatical year in Germany that began in September 2001, first at the **Social Science Research Center (WZB)** in Berlin and later at the **Max Planck Institute for Research into Economic Systems** in Jena, provided the necessary time to finish the book. **Lars-Hendrick Röller** and **Jürgen Kocka** at the WZB and **Ulrich Witt** at the Max Planck Institute provided me with ideal conditions to bring this project to a closure.

Of the many people involved in putting my ideas into a physical book, I thank especially **Frank Smith**, **Catherine Felgar**, **Eleanor Umali**, **Virginia Marcum**, and **Bill Wondriska**. Frank Smith, my acquisitions editor at Cambridge University Press, skillfully managed this book from beginning to end and was a great partner in publishing a book we can all be proud of. A good copyeditor is worth gold; Virginia Marcum made sure my prose would not be an obstacle in communicating my ideas. Catherine Felgar at Cambridge and Eleanor Umali at TechBooks acted as competent production managers who kept the book on schedule. Finally, given that human beings take in most of the information they encounter through their eyes and the fact that this book deals with synthetic colors, this combination presented a once in a lifetime opportunity to produce a book that would be a feast for the eyes. Bill Wondriska's artistry turned this opportunity into reality.

Last but not least, I would like to thank especially **my family** for letting me go where curiosity would lead me and for supporting my endeavors in many ways over the years. Take this as the first report from my journey. Stay tuned for more.

Jorge Louis Borges (2000, p. 69) noted that "the concept of a 'definitive text' corresponds only to religion or exhaustion." Although I tried to remove all errors concerning the facts, any remaining mistakes will need to get fixed in a future text. I am confident, however, that the central empirical descriptions of how the synthetic dye industry developed can be relied on by generations of scholars to come. What may change are our theoretical interpretations that relate the facts in a web of causation and the relative importance of each of the causes. I urge the scholarly community at large to learn about my theory of coevolution and try it out in new arenas!

Timeline of Key Events in Development of the Synthetic Dye Industry before 1914

1856	Perkin discovers first synthetic dye, aniline purple (mauve), in London
1857	Perkin & Sons begins production of aniline purple
1858	The German firm Jäger enters the industry
1863	The German firm Friedrich Bayer enters the industry
1864	German immigrants form the British firm Levinstein near Manchester
1865	Professor Hofmann leaves London for Berlin
1866	Kekulé publishes his benzene ring theory
1868	The British firm Brooke, Simpson & Spiller (BS&S) is formed
1869	Graebe and Lieberman in Germany and Perkin in Britain develop synthetic alizarin
1874	Perkin sells his plants to BS&S and retires from the dye industry
1875	American Aniline is formed by German-born Victor Bloede
1877	All-German patent law is passed
1877	German Chemical Industry Association is formed
1879	The American firm Schoellkopf is formed in Buffalo, NY
1880	Professor Baeyer synthesizes indigo on laboratory scale
1881	Society for Chemical Industry is formed in Britain
1883	First patent for a direct azo dyestuff is issued
1883	Carl Rumpf hires the first three research chemists for the Bayer Company
1891	German patent office changes the application of patent law
1897	BASF produces commercially synthetic indigo
1905	Professor Baeyer receives the Nobel Prize in chemistry
1914	World War I disrupts German supply of dyes to the world market

1 Introduction

[M]ost of the fundamental errors currently committed in economic analysis are due to a lack of historical experience more often than to any other shortcoming of the economist's equipment[.]

> —JOSEPH A. SCHUMPETER (1954) in *A History of Economic Analysis* (Schumpeter and Schumpeter, 1986 edition, p. 13)

[The master economist] must reach a high standard in several different directions and must combine talents not often found together. He must be mathematician, historian, statesman, philosopher – in some degree.

> —JOHN MAYNARD KEYNES (1933) in *Essays in Biography* (1971 edition, p. 173)

I concluded in my most recent research that detailed longitudinal case studies, covering long periods of time, were necessary to study [competitive success] . . . This style of research nudges strategy research, and indeed industrial economics, into the world of the historian.

> —MICHAEL PORTER in *Strategic Management Journal* (1991, p. 116)

The Mecca of the economist lies in economic biology . . . But biological concepts are more complex than those of mechanics.

> —ALFRED MARSHALL (1890) in *Principles of Economics* (1997 edition, p. xx)

[E]xplaining many things about the coevolution of populations in a community requires narrative history as a complement to statistical analysis.

> —PAUL DIMAGGIO in *Evolutionary Dynamics of Organizations* (1994, p. 446)

There are few things – perhaps only one – that can arouse the passions of human beings as much as wealth. Humans need material objects to survive. But as social creatures, human beings desire wealth often not in an absolute sense of possessing more than before but in the relative sense of possessing more than one's neighbor. Thorstein Veblen (1899, p. 290) called this passion "the emulative predatory impulse," which he regarded as an evolved cultural modification of the basic instinct of workmanship that gave human beings a predilection for worthwhile achievement. It is not a coincidence that Adam Smith's classic text *The Wealth of Nations* (1776) was preceded by his *Theory of Moral Sentiments* (1761), in which he inquired into the passions that were necessary for creating a society capable of generating wealth. A close reading of Smith reveals that understanding economic inequality – a topic that became a key issue a century later in the development of sociology – was for him quite essential in identifying wealth-generating processes (see, for example, *The Wealth of Nations*, Book V, Chapter 1). Despite this longstanding human passion for wealth and the almost equally long-standing fear of destabilizing inequalities in modern societies (Hirschman, 1977), economics and sociology have not yet provided a complete understanding of how nations generate wealth and how they can distribute it relatively evenly. Even when we narrow the question considerably and inquire why nations differ dramatically in the performance of a particular branch of industry, existing theories do not provide us with an adequate explanation (Porter, 1990; Mowery and Nelson, 1999). Consider the following intriguing puzzle.

The Puzzle

London, 1856: William Henry Perkin serendipitously invents the first synthetic dye while trying to synthesize quinine, a medicine for malaria. Against the advice of his professor, August Wilhelm Hofmann, the nineteen-year-old Perkin leaves the Royal College of Chemistry and quickly commercializes his aniline purple dye, thereby launching the synthetic dye industry. From this time on, the industry continued to dazzle the eye with ever-new and appealing dye colors. Perkin, along with en-trepreneurs from Britain and France, dominated the synthetic dye industry for the next eight years. During this period, British and French firms introduced most other innovative synthetic dyes onto the market and held the largest global market share.

Contrary to contemporary predictions, however, these firms were not able to sustain their leadership position in the new industry. German firms such as Bayer, BASF, and Hoechst[1] (some of the largest firms in the global chemical industry at the turn of twenty-first century) started to gain in market share. By 1870, Germany had about 50 percent of the global synthetic dye market. Britain fell to second place. By 1900, Germany's worldwide share climbed as high as 85 percent,[2] where it stayed with relatively minor fluctuations until World War I. From the 1860s on, American firms also tried to be successful participants in the U.S. market but could not compete with

---

[1] Hoechst merged on December 15, 1999, with the French firm Rhône-Poulenc. The combined company was renamed Aventis.

[2] This is Reader's (1970, p. 258) estimate. Thissen (1922) provides a lower estimate of 75 percent for Germany's global market share. If one includes German plants in foreign countries, the share may have been as much as 90 percent. Even though there is no agreement on the exact figure, everyone concurs that German firms collectively dominated the world market on the eve of World War I by a wide margin.

German and Swiss firms before World War I; they remained relatively small players or went out of business.

Any explanation of the shift in industrial leadership from Britain and France to Germany quickly becomes mired in an intriguing puzzle where the obvious suspects have surprising alibis. Possessing cheaper raw materials or a larger home market cannot account for why German firms left British and U.S. firms in the dust, because both latter countries had more raw materials and a larger home market. Why, then, did Britain lose its leadership position? Why did the American dye industry remain so small before 1914? This book takes a new tack to resolve the puzzle by engaging in a detailed historical analysis of what caused this transition in industrial leadership.

The purpose of trying to solve this particular puzzle of why industrial leadership shifted during the first fifty-seven years of the synthetic dye industry is to make a contribution to two important intellectual agendas pursued by scholars in a number of different fields. Adam Smith (1776) and David Ricardo (1817) and, more recently, Michael Porter (1990) and David Mowery and Richard Nelson (1999) are prominent examples of a wide array of social scientists who have tried to identify the factors that lead nations and firms to prosper. For economists and management researchers, the question of how economic success is generated remains a key intellectual challenge (Kogut and Zander, 1996; Landes, 1998; O'Sullivan, 2000). In tracing the development of one industry within the context of three countries, I hope to make a significant contribution toward formulating a much-needed dynamic theory of industrial leadership. At the heart of the theory lies the concept of coevolution, which has been employed with much success by researchers of biological (Kauffman, 1993, Chapter 6; Thompson, 1994) and cultural (Lumsden and Wilson, 1981; Durham, 1991) change. Recently, ideas of coevolution have been introduced in the discourse on industrial leadership (Nelson, 1995a), technological change and economic growth (Mokyr, 2002), and development of firms (Lewin, Long, and Carroll, 1999). What we need now is a theory that does more than explain industrial leadership at a particular time. I believe a coevolutionary theory that models firms as interacting with their social environment takes a significant step toward explaining how industrial leadership is gained and lost and how small initial differences in performance can translate into large differences over time.

In placing national institutions and technology into the center of my analytical framework, I continue an unduly neglected tradition that flourished around the turn of the twentieth century. Prominent social scientists such as Thorstein Veblen (1915) saw national institutions and their effects on technological development as a key to understanding why Germany, for instance, achieved higher rates of economic growth than Britain in those years. More recently, scholars from various disciplines have relied on institutional accounts to explain both Japan's rise to economic leadership after World War II (Fruin, 1992; Gerlach, 1992) and its recent economic troubles (Thomas, 2001). Nobel laureate Douglass North (1990) has argued in a recent book for an important role of institutions in shaping economic performance. However, institutional arguments have long been given scant attention in economic analysis (Hodgson, 1998; Hall and Soskice, 2001).[3] The goal is to help move these arguments

---

[3] To be sure, in some areas of sociology, institutional arguments have been more prominent in the last couple of decades (Hollingsworth and Boyer, 1997). Scholars who compare the development of

once again onto center stage and to focus our attention on a critical missing piece in institutional analysis, namely, how institutions are created in the first place.

The book also tries to make a contribution to a second important line of work that concerns itself with the rise and development of the large managerial firm as a new economic institution. The business historian Alfred Chandler (1962, 1977, 1990), who pioneered the study of this corporate entitity that appeared on the scene in the second half of the nineteenth century, identified this new organizational form as a key source of economic growth over the past century. On the Chandlerian model, large firms – those run by professional managers rather than owners – came to dominate industrial activity in modern industrialized economies because they could operate more efficiently by exploiting the scale and scope economies made possible by cheap transportation (railroads) and communication (telegraph). Sociologists Neil Fligstein (1990) and William Roy (1997) have argued that Chandler's analysis is incomplete because it leaves out the political context in which large managerial firms originate. I attempt to integrate the writings on the rise of the large managerial firm in business history and sociology by focusing on how collective action on the part of firms molded the social and institutional environment in which firms operate. I marshal considerable evidence to show how the rise of the large managerial firm required the construction of an institutional regime that would favor such firms over other forms of organization. As we shall see, German firms in the synthetic dye industry were much more successful in molding their institutional environment than were their British and American counterparts. In Chandler's analysis of the rise of large firms in Germany, Bayer figures prominently (Chandler, 1990, pp. 474–81) as an example of how a sophisticated managerial hierarchy was created that could organize more efficient production than smaller firms could. I will argue that Bayer could only realize its economic advantage precisely because it became a key player in lobbying efforts to create a favorable institutional environment. Bayer's leaders sought prominent roles in the chemical industry trade association and participated in collective action to improve the German education system in chemistry as well as change German patent laws to give large firms an advantage over foreign competitors and smaller domestic rivals.

One of the key propositions of this book is that the creation of German dominance in the synthetic dye industry before World War I cannot be understood without coming to terms with successful and unsuccessful patent law, science funding, and tariff lobbying efforts in the three countries. My analysis of the synthetic dye industry shows that we need to rediscover scholarship that recognized the importance of lobbying in industrial development, such as Galambos's (1966) *Competition & Cooperation: The Emergence of a National Trade Association* and Hirsch's (1975) *Organizational Effectiveness and the Institutional Environment*. Comparing the fates of firms in the three countries, this study shows that firms depended on their social environment for resources to prevail against foreign competitors. In the case of Germany, firms were able

---

professions across different countries (Gispen, 1989; Cocks and Jarausch, 1990; Jarausch, 1990; Lundgreen, 1990; Guillén, 1991) cannot but notice the importance of institutional differences. Similarly, scholars of comparative management such as Mauro Guillén (1994) frequently appeal in their explanations to institutional arguments. Comparative political scientists have also frequently resorted to institutional arguments in explaining differences in behavior across countries. See Thelen (1999) for a recent review of this literature.

to obtain more resources from their social environment than were their British and American counterparts. My analysis of why German firms overtook their foreign rivals and then cemented their leadership is consistent with Pfeffer and Salancik's (1978) theory of resource dependence, which highlights the political nature of creating successful organizations. One of the critical resources that firms in the synthetic dye industry needed to obtain was access to organic chemical knowledge and dye innovations. Because this knowledge, as well as dye innovations, was heavily concentrated at universities in the early period of the synthetic dye industry, firms needed to develop ties to university professors and their students. Examining the dependencies of a dye firm through Burt's (1992) more formal, network version of resource dependence theory makes apparent that firms were competing for access to the leading organic chemists in the world.[4] Those firms that were able to maintain ties to the best chemical talent of the day outperformed rivals that were not as well connected. After working in a professor's university laboratory, chemists often moved from academia to industry, from one firm to the next, and sometimes back to a university position. This created an informal network of ties that connected players in industry and academia. Mapping the network on a worldwide scale for the period before World War I reveals not only that this informal network was overwhelmingly constituted of Germans but also that the central positions were occupied by players from Germany. Explaining the shift in industrial leadership in the synthetic dye industry is intimately bound up with being able to account for the strong and weak ties in what I will call the academic–industrial knowledge network.

The informal network assumed a second function beyond simply transferring knowledge about chemical synthetic dyes. It served as a mechanism for organizing collective action. A key reason why German firms engaged in significantly more successful collective action to shape domestic patent laws and university policies is that they could rely on a much stronger network of actors spanning industry, academe, and government.[5] To be effective in orchestrating lobbying efforts, the informal academic–industrial network was enriched by ties to high-level government officials. Where this industrial–academic–government network was large and close-knit (Germany), collective action on behalf of the dye industry tended to succeed; where the network was small and distant (Britain and the United States), collective action was more likely to fail.

Is This Book for You?

Having made a careful investigation of the synthetic dye industry, I attempt to articulate a theory of coevolution of firms, technology, and national institutions so that other scholars can join the effort to formulate a rigorous theory of coevolution and to collect empirical support for it. My goal is to stimulate debate and new research rather than to provide the definitive word on the subject. I have not studied in detail all industries that ever existed from the industrial revolution until current times and hence it is an open question whether the theory I develop in this book is universal in scope. But my reading of other industry studies (e.g., Mowery and Nelson, 1999)

---

[4] My empirical analysis does not present a full-fledged test of Pfeffer and Salancik's (1978) or Burt's (1992) theories. Rather it draws on these theories to illuminate the historical dynamics in the synthetic dye industry.

[5] For an overview of the literature on organizational networks and alliances, see Gulati (1998).

gives me confidence that the theory provides a powerful analytical lens for industrial development in general.

Two communities – analysts of industrial leadership and scholars working on the rise of large managerial firms – are likely to find the study of the synthetic dye industry rewarding. If one surveys the literature in business strategy and organization theory, it becomes clear that both fields would benefit from devoting more attention to business history (Chandler, 1990; Galambos and Sewell, 1995; McCraw, 1997b; Jones, 2000; Lazonick, 2002).[6] Management scholars in business schools have become very competent over the past 25 years in conducting rigorous cross-sectional studies that relate differences in the structure of firms at a particular time to differences in their outcomes. But apart from organizational ecologists (Hannan and Freeman, 1989; Carroll and Hannan, 1995b; Rao and Singh, 1999) and several other scholars (e.g., Tushman and Anderson, 1986), not enough research on business strategy and organization theory is longitudinal in nature (Lewin and Volberda, 1999). Business historians, in contrast, take it as a given that understanding the actions of a particular firm requires the analyst to examine the development of the firm over time. Through a detailed study of the evolution of the dye industry, I hope to persuade management scholars that the field would be able to build more robust models of organizational development if it could draw on more historical studies.

This book also brings the sampling methods of organizational ecologists to business history. In doing so, I examine the entire population of dye firms that existed from 1857 to 1914 – large firms and small firms, short-lived and long-lived, failures and successes. Conclusions derived from the study of an entire industry become much more convincing if they are supported by detailed evidence from specific firms. Hence I also conduct matched comparisons of three pairs of firms – a winner and a loser from Britain, from Germany, and from the United States. These case analyses will demonstrate the benefit of examining causal processes with a higher resolution lens at the level of specific firms.

The resource-based theory of the firm (Wernerfeld, 1984; Dierickx and Cool, 1989; Barney, 1991; Teece, Pisano, and Shuen, 1997; Kraatz and Zajac, 2001) has received wide attention in the field of business strategy during the past decade and, given the current trend of viewing knowledge management as the key to success in a globalizing economy, the theory is likely to remain at the forefront of the research agenda. (See Kogut and Zander [1992] and Zander and Kogut [1995] for pioneering statements about the importance of knowledge in firm success, and Loasby's [1998; 2001] contributions on the cognitive foundations of organizational capabilities.) This literature identifies firm resources and capabilities that are hard to trade and hard to replicate as the key source of competitive advantage. Because empirical support for the theory has been collected generally within the context of one country, the resource-based theory of the firm has never dealt with the question of how the larger social environment rather than a particular firm itself may be an important source of

---

[6] Although many strategy scholars cite Chandler's (1962) book *Strategy and Structure: Concepts in the History of American Industrial Enterprise* as the pioneering study in the field of strategy, the share of historical analyses is much smaller than one would expect for a field that refers to *Strategy and Structure* as a foundational study.

competitive advantage. I show that bringing the resource-based theory together with ideas from institutional theory can refine the resource-based theory of the firm.

The new institutionalists in sociology and organization theory (Meyer and Rowan, 1977; Powell and DiMaggio, 1991; Dobbin, 1994; Scott, 1995) have argued against taking an atomistic view of organizations in which causal processes originate and end within the boundaries of the firm. Understanding why organizations fail and succeed, why they take on a particular form and not another, must be analyzed at the level of the field or, to use Marshall's (1923) term, the industrial district. The field comprises not only buyers, sellers, and suppliers but also regulatory organizations and a host of other supporting institutions. In bringing together the literatures around the resource-based theory of the firm and the new institutionalism, I develop the concept of "raw capabilities," which are created by the social environment and not within the boundaries of the firm. Comparing firms in the different national settings reveals that what firms do, to a significant extent, is to combine these raw capabilities into firm-specific capabilities that may be competitive in the global marketplace. The institutional environments in which firms are embedded frequently confer competitive advantage precisely because the institutional environments are hard to replicate and hard to imitate: They typically develop incrementally over long periods, their causal structures tend to be imperfectly understood, and changes in their makeup typically require agreement among a large number of actors, whose interests often do not coincide.

Institutional theorists in sociology have marshaled considerable evidence that institutions assert control over organizations (Dobbin and Dowd, 2000); with the notable exception of Holm (1995) and Ingram and Inman (1996), however, few studies have examined how institutions come about. My detailed account of how universities and patent laws were shaped through collective action should, therefore, prove valuable reading for the institutional scholar who wants to develop a deeper understanding of how institutions come about.

Evolutionary economists (e.g., Dosi, 1984; Metcalfe and Gibbons, 1989; Klepper and Graddy, 1990; Winter, 1990; Saviotti and Metcalfe, 1991; Witt, 1992; Nelson, 1995a) can profit from this study in at least two ways. Ernst Homburg and I argued in an earlier paper (Murmann and Homburg, 2001) that empirical studies of industry evolution have typically focused on one particular country. As a result, we have very little understanding of how patterns of industry evolution may differ from one social setting to the next. Are firms founded and dissolved at the same rates? Why are some national industries much more successful than others? Do industry shakeouts occur in every setting? Do industries run through the same stages of development in each country? Because the synthetic dye industry started at the same time in different national settings, a study of this industry can provide some answers to these questions. Although the specialist in evolutionary economics will read this book primarily for its empirical evidence, my formulation of a coevolutionary theory may provide the impetus for a vigorous debate about how to model coevolutionary processes of economic phenomena.

Economic historians have debated for some time why Victorian Britain lost its economic leadership position to the United States and, in some industries, to Germany. The study of the synthetic dye industry before World War I can be read as another chapter in trying to come to terms with the relative decline of Great Britain. The theme that the economic historian may find most intriguing concerns the less powerful social network and the resulting collective action problems that the British dye industry faced in mounting successful lobbying campaigns against established industries. The British dye industry and the other new science-based industries were at an inherent disadvantage against powerful existing industries such as textiles. Germany industrializing later would, of course, encounter the same problems, but to a significantly smaller degree than Britain because the textile industry in Germany was not nearly as large in relative terms as in Britain. As Gerschenkron (1962) highlighted some time ago, it is crucial to pay attention to both when a new industry arises and how existing institutions may help or hinder the development of a new branch of industry.

Finally, a few words about what this book is not: It is not new history of the synthetic dye industry. The specialist historian of the synthetic dye industry will thus not find a revisionist interpretation of the synthetic dye industry before World War I. I have not uncovered new data that would call into question all existing accounts. Because a comprehensive database on all synthetic dye firms before 1914 has never been assembled, my data collection efforts with Ernst Homburg allow me to offer a systematic investigation of the organization of dye industry, shedding new light on how Germany was able to become and remain the dominant player in dye-making for so long. While I have made all efforts to get the history of the industry right, the purpose of the study is not to record all facts that are available on the synthetic dye industry or to provide the reader with a comprehensive handbook on the synthetic dye industry up to 1914. The reader who requires econometric analyses to be persuaded by an empirical argument will also be disappointed. I do not attempt to estimate an econometric model. The purpose of this book is to articulate a coevolutionary argument about the dynamics of industrial leadership and provide empirical data that give such arguments face validity. I hope the book can stimulate other scholars to test the arguments in a more systematic fashion.

Key Ideas in Evolutionary Theory
Let me preview the theoretical argument that I develop throughout the book. I have formulated the precise mechanisms of my coevolutionary theory after constructing a comparative narrative about the development of the synthetic dye industry in Britain, Germany, and the United States. All good theory development in the empirical sciences is a mixture of deductive and inductive reasoning that involves shuttling back and forth between the two modes of thought (Glaser and Strauss, 1967; Stinchcombe, 1968; Skocpol, 1984; Ragin, 1987; Eisenhardt, 1989a). By first studying in detail the evolution of the industry, I have placed more emphasis on the inductive aspect. I will now present a sketch of my coevolutionary theory, but a full articulation of the mechanisms that allow us to construe firms, technology, and institutions as coevolving will wait until I have given readers an opportunity to learn about the development of the synthetic dye industry. This will permit readers to develop their own notions about the causes of industrial leadership before they see the details of my model. Furthermore, those who are not predisposed to accept coevolutionary arguments can learn about the developments in the synthetic dye industry without having to see it through the lens of coevolution.

Evolutionary theory in the social sciences is sometimes misunderstood and seen as advocating social Darwinism, a view in which "successful" individuals in society have the right to trample and exploit its weakest members because nature works to let the strong prosper and the weak die out. Quite rightly, this so-called social Darwinism has been rejected as pseudoscience, and many people now greet the unreflective application of biological concepts to the social world with strong skepticism. Unfortunately, many people who for good reasons reject social Darwinist doctrines throw the baby out with the bath water by rejecting evolutionary arguments altogether. Moreover, many do not realize that the logical structure of an evolutionary theory is much broader than its biological versions (Campbell, 1969; Dawkins, 1976; Dennett, 1995; Hull, Langman, and Glenn, 2001). Evolutionary explanations have been applied to a diverse set of phenomena such as the development of the earth's geological features, economic change, and the development of languages.[7] Given that evolutionary theories of language existed long before Darwin, an evolutionary theory should not be interpreted as "biologizing" social theory before one has studied the specific arguments set forth.

The development of languages is perhaps the best example of evolutionary arguments that carry a much-needed neutral connotation and do not come with the heavy ideological baggage of biological concepts. The proposition that all languages spoken across the world today have evolved from one or a few common ancestor languages that branched out into families and subfamilies as people migrated to new places over the course of human history is widely accepted (Samuels, 1972; Ruhlen, 1994).[8] Similarly, the idea that today's vocabulary is evolving through a process of creating words for new phenomena – the World Wide Web, the Web, the Internet, electronic mail, e-mail, and so forth – (variation on existing words) and winnowing out a few of them that become most commonly used over the long run (selection) is not controversial (Müller, 1870).[9] In fact, in 1859, Darwin in *On the Origin of Species* (1964 facsimile, p. 422) appealed to the work of linguists to illustrate his ideas of a biological genealogy, underscoring the fact that evolutionary ideas existed before Darwin's application to the biological world. Hull (1995) recently examined the formal structures that characterize the evolution of language and biological life and concluded that they are essentially the same. Clearly, language is a better entry point to rigorous evolutionary theories in the social sciences than biology is.[10] One must

[7] Lewontin (1974, p. 6) has argued that an evolutionary perspective is equivalent to being interested in the change of the state of some universe in time, whether that universe consists of societies, languages, species, geological features, or stars. This definition is a bit too broad because it turns almost any development into an evolutionary account. As I will discuss later, the criteria for a rigorous evolutionary explanation are more narrow. But Lewontin also underlines the key point that evolutionary explanations are much broader than their biological versions.

[8] For an overview of the early connections between evolutionary thought in linguistics and biology, see Schleicher (1850) for the state of linguistics before Darwin. The essays by Schleicher, Bleek, and Haeckel presented in Schleicher (1850) give an early reaction in linguistics to the ideas of Darwin. For a comparison of intellectual developments in linguistics and geology in the nineteenth century, see the edited volume by Naumann, Plank, and Hofbauer (1992).

[9] For a contemporary evolutionary theory of language change, see Croft (2000).

[10] The best model for the evolution of firms, technology, and institutions is evolutionary epistemology, developed by Campbell (1974), Hull (1988), and others. As Hull (1995) points out, the evolution of languages has the property that evolutionary lines do not cross. Linguists report that two distinct languages

realize, however, that evolution does not necessarily imply progress or improvement, but rather cumulative and transmissible change. No society ever creates a new language from scratch without borrowing heavily from previous languages. Similarly, no society ever creates new industrial practices without drawing heavily on existing practices. As a general principle, novel things come about by changing and recombining existing things. The excellent summary description "descent with modification" crystallizes the key point of evolutionary theory into three words.

Identifying the formal structure that any evolutionary argument must possess to constitute a complete explanation[11] will make it easier to judge whether the theory I am proposing meets the formal requirements of an evolutionary explanation. More general than Nelson and Winter's (1982) articulation of evolutionary economics, evolutionary epistemology as articulated by Campbell (1974) and Hull (1988) provides, in my view, the most useful starting point for an evolutionary theory of industrial, institutional, and technological development. Expanding on Campbell's (1969) variation, selection, and retention model of evolutionary change, Durham (1991, p. 22) identifies five system requirements for an evolutionary theory of change:

R1. Units of transmission
R2. Sources of variation
R3. Mechanisms of transmission
R4. Processes of transformation
R5. Sources of isolation

An evolutionary explanation needs to identify clearly a unit of transmission – for example, genes, ideas, values, words, or even entire languages (R1).[12] It has to specify how these units are transmitted through time and space – for example, sexual intercourse in biology or social intercourse in culture (R3). It needs to say where variations come from – for example, gene mutation in biology or invention in culture (R2). And it has to articulate clearly the process that transforms the system through selection – for example, changes in the frequency of a trait in a population based on

---

have apparently never merged into one common language. Languages borrow words from one another, but linguists have not been able to find a true merger of two distinct languages. Industrial and conceptual evolution, by contrast, are replete with mergers of distinct lines of development. Industrial firms often merge and so do schools of thought. Because industrial evolution and evolutionary epistemology share key properties, evolutionary epistemology is, in my view, the best model for studying industrial phenomena.

[11] I draw here mostly on the excellent work of the philosopher David Hull (1988, 1989a) and the anthropologist William Durham (1991).

[12] Units of transmission come in different scales. Both individual words and entire languages can function as a unit of transmission. Later I will say more about how to deal with the different sizes of units of transmission and the relationship between them. The term "meme" is becoming increasingly popular to refer to nongenetic units of transmission. Susan Blackmore's *The Meme Machine* (1999) provides a useful introduction to memetics. I disagree with her insistence that memes are the only units of selection in cultural evolution. Sober and Wilson (1998) provide the most comprehensive argument for "group selection" as opposed to the "individual selection" that Blackmore, following Dawkins and other neo-Darwinians, is committed to. For a recent critical evaluation of meme literature, see the useful collection of essays for and against meme theory edited by Aunger (2000). Aunger (2002) lays out in more detail a neurological, brain-based model of memes.

natural selection through differential birth or death of variant organisms in biology or differential adoption of variant ideas in culture (R4). To account for stable differences in systems of the same kind (for example, how it is that two societies speak different languages), an evolutionary explanation needs to provide for sources of isolation (R5). If we are concerned with the evolution of one particular population, a source of isolation is not required. However, when we are trying to account for differences among populations, we need a source of isolation that introduces a boundary around each population and allows each to take its own specific path. Boundaries do not have to be sharp; they can operate as gradients, such that a population is very dense at a center but further out into the periphery becomes sparse. In principle, anything that fulfills these five systems requirements can evolve.

Another, complementary, way to assess the analytical rigor of an evolutionary account is to examine it through the lens of the conceptual tools developed by the philosopher David Hull (1989c, p. 96), who argues that a successful evolutionary explanation has to specify two entities, an interactor and a replicator. Hull defines a replicator as an entity that passes on its structure largely intact in successful replications and an interactor as an entity that interacts as a cohesive whole with its environment in such a way that this interaction causes replication to be differential. Essentially, the concept of a replicator fuses together Durham's concepts of a unit and a mechanism of transmission. Because genes are the replicator in biological evolution, the term meme has been coined by Dawkins (1976) to designate a nongenetic replicator for sociocultural evolution. The concept of an interactor maps into the concept of a process of transformation in Durham's scheme. What is replicated is information that is contained in the structure of the replicator. In more concrete terms, an interactor is an entity that exists in an environment characterized by competition for resources, survival, and replication. In the realm of biology, the human organism would constitute an interactor and the human genes a replicator. Using these two technical terms, Hull then can define selection as a process in which differential extinction and proliferation of interactors cause the differential perpetuation of the relevant replicators. Selection can be interpreted as a filtering device of information in which some information is passed on while other information is discarded. Notice that Hull's definitions do not make references to concrete entities. Quite purposefully, he defines replicators, interactors, and the selection process as abstractly as possible so that they can be applied to all phenomena that may be generated by an evolutionary process.

In applying the evolutionary model of variation, selection, and retention, the challenge for the researcher of a concrete phenomenon – in the present case, the evolution of industrial structures – is to specify how variants are introduced, how selection leaves behind variants that were not as fit according to the prevailing selection criteria (criteria that in turn need to be identified), and how some variants are retained over time to create a historical trajectory or genealogy captured by descent with modification.

Selection processes can vary dramatically across different phenomena. A powerful evolutionary theory needs to specify the most important selection process among a host of processes that transform a population of particular entities. In 1859, Darwin (1964), for instance, brought a great deal of specificity to his theory of biological evolution by arguing that natural selection (birth and death rates of individuals), not other forces[13] that are clearly also operating, was the most important force behind organic evolution. Trying to model Darwin's precision, Durham (1991) in his theory of cultural evolution identified selection by internal choice of individual human beings and not imposition by powerful external people (e.g., in a conquest of a particular society) nor the birth and death of individuals (natural selection) as the key driver behind cultural evolution.

Analogously, a theory of industrial evolution needs to specify its primary selection processes. In my view, there are two key selection processes in the case of populations of industrial firms. Organizational ecologists (Hannan and Freeman, 1989; Carroll and Hannan, 2000) have focused on births and deaths of individual firms. Evolutionary economists such as Nelson and Winter (1982), in contrast, and scholars of organizational adaptation (Child, 1972; Nadler, Tushman, and Nadler, 1997; Kraatz and Zajac, 2001) have stressed that organizations possess some capacity to adapt to changing environment by changing their strategies and structures. But scholars differ widely in their theoretical positions on how readily organizations can adapt to changing environments. Evolutionary economists view firms as strongly constrained in their ability to change, whereas scholars of strategic management typically grant organizations a much greater capacity for change. On the adaptationist model, selection of particular organizational traits takes place through managerial decision making. The relative importance of these two selection processes is one of the big questions that has not been sorted out; in my mind, this should be a key item on the agenda of organization theory. Although addressing this question is beyond the scope of my book, I note, however, that selection by individual and collective choices played an important role in the evolution of the synthetic dye industry. The characteristics of national patent laws and university systems were clearly selected in part through the collective lobbying efforts of actors in industry, academe, and government.

For a long time researchers in many fields have debated what constitutes appropriate units of selection in evolutionary models. Hull (1989c) introduced the concept of replicators and interactors in part to clarify that there are two processes in selection, the making of copies of an entity (replication) and the differential survival of copies caused by environmental interaction. Hull et al. (2001) have argued persuasively that instead of asking, "What is the appropriate unit of selection?", researchers need to pose two distinct questions, namely, "What is the unit of replication?" and "What is the unit of environmental interaction?" Another key challenge, then, in constructing an evolutionary theory is to identify clearly what is the unit of replication and what is the unit of interaction with regard to the phenomenon to be explained. Before moving on to the evolution of industrial phenomena, I will identify a few other important features of a successful evolutionary explanation. We will see a little later how important it is to clarify what constitutes the unit of analysis to be able to study effectively the evolution of industrial phenomena.

In the debate about appropriate units of analysis, it is often forgotten that evolutionary theory is inherently a multilevel theory. Any evolutionary analysis requires at

---

[13] Darwin (1859) ended the introduction to *On the Origin of Species* with the line, "I am convinced that Natural Selection has been the main but not the exclusive means of modification" (1964 facsimile, p. 6). Later in the book he identified migration (p. 81) and sexual selection (competition for mates; pp. 87–8) as other, less important forces in the evolution of biological populations.

least two levels, a level identifying particular individuals that reproduce at differential rates and a level specifying a particular population that is the locus of evolutionary change. A simple abstract example illustrates this point. Consider a population of 100 individual balls, 50 being red and 50 being white (the example is chosen to underscore that evolutionary explanations apply broadly and not just to biology). Let red balls replicate at a greater rate than white balls but let both groups go out of existence at the same rate. If we examine what percentage of balls in the population is red from period to period, we would find that the initial 50 percent increases gradually to 100 percent. In evolutionary terms, the population of balls evolved with respect to its color distribution. If the relative rate of the replication and destruction of red and white balls is different from the one in our example, we would see very different evolutionary outcomes in the relative frequencies of white and red balls. Note that none of the individual balls "evolved" in any sense, because none changed its color. The first key point is that populations, not individuals, evolve. The second is that an evolutionary explanation requires the analyst to specify who are the "individuals" and what is the population in the analysis.[14]

Just as in other sciences, researchers of industrial evolution have debated extensively as to what constitutes appropriate units of selection and what units of selection are more important than others for industrial change (Aldrich, 1999, pp. 35–41, 336–40). Most studies have focused on routines or entire organizations as the units of selection (Aldrich, 1999, p. 35). But there are clearly other possibilities. Social activity is analogous to the physical and biological world, in that it is organized in multiple levels (Simon, 1981). Starting at the microlevel are the actions and reactions of individual human beings (Weick, 1979); at the next higher level are work groups and teams in organizations; and then business units within organizations; entire organizations; entire industries; communities of industries; the organization of national economies; and finally, at the most macrolevel, the world economy.[15] Given that an evolutionary analysis always requires two levels – individuals and a population – the most macrolevel, the entire world economy, logically cannot serve as a unit of selection. In principle, all lower levels could function as units of selection.

The primary units of selection used thus far in organization theory have been either entire organizations or routines/competencies (Aldrich, 1999, p. 35). There is of course no theoretical reason why other units of analysis at intermediate or higher levels of aggregation, such as groups within organizations or organizational divisions or even entire industries, cannot serve as units of selection in evolutionary analyses. As anthropologist Durham (1991, p. 428) remarks regarding organic evolution, "In principle, of course, the potential exists for natural selection to operate at any level in the organizational hierarchy of life where there are variable, reproducing entities (see for example, [...] Vrba and Eldredge 1984; Eldredge 1985)."[16] Just as is the case

---

[14] Organic evolution traditionally was conceived as a process that involved three distinct levels of organization. The standard formula for organic evolution went as follows: Genes mutate, organisms compete and are selected, and species evolve. Hull (1989b, p. 83) reports that biologists now know that this formula is too simple. The central idea in the present context is that evolutionary explanations require the researcher to track at least two levels.

[15] This list is not exhaustive. Other possible units of analysis lie in scale between the ones I mention.

[16] Evolutionary biologists have not as yet reached a consensus on whether selection processes occur at any level in the organizational hierarchy of life.

with organic evolution (and I suspect with other domains too), we have very little systematic understanding of the relative importance of the selection process at each of the different levels of analysis in shaping social and industrial evolution. In my analysis of the synthetic dye industry, I operate at different levels of analysis – routines within specific firms, individual products, firms, national industries, the global industry – without systematically sorting out the relative importance of each level. Unfortunately, I can again only highlight what is still missing in a complete theory of organizational evolution and must leave the task of filling this gap for future research.

An important step toward collecting the necessary data that will make it possible to sort the relative importance of different levels of analysis in industrial change is that researchers become much more careful in specifying their level of analysis. Michael Tushman and I (Tushman and Murmann, 1998) recently undertook a systematic analysis of the literature on technological evolution and dominant designs. We found that researchers more often than not confused these different levels. As a result, empirical investigations of a large number of technologies have not led to a cumulative body of knowledge. What is needed in the study of industrial change, just as in the study of technological change, is that researchers clearly specify their level(s) of analysis. In particular, this requires that researchers identify the level of analysis that lies directly above and directly below the level that is the focus of their investigation (Murmann and Tushman, 2001).

Until now the debate in organization theory has not incorporated Hull's (1989c, p. 96) insight that an evolutionary analysis becomes more transparent by specifying two units, an interactor and a replicator. Another step toward achieving greater precision in regard to the units of analysis in organizational analysis is to specify clearly the replicator and the interactor in a particular analysis. Hull (1989c, p. 95) explains that good candidates for replicators meet the general criteria of longevity, fecundity, and fidelity. Ideas, mental representations, models of management, organizational cultures, and rules in operating manuals in firms are examples of possible units of analysis for replicators in organization theory. Candidates for interactors, entities that interact with the environment and cause replication to be differential, are standard behavior (or routines, in the language of Nelson and Winter, 1982[17]) – individual human beings, work groups, divisions, entire organizations, and so on.

Many writers make the point that evolutionary theory is explanatory but not predictive. While true that an evolutionary theory cannot make point predictions – that is, foretell exactly, in every conceivable detail, what is going to happen in an evolutionary system tomorrow – in many instances knowledge about the path and present state of the system that is evolving allows one to make broad predictions. Just as we can predict with confidence that dinosaurs will not evolve by tomorrow out of today's existing animal species, it is safe to predict that the African nation of Uganda will not emerge tomorrow as the largest chip producer in the world. Evolutionary

[17] Nelson and Winter (1982) not only use the term "routines" to refer to expressed behavior but also liken the role of routines in organizations to genes in biological evolution. As the ambiguities in the subsequent literature shows, I believe it is better to reserve "routine" to indicate expressed behavior (the interactor) and not the mental representation (the replicator). See Cohen et al. (1996) for a good discussion of routines.

theory does not provide exact predictions of future outcomes, but it does provide scientifically rigorous explanations.

Finally, another important characteristic of evolutionary explanations is that they are probabilistic rather than deterministic (Sober, 1984, pp. 110–34; McKelvey, 1997; Aldrich, 1999, pp. 33–5, 200–1). While some theories predict that, given condition x, y is going to follow, evolutionary theory can only make statements of the kind that, given x, y will follow with a probability of z. Let x be the selection environment and y the fate of a particular individual in the population. Rigorous evolutionary theories will make probabilistic statements like this: There is a z probability that individual y will not replicate (die when the entity has a limited life span) under the selection environment x.

In economics, management, and organization theory, evolutionary theories have been developed for two important sets of reasons: (1) to explain industrial and organizational structures not solely in terms of the agent's intentions but in terms of the consequences of the agent's actions, and (2) to recast the fundamental assumptions of how human beings make decisions and behave. Unlike many other theories of action, an evolutionary account focuses on consequences and not intentions. If actions generate positive outcomes under the prevailing selection criteria (even if the outcomes are unintended), they are selected for by the environment and persist. If they generate negative outcomes, actions will be selected against and fade away.

Evolutionary theories try to overcome unrealistic assumptions about human beings in rational choice theories. Instead of viewing individual human beings as perfect calculating machines that can consider all possible alternatives for a particular decision, know the future perfectly (at least in probabilistic terms), and then calculate the optimal course of action, evolutionary theories see human beings as fundamentally limited in their ability to consider alternatives, foresee the future, and make error-free calculations (Potts, 2000). In Nelson and Winter's (1982) evolutionary theory of economic change, for example, behavior is less guided by calculating consequences than by following rules that have been developed for a specific situation. Because human organizations are composed of collections of boundedly rational individuals – to use Simon's (1981) famous term – they also make decisions largely by following rules or routines, Nelson and Winter's term for the predictable aspects in the behavior of organizations. (How preferences of individual human beings are integrated to form a "preference function" of an organization is, of course, one of the fundamental questions in organization theory.)

For the most part, organizations act on a simple principle: If a given routine works, let's do more of it; if it does not work, let's do less (March, 1999). In the language of evolutionary theory, actions or routines within organizations are selected for the perceived benefits they generate. Because the organization-wide implications of particular routines are often difficult to determine – especially if routines are highly interdependent with other routines – it is bundles of routines and not individual routines that are selected. The selection mechanism in this case is the market, which eliminates entire organizations that do not return an adequate profit.[18] When

---

[18] In line with the preceding discussion of units of analysis in social organization, it is, of course, possible that an organization is a division of a larger organization. Then the proximate selection mechanism

organizations fail because their collection of routines is not efficient compared with that of rival organizations, a particular routine goes out of existence together with all the other routines of the organizations.[19] Notice that we are dealing with two different units of analysis, an individual routine and an entire organization.

An evolutionary view of organizations has profound implications for how one will see industrial development, as will be detailed in Chapter 5. Here, I just want to make a few introductory remarks on how "the world of industry" looks through the perspective of an evolutionary theory. Because organizations consist of routines that interact in highly complex ways, managers more often than not find it difficult to figure out what makes their organization successful. This causal ambiguity is not a problem as long as the environment does not change. Managers can guide their organizations to replicate existing models of action as faithfully as possible without understanding the causal microstructure that makes their collection of routines successful. When the environment changes, however, this causal ambiguity makes it difficult to determine what the organization will need to do differently. The very process of constructing complex organizational routines that make an organization reliable poses an enormous challenge in the face of changing selection criteria. The evolutionary perspective of organizational change takes into full account the inertia that arises from existing routines. It highlights the fact that the historical path of a specific organization imposes significant constraints on where it can go (Aldrich, 1999, pp. 200–22).

The literature on organizations is filled with examples of organizations that were unable to transform themselves despite the best intentions of top management (Tushman and Anderson, 1997; Tushman and O'Reilly, 1997). After many unsuccessful attempts to change its organization, General Motors (GM), for instance, realized that introducing new work and management processes into its existing divisions for the purpose of producing small cars at high quality and low cost was likely to fail. Instead, it decided to create from scratch a new division to make small cars, Saturn (Woodruff, 1992). Saturn was given an enormous amount of independence because GM wanted to build an organization with entirely new routines and not allow the existing divisions to impose their routines, values, and structures on the small car operation. The GM example highlights that change within an organization often comes about by creating new, relatively autonomous, divisions, by removing resources from existing divisions, by selling off divisions, or by closing them down altogether.

Individual organizations are constrained not only because of their own history but also because they exist in larger social environments that impose additional limits on the directions an organization can take. Implicit in the framework of this book

involves managers at headquarters, and not the market, to decide whether to sell or close the division. Business units that vary in their profit rates contain variable reproducing units, which interact with an environment. Managers play the role of the proximate agents of selection by giving more money to invest in growth to (selecting for) profitable business units and by pulling resources out of (selecting against) relatively unprofitable units.

[19] Arthur Stinchcombe (personal communication, 2000) reminded me that strictly speaking this statement is not true if the same routine exists in another organization where it can reproduce. As long as the routine has a separate evolutionary dynamic, it can flourish even after the "death" of the organization. Stinchcombe pointed out that many of Napoleon's tactics and strategy routines survived because of the successful adoption by his enemies, which, for example, destroyed the French army that had conquered parts of Italy and much of Russia and Germany.

is that individual countries often are the appropriate unit of analysis for the impact of the larger social environment on a particular organization. Organizations typically borrow blueprints and management models from other organizations, whether they be competitors, suppliers, or customers. Practices that are prevalent or even taken for granted in a particular social environment are easier and cheaper to import into the organization than are practices that run counter to the way actors and organizations that are close in social space are organized (Tilly, 1998, pp. 76–83).

If individual organizations and clusters of organizations surrounded by the same social environment are limited in their capacity to adapt to an environment in flux, what are the public policy implications for change at the industry level? One key implication is that significant change at the industry (or population) level is likely to come from the birth of new organizations with different organizational routines and the exit of established organizations. Efforts to encourage existing organizations to transform themselves radically, as in the case of converting defense contractors to makers of consumer products, may be bound to fail. The routines that make an organization successful in getting repeat business from the military are quite different from the routines for marketing and selling to the private sector. Hence, public policy makers have to weigh carefully whether a better way to foster innovation and change in an industry may be to encourage the formation of altogether novel enterprises that are not constrained by historically accumulated and well-entrenched routines.

Evolution of Technology

Before offering a sketch of my coevolutionary theory, let me briefly lay out what it means for technology and national institutions to evolve. Having now identified the general requirements for a rigorous evolutionary theory, it is not difficult for us to identify the key features of an evolutionary view of technology and national institutions. Articulating an evolutionary framework for each domain will make it easier to spell out the more complex coevolutionary model that links the two with the evolution of industrial structures.

Scholars have long recognized that technological change plays an important role in industrial dynamics and economic growth (Usher, 1954; Landes, 1969; Rosenberg, 1982). Over the past two decades, empirical research has documented that technological innovations not only are able to create new products and industries but also can radically destroy the fortunes of existing firms or even eliminate entire industries altogether (Schumpeter, 1934; Gort and Klepper, 1982; Nelson and Winter, 1982; Tushman and Anderson, 1986; Anderson and Tushman, 1990). Many historians of technology have argued that the development of technology is best understood as an evolutionary process (Basalla, 1988; Vincenti, 1990; Petroski, 1992; Ziman, 2000).

Evolutionary approaches to technological change come in a variety of flavors. Let us first identify what they have in common. All theories share the idea that the invention process by scientists, engineers, and tinkerers provides the sources of variation (Durham's R2) necessary for an evolutionary account of technological change. Scholars also agree that social intercourse provides the mechanism of transmission (Durham's R3). The most important difference between theories lies in their object of analysis, that is, the "thing" that is seen as evolving. Some scholars such as Basalla (1988) and Ziman (1999) conceptualize technology primarily in terms of the physical artifact. Basalla studied in detail how physical attributes of artifacts, for example, the shape of axes, have changed over the centuries. On this materialist view, technological evolution occurs because the relative frequencies of artifacts with a certain shape change over time. Other scholars argue that what is central in technological evolution is not the physical artifact but the science, engineering, and design knowledge that goes into making a particular artifact. In the language of Hull (1989c) these scholars argue that technological evolution needs to be understood in terms of both a replicator (ideas, knowledge, etc.) and an interactor (the physical artifact). Behind this view lies the observation that particular technological principles often diffuse widely in the economy. Steam technology a couple of hundred years ago or integrated circuits during the past few decades, for instance, are seen as such important technologies because the knowledge behind these two technologies found their way into a great many different artifacts and thereby transformed the economy.

Following the pioneering work of Nelson and Winter (1982), Mokyr (1999) recently proposed a selectionist model of technological change that focuses on knowledge, not concrete physical artifacts, as the most relevant object of analysis. Mokyr's (1999) model distinguishes between two types of knowledge, knowledge of what and why (a type he calls omega) and knowledge of how (a type he calls lambda). Scientific and basic engineering theories, for example, would fall into the what and why category. In contrast, blueprints and instructions of how to make things (be they verbal, oral, or pictorial) would fall into the how category. Because the different pieces of knowledge in omega can be combined in a multitude of ways, they give rise to a virtually endless number of possible procedures (or techniques, as Mokyr calls them) for making things. From this set of all possible techniques, few are in use at any time. What evolves in Mokyr's theory is the relative frequency of techniques in existence at any time. Ideas serve as the units of transmission (Durham's R1). Given that there are always a variety of alternative ways to accomplish a particular technological goal, techniques compete with one another for adopters. The selection mechanism that transforms populations of techniques (Durham's R4) is the choice of users to adopt or abandon a certain technique. Those techniques that find a larger number of adopters become more prevalent in a particular technological domain, and those that lose users and do not gain new adopters shrink in importance or may go out of existence altogether.

Scholars of technological change also differ in their views of the selection criteria that lead to differential replication among technological variants. On the one extreme are those who believe that the best technology always succeeds against inferior alternatives. Let us call them the "strong technological efficiency school" (see Liebowitz and Margolis, 1999, for a statement of the technological efficiency position). On the other extreme are scholars who believe that social criteria, such as political and economic power of particular groups, determine which technological variants thrive and which ones fail. Let us call them the "strong social constructionists" (see Bijker, Hughes, and Pinch, 1987, and Bijker and Law, 1992, for a statement of the social constructionist position). Many scholars lie somewhere in between these extremes, holding the view that under some circumstances social factors dominate selection, and under other conditions technical factors dominate (see Vincenti, 1991, for a statement of this position). Our previous discussion of the requirements for a rigorous evolutionary theory makes it plain that both views can be incorporated into an evolutionary model. As long as the theory specifies clearly the selection criterion – be it efficiency or social power or something else – it can constitute a proper evolutionary explanation. A little later, in discussing the economics of dye-making, I will give evidence that technical efficiency was the most important selection criterion in the case of synthetic dyes.

Let us return to the debate about the appropriate object of analysis in the evolution of technology. Ziman (1999) is well aware that technological artifacts are embedded in bodies of knowledge and social practices, but he argues that focusing on artifacts avoids the enormous problems of operationalizing a theory, à la Mokyr, that is based on knowledge and ideas as the objects of analysis. Let us recognize again that the formal requirements of an evolutionary theory are flexible enough to make it possible to conceptualize the evolution of technology in terms of both artifacts and ideas. In the long run, I believe, we should strive to build a rigorous evolutionary epistemology of technical change as conceived by Nelson and Winter (1982) and Mokyr (1999). We need to work out the specifics of how to operationalize and measure the key concepts in such a theory. Fortunately, there is no need to start from ground zero because Hull's (1988) work on science as an evolutionary process can provide important guideposts on the road toward a rigorous evolutionary epistemology of technology that articulates precisely what would constitute a compelling replicator and what would constitute an appropriate interactor for an evolutionary model of technical change. In the short run, however, we should not be rigid in terms of what aspect of technology we regard as evolving because this would put a brake on doing empirical studies of technological evolution. In my analysis of synthetic dye technology I take such a pragmatic approach. At times I find it useful to talk in terms of knowledge evolving and at other times I find it convenient to point to dyes (defined by their chemical structures) as the things that evolve.

Evolution of Institutions

In this book, I will focus on the evolution of national institutions, but the arguments I develop can be applied equally to lower levels of aggregations such as states, regions, or cities. Generally, institutions are defined either in terms of persistent patterns of actions or in terms of enduring patterns of ideas and values. Because there are almost as many uses of the word "institution" as there are authors (see Nelson and Sampat, 2001, for a recent overview), it is important that I state clearly what I mean by the term. I use the term to denote actions, rules, social structures, and practices that persist over time and are features of social aggregates that are larger than a single organization. If one dye firm has certain practices that remain moderately stable for many years, I would not count that practice as an institution. Only when a practice exists in many dye firms operating in the same environment would it qualify as an institution by this definition. Remember that for an evolutionary explanation we need both a population and an individual exemplar. Patent laws and associated practices, for example, apply to all firms in a particular country and typically remain stable for considerable periods of time. Similarly, universities in the same country share many features (appointment requirements, department versus chair structure, kind of degrees offered, etc.), which allows me to talk about these features as (national) institutions on my definition.[20] Because alternative institutions differ in how efficiently they coordinate human

---

[20] The way I use the term "institution" may remind some readers of North's (1990, p. 4) useful distinction between institutions, which he defines as the rules of the game, and organizations, which he defines as the players in the game. I differ from North in emphasizing that organizations are very active in shaping the rules of the game.

efforts for a particular purpose, institutions can have a profound influence on the performance of a particular industry or economy (North, 1990; Nelson and Sampat, 2001).

As discussed earlier, a rigorous evolutionary analysis needs to operate at both the level of a population and the level of individuals that are selected. What, for example, are possible populations and individuals in the case of patent laws? One approach is to see all different formulations of patent laws that exist the world over at any one point in time as the population from which each country selects its particular patent law. Scholars of comparative patent law have documented that when a country is about to implement, change, or abandon its patent laws, it always surveys the different patent laws around the world for ideas of how to design its own system (Penrose, 1951). On this first approach, a country's patent law serves as the individual that is selected for or against based on the selection pressures that are prevailing at the time. A second approach moves the unit of analysis down a level and treats each national patent law and associated practices as a population. In this case the individuals that are selected for and against could be, for example, (1) the individual rules that make up a national patent law and practices or (2) court cases. One could track how the frequency of rules that favor inventors over other parties changes over time. Or one could track the frequency of court rulings that nullify patents after they were granted by the patent office. Judges in this case would be the proximate agents of selection, who select particular practices based on their understanding of the law and the prevailing social climate. Focusing on court rulings is analytically appealing because sometimes patent laws do not change in their wording but their interpretations do.

Why is it useful to conceptualize changes of patent laws over time as an evolutionary process? First of all, national patent laws are marked by substantial diversity, especially as we go back in time. The history of patent laws shows that there is a great deal of trial and error in countries' attempts to design their patent laws. The Netherlands, for example, had a patent law but abolished it in 1869 because it was seen as hurting the economic development of the country (Penrose, 1951). Just as The Netherlands was abolishing its law, newly unified Germany created a national patent system that had a dramatic impact on the innovation strategies of dye firms. Some countries grant patents to the first person to file the patent claim, whereas other countries grant patents to the first to invent. Typically, policy makers introduce new regulations without being able to foresee the consequences of implementing a particular rule (Hayek, 1973). Only over time does it become apparent whether a particular patent rule has desirable consequences for the people who have the power to make rules. Patent laws evolve over time precisely because desirable rules are retained and undesirable rules are selected out by the prevailing selection regime. But as we shall see, the evolutionary explanations for the development of patent laws are not nearly as well worked out as those for industrial development because in the former case it is much more difficult to specify as clear and simple a selection criterion as profitability in the case of industrial evolution.

Similarly, the development of the global population of universities or, at a lower level of aggregation, national populations of universities meets the criteria of an "evolutionary system" à la Durham. Universities or colleges shutting their doors does not make the headlines these days. But looking back in time, one finds that a sizable number of universities have closed, leading to change in the population of national universities. Of the 1,990 four-year colleges founded in the United States between 1636 and 1973, 515 had gone out of existence by 1973 (Marshall, 1995). A map of German universities in 1900 by Franz Eulenberg (1904) shows a surprisingly large number of universities that existed for some time and then were closed. Preceding the wave of the last two decades, private universities were already formed in Germany in the beginning of the twentieth century but they invariably failed or were taken over by governments and turned into public institutions. I will focus in my analysis on national university systems as the populations whose evolution we will track. I chose this unit of analysis because the organizational structure of universities typically displays more variations across than within countries. An evolutionary analysis of national university populations could track, for instance, the relative frequencies of private versus public universities. Or, as Aldrich (1999, pp. 177–80) points out, one could examine the relative frequencies of single-sex versus coeducational colleges in the United States. Recall that an evolutionary analysis can pick out any trait or characteristic and then trace how the frequency of that particular trait or characteristic changes over time in the population.

Given my focus on the synthetic dye industry, I examine over time the relative importance of research and teaching in organic chemistry in the British, German, and U.S. university populations. Among the variables I track for each national population are the frequencies of chemistry professors and students in chemistry.[21] To support an evolutionary line of argumentation, one must show that certain variants fail because of the particular selection criteria for universities prevailing in a country at a given time. I will show that the differences in the characteristics of the three national university populations can be attributed to differences in the selection environment. But to reemphasize the key argument of this book, the selection criteria prevailing in each country have in part been shaped by the collective actions or inaction of dye industry participants. Because the evolution of the three national university populations were causally linked to the evolution of the three national dye industries, it is proper to speak about a coevolutionary process.

A Sketch of Coevolution

Such a diverse group of scholars as Kauffman (1995, e.g., pp. 279–98), Lewin et al. (1999), Nelson (1995a), and Ziman (1999) have argued that we need to develop coevolutionary models to better understand the dynamics of industrial change. This book responds to their call and takes a significant step forward in articulating a powerful coevolutionary theory that links industrial, technological, and institutional dynamics. To avoid any misunderstanding, it is important to clarify at the outset that I use the prefix "co-" in coevolution not in the restricted sense that two things are evolving together but in the broader sense that multiple things are jointly evolving. Unlike those writings in which coevolution means the parallel development of two entities, my study analyzes the coevolution of national firm populations, technology, and two different kinds of national institutions, namely, research and training systems and patent practices. I will now briefly introduce the key ideas behind my coevolutionary model. It is fleshed out in full detail in Chapter 5.

---

[21] Ideally, one would have tracked the funding provided for chemistry research relative to funding for other disciplines. Unfortunately, these data are not available on a systematic basis before World War I.

In the preceding pages we have developed a general theory of evolutionary change. But what does it mean for things to coevolve? Scholars have used the term coevolution in several different ways. To make a theory testable, one must be very clear about the meaning of its central concepts. Coevolutionary arguments are beginning to receive more attention in organization and management theory (Kieser, 1989; Yates, 1993; Baum and Singh, 1994; March, 1994; Levinthal and Myatt, 1995; Barnett and Hansen, 1996; Haveman and Rao, 1997; McKelvey, 1997, 1999; Coriat and Dosi, 1998; Koza and Lewin, 1998; Baum and McKelvey, 1999; Lewin and Volberda, 1999; Lewin et al., 1999; Van De Ven and Grazman, 1999; Eisenhardt and Galunic, 2000), but because researchers are using coevolutionary language often in a very imprecise or inconsistent manner, they have invited unnecessary criticism. Some observers of the present state of coevolutionary scholarship in organization theory jump to the invalid conclusion that in coevolutionary explanations everything seems to be coevolving with everything else and hence cannot provide a parsimonious explanation. In biology, for instance, it is not the case that every species is coevolving with every other species in the world. In many cases, coevolution takes place between two species, for example, a particular plant and a particular insect, the former serving as food and the latter as an instrument for spreading the pollen (Thompson, 1994). Coevolutionary relationships frequently also exist between a predator and its prey (Nitecki, 1983). Similarly, a particular industry coevolves to a significant extent only with a very restricted number of other industries and surrounding social institutions. Often a coevolutionary relationship exists between producers and user populations, as in the case of the tabulating industry and the life insurance industry documented by Yates (1993). At other times a coevolutionary relationship exists between two populations of competing technologies, such as propellers and jet engines that power airplanes.

Let me try, then, to provide a precise definition of my use of the term coevolution. Two evolving populations coevolve if and only if they both have a significant causal impact on each other's ability to persist.[22] Such causal influence can proceed through two avenues: (1) by altering the selection criteria or (2) by changing the replicative capacity of individuals in the population without necessarily altering the selection criteria. Kauffman (1993) uses the idea of coupled fitness landscapes[23] to express this conception of coevolution. In coevolution à la Kauffman, one partner deforms the fitness landscape of the second partner and vice versa. As a result, a coevolutionary relationship between entities can increase the average fitness of both populations, decrease the average fitness of both, or have a negative or positive impact on the average fitness of one but not the other. Whether a coevolutionary process is beneficial or harmful for the parties involved depends on the particular causal

---

[22] My definition of coevolution is very similar to Nitecki's (1983, p. 1): "Coevolution occurs when the direct or indirect interaction of two or more evolving units produces an evolutionary response in each."

[23] Borrowing from Wright (1931, 1932), Kauffman (1993, pp. 33–4) defines a fitness landscape as the distribution of fitness values over the space of possible genotypes for individuals in a population. According to Kauffman, each possible genotype has a particular fitness value. The population on this view is a tight or loose cluster of individuals located at different points in the landscape. In this model, adaptive evolution in a population amounts to a hill-climbing process. When a population evolves, selection will lead to the reduction of some genotypes and the proliferation of others. As a result, over time the cluster of individuals representing the population will "flow" over the fitness landscape.

relationship that links the parties; therefore, this relationship needs to be specified in the empirical analysis.

My definition differs from Durham's (1991, pp. 171, 205–13) meaning of coevolution. Durham uses the term more broadly to include the case in which two factors (in his case genes and culture) have an effect on a third factor (in his case human behavioral diversity) without necessarily standing in a causal relationship with one another. In Durham's scheme, genes evolve and culture evolves, and they both have independent causal effects on diversity in human behavior. Whereas Durham allows parallel evolution to count as coevolution, I restrict my definition to Durham's narrow meaning of coevolution in which two evolving entities interact causally with one another. This restriction helps make a theory of coevolution in the social sciences sufficiently precise to lead to compelling explanations.

What is central about a coevolutionary process, in my use of the term, is the bidirectional causality linking the two parties in the relationship. To understand why Germany's dye industry was able to capture a dominant market position and maintain it for a number of decades before World War I, it is necessary, I argue, to examine the causal links between the national populations of industrial firms and the national populations of universities. Coevolutionary dynamics can lead to self-reinforcing processes that translate small initial differences in the performance of national industries into large differences over time. The key challenge for such arguments is to establish that causal processes indeed do connect the two partners in a coevolutionary relationship. To claim, for example, that technology coevolves with national firm populations, one must establish a precise mechanism by which this reciprocal influence takes place.

Arthur Stinchcombe (2000) proposes that we need to examine the "physiology" of the evolving social system to do a proper evolutionary analysis. By extension, a coevolutionary analysis should examine the physiology that links two or more evolving systems. In the case of the synthetic dye industry, we need to investigate flows that link firms with universities and patent practices. I will argue that the transfer of synthetic organic chemists between firms and universities constituted one important such flow that allowed this reciprocal influence to take place.

A second important flow involved university professors, who offered their expertise and reputations in the realm of patent laws and practices. University professors were typically used by the state to help draft patent laws or they were hired as expert witnesses in patent litigation, providing the professors the opportunity to influence patent laws and practices. Because these cross-flows varied from one country to the next, the competitive strengths of the three national dye industries evolved along very different paths. In Germany, dye industry firms were much more able to alter selection criteria in their favor than were firms in Britain or the United States.

Using cross-flows to establish evidence of reciprocal influence between two coevolving partners is particularly important because not everything that looks like coevolution is really coevolution. As Nitecki (1983) points out, coevolution may be mimicked by such things as sequential adaptations from different causes or simultaneous adaptation to the same environment. The only way to establish true coevolution as opposed to spurious coevolution is to gather evidence of cross-flows among the alleged coevolving systems. I try to do so in the body of this book by examining closely the career biographies of academics, industrialists, and members of relevant political organizations. I uncover links between these different populations of actors to show that they influenced each other's evolutionary trajectory.

Before attempting to solve the dye industry puzzle, I need to equip the reader with sufficient knowledge about dye technology, the changing role of science in the innovation process, and the economics of dye-making. Without such knowledge, one easily could get lost along the way. For those readers who have no knowledge of dye chemistry and dyeing processes, it will be useful to read Appendix I, which provides a more detailed technological history of dyes and dyeing, before starting Chapter 2. I begin with a short overview of the economics of dye-making and then move into a discussion of dye technology.

The Economics and Science of Dye-Making

The well-established market for natural dyes made it relatively simple to determine how synthetic dyes in 1857 might be competitive. For Perkin to win customers for the first synthetic dye, his novel purple aniline dye had to meet two economic criteria. First, the cost of the new dye had to be low enough for some segments of the dyeing and printing trade to find the product appealing. The actual cost of a dye was determined not only by what the dye maker charges for a certain quantity but also by how expensive it was to apply the dye to a textile and how long the color will resist wear and tear. (Not surprisingly, fashion concerns sometimes turn normal quality concerns on its head: Nowadays many blue jeans are colored on purpose with a dye that fades readily so that the fashion-conscious owner can enjoy worn-looking pants after a short while [Seefelder, 1994]). Second, if the cost were equal to or more than that of natural dyes, the dye had to offer greater quality either by delivering a shade that was not available in natural dyes or by offering a more consistent shading from one product shipment to the next. (Appendix I provides a detailed account of the differences between natural and synthetic dyes.) As Perkin found out by consulting with dyers, his aniline purple was clearly competitive along the quality dimension. Hence the crucial question in pioneering the production of the first synthetic dye became, "Can the product be made cheaply enough?" The key factor in this equation was how much the chemicals would cost that were required to make aniline dyes. The basic chemicals were widely available in the market, making their costs rather straightforward to forecast. But how expensive would it be to make nitrobenzene and then aniline, which Perkin converted into the purple dye? Because no market existed for nitrobenzene and aniline, two of the key organic raw materials, Perkin had to learn how to manufacture himself the two compounds on a commercial scale. By making a series of production innovations – for instance, using iron instead of glass vessels as was then common practice in chemical laboratories – Perkin was able to manufacture the intermediates cheaply enough to make aniline purple a big commercial success, especially once the color became popular in French fashion circles in late 1858.[24]

This short description of the first dye production already gives an indication of the multiplicity of production steps that were typically involved in converting the basic raw material, coal tar, into commercial dyes. For the lay person it helps to conceptualize a synthetic dye company by drawing an analogy to a kitchen in a large

---

[24] *Mauve*, a recent biography of Perkin (Garfield, 2001), portrays in detail (pp. 60–73) the fashion craze that surrounded aniline purple once it was popularized in France under the name of mauve.

restaurant. Basic foods and ingredients are bought from outside vendors. The chef mixes basic ingredients to make sauces and flavors that are stored for later use. In preparing a particular dish, the chef then draws on many basic foods and materials, as well as preassembled sauces and flavors, and combines them according to the proper recipes. Some chefs like to make the "intermediate" sauces and flavors themselves. Others buy them ready-made from vendors. Similarly, synthetic dye firms in the later stages of the industry had the option of buying dye intermediates from the market or making them themselves.

Perkin held a British patent on aniline purple and hence possessed a monopoly on its manufacture, but other aniline dyes, such as fuchsine, marketed only a year later, were made by several firms. As a result, price competition between firms became a regular feature of the synthetic dye industry early on. Market prices for synthetic dyes were constantly falling, similar to those for personal computers in our own day. A few datapoints illustrate this trend: By 1864, the price of fuchsine (aniline red) had fallen to about 10 percent of the 1860 levels (Morris and Travis, 1992, p. 65). Borscheid (1976, p. 132) reports that alizarin prices fell from 270 marks (1869–1871) to 40 marks in 1877 and to 9 marks in 1886. Prices for dyes in part came down because raw material prices declined. According to Hückstädt (1967, p. 387), British benzene prices declined in a short two-year period from 12 shillings (1883) to 3.5 shillings (1885). These constant price drops between 1857 and 1914 reflected both the improved methods of large-scale production and the high level of competition. To stay competitive, a dye firm had to be able to make its own production cheaper; those who could not were forced to close.

At the start of the synthetic dye industry in 1857, participants could have hardly foreseen that by World War I synthetic dyes would virtually replace natural dyes. Just as in the case of electric lighting and the internal combustion engine, which replaced gas lighting and steam engines, respectively, the new synthetic dye technology in time proved to be vastly superior in cost and often in quality, relegating natural dyes to small niche markets. The size of the market for synthetic dyes increased dramatically. Between 1862 (the first year for which data are available) and 1913, output increased by 3,800 percent in terms of monetary value. Because of continual price decreases, however, the increase in volume was substantially higher. The expansion in production from 1871 (the first year for which an estimate is available) to 1913 was 4,000 percent (from 3,500 to 162,000 tons). A larger market could, in principle, either accommodate more firms or, if no new firms should enter the industry, result in enormous growth for existing players, or anything in between.

This immense increase in output was made possible in part by the large proliferation of dyes sold in the market. By conservative estimates, on the eve of World War I, dyers and printers could choose from 900 distinct dyes made from about 270 chemical intermediates. From the very beginning of the synthetic dye industry, a frenzied search broke out to find synthetic routes to the commercially most significant natural dyes, alizarin and indigo. Perkin in Britain and the team of Graebe and Liebermann in Germany invented synthetic alizarin concurrently in 1869. Within a few years, farmers in Europe had to give up planting madder, the crop from which alizarin was made. But synthetic dyes not only competed with their natural counterparts, they also competed with one another: New synthetic dyes often made older ones obsolete because they were cheaper or better, as was the case with the first synthetic dye, aniline purple, which had a commercial life of only a few years. By the 1860s, many firms already made more than one particular dye. As the number of distinct synthetic dyes proliferated, some firms offered their customers a full spectrum of synthetic dyes. This product strategy transformed the economics of the dye business.

On the production side, firms not only could exploit some scale economies,[25] but even more importantly, they could organize to reap the benefit of scope economies. The demand for many dyes was not so large that a production line would be occupied all the time. To use production equipment continuously, firms like Bayer produced a wide range of dyes and intermediates in the 1890s, using the same production lines. To do so, firms needed to be able to make some predictions about demand for various dyes and then figure out an elaborate schedule as to when to make what dye or what intermediate and how to deal with unexpected downtimes in the production lines. The cost reduction made possible by using chemical intermediates for many different dyes and by cross-utilizing production lines depended on having relatively steady demand for a firm's product. Without sufficient orders, even the most efficient producer cannot stay in business. The economics of large scope and reasonable large-scale production required that competitive firms find a way to secure relatively steady demand for their product. We will explore later in more detail how a firm such as Bayer solved this problem by building a sophisticated marketing and distribution organization.

But where did all the novel dyes come from that would keep a large factory occupied? Dye innovations in the 1860s occurred in very different ways from those in the 1890s. Some chemical knowledge was always required to find synthetic dyes. Before Kekulé published his benzene ring theory in 1865, however, even leading organic chemists had little knowledge about how a particular molecule would create a particular color. Chemists would try out a large number of reagents on aniline without having a good idea of how the reagent transformed aniline to give it a coloring property. More trials and serendipity led to success. Because laboratory skills were involved in making dyes, most important dye innovations came from university-based researchers and were then commercialized by industrial firms.[26]

It took more than a decade until Kekulé's benzene ring theory and subsequent progress in organic chemistry had a significant impact on the development of new dyes (Ernst Homburg, personal communication, 2001). But by 1880 more precise understanding of the chemical structure underlying synthetic dyes provided scientists a powerful tool to search more systematically for dyes. When in 1877 German patent law protected dye innovations, a few German firms such as Hoechst, BASF, and AGFA saw the advantage of hiring organic chemists whose sole task would be to synthesize

---

[25] Compared to heavy chemical production, for example, of soda and sulfuric acid, scale economies were not nearly as important in dye making, but they clearly did exist, often giving larger firms an economic advantage over smaller ones. Scope economies, however, especially the ability to use the same production equipment for many dyes, were competitively much more significant in the synthetic dye industry.

[26] The empirical pattern that most major innovations came from university laboratories left traces in the socialization of chemistry students and their expectations. In 1883 Hoechst hired Dr. Eduard von Gerichten, a student of Emil Fischer, from the University of Erlangen. Bäumler (1988, p. 118) reports that "the young man had very ambivalent feelings toward his new job. On the one hand he would earn 300 Taler, and that meant much more than as an assistant at the University of Erlangen, his last job; but on the other hand, he had been taught that great inventions were to be made not by the chemical firms but by the universities and technical universities" [all translations of foreign language material are mine].

new dyes. After these research chemists turned out economically successful dyes, firms hired more and more chemists and pioneered an entirely new corporate function, formally organized research. The birth of corporate research and development (R&D), which today is a standard activity in high-tech industries (for overviews see Nelson, 1962; Freeman, 1982; Rosenberg, 1982), can be traced to the German synthetic dye firms in the 1880s. By the 1890s the vast majority of dyes were being discovered in the R&D laboratories of Bayer, Hoechst, and BASF.

Whereas in the early days of the industry a firm could exist by copying dyes invented somewhere else, patent laws made the systematic application of science within the boundaries of a firm a critical dimension of remaining a leader in the industry. The organization of innovation evolved from hiring one chemist to employing a cadre of chemists who would systematically search for new dyes to complement the existing product portfolio of the firm or would find a novel synthesis that could circumvent the patent protection a competitor had on a specific dye. From the mid-1880s onward, firms needed to master the forefront of synthetic organic chemistry to remain significant players.

The Road Ahead

To provide empirical support for a coevolutionary view of industrial leadership, I mainly operate at two distinct levels of analysis – the level of the national industry and the level of the individual firm. At the industry level the key questions are, Why was Germany able to surpass Britain and acquire an 85 percent world market share? Why did the U.S. dye industry fail to catch up with Germany? And, more generally, what was the mechanism that translated small initial performance differences into large differences over time? The record of the dye industry shows that the environment does not automatically bring about high-performance firms. Firms need to take advantage of favorable conditions.

To observe in greater detail how national institutions help or hurt the competitive position of domestic firms, I will examine the development of two companies in each of the three countries. At the level of the firm, the central questions are, How were individual firms able to take advantage of abundant resources in their immediate national environment or compensate for the lack thereof and become successful? Specifically, why were particular firms within the same country environment more successful than their domestic rivals? This study design makes possible another interesting question: Why was the German firm Bayer so much more successful than any British or U.S. competitor?

I begin the analysis at the level of national industries (Chapter 2), trying to answer the question of why the three national dye industries – of Britain, Germany, and the United States – followed very different development paths. The central puzzle is why Britain was unable to maintain its initial leadership position; for instance, the leading organic chemist Hofmann predicted in 1863 that Britain would dominate the industry for decades. I survey a host of performance factors – share of dye production, patent frequencies, number of firms participating in the industry, and so forth – to establish beyond doubt that Germany overtook Britain and came to dominate the synthetic dye industry in the decades before World War I.

Because industries are embedded in a larger social environment (Zukin and DiMaggio, 1990), understanding an industry's particular path requires knowledge of the specific opportunities and constraints would-be entrepreneurs faced in the three national contexts. In the next section, I paint a rough sketch of the differences in three countries before 1856 to give the reader sufficient knowledge about the histories of the three countries to fully understand the subsequent institutional analyses. I then analyze what features of the national environment caused the performance differences in the synthetic dye industry, beginning with the educational and training systems and then moving to the development of professional and trade associations, the role of the organic chemistry knowledge network, the social organization of production at the shop floor, and finally intellectual property right regimes.

I highlight the fact that the German educational and training system gave German firms a large advantage, particularly after science became a more precise tool in developing dyes. The formation of professional and trade organizations that supported the dye industry proceeded at different speeds in the three countries. In Britain, the infrastructure supporting the trade in natural dyes was much larger than in Germany, creating more obstacles and inertia in the process of developing supporting institutions specific to the synthetic dye industry. Earlier in this introduction, I touched on the critical role of synthetic organic chemical knowledge in creating successful enterprises in the synthetic dye industry. The educational system was a place where not only knowledge was created but also strong ties between professors and students. Many students came to work for industrial firms and thereby provided the link back to the university laboratories, where important new knowledge and discoveries were made.

Following Tilly's (1998) relational analysis of social processes, I dissect in some detail the academic–industrial knowledge network that developed alongside the industry. The analysis shows that the central players in this network were professors such as Hofmann and Baeyer.[27] Because the international network had its centers in Germany, German firms were, on average, closer in social (and geographic) distance to the sources of new knowledge and inventions than were British and U.S. firms.[28] Being located more on the periphery of the knowledge network, Britain and the United States possessed an inherent competitive disadvantage in recruiting talent and discovering new technological threats and opportunities.

Inventing new products, however, is not sufficient for commercial success. Firms also have to manufacture the product efficiently. German firms apparently were more frequently able to make the transition from having a foreman control the shop floor to letting chemical scientists and engineers make the calls about how to organize and manage production. Bringing scientific methods (i.e., rational and systematic analyses) to the shop floor allowed German firms to push the forefront of production efficiency. All firms who entered the dye industry in the very early days had to experiment to produce dyes on a large scale in a factory rather than on a small scale in a laboratory. Shop floor experimentation appears to have been more extensive in Germany because differences in patent regimes in 1857 across the three countries led to a larger number of plants there than in Britain or the United States. The patent laws and associated practices acted as important selection mechanisms on the populations of firms that

---

[27] Baeyer was not related to the founding family of the firm Bayer.

[28] For an application of network ideas and the concept of embeddedness to the study of economic action, see Uzzi (1997).

would come to exist in the three countries. Because Britain offered patent protection on dyes in 1857, firms with patents on particular dyes, such as Perkin & Sons, were shielded from fierce competition and realized large profits based on their monopoly. By contrast, the absence of effective patent protection in Germany until 1877 led to a very different selection regime. Firms could enter freely, and the forces of competition would eliminate firms that could not keep up with the efficiency gains of the best producers.

The passage of the all-German patent law in 1877 was fortuitous in its timing because it came after the industry had already developed strong firms and science was providing the tools to do systematic R&D on new dyes. German firms could pay for their R&D efforts after 1877 by getting fifteen-year monopolies on new dye-process inventions. The experience of the German and British dye industries shows that having a patent system is not necessarily as advantageous for the long-term development of an industry as is now often assumed. It also strongly suggests that the timing of the German patent law was crucial for its later beneficial effects. Had the German patent law arrived in 1858, it is doubtful that as many German firms would have developed into such strong competitors. Fewer firms would have entered the industry, and inefficient firms would have been more likely to survive, as was the case in Britain. The most important institution in the early success of the German dye industry was the university system, but patent laws were a second key factor that allowed the German firms to capture a dominant position.

By no means was every German firm a success. Quite to the contrary, 91 (or 185, if we count distinct legal entities as opposed to continuing economic units) of the 116 (200) entrants before 1914 went out of business. The figures for Britain are 36 (60) out of 47 (70) firms and for the United States 25 (27) out of 35 (40) firms. Chapter 3 examines in detail why some firms became more successful than others by tracing the development of six firms from their beginning until they went out of existence or until 1914, the end of the period studied in this book. A matched comparison of a winner and a loser in each of the three countries (Bayer and Jäger in Germany, Levinstein and Brooke, Simpson & Spiller [BS&S] in Britain, Schoellkopf and American Aniline in the United States) allows us to identify strategies that led to success.

The winners in all three countries shared one thing in common: In contrast to the losers, they had strong ties to the centers of organic chemistry knowledge. The German firm Bayer, which was closer in social space to the central nodes of the university knowledge network, was able to establish the strongest ties to leading researchers in organic chemistry and thereby assured itself more timely access to new chemical knowledge and talent that could run the firm's operations.

Confirming Chandler's views (1990), Bayer, unlike Jäger and the other four foreign firms, became a world leader because it invested its profits into building new organizational capabilities in marketing, production, R&D, and administration. Furthermore, Bayer, in contrast to the other five firms, also made a transition from a family firm to a joint stock company controlled by a team of professional managers, providing it with more growth potential than any owner-managed firm. Last but not least, in the first twenty years as synthetic dye firm, Bayer had an entrepreneur in its leadership ranks who took considerable risks. Bayer once came close to going out of business, but the gamble on a new dye factory (the alizarin plant) paid off handsomely and the firm returned to a profitable path. Jäger never took such risks and became relegated to the role of a niche player. The entrepreneurial spirit that pervaded Bayer, even when it was later run by professional managers, clearly mattered for becoming a world leader that could renew its product portfolio through systematic R&D.

Chapter 4 expands the Chandlerian view of the rise of the managerial firms to include political processes stressed in the writings of Fligstein (1990) and Roy (1997). The preceding chapters work with the assumption that national institutions have beneficial or harmful effects on local firms, but that firms themselves have no significant effect on the structure of these institutions. In Chapter 4, I abandon this working assumption and investigate the extent to which firms were collectively able to influence key institutional features of their national environment. This chapter represents the core of my empirical analysis because, although many scholars have long recognized the need to examine how firms shape their environment, few have done so systematically. The chapter also integrates Chandler's (1990) views with those of Fligstein (1990) and Roy (1997). We see that German firms were more successful than British and American firms in their lobbying efforts to upgrade educational institutions and to change patent laws and practices in their favor. I show, by conducting a careful study of the political dynamics that led to changes in the German patent laws and the failed attempts to change laws by British firms, that German firms' collective organization allowed them to shape German patent laws and practices to their competitive advantage.

The final chapter (Chapter 5) assesses the adequacy of existing theories in accounting for Germany's long dominance of the synthetic dye industry; in it I develop a coevolutionary model to explain how Germany moved from a laggard to an uncontested leader in this industry. I argue that although academic disciplines from economics to strategic management have provided a variety of theories to account for industrial success and failure, no one theory can adequately explain how and why Germany dominated the synthetic dye industry for so long and why firms within Germany differed so dramatically in their fortunes. Whereas international economics can explain quite well the success of the German industry as a whole, it cannot deal with the vast differences in performance of firms within the same national environment. In contrast, a theory such as the resource-based view of firms, developed by management scholars, has difficulty explaining why most of the successful players cluster in a particular national environment, rather than being spread out evenly across countries. Both kinds of theories, however, have difficulty explaining the dynamics of how competitive advantages change over time. The shortcomings in current theoretical arguments provide the starting point for the second part of Chapter 5, in which I develop an institutional theory of competitive advantage that deals with the national industry and firm level at the same time. To make coevolutionary arguments persuasive and not a catchall label for the analysis of organizational and environmental change, we need to know the specific mechanisms that characterize coevolution. After showing that the industry, technology, and institutions evolved, I articulate a more detailed coevolutionary model of industry development that I sketched earlier in this chapter. Besides highlighting the three abstract causal mechanisms of evolutionary explanations (variation, selection, and retention), I identify the exchange of personnel, the formation of commercial ties, and lobbying on behalf of the other social sphere as the more specific causal mechanisms that connected the evolution of national firm populations with the evolution of national populations of universities.

In this final chapter I also discuss the implications of the present study for evolutionary economics, corporate strategy, and business history. Because scholars from these different domains are all interested in the study of industrial change, the last section of the book proposes future research that should be carried out in the fertile triangle of evolutionary economics, management, and business history. I hope this overview has stirred your interest to read a detailed analysis of the evolutionary dynamics in the synthetic dye industry. Let us return to the beginning of the industry.

2 Country-Level Performance Differences and Their Institutional Foundations

Intriguing Questions about Industrial Leadership

Tomorrow or the day after tomorrrow, we believe, a process will be discovered by which the magnificent dyestuff of the madder plant or the soothing quinine or morphine will be made from coal-tar.

—JUSTUS VON LIEBIG[29] in *Chemische Briefe* (1844), as quoted in *Im Reiche der Chemie* (Roggersdorf, 1965, p. 26) [my translation]

[A]t no distant date... [England will be] the greatest colour producing country in the world; nay, by the strangest revolutions, she may, ere long, send her coal-derived blues to indigo-growing India, her tar-distilled crimson to cochineal-producing Mexico and her fossil substitutes for quercitron and safflower to China and Japan, and the other countries whence these articles are now derived.

—AUGUST WILHELM HOFMANN (1863, p. 120)

The year is 1857. Justus von Liebig, the most prominent chemist in the middle of the nineteenth century, was correct in his prediction that one day synthetic dyes could be derived from coal tar. But despite his purposefully optimistic preview of the ability of chemical research to improve the material condition of humanity, he probably was surprised himself how quickly serendipity paved the way for the creation of the first synthetic dye. Only thirteen additional years of chemical research and development (R&D) were necessary for the first commercial coal-tar dye to become available. Great Britain was the starting place of the synthetic dye industry. The start-up firm Perkin & Sons erected the first plant in Greenford Green near London in 1857 and sold a purple dyestuff to silk dyers all over Europe. For the first eight years, Britain was the home of the largest dye firms, but its leadership status was short-lived. In 1870 Germany had about 50 percent of the global synthetic dye market. Britain fell into second place. By 1900, Germany's share climbed as high as 85 percent, where it remained with relatively

---

[29] In 1844 his name was Justus Liebig because he had not been knighted at that point.

minor fluctuations until the First World War (Beer, 1959). If one also counts plants owned by German firms in other countries, Germany reached a market share of around 90 percent (Plumpe, 1990). Meanwhile, in 1913 Britain's position was reduced to 3.1 percent of world production.[30] By 1913, five firms (BASF, Hoechst, Bayer, AGFA, and Cassella) controlled more than 90 percent of German production, or 76.5 percent of world production if one uses the 85 percent world figure (Redlich, 1914, p. 18).

The United States failed to develop a significant dye industry until World War I. In 1913, U.S. firms produced a mere 1.9 percent of total world production. The dye firms that were started could not take hold in the industrial context of the United States and for the most part died when they could not compete against German imports. In a few cases, U.S. firms survived when they catered to niche markets. Given that these three countries experienced such very different levels of success in the synthetic dye industry, we can ask what national institutions were responsible for the high performance of Germany and the low performance of Britain and the United States.

Without the crisis associated with the war and the resulting government interventions in Britain and the United States to create self-sufficient national industries, there is no reason to believe that German dominance would have ended any time soon. Even until 1914, the dye industry presents a remarkable example of long-lasting dominance of firms from a particular country.

The dye industry thus is not only an example of a few firms achieving dominance but also a striking case of firms from *a particular nation* achieving dominance. Although international economists would not be surprised that a nation dominates an industry, they would find it extremely difficult to account for the long-term leadership of particular firms in their theoretical models. In contrast, whereas students of corporate strategy have offered explanations for why a small number of firms can achieve a dominant position in an industry, they have until now provided little guidance in understanding why dominant firms in an industry should all originate in the same country. The synthetic dye industry may be on the extreme end of the continuum that leads from virtually no clustering to full clustering of successful firms in a particular nation, but it is clearly not the exception. The dominance of American firms in the computer and software industries since World War II is another prominent case among many more.[31] For this reason, the dye industry offers a rich cross-national and historical arena for examining the question that is at the heart of firm strategy: How can firm managers create sustainable competitive advantages?

---

[30] All the figures rely on estimates because comparable statistics were not collected in the three countries at this period. They should be taken as approximations rather than exact numbers.

[31] In fact, in many industries, successful firms are clustered in very few nations, often in a single one. Take as other examples movies, fast food restaurants, or credit cards. These industries are all dominated by American firms. The popular music, oil, and cigarette industries are dominated by British and U.S. firms. French firms dominate the high fashion and luxury goods industries. Japanese firms dominate consumer electronics. Furthermore, it is quite often the case, not only in the dye industry, that particular firms dominate their industry for long periods of time. In the nineteenth century the Singer company dominated the international sewing machine industry and International Harvester dominated the farm equipment industry. General Motors and Ford dominated the international auto industry for many decades in the twentieth century; only in the last two decades, with the rise of Japanese producers, have they lost their unique position. IBM dominated the mainframe computer business for decades after World War II in the same way that Microsoft today dominates the operating system business for personal computers. See also Porter (1990) for many other examples of nations dominating industries.

Six years after the birth of the synthetic dye industry, August Hofmann, at the time one of the leading organic chemists in the world and a close observer of the early dye industry, predicted in his official report on the dye section of the London Exhibition that Great Britain was to become the largest producer of synthetic dyes. On what basis did he state so confidently that Britain was destined to develop the largest synthetic dye industry in the world? Surveying the different countries, he would see that Britain possessed in great abundance the necessary raw materials and was home of the largest textile industry in the world.

A numerical comparison of the supply and demand conditions in the three countries reveals a striking pattern. The basic raw material for synthetic dyes was coal. In 1859, Britain produced about six times as much coal as Germany and was still ahead by 1913. The United States produced 25 percent more coal than Germany in 1859 and twice as much in 1913. Looking even more closely, one sees that the most immediate raw material for dye production – coal tar – was actually largely imported by Germany from Britain.

Examining the size of the textile industry in the three countries gives an indication of the demand for dyes in the three countries. Driven by a strong consumer demand for colorful textiles, the textile industry developed a voracious appetite for brilliant dyes. In 1852, the largest textile industry in the world was that of Britain. Britain had a capacity of cotton spindles that was twenty-three times larger than Germany's, and four times larger than that of the United States. Even though most countries improved their relative position until 1913, British spindle capacity at that point was still five times larger than that of Germany and almost twice as large as that of the United States.[32]

If raw materials or dye demand were a decisive advantage, Britain should have developed the largest dye industry and not Germany. And the United States should have at least matched Germany's performance. Given that both demand and supply conditions were so favorable in Britain, one of the large mysteries about the early dye industry revolves around the question of why Britain lost its leadership position in the late 1860s and became almost entirely dependent on German dyes.

Alfred Chandler's seminal (1990) work on the development of corporate capitalism in Great Britain, Germany, and the United States covered the chemical industry as a whole but did not specifically analyze the dye sector. Because many of the chemical firms he discussed (in the case of Germany, the majority) had their origins in the synthetic dye industry, his general findings apply to the dye industry as well. Chandler showed that those firms that were quick to invest in large production facilities, to create managerial hierarchies, to organize R&D laboratories, and to build marketing and distribution networks assuring steady sales were the ones that became large and successful. The German and U.S. chemical industries caught up with and later surpassed the British chemical industry because there were more firms in Germany and the United States than in Britain that made these large investments in what Chandler calls organizational capabilities.

---

[32] Because dyeing and printing became increasingly divorced from textile production, a more precise measure for demand would be the relative size of the dyeing and printing industry. A bit later in this chapter, I will present more precise estimates for actual dye demand in 1913, which confirm that the United States and Britain both consumed more dyes than Germany.

Chandler's analysis can be taken a step further back in the causal chain by asking why there were more entrepreneurs in Germany than in Britain who were willing and able to create large dye firms. The goal of this chapter is to expand Chandler's analysis and examine how firms – because of their national environment – possessed advantages or disadvantages that led to these strong differences in country performance. Given that neither supply nor demand conditions can really explain the dominance of German firms, I will argue in this chapter that the institutional arrangement in the three countries was to a large extent responsible for the performance of domestic firms.

For this purpose, I will track the institutional developments in the three countries from 1856 to 1914. Working only with three countries and a large number of factors that interact in producing winners and losers in an industry, it is necessary to admit many different pieces of data into the analysis and accept different kinds of methods for supporting the argument. Although I will look at several different national factors in explaining the relative failures of Britain and the United States, the national patent system – and particularly the research and training system – takes a central position in the analysis.

I have organized the presentation with an eye toward being able to abstract factors and mechanisms that may also apply to other industries. This will make it easier to derive some general propositions about the nature of industry leadership. I will pay particular attention to the timing of events because there may be a critical period during which a particular national industry gets ahead and after which catching up with it becomes increasingly difficult.

Performance under the Microscope

Self-Destruction
Like William Perkin I personally aspire
to metamorphose lower into higher.
His transforming coal-tar into brilliant dyes
has come for me of late to symbolise
chemistry at its most profound and true
creating radiance out of basest residue.
It is infinitely satisfying
to see what was black dreck serve the art of dyeing.

Those are the powers and forces that are needed
if the Western World is not to be superseded.
William Perkin's ingenious transformation
could have benefited the British nation
But unfortunately Great Britain still relies
on Germany for all synthetic dyes.
The coal tars of the Ruhr and Rhine
metamorphosed in industrial bulk into aniline.
If more of us in Britain had done work in
the processes pioneered by William Perkin
we would not now as a nation still have to rely
on Germany for all synthetic dyes.

*Like many a physical or chemical invention
pioneered by the British I could mention
Perkin's valuable synthetic dyes
which will always, for yours truly, symbolise
the magic of chemistry, Germans monopolise.*

> —SIR WILLIAM CROOKES, historian, physicist,
> spiritualist, and chemist (trained under August
> Wilhelm Hofmann), as portrayed in Tony
> Harrison's (1992, pp. 19–20) play *Square Rounds*

*Why the other countries have failed is probably due to the fact that they contributed
little or nothing to the real upbuilding of the business, and to its creation, for the
coal-tar dye business is a created business; those who aided in its creation were first in
the position to reap the benefits – an advantage they have no doubt earned and
deserved through the effort they expended and the risks they assumed... The
transplanting of that industry out of Germany is an undertaking properly and fitly to
be described as titanic.*

> —BERNARD HESSE (1914, p. 126), in his analysis of
> the dyestuff crises in the United States after the
> outbreak of World War I

Existing historiography of the dye industry agrees that British and French firms pioneered the dye industry and were responsible for a great many innovations, even after Perkin's first synthetic dye came on the market in 1857. There is also broad agreement that German firms in the very early period simply copied product innovations that were achieved abroad. But how and why this transition in leadership occurred has not been answered satisfactorily.

A look at trade journals (e.g., *Chemical Review*) and the accounts of leading participants (Perkin, 1885) indicates British manufacturers and chemists by the early 1870s had begun to realize that German firms had become formidable competitors, overtaking British firms even in their home market. However, this realization did not lead to effective action that would have recaptured lost market share from German firms; instead, the German dye industry steadily increased its market share from 1870 to 1900.

The first synthetic dyes in the United States were produced in 1864, seven years after their synthesis in Britain. The British firm Read Holliday started the production of a red aniline-based dye (magenta) in Brooklyn, NY, after importers had made large sums of money with the new aniline dyes. Although several new firms entered the industry before 1914, the United States never established a dye industry that could compare with that of Germany or even the much smaller country Switzerland.

To provide a sound empirical ground for analyzing the competitive fortunes of the three national industries, let us tour the evidence I have been able to assemble on their individual performances. To date, no good data on the evolution of the industry in the three countries have been available. Now the database construction efforts of Ernst Homburg and myself have put us in position to examine in detail the structure of the industry, the exit and entry patterns, and so forth from 1857 to 1914.

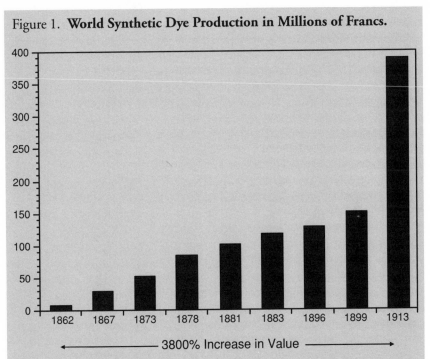

Figure 1. **World Synthetic Dye Production in Millions of Francs.**

3800% Increase in Value

Source: Compiled from multiple publications. Ernst Homburg located much of the production data on which this figure rests. Another source for such data (calculated in German currency) is Redlich (1914, p. 43 ff.). Note that number of years between bars is not constant.

Increase in Production Volumes

Production of synthetic dyes increased dramatically from 1857 to 1913. From 1862 (the first year for which data are available) to 1913, output increased by 3,800 percent in terms of value (see Figure 1). Because prices, just as in the personal computer industry in recent times, declined rapidly and continually as new and improved dyes appeared on the market, the production increase in terms of volume produced was even much higher. The jump from 1871 (the first year an estimate of volume production is available) to 1913 was 4,000 percent (from 3,500 to 160,000 tons).

Dye Production and Consumption in 1913, Imports and Exports

Beginning as an importer rather than as a producer of synthetic dyes, the United States never achieved a significant degree of independence from foreign supplies. By 1913, the United States had become the second largest market for dyes, importing a full 88 percent of its dye needs (see Table 1).[33] Domestic firms that made the remaining 12 percent of dyes consumed imported virtually all dye intermediates from abroad (Haynes, 1954, p. 314). Britain, in contrast, which initially produced most of its dyes

[33] In terms of value, the United States was the largest market because it imported a larger proportion of high-value synthetic dyes than China. I suspect that in terms of value the British and German markets were also larger than the Chinese one. Unfortunately, I have not found concrete data on this as yet.

Table 1. Estimated World Dye Production and Consumption in 1913

	Production in tons	Consumption in tons	Trade balance
Germany	135,000	20,000	115,000
Switzerland	10,000	3,000	7,000
France	7,000	9,000	−2,000
United Kingdom	5,000	23,000	−18,000
United States	3,000	26,000	−23,000
Other producers	2,000		
China		28,000	
India		8,000	
Italy		7,000	
Russia		7,000	
Japan		5,500	
Canada		1,200	
Mexico		600	
Australia		500	
Africa (including Egypt)		1,000	
Others in			
Europe		18,000	
Asia		3,000	
South America		1,200	
Total	162,000	162,000	

Source: Reader (1970, p. 258).

in domestic factories, began importing dyes in large quantities in the early 1870s. Both in terms of quantity and value, imports rose from year to year, such that in 1913 Britain had become highly dependent on Germany and to a lesser extent on Switzerland for its dyes. Being at this point only the third largest dye market in the world, Britain imported 78 percent of its dye needs. Although Germany had become the fourth largest market for dyes just before World War I, the country nonetheless exported 85 percent of its domestic dye production.

Relative Shares of Patents around 1877 and 1900

The relative position of the three national dye industries is also nicely revealed by their share of dye patents of each of the three countries. Because Germany did not have a unified patent system until 1877, useful cross-national comparisons are possible only from the mid-1870s onward. Figures 2 to 4 present dye patent statistics for Germany, Britain, and the United States, respectively.[34] To give a sense of the change in relative

---

[34] The raw data come from a research project on the internationalization of technology by Ross Thomson and Richard Nelson, in which I have been peripherally involved. For the details on the sampling methodology, see the appendix of their 1997 paper.

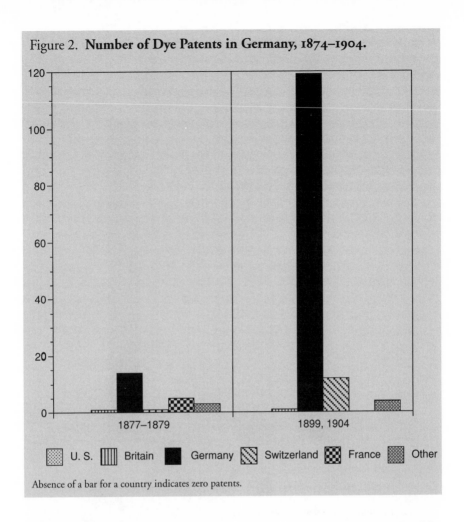

Figure 2. **Number of Dye Patents in Germany, 1874–1904.**

Legend: U. S. | Britain | Germany | Switzerland | France | Other

Absence of a bar for a country indicates zero patents.

patenting share of the three national dye industries, the figures show a sample of dye patents at two different time windows.[35]

Period I: All three countries had relatively little dye patenting during this first period. Not surprisingly, in Germany most patents were held by German individuals and firms; French firms and individuals held the second most patents. In Great Britain, the largest share was held by French individuals and firms, then German, and then British. In the United States, the very few patents filed were held by either Americans or Germans, with Americans in the lead.

Period II: Twenty years later, at the turn of the century, dye patenting shot up dramatically in all three countries. As Figures 2 to 4 show, German individuals and firms captured the vast majority of dye patents in all major industrialized countries

[35] The first time window represents the average number of dye patents in the years 1874 and 1879 (in the case of Germany, it is the average of 1877, 1878, and 1879; for Britain, the years averaged are 1874 and 1878). The second time window represents the average of the years 1899 and 1904.

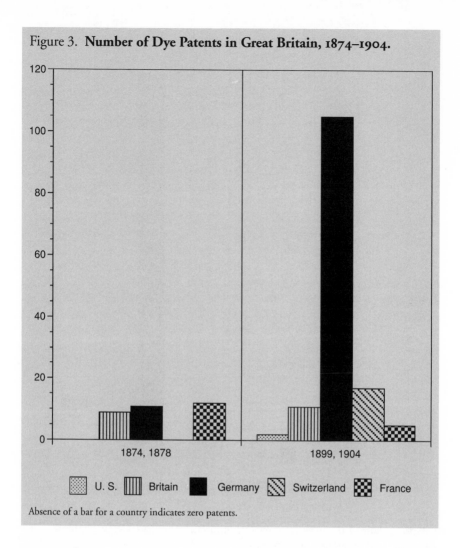

Figure 3. **Number of Dye Patents in Great Britain, 1874–1904.**

Legend: U.S. | Britain | Germany | Switzerland | France

Absence of a bar for a country indicates zero patents.

in 1899 and 1904. At home, German individuals and firms held 87 percent of all dye patents, 9 percent being in Swiss hands. In Britain, German firms and individuals received 75 percent of the dye patents and the Swiss 12 percent, whereas only 8 percent were British controlled. In the United States, 79 percent of all dye patents were held by Germans and 14 percent by the Swiss. As you can see, patent shares by national industry and their respective world market share are almost perfectly correlated, indicating a strong link between patents and market power.[36]

---

[36] Other sources on patents paint essentially the same picture. In 1915, Mason (as quoted in Donnelly, 1987, pp. 303–4) compared the number of dye patents issued to Britons (B) and Germans (G) in Great Britain and showed the change in the relative position of the two national industries. 1856–60: B 20, G 8; 1861–5: B 54, G 21; 1866–70: B 23, G 17; 1871–5: B 11, G 8; 1876–80: B 13, G 47; 1881–5: B 15, G 113; 1886–90: B 39, G 201. Landes (1969, pp. 352–3) reports that whereas the six largest German firms for coal-tar products took out 948 patents between 1886 and 1900, the corresponding British firms took out only 86. Liebenau (1988) found that Germans held 81.3 percent of the 862 U.S. organic color

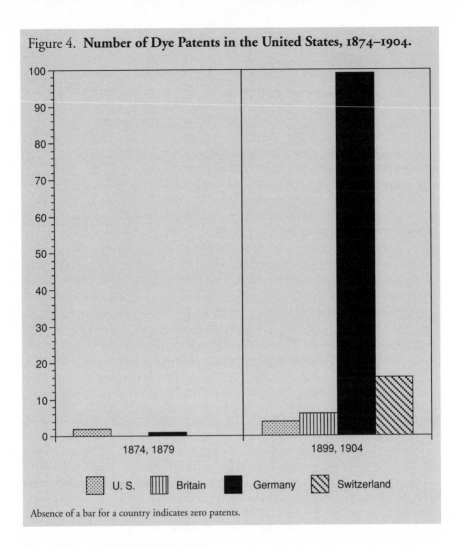

Figure 4. **Number of Dye Patents in the United States, 1874–1904.**

	U.S.		Britain		Germany		Switzerland

Absence of a bar for a country indicates zero patents.

Entry, Exit, and Density Patterns[37]

These market-share data show that Germany had a global monopoly[38] in dyes before World War I. Given that all the leading firms originated in Germany, it would be relatively easy to jump to the conclusion that all German firms did much better than their British and American rivals, that every German firm somehow picked the right

patents issued between 1900 and 1910 (the Swiss held 13.3 percent, Americans 2.2 percent, and Britons 1.3 percent). Munroe and Doyle (1924, p. 419), covering a more extensive time period, report that of the 3,765 U.S. patents for dyes and related products issued between 1860 and 1923, 2,203 (60 percent) were of German origin, 864 (23 percent) were of American, 345 (9 percent) of Swiss, 147 (4 percent) of French, 154 (4 percent) of British, and 52 (1 percent) of other origin. Redlich (1914, p. 181) notes that the total number of patents issued in Germany for dyes and related products (Class 22) in the period from 1877 to 1911 amounted to 4,978 (789 for period 1881–90, 1,866 for 1891–1900, and 1,951 for 1901–10).

[37] The data on firms come from the Homburg–Murmann database described in Appendix II.

[38] I use the term "monopoly" here in its meaning as dominant market position rather than its legal connotation of enjoying the exclusive right to serve the market.

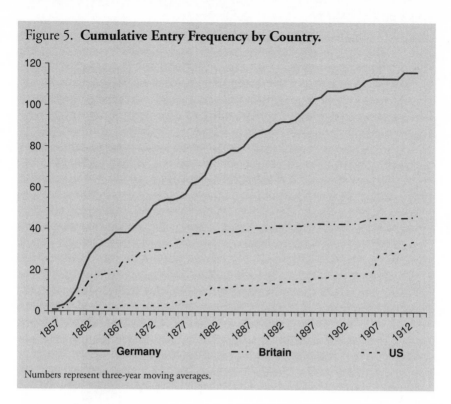

Figure 5. **Cumulative Entry Frequency by Country.**

Numbers represent three-year moving averages.

strategy and every British and American firm the wrong strategy for the industry. The firm entry and exit data for the three countries, however, show some remarkable evolutionary patterns underlying Germany's path toward industry dominance. Entry and exit occurred in all countries over the entire period. By 1914, about 116 dye firms had entered the industry in Germany, about 47 in Britain, and about 35 in the United States (see Figure 5). Germany achieved its superiority not only by experiencing more foundings of firms than any other country but also by witnessing the highest number of failures. Altogether, about 91 firms failed on German territory, about 36 on British, and about 25 on U.S. territory (see Figure 6). In Britain, the number of dye firms participating in the industry never exceeded about 17; in Germany it reached 43 in 1897, and in the United States the maximum number of firms was about 15 (see Figure 7).

In all countries, dye production became heavily concentrated among a few firms. In Germany, BASF, Bayer, and Hoechst were each responsible for about 22 percent of national production and, given Germany's world market share, almost 20 percent of world production each.[39] Levinstein and Read Holliday also had a dominant position among domestic producers in Great Britain with a share of about 30 percent each of domestic production.[40] In the United States, Schoellkopf held a 50 percent share of

[39] These figures are calculated from data provided in Redlich (1914, p. 18) and Beer (1959, p. 138).

[40] It is very difficult to come by exact numbers. I have estimated this figure from the information that Levinstein and Read Holliday were the two largest dye firms of comparable size (Reader, 1970, p. 263) and also from the fact that after their merger the combined firm held about 75 percent of domestic production in 1918 (Richardson, 1962, p. 117).

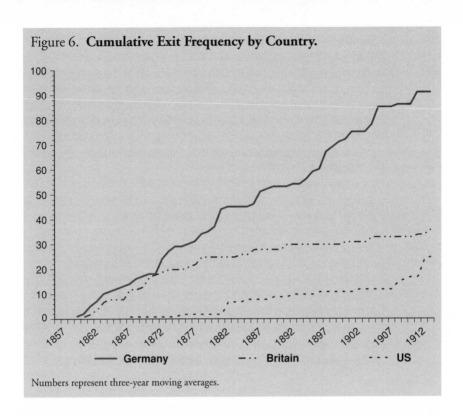

Figure 6. **Cumulative Exit Frequency by Country.**

Numbers represent three-year moving averages.

domestic dye production, Heller & Merz had 21 percent, and the Bayer subsidiary, Hudson River Aniline, had 17 percent (Haynes, 1954, p. 313).

The data on the industry clearly suggest that the German industry evolved toward a dominant position in two important senses of the word. First, the leading firms over time added features to their organization (R&D laboratories, international marketing networks) that allowed them to capture ever larger market shares. Second, German dominance coincided with the failure of a large number of German domestic firms.

Given the dramatic growth in market size up to 1914, there was much room for new firms to come into the industry. Apparently, long-term success for national dye industries was directly proportional to the number of corporate failures a country could sustain without jeopardizing the strength of the industry as a whole. More failures and more successes seem to have been parallel processes. Experiencing a larger number of start-ups, the German dye industry had more room to experiment with different firm strategies and structures. Even though most of these experiments turned out failures, the successful ones evidently had found the right recipe for capturing a large portion of the world market.

A comparison of the global entry and exit graphs (Figure 8) shows that the patterns for the two processes are remarkably similar. Spikes in exits very often followed spikes in entry with a one- or two-year delay. Large numbers of new entries invariably seemed to lead to exits either because incumbent firms experienced more competition

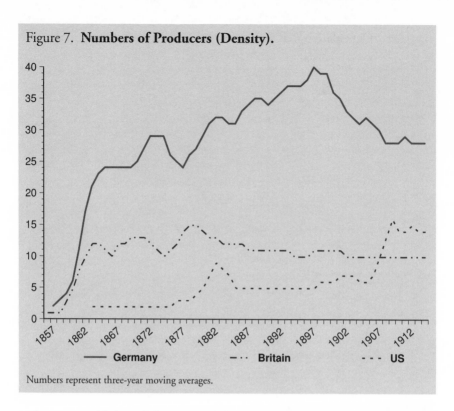

Figure 7. **Numbers of Producers (Density).**

Numbers represent three-year moving averages.

and were more likely to fail or because the new entrants did not have the strength to survive in the industry and were quickly forced out of the industry again. Because students of industry evolution to date have typically focused on one country, it is interesting to note that entry and exit patterns differed across countries. Although Britain and Germany periodically experienced steep declines in the number of firms, the declines often did not coincide.[41] Similarly, periods of high entry often did not occur at the same time in the two countries.

In all three countries, the frequency of entry varied throughout the period from 1857 to 1914. The German and British industry experienced the greatest number of entries in the period from 1876 and 1885, which coincided with new technological opportunities created by azo dyes. Germany also had a particular surge in entry in the early period before 1863, during which aniline dyes offered new market opportunities. In general, one can observe that new broad technological opportunities lead to market entry, everything else being equal. However, national characteristics apparently can amplify or compress this empirical relationship substantially.

To organize the discussion of how national factors shaped the competitive advantage of local firms, it is useful to distinguish among three periods, each of which is marked by different industry dynamics.

---

[41] A true shakeout of firms occurred only in France, one of the countries not covered in this book. It happened relatively early, during 1862 to 1872. For a more detailed comparison of industry dynamics in France, Switzerland, and the three countries discussed in this book, see my paper with Ernst Homburg (Murmann and Homburg, 2001).

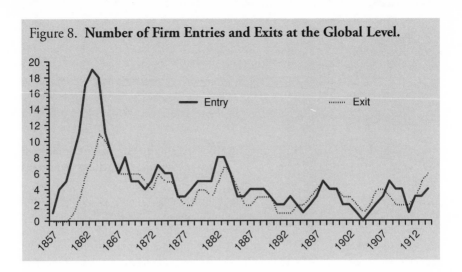

Figure 8. **Number of Firm Entries and Exits at the Global Level.**

Period 1, 1857–1865: Early synthetic dyes
Period 2, 1866–1885: The rise of scientific theory in dye innovation
Period 3, 1886–1914: The age of corporate R&D laboratories

During these three periods, the formulas for competitive success changed. As the industry was developing, entry barriers became higher and higher because German firms invested large sums in international marketing networks. Even technological innovation became an ineffective tool for dislodging incumbent firms because by 1900 the leading dye firms had all developed expensive R&D laboratories that could match without much delay new dye products. The large increase in dye patenting from the late 1870s to the turn of the century reflects the move toward systematic search for new dyes among many firms. In the second half of the 1870s, German dye patenting in Great Britain became larger than dye patenting by Britons themselves, cementing the decline of the British dye industry that would not stop until World War I. The R&D laboratory and its complement – the patent office – as part of the organizational form became a formidable weapon for protecting incumbent firms from technical obsolescence. This made it increasingly difficult for new firms to enter and become significant players. Why German firms more frequently than their British and American rivals went international early and why they more frequently built R&D laboratories is the question we now shall pursue in detail.

Background Information on the Three Countries

What one can say is that [in Germany], even in middle-class circles, there was a far greater emphasis upon deference to authority, upon the role of the state in political life, and upon the individual's acknowledgment that he was part of a larger, corporate whole[.]

—PAUL M. KENNEDY (1980, p. 6) in *The Rise of the Anglo–German Antagonism, 1860–1914*

Looking at the large firms such as BASF, Bayer, and Hoechst that dominated the dye industry in 1914, it is easy to forget that these globally reaching managerial hierarchies started on a very small scale, typically with the founders and a few workers. Organization theorists long ago (e.g., Stinchcombe, 1965; Parsons, 1966) highlighted the importance of the larger social environment in understanding the functioning of individual organizations. These theorists stressed that organizations have to play according to the rules and norms set by a larger social environment. Stinchcombe (1965) in particular pointed to the long-lasting influence of social conditions at the time of founding. He argued that organizations are imprinted with the social conditions at the time of birth and subsequently find it difficult to change. Recently, several economists (North, 1990; Baumol, 1993) have rediscovered the importance of the social context in setting the incentive structures for entrepreneurs. Until now, however, teaching and research in firm strategy have neglected the larger social environment as an important causal factor of firm success.

To understand the obstacles entrepreneurs would have to overcome in creating a successful dye business in their specific social context, we need to know something about the general economic, social, and political conditions of the three countries. A brief survey of the state of economic development and the political and economic organization in the three countries before World War I will help explain why large managerial hierarchies were more likely to rise in Germany and the United States than in Britain.

Economic Development in 1850 and 1913

In 1850, Britain was the dominant industrial country in the world while Germany was still largely an agrarian economy with much lower income levels. The United States fell in between. Steam engines producing a total of 1,290,000 horsepower were installed in British factories compared to 1,680,000 in the United States and only 260,000 in Germany (Landes, 1969, p. 221). By 1870 (the first year for which comparable figures are available), British gross domestic product (GDP) per head of population had increased to twice as much as Germany's ($2,610 versus $1,300 in 1985 U.S. dollars) and was still about 16% greater than that of the United States ($2,247) (Maddison, 1991). In 1913, the United States had surpassed all countries with a GDP per capita of $4,854. British gross domestic product per capita, however, remained 1.5 times as large as that of Germany ($4,024 versus $2,606 in 1985 dollars). These figures show that the economies of Germany and the United States were growing much faster than that of Britain in the period under study here. One of the key reasons for the faster growth of the U.S. and German economies during this period before World War I was that they experienced larger increases in labor productivity in the manufacturing sector than Britain did (Broadberry, 1997).

Political Systems and State Machinery

The year the synthetic dye industry started, Britain not only was the most industrialized and richest country in the world but also was at the peak of its imperial power. A state machinery had been perfected that was capable of administering far-flung possessions. The country possessed excellent research and teaching facilities in botany and mining to exploit the natural resources of the colonies (Brockway, 1979). Understanding Britain's relative inability to respond in a systematic and concerted fashion to the new technologies of the second industrial revolution (triggered by advances in chemicals, electrical machines, and the internal combustion engine) is very difficult unless one realizes that the organization of the British government was optimized for running a colonial empire, not for orchestrating the ability of society to harness the opportunities for economic growth presented by the electrical and chemical revolutions. Leading the first industrial revolution turned out to be a handicap for leading the second industrial revolution.

Tushman and Anderson's (1986) concept of competency-enhancing and competency-destroying innovations appears very useful for characterizing not only firms but also larger social aggregates such as countries. Taking advantage of the second industrial revolution required large investments in educational facilities and the creation of large managerial hierarchies. But Britain's governmental bureaucracies had no particular competencies in organizing universal education or implementing proactive industrial policies. Since the seventeenth century, Britain had been the role model for a liberal state, in which the political authority was vested in a democratically elected parliament,[42] the press was free, and the rule of law reigned supreme (Webb, 1980). This political organization had all the right ingredients to trigger the first industrial revolution but not to move industry into the age of large firms.

Germany was less unified, less democratic, and less free in 1857. The political history of the German-speaking territories in Europe from the Middle Ages onward was one of disintegration and fragmentation. Unlike Britain (an island) and France (largely separated from the rest of Europe by water and high mountains), the German-speaking territories had no natural borders, making it much more difficult to create a unified nation. From the fourteenth century onward, local rulers gained power and autonomy at the expense of the German emperor. Toward the end of the eighteenth century, the German lands consisted of 314 imperial territories and 1,475 imperial knights, giving it 1,789 sovereign political powers (Schnabel, 1937, p. 84). The Napoleonic Wars led to some political unification, but Germany still consisted of 39 sovereign states until 1871, when a new German Empire with strong central powers was formed. Although parliament had the powers to determine the budget in the new unified nation, the government served at the pleasure of the emperor.

At the beginning of the nineteenth century, Germany was lagging far behind Britain in economic development. The first step toward economic unification was

---

[42] Democratic representation in the polity applied to the home country and not to the possessions. Because the residents of many American colonies were unhappy with this, they broke away from the Empire and formed an independent United States. Furthermore, compared with today, Great Britain had a far less extensive democratic process. The essential point here is that relative to other continental countries, Britain was more democratic in the eighteenth and nineteenth centuries.

Table 2. Population Levels 1860 and 1914 (in Thousands)

	Britain	Germany	United States
1860	28,840	36,840	31,513
1914	46,049	67,790	99,118

Source: Maddison (1991).

taken in 1834 with the creation of the so-called Zollverein, which eliminated duties between many German states and, as we shall see later in detail, had an important impact on patent law practices among the states. The competition for prestige and influence that lasted until 1871 among the individual German states had important influences on the educational and industrial policies on German territory. Besides the creation of one large market, the economic significance of the German unification in 1871 lay in the incorporation of Alsace, formerly under French rule. Because the Alsace region was a large center of textile manufacturing, the German home market for dyes was enlarged significantly.

Just as the dye industry was taking off, the United States was sliding into a devastating civil war that lasted from 1861 until 1865. The war disrupted the export of large quantities of cotton from the South and led to a temporary decline of the cotton textile industry all over the world. The economic significance of the outcome of the war was to preserve a unified market that became larger than the British and German ones by 1914 (see Table 2). With the political issue of slavery resolved, the country was in the position to take advantage of the large latent opportunities for industrialization (McCraw, 1997a).[43]

From the beginning of the United States, a principle of dual sovereignty of the federal government and the individual states of the union was enshrined in the constitution. The states, for example, could not interfere with free trade among members of the union but had large autonomy in most areas that mattered for the development of industry – for example, education. In this respect the United States was closer to Germany. However, in terms of general political institutions such as free speech and democratic organization of all aspects of political life, the United States was closer to Britain. This is not all that surprising, given that the original states as colonies were administered according to British law.

---

[43] McCraw (1997a) provides an excellent overview of American capitalism. His book, *Creating Modern Capitalism* (McCraw, 1997b), is a book very close in spirit to the present volume, in that it works with the convictions that comparative historical studies are absolutely essential in understanding industrial change. The book also has excellent chapters on the development of German capitalism by Jeffrey Fear and British capitalism by Peter Bottichelli and contains two case studies of successful firms in the United States, Japan, Britain, and Germany. Incidentally, I should add that I knew nothing about these efforts when I was designing my own study. From an evolutionary perspective, such independent "discoveries" of scientific strategies are of course not surprising. Given the abundance of studies at the national level and the relative scarcity of cross-national comparisons, it is a small step to conclude that cross-national studies are likely to offer substantial scholarly returns. Carrying out such a study, however, is much more complex and labor intensive.

Organization of Industry

Because Germany and, to a lesser extent, the United States were industrializing much later than Great Britain, both countries had very different challenges to overcome than Great Britain did in moving from a largely agrarian society to one characterized by large-scale industries. Whereas Britain had to create the new technologies (steam engine, textile machinery, and the like) on its own, Germany and the United States, coming later, could simply borrow these technologies from Britain. Yet borrowing technology often does not require the same social organization as creating the technology in the first place (Veblen, 1915). Britain created and absorbed the technology of the first industrial revolution with the help of practically minded tinkerers and entrepreneurs who created very competitive, personally controlled firms. The textile industry represents the quintessential model of how industry was organized in general: Large numbers of relatively small firms competed fiercely, bringing down prices, and they tinkered very successfully with existing machinery to make it more efficient (Rose, 2000).[44] However, this highly successful industrial model of the first industrial revolution proved to be inadequate for later technologies (Elbaum and Lazonick, 1987). Germany and the United States were largely unencumbered by an existing model of industrialization and thus could go down a path that differed from that of Great Britain. In both countries, the large managerial enterprise rather than a large number of small, personally controlled firms came to dominate complex and capital-intensive industry (Jones, 1997), although the details of corporate governance were quite different (O'Sullivan, 2000).

Role of the State in Economic Affairs

The role of the state in economic affairs was very different across the three countries. Before World War I, Britain was dominated by the nineteenth century liberal belief that it was best to keep the state out of economic affairs and let the individual entrepreneur be responsible for the well-being of the economy. Initially, the British polity protected the individual entrepreneur from "their neighbors, the Crown, and the state bureaucracy" (Dobbin, 1994, p. 2). Later these laissez-faire attitudes were followed by the active protection of individuals from the intrusion of market forces that might have created larger organizations and from political forces that would have given labor a greater say over enterprise affairs. In the United States, state governments were initially active in facilitating the construction of railroads and other key industries. Later, however, the polity counted on the free market to deliver economic growth and on the federal government to play the role of the referee, ensuring that individual players would not monopolize industry (Dobbin, 1994, p. 2).

At the other end of the spectrum, the individual German states and later the imperial government were heavily involved in creating an industrial economy, starting at the beginning of the nineteenth century and lasting all the way until 1914 (Gerschenkron, 1962). German industrial reformers in the early nineteenth century were faced with a simple question: How do you take an agrarian society quickly into the Industrial Age? As the case of Prussia – by far the largest German state – illustrates,

---

[44] It is no accident that the propositions of neoclassical economics developed in the nineteenth century reflect the features that characterized British industry at the time.

their answer was not to rely on the initiative of the individual entrepreneur but rather to import machinery from Britain, create model factories and firms, erect mines and steel mills, and provide subsidies of all kinds for new industrial firms (Herrigel, 1996).[45] Furthermore, Prussia instituted compulsory military service, to teach labor the discipline needed for industrial work. Military life in barracks was perceived as the right model for preparing the surplus population from farms for the rigors and rhythm of factory life (Schnabel, 1934, pp. 292–4). Furthermore, the government became highly involved in the education of the population because this was perceived as an important policy tool for catching up with Great Britain. (The sources and consequences of differences in the research and training systems among the three countries will be extensively discussed in the next section.)

In making such a quick transition into the industrial age with the norms of feudalism still holding great sway, German governments and industrialists were forced to pay more attention to the well-being of workers. The German empire under Bismarck was the first industrialized nation to institute unemployment, health, and disability insurance schemes. Because the state assumed such a large role in guaranteeing their welfare, workers were more willing to accept the more authoritarian form of government prevailing in Germany.

In essence, the industrial governance structures that prevailed or emerged in the second half of the nineteenth century in these three economies differed in their ability to accommodate the creation of the large, managerial firm that became the successful organizational form in the dye industry (Chandler, Amatori, and Hikino, 1997). Because of an outdated but firmly entrenched model of industry, a social structure that put a great distance between workers and owners, and a government without industrial policy, British firms were at a serious handicap compared to their German competitors in building large organizations that could have exploited economies of scale and scope. Having painted this larger canvas of national differences, we can now examine in detail how these nations successfully developed or failed to develop institutions that were directly relevant for the success of the local dye industry.

National Research and Training Systems

[T]he German population has reached a point of general training and specialized equipment which it will take us two generations of hard and intelligent work to attain... Germany possesses a national weapon of precision which must give her

---

[45] Economist Alfred Marshall (1923, p. 132, footnote 1) captured the involvement of the Prussian state in economic development in these telling words:

The Committees on Import Duties and on the Exportation of Machinery of 1840, 1841, already referred to, were told that in Prussia "every man is intelligent, and every man thinks." In spite of the prohibition of exportation, every new English machine was bought at Government expense and sent to the Gewerbe Institut at Berlin. It was there tried; and, if successful, a working model was made of it for preservation in the Museum; while the machine itself was given to some progressive manufacturer.

The Gewerbe Institut was the place where Graebe and Liebermann in 1869 invented synthetic alizarin, a very important synthetic dye. The Gewerbe Institut later became the Technical University of Berlin.

an enormous initial advantage in any and every contest depending upon disciplined and methodised intellect.

> —SIR J. DEWAR, 1902, in his presidential address to the British Association, reprinted in Gardner (1915, p. 226)

The PhD ... will be a real and very great departure in English education – the greatest revolution, in my opinion, in modern times.

> —ERNEST RUTHERFORD, 1918, as quoted in Simpson (1983, second coverpage)

A half a century ago, ... opportunities for advanced or critical training in America were very scarce and very limited. The change, since that day, has been amazing ... Sums of which no one could then have dreamed have been assembled; ... in the realm of higher education America has become in certain fields a country with which Europe cannot any longer dispense.

> —ABRAHAM FLEXNER (1930, p. 42), authority on American and European universities

Overview of the Argument

Before the birth of the dye industry, Germany was the home of a small, by later standards, but nonetheless very good research and teaching system in organic chemistry. The system became better over time and provided German firms with highly qualified scientists not available to the same degree in Britain and the United States before 1914. Given that knowledge in synthetic organic chemistry was a critical, hard-to-imitate resource, German firms enjoyed a substantial advantage that they were able to translate into a domination of world dye markets. Possessing no institutions that offered graduate training in science and engineering in 1850, the United States experienced a dramatic growth of universities that provided training in engineering and to a lesser extent in science after the Land Grant Act of 1862. But until World War I, American universities offered almost no advanced training in synthetic organic chemistry, which formed the key knowledge base for the dye industry. This made it difficult for American firms to build up the necessary capabilities to compete in the international dye industry. In essence, the German dye industry marched toward its global dominance by residing in a social context that provided a small, but undeniably better, university system in chemistry at the start of the industry and that later provided even larger numbers of highly trained science and engineering students who could give local firms a competitive advantage.

Comparing Britain and Germany

In many ways, Germany had it easier than Britain in bringing forth competitive firms. When synthetic dyes appeared on the scene, there were many more chemists in Germany who had the knowledge to start up a dye plant (Borscheid, 1976). This is evident from the data on firm entry we saw in Figure 5: Germany quickly overtook

Britain in the number of firms entering the industry. In the first period the advantage of residing in an institutional environment that provided more organic chemists was related to a larger number of start-ups that could experiment with the right formula of success for the new industry; in the second and third periods, however, the chief advantage had to do with the ability of dye firms to hire academically trained chemists who could apply scientific theory for the development of new dyestuffs. These important developments deserve to be described in more detail.

The innovative capabilities of the German dye industry rested to a large extent on the human capital that was embodied in the highly skilled organic chemists and engineers employed in corporate R&D laboratories to create new products and processes. Neither the German nor the British dye industry would train their scientists and engineers fully in-house. They would rely rather on universities, polytechnical institutes, and trade schools to provide their scientific and technical personnel with fundamental education. Firms then hired these well-educated individuals and taught them the skills peculiar to the specific tasks required in the industrial context of the synthetic dye industry. The key point here is that dye firms in both countries relied (as they still do today) on their social environment for the training of their scientific and technical human resources.

After the early period that lasted from 1857 until around 1865, the German synthetic dye industry enjoyed substantial competitive advantages over Britain's because it was geographically and culturally closer to the human resources that were produced by a superior educational system.[46] The German system from the 1830s onward became the center of the most advanced system of higher education in the world for the next 100 years (Ben-David, 1977). Germany's institutions of higher learning, unlike their British counterparts, could rely on a very strong primary and secondary school system. For instance, Prussia, by far the largest German state, had instituted compulsory primary education by 1772. Britain had no such laws until 130 years later, after it became apparent that a large, relatively uneducated population was a great disadvantage for a modern industrial society (Wrigley, 1987). Because talent tends to be distributed randomly through a population, a society that is relatively more successful in dispensing primary and secondary education to all segments of the population is able to create a larger number of talented and well-educated individuals who are in a position to take full advantage of higher education programs. Britain had several excellent secondary schools, but they did not reach as widely into different classes of society as did Germany's highly regarded secondary schools. Germany thus created a larger number of students who could meet the challenges of university education. This was an important prerequisite for building a superior system of higher education.[47]

---

[46] This theme of social distance between producers of human resources (universities and polytechnical institutes) and users of human resources (dye firms) will be discussed in much greater detail in the chapter on the academic–industrial knowledge network surrounding organic chemistry.

[47] Why was Britain so much behind in creating compulsory primary and widely available secondary education? Among the variety of factors that contributed to this delay, two stand out. As described earlier, Britain had become the most successful economy in the world without any systematic efforts by government to create an educational system. In Prussia, the education of the population was perceived to be one of the key policies for catching up with Britain. Closing the gap in industrial output was a high priority of the Prussian regime because that would provide the necessary funds for consolidating

Driven by the utilitarian desire to create better-trained mining engineers, tax collectors, and state officials who could direct economic development, German universities and technical colleges increased the numbers of professors who would teach chemistry at this point, often along with a number of other subjects (Homburg, 1998, pp. 45–8). As the number of German academies that taught some chemistry grew enormously, the demand for teachers of chemistry surged as well, prompting universities to develop courses focused on the teaching of chemistry. Previously university professors had taught chemistry largely to students of pharmacy and medicine. The demand for chemistry teachers, however, allowed professors to offer courses designed specifically for students who majored in chemistry.

A second dynamic provided university chemists liberty to focus on basic science and not just the immediate practical problems of society – although utilitarian goals were ever present in the growth of university chemistry. The research universities, which were being created in Germany as a result of the reform movement that found its first significant expression in the creation of the University of Berlin in 1810, became the institutional home of the scientists who made the largest number of important contributions in the natural sciences between 1830 and 1930 (Ben-David, 1971). Although the reform movement was primarily led by humanist scholars who wanted to break the hold over the German universities by traditional scholarship in classical learning and theology, the new emphasis on original research as a fundamental part of a professor's job and a student's educational experience was enormously beneficial for the development of the natural sciences in Germany. Professors in these subjects were now given a large amount of their official working time to pursue serious investigations of the natural world. Despite the fact that German universities did not regard empirical research as the highest calling of its staff, professors were given to freedom to follow their own methodological instincts, even if this led them to English empiricism à la Bacon and his intellectual successors.

In this context, Liebig was able to open his famous laboratory in Giessen and become the leader in the relatively new field of organic chemistry (Holmes, 1989). Liebig, a man of considerable rhetorical skills, artfully combined the rhetoric of the humanist ideal of developing knowledge for its own sake and the utilitarian ideology of developing knowledge for the improvement of society. He argued that doing basic research would have the greatest long-term benefits for society (Homburg, 1998, p. 68), which allowed him to both obtain support for a research program that fit in the ideology of the Germany university and appeal to industrialist and students who saw chemistry as a tool to make money or a career. Students from all over the

and fortifying the expanding Prussian state. This explains the incentive side of the question. It is one thing to have the incentive to do something but quite another thing to possess the ability to pull it off. Why did Prussia manage to convert the 1800 society, in which literacy was the exception, into the society of 1850, in which illiteracy was the exception (Schnabel, 1934, p. 301)? Unlike Britain, the state and not the church was largely in charge of education. More importantly, the rise of Prussia as a continental power was achieved by developing the ability to administer a large army. Britain's power rested chiefly on the supremacy of its navy, and because navies are typically dispersed, Britain did not build up a centralized administrative apparatus for managing a large, land-based standing army. With a virtual state monopoly in education and experience in running a big authoritarian bureaucracy, Prussia had not only the incentive but also the necessary tool (not available to Britain) to achieve a revolution in primary education in the relatively short period of 50 years until the middle of the nineteenth century. For details on these developments, see Fischer and Lundgreen (1975).

world flocked to Giessen in the 1830s and 1840s to receive their training in organic chemistry. The large numbers of British students who studied under Liebig (eighty-three, or 12 percent of the entire student body of his laboratory between 1830 and 1850; Fruton, 1988, p. 16), and who subsequently became the leaders of British academic organic chemistry, are a testimony of how far ahead German laboratory teaching was compared to what was being offered in Britain in the middle of the century.[48]

To be sure, Britain had a significant number of scientists with international reputations in the nineteenth century. But such eminent figures as Michael Faraday, Humphry Davy, John Dalton, and William Wollaston did not create research schools as Justus von Liebig, Friedrich Wöhler, Hermann Kolbe, Robert Wilhelm Bunsen, and others did in Germany. Britain excelled in producing a large number of world-class "private" scientists, who were often associated with learned societies and academies, but did not develop the institutional framework for producing large numbers of qualified students who could be employed by industry. German universities, in contrast, were often educating more chemists than society needed (Flechtner, 1959; Titze, 1987). Men such as Heinrich Caro, Carl Alexander von Martius, Johann Peter Griess, and Otto Witt – to name a few – in part went to Britain not because it was an excellent training ground[49] for any aspiring young man but because jobs for chemists in Germany were probably often much scarcer than the number of qualified applicants.

The overproduction of chemists in Germany was of course a good fortune to Britain, which thus could make up for the lack of local training by hiring Germans. However, when the expansion of the German dye industry and academic chemistry created excellent opportunities for German chemists at home, hiring German talent for British firms became increasingly difficult. The creation of the Royal College of Chemistry in 1845 was already an attempt by British agriculturists and Prince Albert, the German husband of Queen Victoria, to bring Liebig's teaching and his famous laboratory instruction to Britain (Beer, 1959). August Wilhelm Hofmann, whom we have already encountered briefly at the beginning of this chapter in his charmingly wrong prediction about the future of the British dye industry, became – on the recommendation of his teacher Liebig – the first professor of organic chemistry at the Royal College of Chemistry. The College was set up as a private institution, but the enthusiasm of the initial sponsors soon declined because they were largely interested in training students in practical chemistry as opposed to creating research scientists who could advance fundamental theory. Within a few years the college found itself in a dire financial situation and was absorbed by the government-backed Royal School of Mines (Beer, 1959). This episode illustrates how much more difficult it was for a Liebig-like research institution to flourish in the context of British society. Nonetheless, until Hofmann's return to Berlin in 1865, the Royal College of Chemistry

---

[48] For a superb account of Liebig's research school in Germany and the less successful research school of Thomson in Britain, see the classic paper by Morrell (1972).

[49] Ernst Homburg (1999, personal communication) stresses that the biography of many of the Germans who left for Britain in 1850–70 confirms that they often went there to learn the chemical trade and bring the skills back to Germany. Britain was perceived to be far ahead of Germany in industrial development, and large-scale chemical manufacturing at the time could be learned only in Britain. The early success of Britain in chemical industry made it attractive for Germans to work in the British chemical industry and acquire knowledge about it.

was the most important provider of home-trained organic chemists for the British chemical industry.

Traditional British universities, particularly the pinnacle of the system represented by Oxford and Cambridge, were slow to create serious research and teaching programs in the natural sciences.[50] Between 1871 and 1880, the Cavendish Laboratory at Cambridge and the Clarendon Laboratory at Oxford were established, thus bringing some new vigor to science research at these prestigious universities (Haber, 1958, p. 76). In addition, seven new colleges of higher education, the so-called civic or red brick universities, were created in this period to educate larger portions of the populations and partly compensate for the lack of science and technology education (Sanderson, 1972). Despite the creation of the laboratories at the two elite institutions, their output of science students remained meager. Only fifty-six students received a Bachelor of Science honors degree at Oxford or Cambridge between 1880 and 1900 (Haber, 1971). The response of Britain remained inadequate because the second industrial revolution rewarded those countries that could exploit the seemingly endless number of technological opportunities by producing an ever-increasing amount of science and engineering talent. German industry in general and the dye industry in particular enjoyed the benefit of the German system of higher education, which was much more able to meet the demands of industry than the British one.

For business enterprises, the establishment of the polytechnic schools that sprang up throughout the German states in the 1830s was at least as important as the universities in creating the technical talent that could propel the German dye industry into a leadership position. Whereas laboratories like that of Liebig channeled a significant number of students into industrial firms (17 percent of his students in Giessen went into industrial manufacture, 30 percent went into pharmacy, and 14 percent took academic jobs in chemistry; Fruton, 1988, p. 17), polytechnic schools formed the backbone of the institutional structure for the training of engineers and skilled craftsmen. Besides the need for scientifically trained organic chemists, the dye industry developed an ever-larger demand for science-based engineering. Because the traditional universities were as least as reluctant as their British counterparts to welcome new subjects into the academy, this demand was met by upgrading the polytechnic schools into technical universities from the 1870s onward and by expanding their enrollments dramatically (Homburg, 1993). The number of full-time students enrolled in technical universities rose from 2,759 to 10,591 in 1910 (Titze, 1987). Professors at these technical universities fought a long battle against the traditional university faculties before they were finally granted in 1902 the right to award doctorate degrees in the engineering sciences. Because these technical universities had developed not only excellent engineering programs but also strong chemistry curricula, and the large German dye firms came to rely more heavily on talent from the new technical universities than from the traditional universities (Haber, 1971).

---

[50] Oxford and Cambridge at the time were not funded by the state. Strongly affiliated with the church, they were independently endowed. This is an important difference in relation to German universities, which were funded and controlled by the individual states. Hence, even if the British government wanted to make changes in higher education, it would have had little leverage with these elite institutions of the country. Oxford and Cambridge only started accepting government grants in 1919 (Alter, 1987, pp. 34–5).

Various social groups resisted the expansion of science and technology teaching in Germany as well as in Britain; however, Britain's misfortune was that these forces were much stronger there than those on German soil. Although the overall British student population increased 20 percent between 1900 and 1913, Germany's climbed 60 percent in the same period. Between 1893 and 1911, the numbers of students at the civic universities in Britain (excluding Oxford and Cambridge) rose only from around 6,400 to 9,000 or by 40 percent. Of those 9,000, only 1,000 were engineering students and 1,700 were science students (Haber, 1971, p. 51). If to the figure of about 11,000 technology and science full-time students at the technical universities one adds the number of science students educated at the regular German universities, it is evident how much larger was the output of scientifically literate manpower in Germany. These differences in university output became reflected at the highest echelons of industrial leadership. Recent research on successful British and German businessmen in 1870–1914 has shown that 13 percent of the British were academically trained versus 24 percent of the Germans (Berghoff and Möller, 1994).

Not surprisingly, a number of Britons were already quite aware of the relative backwardness of British educational institutions in the 1860s. The Liebig student Lyon Playfair was among the most vocal critics of the British efforts in science and technology education. He played a key role in the first of a series of special government committees that examined the state of British education. Every new committee issued clear recommendations that it was very important to upgrade the British educational system. The creation of the civic universities in the 1870s and of the science laboratories at Oxford and Cambridge was already a response to these committee reports. However, unlike the prescient voices who predicted that Britain would lose her industrial leadership position if she did not match the educational programs of Germany, British society as a whole and its government were not convinced until many decades later that putting as great an emphasis on education as Germany had been doing for a long time was in the vital interest of the nation. Consistent with Schmookler's (1965) observations about the link between support for research and education and the general conditions of society, only a real national crisis would provide the impetus for radical change in policies of higher education.

Interface between Technical Education and the Dye Industry

By that time, competitive advantages had passed into the hands of the German industry because firms there could not only draw on a larger body of talented chemists and engineers but also join forces with German professors in their quest for developing new products. A very large number of contacts between academia and industry were initiated and cemented through teacher–student relationships. When Hofmann was lured back to Germany in 1865 to head a large new university laboratory in Berlin, the British dye industry lost one of its most important collaborators. After his student Perkin had synthesized aniline purple, Hofmann used his laboratory in London to discover other dyes.[51] He consulted widely and channeled students into British dye firms. When he moved to Berlin, he continued this pattern. Not only did he become

---

[51] Hofmann received a British patent for a violet aniline in May 1863. He licensed the dye to Simpson, Maule & Nicholson; Knosp of Stuttgart (Germany); and later Renard Frères in France (Travis, 1993, p. 79).

the most important consultant to AGFA (there is evidence that he held stock in the company), he also became a tireless organizer of German academic chemistry and its relationship to industry.[52]

Hofmann was by no means an exception. Firms could draw on a large number of university researchers who were willing to interact in a variety of ways with industrial firms. The most famous episode is the alliance Carl Graebe and Carl Liebermann formed in 1869 with Heinrich Caro, the research director of BASF, to pool their discoveries and jointly file a patent for alizarin in Britain (Travis, 1993). Even before Bayer had established its own central research laboratory, the firm made use of the superior research facilities that existed at many German universities. The first assignment Bayer handed to newly hired chemist Carl Duisberg was to work for six months (1883–4) in the organic chemistry laboratory at the University of Strasbourg and research various basic problems of interest to the company (Duisberg, 1933).[53] When Bayer had difficulty getting high yields in their newly set up acid plant in Leverkusen in the 1890s, the firm could tap the advice of the leading expert for inorganic chemical technology and famous textbook author Georg Lunge, a German chemist who was for many years on the faculty of the Zurich Technical University (Flechtner, 1959, p. 151).

British firms, of course, also interacted with institutions of science in addition to their traditional reliance on the chemical consultants who traveled from one firm to the next.[54] Levinstein, for example, relied on universities for human talent just as the German firms did. Levinstein also acted as the president of the Society of Chemical Industry (SCI), founded in 1881 by, among others, Professor Henry Roscoe, the country's leading academic chemist,[55] and by the industrialist Ludwig Mond. The purpose of the society was to facilitate interaction between academia and industry (Miall, 1931). However, because the British academic system for chemical research and training was so much smaller than Germany's, the opportunities for British firms to draw on their local universities were more limited. By hiring many German chemists, Levinstein and Holliday and others overcame some of the shortcomings of the British education system, but British firms would not get the first-rate students who had the closest ties with German professors when these students could find employment in German firms. British firms had a second disadvantage: It was more difficult to learn about the newest research findings of German chemistry professors by hiring students who had moved to Britain and therefore had more difficulty interacting with their

---

[52] Recently an edited volume was published to commemorate the 100th anniversary of Hofmann's death by focusing specifically on his role in facilitating the interaction between science and the chemical industry (Meinel and Scholz, 1992). For other details on Hofmann's relations with the industry, see Travis (1993). I will return to Hofmann's importance for the early dye industry when I discuss his role in the organic chemistry network.

[53] Duisberg later developed into a towering figure in the German chemical industry. He became CEO of Bayer, the principal architect of the German dye cartel, leader of the German Association of Chemists, the Chemical Industry Association, and, after his retirement from executive duty at I. G. Farbenindustrie Aktiengesellschaft, the representative of the Association of German Employers (Flechtner, 1959). Duisberg will figure prominently in the case study of Bayer that lies ahead.

[54] One of these traveling consultants, George E. Davis, became a cofounder of the Society of Chemical Industry and in 1901 was author of the first English-language handbook on chemical engineering.

[55] Roscoe was also trained in Germany, albeit in his case not under Liebig but Bunsen, another leader of academic chemistry.

former teachers than did those students who had remained in Germany.[56] Because industrial firms are primarily profit-oriented institutions, the level of involvement of academic scientists and their support of public research activities depends largely on the perceived benefits that will flow from this activity. Given that the German academic system was much more advanced in this period than the British one, not surprisingly German industry cultivated the interface with academia more extensively than did British industry. German entrepreneurs simply had more to gain from interacting with their local university system.

Government Policies

One important reason why the German system of higher technical and scientific education was superior to that of the British lies in the higher level of financial support by German governments. At the end of the nineteenth century, the British government paid £26,000 to universities for all purposes. Prussia alone, albeit the largest German state, supported her universities with £476,000. The respective figures for the academic year 1911–1912 amount to £123,000 and £700,000 (Haber, 1971, pp. 45, 51).[57]

This dramatic variation in the public support of education can only be properly understood in view of the very different historical experiences of Britain and the German states. Whereas the British industrial revolution was more or less carried out by the hands of private individuals, Germany's entry into the industrial era was to a large extent orchestrated by government bureaucracies (Herrigel, 1996). In many cases, German states were eager to stimulate and sponsor industry in their territories to increase the income for the crown and thus further the power of the ruler. Education of highly qualified bureaucrats (who could mastermind industrialization efforts) and engineers (who could transfer British technological achievements) originally constituted the primary aim of the high level of financial support that German governments afforded their system of higher education.

As an explanation of the meteoric rise of the German university system, many commentators have cited what they call German society's uniquely strong emphasis on cultivating a person's self through Wissenschaft (scholarship) for its own sake, and the inability of Germany to express her national identity[58] other than through the cultivation of a shared culture (Paulsen, 1906). Although there may be an element of truth in this social-psychological explanation, I am more persuaded by the arguments along the lines of Schmookler, who argued that utilitarian goals (making the German states stronger) and national crisis (being run over by Napoleon) are primarily

---

[56] Nationalistic sentiments of German professors may have made them also less inclined to share new discoveries and knowledge with students who took positions in the British dye industry. Nationalism was on the rise in the nineteenth century and the German unification made it a potent mood in Germany.

[57] In his informative book *The Reluctant Patron*, Alter (1987) provides many more details about the role of the state in the financial support of science in Great Britain.

[58] The argument by such eminent scholars as Paulsen in his history of the German universities runs as follows: In the beginning of the nineteenth century, France controlled continental Europe politically and Britain controlled the seas and commerce. Germany, being split into 39 states, could express her national identity only through the creation of a culture that was to be shared across all states. The universities were the institutions that could create this unified culture because they were truly national, students and faculty coming from all parts of the German-speaking territory. Conspicuously absent from this line of argument is any reference to utilitarian goals of the universities.

responsible for societies' support of higher education (Schmookler, 1965). Homburg's (1998) detailed investigation of the rise of chemistry as a profession has also called into question the idealist, nonutilitarian argumentation of Paulsen (1906). In support of this line of revisionist thinking, Borscheid (1976, pp. 50–71) has documented in fine detail that the food crisis and the revolutionary movements of 1848 prompted the Government of Baden (one of the German states) to increase dramatically research and educational funding for chemistry and agricultural sciences. The goal was to increase agricultural productivity and avoid future hunger crises by understanding the relationship between mineral fertilizers and plant growth. After 1850, enrollments in chemistry shot up not only in Baden (as shown in Borscheid, 1976, pp. 67–8) but also in Germany in general (as indicated in Homburg, 1993, pp. 394–5).

In the first half of the century, while German public support was laying the foundation for what would become the leading system of higher education, British universities were financed locally, largely with private grants and tuition fees (Sanderson, 1972). The central government in London played virtually no role in the governance and finance of the British universities. Furthermore, because the industrial revolution in Britain was conducted by men of practice, who in most cases had no academic education, Britain had not developed a public spirit that associated industrial success with a highly developed industrial system. In contrast, by the 1860s a national myth of "Wissenschaft" had taken hold in the leading circles of German society, in which the rapid industrialization of Germany was interpreted as directly connected with advances achieved in the natural sciences since the 1830s (Turner, 1989). These differences in the way the British and German institutions of higher education had evolved and in how the two societies interpreted their industrial achievements had important consequences for how governments responded to the opportunities that arose with the second industrial revolution. The German imperial government and the individual states upgraded the polytechnic schools to technical universities in the 1870s, began to form schools of business administration in the 1890s, and expanded enrollments, particularly in the traditional universities. The British government also increased its support for science education by giving grants to local institutions, expanded its support of universities, and upgraded the existing London technical colleges by merging them in 1907 to form the Imperial College, which was modeled after the Technical University of Berlin. But because the British government started from a much lower level of involvement and with less support in society for education, it had to respond more slowly, less systematically, and above all with fewer resources than Germany.[59]

The Case of the United States

Nelson and Wright (1994) have found that students of economic growth widely conclude that the American economy after the Civil War outperformed all other countries because of its superior educational system. This proposition is generally derived from comparisons between the United States and Britain. However, in comparing the

---

[59] Julia Wrigley's (1987) excellent paper on technical education and industry in nineteenth century Britain provides the best overview of how Britain fell behind. Incidentally, it is telling of British management philosophy that the country did not find it useful to create Schools of Business until the 1960s, lagging Germany and the United States by roughly three generations. See Locke (1984) for the history of business education in Germany and in Britain.

United States and Germany, it becomes clear that this view requires revision, given that Germany had achieved higher levels of education – particularly in science – than the United States did before World War I. Indeed, the relative failure of the U.S. synthetic dye industry before 1914 can be traced in large measure to the lack of research and teaching in synthetic organic chemistry available in the country. The quote at the beginning of this chapter indicates that the American system of higher education made great advances in the late nineteenth century. A close examination of the system reveals, however, that it became strong in many disciplines, but not in the one crucial for the dye industry – synthetic organic chemistry.

In 1850, the United States had no universities that offered graduate training in science or engineering. To compensate for this deficiency, about 10,000 Americans went to Germany to receive graduate training in the nineteenth century (Stern, 1987, p. 248). Among them were many people who went to places like Giessen to obtain advanced training in organic chemistry. In the middle of the century, Yale and Harvard attempted to create rigorous science research and education, but these attempts invariably met with little success because of a lack of support by society at large (Rossiter, 1975).[60]

Starting with the Land Grant Act in 1862, the United States began to build a very large university system, creating many new campuses and upgrading existing ones (Rosenberg and Nelson, 1994). The Land Grant colleges in the individual states were typically set up with the explicit purpose of training students to serve the practical needs of agriculture and industry within the state (Ferleger and Lazonick, 1994). Reflecting the pragmatic attitude of the larger culture (Hughes, 1989), engineering dominated the new universities. By 1872, the number of engineering colleges had increased from six to seventy. By 1917, the number had reached 126. Enrollments in engineering schools increased from 100 in 1870 to 4,300 at the outbreak of World War I (Noble, 1977, p. 24). The universities were clearly set up to produce engineers and scientists who could serve the important sectors of American economy at that time, such as agriculture, light machinery, and steel.

It was much more difficult for a physical science such as chemistry to take off. When the sciences received support, they did so because the benefactors or state policy makers perceived them as being useful in advancing the engineering and agricultural

---

[60] The most famous European visitor to the United States in the nineteenth century, Alexis de Tocqueville, explained in his books *Democracy in America*, originally published from 1835 to 1840, why pure science would not flourish in this new country:

It must be acknowledged, that in few of the civilized nations of our time have the higher sciences made less progress than in the United States... In America, the purely practical part of science is admirably understood and careful attention is paid to the theoretical portion, which is immediately requisite to application. On this head, the Americans always display a clear, free, original, and inventive power of mind. But hardly any one in the United States devotes himself to the essentially theoretical and abstract portion of human knowledge... every new method which leads by a shorter road to wealth, every machine which spares labor, every instrument which diminishes the cost of production, every discovery which facilitates pleasures or augments them, seems [to such people] to be the grandest effort of the human intellect. It is chiefly from these motives that a democratic people addicts itself to scientific pursuits... In a community thus organized, it may easily be conceived that the human mind may be led insensibly to the neglect of theory; and that it is urged, on the contrary, with unparalleled energy, to the applications of science, or at least to that portion of theoretical science which is necessary to those who make such applications (1898, vol. 2, pp. 40, 48, 52–3).

sciences. Not until Johns Hopkins University, initially solely a graduate school, opened its doors in 1876 was German-style chemistry research and teaching practiced in the United States. Under the direction of the German-trained professor Ira Remsen, Johns Hopkins offered the first doctoral program in chemistry. This innovative university then served as the model for graduate education in the United States, and the University of Chicago, Harvard, the University of California, the University of Michigan, and the University of Wisconsin began to add serious graduate programs to their educational offerings (Ben-David, 1971, 1977). Johns Hopkins dominated the training of Ph.D.s in chemistry until the turn of the century. One hundred of the 251 chemistry Ph.D.s granted in the United States between 1860 and 1899 were granted by Johns Hopkins (Thackray, Sturchio, Carroll, and Bud, 1985). The number of degrees granted accelerated quickly. In the 1870s, one Ph.D. in chemistry was granted; in the 1880s, twenty-four; and in the 1890s, seventy-five. By 1900, the face of American higher education had been changed dramatically. Research in science had become institutionalized among the leading universities. But I emphasize that this research was driven by practical concerns. The U.S. university system did not develop strength in pure science that was in any way comparable to what was achieved in Germany before the First World War.[61] With many fewer professors in organic chemistry in the United States, fewer man-hours could be devoted to solving more basic research questions that could lead to such breakthroughs as Kekulé's benzene ring theory, which allowed professors such as Adolf Baeyer to work on the problem of synthesizing indigo in the laboratory.

American spending on universities even exceeded Germany's after 1895, leaving Britain a distant third. A study by the Prussian Ministry of Education in 1910–11 compared twenty-one German universities with twelve leading American public and private universities and found that the average budget of the American schools amounted to 5.80 million marks annually compared to only 1.67 million marks for German schools.[62] Since the mid-1890s, American expenditure per university had quadrupled, growing at twice the rate of Germany's; American spending per student nearly doubled in this period, whereas German spending grew very little on a per student basis.

Education statistics for the entire United States show the explosive growth of the American system of higher education. Starting at a lower enrollment level than Germany, the increase in the United States is even greater than in Germany for the same period. Because U.S. degree statistics for the period before World War I are already broken down by subject, it is possible to gain a quantitative picture about the growth of individual disciplines. The yearly number of U.S. bachelor's degrees in all fields and in chemistry increased by over 400 percent in the period from 1890 until 1914 (from 7,228 to 31,540 and from 631 to 2,573, respectively). During the same period, the yearly number of doctorates in chemistry increased by about the same percentage, from 28 to 107 (Thackray et al., 1985). Germany at the time produced more than three times as many Ph.D.s in chemistry, but the United States was clearly catching up

---

[61] A notable exception is Josiah Willard Gibbs, who went to study in France and Germany after taking his doctorate at Yale in 1863; on appointment as a professor of mathematical physics at Yale in 1871, he made significant contributions to the thermodynamics of fluids.

[62] I am relying on Johnson (1990, p. 18) for the details about the study.

because its output of Ph.D.s in chemistry grew faster than that of Germany (Johnson, 1998).

Virtually none of these American Ph.D.s, however, was in synthetic organic chemistry. The university system trained analytical chemists that could do excellent soil analyses for American agriculture, analyze the quality of ore for steel magnates like Carnegie, and set up oil refining operations for oil tycoons like Rockefeller (Skolnik and Reese, 1976).[63] The heavy chemical industries making sulfuric acid, soda, and fertilizers had no trouble becoming competitive by international standards because they required little cutting-edge science. However, the entrepreneurs that started dye firms in the United States had to cope with a total absence of domestically trained talent. Entering the dye business required that entrepreneurs either had themselves received chemical training in Germany (as was the case with Schoellkopf) or relied on talent that had been educated in Germany or Switzerland (as was the case with Heller & Merz).[64] But, of course, the number of people who would go to Germany to receive an education and the number of German chemists who would come to the United States at the same salary level as in Germany was limited. Unlike the situation in Britain, where the Royal College of Chemistry (under Hofmann's leadership until 1865) educated students who could staff the new synthetic dye industry, the United States did not possess a center of organic chemistry that would educate potential entrepreneurs. (I will return later to the importance of the network of academics and industrialists in determining the competitive strength of Britain, Germany, and the United States.) It is not surprising, then, that the American dye industry started with delay, and that a much lower number of firms entered the industry before World War I.

Without a large number of firms that could experiment with different strategies for the new dye business, the United States was at a serious handicap. This handicap was turned into a formidable entry barrier by the actions of German entrepreneurs and later managers, who built large international firms that exploited economies of scale and scope and industrialized the innovation process. Once the Germans had transformed the competition in the dye industry onto a plane where large R&D laboratories were an essential component of corporate strategy, American firms had no chance to catch up and become significant players in free competition with German firms.

Supporting Organizations and the State

To Our Readers

It is a matter of surprise that the first commercial country of the world does not possess a single journal which, in a popular way, deals with the practical application of Chemical Sciences to the different branches of Art and Industry.

In Germany and France there appear more than forty journals, publishing and reviewing, in a more or less popular manner, the latest improvements, discoveries, &c. which have been made in Chemical Science in its relation to arts

---

[63] Only in response to the shortage of organic chemicals during World War I did the United States build up capabilities in synthetic organic chemistry. For details, see Kathryn Steen's (1995) dissertation.

[64] For biographies of leading dye entrepreneurs in the United States, see Hendrick (1924), Prochazka (1924), Derrick (1927), Merz (1944), and Haynes (1954).

*and manufactures. To this reason, it is mostly to be ascribed that both of these
countries have made, during the last twenty years, by far more rapid strides in the
knowledge and application of Chemistry than Great Britain.*

—Unsigned note in the Ivan Levinstein-founded
Chemical Review (1871, vol. 1, no. 3, p. 33)

Artificial Indigo
From the Chemiker Zeitung *(Coethen) we copy the following satisfactory
announcement.*

*According to information which we have personally obtained from Professor A.
Baeyer, the manufacture of indigo on the large scale is as yet* not even thought of.
*The artificial indigo lately exhibited at Nurnberg was specially produced and it is
simply to be regarded as a "preparation" – i.e., it cannot compete with natural indigo
as regards the cost of production. It is altogether questionable whether and when
indigo can be manufactured on the large scale.*

*This report is confirmed by the circumstances that the prices of indigo at the London
and Amsterdam sales show no symptoms of a decline. For all this the British public
and their rulers ought not to fold their hands in a fool's paradise. The production of
indigo in India is capable of improvement, and to effect this is a national concern.*

—Report in *Chemical Review* (1882, vol. 9, Dec.,
p. 40)

The Argument

Firms do not create all the resources, infrastructure, and knowledge that are required to
make a product by themselves. If one considers the variety of supporting organizations
associated with a particular industry, it becomes apparent that competency-enhancing
or -destroying innovations can occur not only at the firm level but also at the level of
what analysts have called the industrial district (e.g., Marshall, 1923; Krugman, 1991).
Besides encompassing firms and their suppliers and customers, industrial districts can
be defined to include such supporting institutions as professional organizations, trade
organizations, trade presses, information services, and government agencies that have
the ability to intervene in the affairs of the industry.

As the dye industry developed from 1857 to 1914, supporting institutions grew
much faster both in terms of size and quality in Germany than in Great Britain and the
United States. This helped the German dye industry cement and protect its leadership
position after the 1870s. Entry barriers were becoming higher and higher in Britain
and the United States because dye firms in these countries could not rely on the same
level of supporting institutions that were growing side by side in Germany with the
success of local dye firms.

Professional Organizations

A body of knowledge that is rapidly advancing requires its users to continue to keep
up with the field even after they leave the university. One of the roles of a professional

Table 3. **Frequency of Membership in National Chemical Societies**

Year	Britain	Germany	United States
1841	77		
1850	221		
1860	323		
1870	551	617	
1880	1,034	2,265	303
1890	1,698	3,440	238
1900	2,292	3,410	1,715
1910	3,073	3,359	5,081

Sources: Britain, Moore and Philip (1947); Germany, Lepsius (1918); Unites States, Thackray et al. (1985).

organization in chemistry was to serve as a forum that would disseminate new knowledge to chemists through such vehicles as meetings and journals. Britain was the first country to have a professional society for chemists on the national level. The London-based Chemical Society was formed in 1841 (Miall, 1931, p. 261); it started publishing proceedings and memoirs in the same year and a regular journal about chemical research in 1848 (Moore and Philip, 1947). Modeled after the British example, Germany saw the formation of a chemical society (Deutsche chemische Gesellschaft [German Chemical Society]) in 1867 and the United States (American Chemical Society) in 1876. The founding dates reflect the development of the local chemical industries, Britain being an early leader and Germany and the United States trailing in industrial development.

The number of members each national chemical society was able to attract gives some indication of how significant each national chemical community was in advancing the science of chemistry, an enterprise that had clearly become an international effort by the midnineteenth century. Table 3 shows how Germany was becoming the center of chemical science by 1870. Just before World War I, the United States had developed the largest chemical society, reflecting the dramatic growth of the inorganic chemical industry and the proliferation of American university chemists. However, organic chemistry was still relatively underdeveloped in the activities of the American Chemical Society. A special division for organic chemistry was established only in 1908 (Skolnik and Reese, 1976), reflecting the late development of organic chemistry in the United States.

In the beginning the British and German chemical societies were also concerned with the problems of industrial chemists.[65] Yet as the chemical industry grew, a single society was increasingly unable to fulfill at the same time the professional needs of academic chemists and chemists employed in industry. In the case of Germany, this led to the establishment of the Verein analytischer Chemiker (Association of Analytical

[65] A large number of factory owners, directors, and industry chemists were part of the German Chemical Society from the beginning. See Borscheid (1976, p. 123) for a breakdown of the professional backgrounds of the members for the years 1867 and 1868.

Chemists) in 1877. Only after some experimentation with the format of the society, reflected in two name changes, first to Gesellschaft für angewandte Chemie (Society for Applied Chemistry) in 1887 and then to Verein deutscher Chemiker (Association of German Chemists) in 1895, did the organization become very influential. When it finally settled on the goal of serving the professional concerns of all chemists in industry and academia, membership grew dramatically. With 3,900 members (4,200 counting the special members), the Association of German Chemists had more members by 1908 than did the German Chemical Society (Duisberg, 1923, p. 506). Citing these figures, Carl Duisberg claimed it was the largest chemical society in the world at the time. If one looks at the membership statistics of the Society for Chemical Industry, which had around 4,000 members, and of the American Chemical Society, which had also about the same numbers, the statement of Duisberg appears to be an exaggeration. But he was certainly correct in stating that in terms of serving professional chemists, the Association of German Chemists was the most successful organization in any country. Its journal of applied chemistry was influential far beyond the borders of Germany.

The Society for Chemical Industry, in contrast, was more narrowly focused on industry concerns. Formed in 1881 by leading British chemists and industrialists to provide a link between academic research and practical application of chemistry, the society over time became mainly focused on the concerns of the various branches of the chemical industry. Its journal covered extensively technical innovations and new patents in the industry but did not represent the professional concerns of individual chemists as was the case with Germany's Association of German Chemists. To some extent, this was simply a reflection of the fact that Britain possessed fewer academically trained chemists. Nonetheless, the Society for Chemical Industry proved to be a very useful forum for the chemical industry community and attracted many foreign members, particularly in the United States, where no comparable organization existed at the time. This prompted the U.S. members to create a special section of the society in 1894. One of the key differences between the British Chemical Society and the Society for Chemical Industry, on the one hand, and the German Chemical Society and the Association of German Chemists, on the other, was that the British organizations were founded and dominated by individuals with a focus on heavy chemicals, whereas in Germany, individuals with an organic chemistry background played a much larger role.[66] This meant that the interests of the dye industry were much more at the center of attention in the German professional organizations than in the British counterparts.

---

[66] The orientation of the Society of Chemical Industry is made evident in a report on its founding:

The first general meeting of this newly-formed society was held on Tuesday and Wednesday . . . The aim of the society is to bring more closely together the scientific chemist and the practical man, or, as it is worded in the laws "to promote the acquisition and practice of that species of knowledge which constitutes the profession of a chemical engineer." The society was intended to include all in any way connected with chemical science, and among its members were technical, analytical, and manufacturing chemists, professors and demonstrators, alkali manufacturers, chemical engineers, brewers, sugar refiners, distillers, &c., &c . . . [T]o enable [English manufacturers] more satisfactorily to meet the inevitable increase of foreign competition was one of the objectives for which the society had been formed . . . (*Chemical Review*, 1881, vol. 10, Aug., p. 217).

For the backgrounds of the founding members of the German chemical industry association, see Ungewitter (1927, pp. 5–14).

Trade Organizations

The Society for Chemical Industry constituted a mixture between the Association of German Chemists and a third German organization of great influence, the Verein zur Wahrung der Interessen der deutschen chemischen Industrie (Association for Protection of the Interests of the German Chemical Industry; Chemical Industry Association, for short). Whereas the Association of German Chemists represented the interests of the individual chemists (who in ever-larger numbers as well as proportion became employed in industry, particularly when the R&D laboratories raised the demand for able researchers), the Association for Protection of the Interests of the German Chemical Industry was founded in 1877 to look after the interests of the chemical firms. Because the interests of chemists were often quite different from those of chemical firms, possessing two separate organizations proved to be advantageous in providing a more supportive environment that allowed chemical firms as well as chemists to prosper in Germany.

In Britain, an association analogous to the Association for Protection of the Interests of the German Chemical Industry was formed only in 1916 (the Association of British Chemical Manufacturers) to respond to the problems created by World War I. Until that time, individual branches of the chemical industry set up more or less successful trade organizations. Britain trailed Germany by thirty-nine years in creating such a specialized industry-wide trade association, in part because the greater cooperative spirit that still prevailed in Germany made it easier to achieve the necessary agreement for such an organization. Furthermore, the German chemical industry was only starting to take off, whereas in Britain different branches of the heavy chemical industry had been operating successfully for decades without a collective coordinating body. The same logic was in part responsible for the early creation of a U.S. trade organization, the Manufacturing Chemists' Association. In fact, when formed in 1872, it was the very first trade association in the Western Hemisphere.[67] Although it was very instrumental in helping support the causes of the rapidly growing and successful heavy chemical industry, the association did not pay much attention to the fledgling dye industry.

A cursory survey of industries and their trade organizations seems to suggest a fairly strong correlation between the success of a national dye industry and the existence of a strong trade association. It is very difficult to tease out which came first – strong firms or a strong industry association – but in many cases trade associations seem to have played a powerful role in protecting the leadership position of a national industry rather than initiating the rise to leadership. In Britain, the successful coal-tar distillers (who were the dominant suppliers of the chief raw material for dyes even to the German firms) formed a trade association (Association of Tar-Distillers) in 1885. Similarly, the very successful textile dyers and printers formed an influential trade organization (Society of Dyers and Colourists), which was organized in the same year. In contrast, the declining dye manufacturing industry of Great Britain was not supported by any significant trade organization. This changed only when the dyestuff crisis provoked by World War I made collective action imperative for the military effort.

---

[67] The organization continues to exist today under the slightly modernized name, Chemical Manufacturers Association. The German industry association is also still active today, although it had to move from Berlin to Frankfurt after World War II and changed its name to Verband der chemischen Industrie. (Chemical Industry Association).

Academic and Trade Journals and Other Information Sources

Because Levinstein (founder of the *Chemical Review*) never hesitated to exaggerate when he could hope to further the causes of his enterprises and his industry, the quote at the beginning of this section may overstate the extent to which Germany enjoyed a better coverage of the developments in the chemical industry. But it is safe to say that from the 1870s onward the most useful information on chemistry (both basic and applied) and the dye industry was published in Germany.[68] The *Berichte der deutschen chemischen Gesellschaft (Reports of the German Chemical Society)*, first published in 1867, became the most important academic journal for chemistry in the world, and the *Zeitschrift für angewandte Chemie (Journal for Applied Chemistry)*, first published in 1887 (and later purchased by the *Verein deutscher Chemiker*), acquired the same status in the field of applied chemistry.[69] The *Chemiker Zeitung* (Newspaper for Chemists), founded in 1878, focused on reporting prices and commercial news. The fortnightly publication *Chemische Industrie (Chemical Industry)* was the organ of industry association and published "excellent statistical series and carried weight in industrial quarters" (Haber, 1971, p. 36). Before World War I, Germany put out the most extensive chemical firm directories (both for Germany and foreign countries). It is no accident that, at the time, the only systematic overview of all the synthetic dyes available on the market was produced by the German dye experts Schultz and Julius.

Because Germany had the manpower and the knowledge to publish the best information about organic chemistry and innovations relevant for the dye industry, German dye firms had easier access to information that was of competitive importance. If British and American firms wanted to avoid this handicap, they had to have talent that could at least read German. It is not surprising, then, that American Ph.D. students in chemistry were forced until World War II to pass an exam in German to demonstrate their comprehension of the language (Ralph Landau, personal communication, 1997). This would give them direct, albeit delayed, access to the leading published research in organic chemistry.

British Organizations and Natural Indigo

Britain's inability to provide the same quality of supporting institutions had much to do with the fact that that country, in contrast to Germany, had large investments in indigo plantations in India. Garfield (2001, p. 125) reports that 2,800 firms in India were producing indigo before the synthetic version of the dye appeared on the

---

[68] A reader (signing as "Analyst") could complain about the deteriorating quality of the *Journal of the British Chemical Society*:

Some months ago a general meeting of the Fellows of the Chemical Society was held at Burlington House. At this meeting, among others things, the condition of the Society's *Journal* was discussed, and various improvements were suggested and promised. So far, however, we are sorry to say, no beneficial results seem to have been produced. The *Journal* appears as late as ever, and the character of the abstracts becomes less and less satisfactory (*Chemical Review*, 1877, vol. 7, no. 75, Dec., p. 288).

[69] The centrality of German chemical journals in worldwide chemistry research is evident from cross-citation indexes. Because scientific leadership in the field of chemistry resided in Germany until World War I, U.S. researchers were required to read and cross-reference German articles very frequently. German researchers, in contrast, could largely ignore American research publications before 1914 (see Thackray et al., 1985, pp. 154–60, for quantitative evidence).

market. The second opening quote of this section conveys powerfully how synthetic dyes were perceived more as a threat than an opportunity in British circles.[70] Because indigo had been one of the most important dyestuffs for centuries, Britain, as the largest producer of textiles, consumed vast quantities of indigo. The British demand for indigo and other natural dyes gave rise to a larger number of firms than in either Germany or the United States that specialized in refining, trading, and selling natural dyes. Given the British involvement in India, synthetic dyes represented a greater destruction of existing competencies in natural dye farming and refining for Britain than for Germany and the United States. Not surprisingly, then, Britain was much more reluctant than the other countries to create supporting institutions for synthetic dyes. Becoming active on behalf of the synthetic dye industry would threaten to make existing investment in the natural dye business obsolete. If the government authorities had wanted to implement policies that could have helped the British dye industry compete with their German rivals, those policies would have always at the same time hurt the British interests in natural dyes.

The State

In studying the competitive dynamics of an industry over longer periods of time, one can scarcely not be struck by the many ways in which political authorities can and actually do involve themselves in setting and enforcing the rules according to which firms compete with one another. Besides providing support for education, research, and training (which has already been discussed), the two most important policy instruments the state possesses to influence the fortunes of the domestic industry are taxes and tariffs. For example, until industrial alcohol became exempted from the spirit duty in 1902 (Haber, 1971, p. 221), British dye firms faced a higher cost for industrial alcohol than Germany. Although this higher tax was certainly not the main reason for the decline of the British dye industry, it did put British firms at a competitive disadvantage.

The ability of the state to influence the fortunes of the local industry is evident from the change in U.S. tariff policy. After imposing a very high tariff for several years to afford the infant dye industry with protection, the U.S. government lowered tariffs on dyes considerably in 1883 (Hesse, 1915; Steen, 1995, p. 70). One year later, five companies (half of all existing dye firms) had been forced out of the market because they could no longer compete with foreign firms (Haynes, 1954, p. 310). (I will return to a more detailed discussion of how tariff policies came about in Chapter 4.)

Taking Stock

It would be wrong to conclude from the experience of the early dye industry that a collection of strong supporting institutions by itself assures the emergence of a strong industry. In the case of the German dye industry, it does appear that strong supporting institutions developed side by side with strong firms. In some cases, strong

---

[70] Already in 1876, the editors of *Chemical Review* saw synthetic indigo as a threat rather than an opportunity:

> In this country we have no reason to wish for artificial indigo, since the bulk of the natural indigo is grown with British capital on British territory. We recollect when the coal-tar colours first came up certain enthusiasts went about phrophesying [*sic*] that henceforth we should produce all our own colours. Alas, we are as far off the mark as ever, for instead of importing dye from our own colonies, we procure them from other countries, to which we actually export the raw material for their manufacture (*Chemical Review*, 1876, Sept., p. 224).

supporting institutions emerged only after the industry had already started and had become successful. With the rise of more supporting institutions, the German dye industry over time became even stronger, explaining why it was able to achieve a near world monopoly. The reverse process seems to have been operating in Britain and the United States. Weaker dye industries did not provide enough of a stimulus for strong supporting institutions to emerge.

In the particular case of trade associations, apparently they were effective only when the dye industry had achieved a certain level of success. The emergence of a chemical trade association can be seen as a tool that buffered incumbent German leaders from foreign challenges. The same logic seems to hold true in industries that were successful in Britain (coal-tar distillers and dyers and printers) and the United States (producers of heavy chemicals). This hypothesis finds additional support by the later developments in the dye industry. Only when the United States and Britain put in place the same kind of supporting institutions during and after World War I did the British and U.S. dye industries start to catch up with the German one.

The Academic–Industrial Knowledge Network

The purpose of this new German Chemical Society is to provide a forum where representatives of speculative and applied chemistry can exchange ideas and thereby reaffirm the alliance between science and industry [my translation].

> —A. W. HOFMANN, 1867, speaking to the constituting gathering of the German Chemical Society; quoted in Johnson (1992, p. 167)

I had never met a technologist in all my life, and I gazed at them as if they were creatures from another planet [my translation].

> —PROFESSOR ADOLF BAEYER, after meeting for the first time Engelhorn, Caro, and Clemm of the BASF corporation in his laboratory and commencing a long collaboration with the firm; quoted in Roggersdorf (1965, p. 27)

As we have seen earlier, Germany among the three countries possessed the best research and training system in synthetic organic chemistry. Because the most important dye innovations before the rise of corporate R&D laboratories came from individuals who were affiliated with university research laboratories, the success of an individual firm depended in many ways on its ability to establish ties with university researchers.[71] After the mid-1880s, when dye innovations more and more came out of

---

[71] In the first few years of the dye industry (until around 1862), colorists, who worked in the dyeing and printing industries and possessed considerable chemical knowledge of a practical kind, were also reponsible for several innovations in the dye industry. But their role faded away as scientific knowledge about dye chemistry advanced and made academic training in the field a prerequisite for inventing new dyes. On the role of colorists in the early dye industry, see Homburg (1983) and Travis (1992).

corporate R&D laboratories, firms were still dependent on the universities to train the staff of the industry laboratories in the art of organic chemistry and to recommend students to take positions in the dye industry. Acquiring the skills to do dye syntheses was not a matter of mere book learning. Hands-on experience in a laboratory was the prerequisite for being able to create new dyes. Because knowledge of synthetic organic chemistry was such a critical resource for firms in the dye industry, strong connections to the holders of this knowledge were a key variable in the long-term success of individual firms.

In this section I will try to establish the following claims: Because the social center of this knowledge network was in Germany (especially after a key actor, August Hofmann, moved from Britain back to Germany), the German dye industry had an important competitive advantage over its British and American competitors. Firms in Britain and the United States tried to overcome this disadvantage as much as they could by hiring people who had gained access to this knowledge network.

Reasons for an Academic–Industrial Alliance

Because knowledge of organic chemistry resided with academics and their students, it is quite obvious why firms were eager to establish ties with university researchers: They wanted to gain access to the most important strategic resource that would allow them to put innovative dyes into the market. Heinrich Caro's (the early research director of BASF) ties with Carl Graebe and Carl Liebermann and their teacher Adolf Baeyer provided the firm with direct and almost exclusive access to the laboratory of one of the most productive dye chemists of the time. Owing to this special relationship, BASF was able to be first on the market with two of the most important dye innovations before 1914: synthetic alizarin and later synthetic indigo.[72]

But why would academics enter in such close relationship with industrial firms? After all, academics were expected to advance and disseminate knowledge that would be accessible for everyone, rather than enter into special relationships with particular firms and grant them preferred access to their knowledge. The biographies of such leading organic chemists as Justus von Liebig, August Hofmann, Adolf Baeyer, Otto Witt, and Emil Fischer are revealing in this respect. Material gains did motivate these academics, although they could not display this too overtly. But personal material interests were not necessary to give academics a strong incentive to interact with industry. Even if they only had been motivated to advance their respective scientific enterprises, they would have found it expedient to forge strong ties with industrial firms, for several reasons.

Let us assume that the chief motive of scientists is to make many important discoveries, become leaders in their fields, and win great reputations during their lifetime, possibly even for the rest of history. To become a leading scientist in organic chemistry, it was important to run a large laboratory with competent students who would participate in the scientific enterprise. Most of these students would not be able to secure a position in academe. If a professor had strong ties to industry, he would be more able to help his students secure a position in a firm. Hence strong

[72] Reinhardt (1997, pp. 335–64) provides short career biographies of the research chemists who worked at BASF between 1873 and 1899. The biographies make it possible to track the movement of chemists between universities and industrial firms.

ties to industry made it easier to run a big laboratory that could attract many good students. Large laboratories even in those days were expensive to build and maintain. Industrial firms could provide academic chemists with expensive chemicals required for lab experiments in return for consulting services. Furthermore, strong and successful contacts to industry were very important in convincing governments to support science. Being able to point out the success of dye firms in creating new products based on chemical science and enjoying strong support from industrial circles made it much easier to secure funding for large laboratories from society at large. Hence, by giving firms access to advanced theoretical knowledge and laboratory know-how, professors could hope to receive favorable press for their field and subsequently greater support. By the same token, a professor in a particular country had stronger incentives to help domestic firms because they could in turn be more instrumental in helping his research endeavors.

A similar logic would also push an academic researcher to establish strong ties to his colleagues, despite the unavoidable competition for prestige and resources that would exist between any two researchers. If a scientist wanted to attract to his laboratory the most talented students who wanted to become professors, he had to have a reputation for being very effective in securing a university position for them. Co-opting other professors who had a large influence over university appointments thus could be very important in running large successful laboratories because students would be more likely to find an academic job working for a professor who had good contacts with other leading chemists.

Anatomy of the Knowledge Network

If one were to map the contacts between academic organic chemists, dye chemists in industry, and dye entrepreneurs, some striking network patterns would emerge. Several leading academic chemists were at the center of the network: Hofmann (in London until 1865, then Berlin until 1892), Baeyer (Berlin, Strasbourg, Munich), and Witt (first in private industry in Britain, France, and Germany, then professor of chemical technology at the Technische Hochschule in Berlin). Similarly, among the industrial members of the network, some players such as Caro at BASF and Martius at AGFA and later Duisberg at Bayer acquired central positions.

The origin of the network can be traced to Liebig, who trained a generation of leading chemists (among them Hofmann, Kekulé – who in turn was the teacher of Baeyer – and many British and some American chemists). Figure 9 is a representation of the early industrial–academic network that connected entrepreneurs with academic sources of knowledge.[73] The early British entrepreneurs in the dye industry almost exclusively came out of Hofmann's laboratory at the Royal College of Chemistry in London (see Fox, 1987, and Travis, 1993, for biographical details). Later Baeyer, Hofmann, and Kekulé trained in Germany many of the chemists who would develop the new dyes.

The structure of this academic–industrial knowledge network (its centers and peripheral regions) is powerfully revealed by examining the migration frequencies of chemists from university to industry (Table 4), of chemists from firm to firm

---

[73] The figure is a simplified representation of the early dye network. It does not contain all relationships and is meant to be suggestive rather than exhaustive.

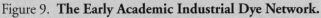
Figure 9. The Early Academic Industrial Dye Network.

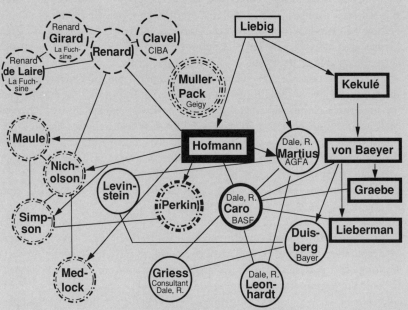

Circles represent individuals in industry (the words in small letters identify firm[s] with which the individual is affiliated if not evident from his name), squares represent academics. Lines with arrows on one end represent teacher–student relationships. Graebe, for example, is the student of von Baeyer. Individuals on the right side of the figure are Germans; individuals in the southwest corner are British; individuals in the northwest corner French; and Muller-Pack in the upper middle is Swiss. Thicker lines indicate that the individual is relatively more important. Hofmann is positioned in the middle of the figure because he assumed the central role in the early period of the academic–industrial network. Some of the information in this figure is drawn from Travis (1993).

(Table 5), and of students who sought advanced training in organic chemistry (Table 6). Although it was quite frequent for German chemists to go to Great Britain to seek employment there, British or American chemists did not possess the training that would have made it lucrative for them or their prospective employers to go Germany. Especially in the early period, German chemists would frequently go to Great Britain to gain experience in the most advanced economy at the time. Along with Hofmann, who was active at the Royal College of Chemistry from 1845 until 1865, chemists such as Carl Alexander Martius (later at AGFA) and Heinrich Caro (later at BASF) gained experience in the British dye industry that proved very useful once they started or became involved in synthetic dye firms in Germany. Others like Eugen Lucius (later at Hoechst) spent time in Manchester to round out their education and learn about the state of the art in textile manufacturing and its associated trades (Bäumler, 1988, p. 33). When individuals had gained foreign experience, it meant that they were willing to immerse themselves in the language and customs of another society. The willingness and ability of German dye firms to go international at an early date had a lot to do with the fact that the leaders of many dye firms had established

Table 4. Movement of Industry Chemists (by Nationality) to Firms[a]

Destination	Nationality of chemist		
	German	British	American
German firm	Very many	Very, very few	None[b]
British firm	Some	Many	None
U.S. firm	Few	Few	Some

[a] The table entries represent the relative frequency of reaching a destination state, given a particular state of origin.

[b] By "none," I mean that I have not encountered a case in my sources and it is plausible that such case, indeed, exists. Of course, there is always the possibility that one or two such cases have occurred without having been recorded.

Table 5. Movement of Industry Chemists from Firm to Firm

Destination state	Origination state		
	German firms	British firms	U.S. firms
German firms	Very many	Some	Very few
British firms	Some	Many	Very few
U.S. firms	Few	Some	Some

Destination state: Chemists in firms in a particular country.

Table 6. Movement of Students to Study Advanced Chemistry

Location of advanced training	Student's geographic home		
	Germany	Britain	United States
Germany	Very many	Some/Many	Many
Britain	Very few[a]	Many	None
United States	None[b]	None	Some

[a] If we were to look at subperiods, it would be evident that before 1865 some Germans went to London to receive advanced training with Hofmann. After 1865, almost no German student went to Britain because Hofmann's departure left Britain with no leader in the field of organic chemistry who had an international stature and strong connections to German academic centers.

[b] See footnote [b] in Table 4.

knowledgeable contacts in foreign lands and were eager to expand their marketing organizations abroad.[74]

The center of the academic–industrial network became located in Germany because the laboratories of Hofmann (Berlin), Baeyer (Berlin, Strasbourg, Munich), and later Emil Fischer (Strasbourg, Munich, Berlin) became leading centers of organic chemistry where new knowledge was created at a faster rate than in British laboratories. Students from the United States and Britain would very frequently come to Germany to receive advanced training in organic chemistry. But a reverse flow did not take place once Hofmann had left London. Britain attracted a substantial number of German chemists because the British pioneers of the dye as well as the large dyeing and brewing industries provided an excellent training ground as well as jobs that were often hard to come by in Germany, where chemists were typically in oversupply. Given the scarcity (or absence in the case of the United States) of strong training programs in organic chemistry and the need to gain access to the dye advances made in Germany, British and American firms hired German- or Swiss-trained chemists. I have not come across a British or American firm in the period before World War I that did not put German or Swiss chemists on its staff at one point or another. Whereas the very large firms such as BASF, Bayer, and Hoechst were typically able to retain their chemists, smaller firms such as Kalle and Oehler lost chemists to British firms that would pay higher remunerations (Ernst Homburg, personal communication, 1997).

British dye firms were also in a number of cases the training ground for British and German chemists who then went on to the United States to pursue opportunities in this rapidly growing market. The academic–industrial network came to be centered in Germany because of its continued leadership role in the training of organic chemists. American and British students continued to flock to Germany, sometimes even after they had already gained some industrial experience and realized that they needed to be taught the advanced knowledge available in Germany to be able to compete.[75]

Although the network branched across all the major dye-producing and -consuming countries, the strongest links existed in Germany. Because German academics had a stronger incentive to help German firms than their British or American rivals, German firms had less difficulty in establishing a strong relationship to academics.

How the Network Was Formed, Maintained, and Expanded

Dissecting the anatomy of the academic–industrial network indeed shows that its centers were located in Germany, but it does not provide a satisfactory account of

---

[74] In the past two decades the largest numbers of foreign students in the United States have come from Japan. The success of Japanese firms in the American market is clearly related to the policy of many large Japanese firms and government agencies to send students abroad for at least a year or two so that they become acquainted with American business practices. Japanese often refer to the M.B.A. programs not as Master of Business Administration but as "Master of Being American," highlighting that the most important thing for Japanese students who typically have received a university education in Japan is to become acquainted with the United States and establish ties. The Japanese are now only repeating on a larger scale what Germans successfully practiced in the nineteenth century.

[75] A good example is Dan Dawson. After founding a dye firm in Great Britain, Dawson, at age thirty-eight, decided to let his brothers run the business while he went to the University of Berlin in 1874 to study with Hofmann (Fox, 1987, p. 141).

how the academic–industrial network came to be formed in Germany and how it was maintained and expanded in such a way that German chemists and firms remained the central actors.

Origins

Justus von Liebig pioneered not only the laboratory method (which today is the standard teaching method all over the world) but also the practice of networking intensely with businessmen, large property owners (the latter particularly in Britain), and government officials. In his famous periodical *Chemische Briefe* (Chemical Letters), he tirelessly articulated the utilitarian benefits that society would enjoy from investing heavily in chemical research and teaching facilities: The promise was nothing short of relieving mankind from hunger and sickness. Many of his students became entrepreneurs in chemicals (Borscheid, 1976), keeping in touch with their teacher, sending him chemicals that would be of use to his laboratory, hiring graduates, and promulgating the message of their master.[76] Liebig also became a partner in business ventures, for example, a fertilizer factory in Britain (Meinel, 1992, p. 32).

The student–teacher relationship was the most important mechanism that created the strong links in the network. Spending long hours together in the laboratory, making joint scientific discoveries, and publishing papers under joint authorship not only transferred the knowledge (often tacit) of how to do organic chemistry but also created strong emotional ties between teachers and students. It was not uncommon that a student would marry into the teacher's family, and sometimes a teacher would marry into the family of the student (Burchardt, 1992, p. 10). Hofmann, for example, celebrated his wedding with the niece of Liebig before going to London in 1845. Liebig's good contacts in Great Britain (the husband of the queen was a German prince) was the reason why Hofmann was appointed first professor of chemistry at the Royal College of Chemistry. Having one of his best students in London established more than a beachhead of the Liebig network in Great Britain.

Although Liebig established the model for academic–industrial collaboration, his student Hofmann must be credited with perfecting it (hence the revealing quote at the beginning of this section). When the synthetic dye industry was started by Hofmann's student Perkin, Hofmann became a true academic entrepreneur, redirecting his own research projects more toward synthetic dyes, filing dye patents, serving as consultant to firms of his British students, serving as a juror at world exhibitions, becoming a witness in patent fights, and playing other roles that would forge numerous ties between science and industry.

Carl Alexander Martius (student of Liebig in Munich, then of Hofmann in London, and chemist at Dale Roberts with Heinrich Caro before returning as Hofmann's assistant to Germany in 1865) reports in his *Chemische Erinnerungen aus der Berliner Vergangenheit* (1918) that Hofmann's decision to return to Germany was based to a large extent on his desire to create a research school in the tradition of Liebig.[77]

---

[76] I mentioned earlier that Liebig's academic enterprise is very well documented. The recent articles by Fruton (1988) and Holmes (1989) provide a particularly detailed account of the career path of the students who left Liebig's laboratory.

[77] The English translation would be "Chemical Memories from the Past in Berlin." The students of Hofmann put together a book containing their memories of the time with Hofmann in Berlin. Martius

The number of students enrolling in his British laboratory was insufficient to allow him to run an operation of comparable size to those of the research schools of Liebig, Bunsen, Kolbe, or Kekulé. The death in 1862 of his chief sponsor in Britain, Prince Albert, the German-born husband of Queen Victoria, meant that his work environment in Britain was going to become more difficult rather than easier.[78] Because Prussia wanted to catch up with the smaller German states in chemical education, government officials started negotiating with Hofmann in 1862 about taking up the vacant professorship at Bonn and later, when two incumbent professors died, in Berlin. Hofmann accepted the position after Prussia agreed to build and fund a large institute with a new laboratory for about 100 students and room for a smaller laboratory that Hofmann could use for his private work. Martius (1918, p. 9) also cites the unwillingness of British firms to enter into a closer cooperation with Hofmann as a reason why Hofmann decided to return to Germany, although he clearly enjoyed his position there. He cherished the stature he had acquired in London society despite the fact that the substantial practical assignments that came with his London position did not give him as much time to do fundamental research as he would have liked (Roberts, 1992).

Although possibly Martius is reinterpreting history through the eyes of his later relationship with Hofmann (in 1867 he had founded one of the most successful dye firms in Germany [AGFA] and obtained a monopoly of Hofmann's research findings and students [Meinel, 1992, p. 45]), we have no reason to doubt that Hofmann had weighed very carefully the pros and cons of leaving his London position.[79] Hofmann, who had lived long enough in Great Britain (he had even taken up citizenship) and was the president of the Chemical Society (1861), was sufficiently well connected to judge in what social context he would be more able to create a network of close relationships with industry and other academics.[80] When he set up his shop in Berlin, Britain no longer possessed a leading center of organic chemisty.[81]

seems to have updated his contribution in 1918 and then published it also as a stand-alone piece, which I was able to obtain and use here.

[78] Garfield (2001, p. 85) provides the text of a letter written by Jaz Clark, a secretary of Windsor Castle, dated 27 March 1865 that demonstrates how important was the support of the Royal Family in bringing Hofmann to Great Britain in the first place.

Dear Dr. Hofmann, I have received the Queen's commands to express to you the great pleasure which Herself and the Royal Family derived from the very interesting and clear lectures on chemistry, and the beautiful experiments by which they were illustrated, delivered in Windsor Castle last week. Her Majesty also admired the numerous beautiful specimens of richly coloured silks and wools, the results of the recently discovered aniline dyes, and perceives clearly great advantage to the material interests of this country which must result from the discovery of these beautiful colours, and it gave her great pleasure to learn that they originated from researches conducted in the Royal College of Chemistry, in which the late Royal Highness the Prince Consort took so much interest...

[79] A report in the *Chemical Review* shows that the nature of the relationship between Hofmann and AGFA was very public. In the May 1878 issue (p. 406) the journal reported that an assistant of Hofmann had invented a dye that was produced by AGFA.

[80] For an overview of his industrial connections in Britain, see Russell (1992, p. 62).

[81] Until the mid-1880s, a smaller center in the dye chemistry network in France supported the early strength of the French industry. However, as Haller (1903) documents on the occasion of the World Exhibition in Paris, the French research center collapsed in parallel with the French dye industry. Ernst Homburg

Maintenance

One way to maintain the network was to look out for the best students. Hofmann gave his former student Martius the job of his Berlin assistant. Similarly, when Adolf Baeyer (Nobel Prize recipient, 1905) received a call in 1875 to become professor for organic chemistry in Munich and to direct a new large chemical laboratory, he took two of his best students, Emil Fischer (Nobel Prize recipient, 1902) and Otto Fischer, with him. Very shortly after their return to Germany, Martius and Hofmann together with Wichelhaus organized formation of the German Chemical Society (1867) to create a place where academic chemists and industrialists could meet, exchange chemical information, and form strong ties (Lepsius, 1918). Hofmann was the leader behind the society until his death in 1892 (Martius, 1918, p. 14).

To maintain the cohesiveness of the knowledge network even after the creation of such other societies as the German Chemical Industry Association and the Association of German Chemists provided other forums for chemists and industrialists, the three societies were held together by substantial overlap of their membership. Particularly at the highest levels, substantial interlock guaranteed a close coordination of the three societies. Because the chemical societies in Britain and Germany were open to foreign members, the knowledge network could be maintained in a looser way even across countries. To make sure that their ideas would travel the world over, leading chemists such as Hofmann would maintain their membership in the British Chemical Society, and the same was true of the British chemists in Germany.

Besides the periodical meetings of national chemical societies, important information was communicated through the various chemical journals. Although the journals in principle were accessible by everyone around the world, replicating and being able to make use of information communicated were somewhat contingent on having shared knowledge to begin with. Hence public journals could maintain only weak ties.

To maintain strong ties, private correspondence was a frequent tool for staying in touch even outside the meetings at chemical societies, world exhibitions, celebrations, court hearings, and the like. During their long collaboration, Heinrich Caro (BASF) and Professor Adolf Baeyer wrote each other hundreds of letters. In a letter dated August 3, 1883, for example, Baeyer informed Caro that he had just clarified the remaining uncertainties about the structure of synthetic indigo; at the end of the letter Baeyer inquires, "How is your wife?" (Seefelder, 1994, p. 57). The case of Caro and Baeyer was very typical: All leading organic chemists maintained elaborate correspondence with their most important colleagues and industrial partners to communicate information they did not want to share with the entire chemical community.[82] Those firms that had established special connections with individual leading professors were, of course, eager to keep competitively relevant information away from their rivals as long as possible.

and I plan to investigate the causal ordering of these two events in an upcoming study. Switzerland, being fully integrated in the German-speaking university system, also had a center of dye chemistry at the Federal Polytechnic in Zurich, which provided excellent dye chemists not only to Swiss but also to German dye firms.

[82] The correspondence of many German chemists of the time (Liebig, Hofmann, Baeyer, Caro, Graebe, and Liebermann, among others) have been put into a special collection at the *Deutsches Museum* in Munich and are accessible for scholars.

Expansion

In a world where knowledge was rapidly expanding, new chemists were to appear on the scene who had not been educated at the centers of the network. For the network to expand without core players losing substantial control, it had to reach out to such talented outsiders and co-opt them into the inner circle. Eduard Ulrich (1839–1917) appears to be one such example of someone who was educated by a relatively peripheral player at the University of Marburg but ended up in as the technical leader of Hoechst's dye shop in the 1880s.

The network also expanded as some players took on jobs in the supporting institutions that were growing along with the rise of the dye industry. Schultz worked at the Martius-founded AGFA firm in Berlin before he became the famous editor of the Farbstofftabellen (dye directory). Another member of the AGFA staff was appointed commissioner of patents (*Chemical Review*, Oct. 1883, p. 301), providing the dye industry with a strong contact at the patent office only six years after the office had been created.

Furthermore, the patent suits that had started in Britain and France in the 1860s and continued to plague the industry until 1914 created the side-effect of bringing together chemists (as expert witnesses) and industrialists (as opponents). This provided players the opportunity to form strong relationships despite the antagonism in the courtroom. Not surprisingly, Hofmann had appeared in court cases in England and France already in the 1860s. Hofmann was so ubiquitous until his death in 1892 that a member of the dye community could have easily exclaimed, "All roads lead back to Hofmann!"

The academic–industrial network expanded much faster in Germany than in Britain and the United States. When Hofmann's new research institute opened its doors in 1869 and Baeyer was given an even larger institute in Munich by the Bavarian government, these two academic centers socialized into the network many more students than in Britain and the United States.[83] Edward Frankland (Hofmann's successor at the Royal College of Chemistry), Henry Roscoe and Carl Schorlemmer at the Owens College in Manchester, and Arthur G. Green at the newly established University of Leeds were part of the larger organic chemistry network; however, because they did not train students on the same scale as their German colleagues, and because on average British dye firms were not as eager as their German rivals to establish close contacts, they did not play as central a role as the leading German professors.

Functions and Consequences of the Knowledge Network

The anatomy of the academic–industrial network had major competitive implications for the dye industries of the three countries. Burt (1992) has provided an admirable

---

[83] After his appointment in Berlin (1865) until his death in 1892, Hofmann worked at breathtaking speed. During this period he graduated 150 doctoral students, and he published alone and with his students 899 pieces of research (Meinel, 1992, p. 44). The other towering figure in dye chemistry, A. Baeyer, had a similar rate of output. From 1875 to 1915, 560 people were associated with his group in Munich, which generated about 1,200 papers on organic chemistry. Of these 560, 395 received their Ph.D. under Baeyer or one of his many lieutenants (Morrell, 1983, p. 106). The design of Baeyer's laboratory space served as a model for chemistry laboratories the world over for the next fifty years. Only because German professors were training so many students was Germany able to "export" organic chemists to Britain and the United States.

overview of how the structure of a social network confers competitive advantages on players who enjoy greater structural autonomy than their competitors. Burt identifies structural holes, the disconnections or nonequivalences between players in an arena, as the underlying causes for the differential performance of individual players (p. 2). In Burt's formulation of social network theory, those players that are in relative terms surrounded by more structural holes enjoy greater entrepreneurial opportunities that, when acted upon, create greater returns. As a location where a network of social relations intersects, players can achieve a competitive advantage if they have access to opportunities, if they are the ones who are informed about these opportunities early, if they can marshal support of others in exploiting the opportunities, and finally if they can achieve some degree of control over these opportunities. These information and control benefits are, according to Burt, the principal mechanisms by which the social ties that connect players provide individuals and firms with better or worse opportunities for extracting economic rents.

What evidence is there that such social network mechanisms played a role in conferring a competitive advantage on German firms, allowing them to outperform their British and American rivals? The structure of the knowledge network as it developed clearly discriminated between the different players. German firms were systematically in a better position to be faced with entrepreneurial opportunities. This does not imply, however, that each firm would actually take advantage of these opportunities.

First, consider access to existing scientific knowledge and know-how. Because the largest number of leading organic chemists were located in Germany, German entrepreneurs (often students of these professors) had much better access to scientific know-how that would allow them to outperform rivals in the long run.

What about the differentials in information about new technological threats and opportunities? Relatively speaking, ties within the knowledge network were stronger and denser within Germany than between Germany and the other states. Given that most dye innovations after 1865 came out of Germany, German entrepreneurs and firms would be more likely to hear about these opportunities earlier. BASF gaining first access to the work of Graebe and Liebermann is an important example. Even when important discoveries were made in Britain, they would travel more quickly back to Germany (the origin of the network) than to the United States. This meant that German firms were more protected against innovations made abroad because they would be quickly informed about them and possessed the capabilities necessary to copy or build upon the innovation. Two examples illustrate this process: Heinrich Caro (BASF) and Otto Witt shared the discoveries on the new class of azo dyes with one another at the London International Exhibition of 1876 (Morris and Travis, 1992, p. 80). The Bayer Company was warned about the threats and opportunities coming from this new class of azo dyes through an indirect contact to Peter Griess, the inventor of azo dyes. The firm quickly created a strong tie to Peter Griess, purchasing the patent he had acquired (Flechtner, 1963, p. 14). The professional societies, the different trade journals, and so forth, all contributed to the information advantages of German firms.

Control over new knowledge was also an important differentiating factor. Once German firms had established contacts with the leading dye chemists, it was relatively difficult, often impossible, for a domestic rival and even more so for a foreign rival to gain similar access to a professor. Professors would grant privileged access to the new discoveries and the best students, typically to one (Hofmann's relationship with AGFA) or sometimes two firms (Baeyer's relationship with BASF and Hoechst). This meant that once a firm was ahead in securing access to critical scientific expertise, it was in the position to translate such a relation into a long-term competitive advantage.

Given these network dynamics, British firms were advantaged over the American firms because they were socially closer to the important research schools in Germany. Not surprisingly, German chemists came to the United States often by way of an intermediate stop in a British firm.

The network of players in the dye industry had other important functions that are most conveniently presented together with the themes of Chapter 4. In that chapter, I will focus especially on how the network was a central instrument in shaping the patent laws in Germany and in setting up nonuniversity research laboratories. Both of these events helped to enhance the competitive advantage of the German institutional environment.

Social Organization of Production at the Shop Floor

In these [dye work] establishments there are two distinct sets of men, between whom there is placed a great gulf. On the one hand, there are the foremen over the different departments... They have all learned their business by apprenticeship, and are left to exercise their own discretion each in his department, being, of course responsible for the results. On the other hand, the great body of workmen are known as "slabs," "mules," and other uncomplimentary names... These men, as a rule, know little about what they are doing, and care less.

> —Unsigned editorial in *Chemical Review* (1874, Nov., p. 27) on the organization of labor in British dye-works

[T]he supervision and the improvement of plants is handed to academically-trained chemists, the stifling influence of uneducated supervisors and "old practitioners" is removed, while abroad the domination of the "contre-maître" and the "foreman" continues to flourish [my translation].

> —HEINRICH CARO (1904, p. 1357), director of R&D at BASF, 1868–1890

Being surrounded by a superior research and training system in the end only matters for the competitive position of a firm if the firm is able to use the technical expertise available in the environment and translate it into lower-cost or higher-quality products. Cost and quality of products are often largely determined by the social organization of the shop floor. When firms in all countries have the same efficiency in their plants, the social organization of production clearly has no bearing on competitive advantage. However, when firms display great diversity in terms of the ability to manufacture at low cost and high quality, the way in which the production process is organized may, in fact, be a leading factor underlying the competitive advantage.

In recent times, the Toyota "just-in-time" production system has been cited as a key reason for why the Japanese automobile industry has performed so well (Clark, Chew, and Fujimoto, 1987). Those who have analyzed this production system point out that not only labor practices within firms but also complementary features of Japanese society at large were key to making the system work (Aoki and Dore, 1994). The Japanese automobile industry highlights the importance of examining the relationship between shop floor practices and general practices in the larger social environment. The national environment may indeed constrain domestic firms in how they can organize the shop floor and confer a relative advantage or disadvantage compared to rivals located in other countries.

How strong is the evidence that German shop floor practices conferred a competitive advantage to German firms over their British and American rivals? A definitive answer would require having detailed productivity measures for plants in all three countries. Such data simply do not exist. Thus we have to rely on the judgment of informed contemporaries and on indirect evidence to piece together a realistic picture of what happened on the shop floor. Because much more information is available for Britain and Germany, I will first discuss the two countries and then offer some speculation about the U.S. case, relying on indirect evidence of general labor practices at the time.

Many German firms appear to have possessed an important advantage over their British competitors because they academically trained chemists in charge of the organization and management of the shop floor, whereas in Britain the traditional foremen continued to rule over the production process and the associated labor practices. The quotations at the beginning of the section make clear that in Britain a foreman had large discretion about how he was going to run the shop floor. Owners would judge him based on the results he achieved and not on how he achieved those results.

In the early stages of the dye industry, German and British firms appear to have organized their production by putting the foreman in charge of all aspects of production – a system with deep historical roots.[84] In the preindustrial era, guilds had control over how handicraft products were to be made. The power struggles between capitalists and workmen that invariably would accompany the change to capitalistic factory production led to a status quo in which the foreman achieved much of the control over the shop floor. As William Lazonick (1990) has documented for the textile industry, this system continued in Britain essentially intact until World War I and contributed to the lower levels of process innovation in the British textile plants.

Around 1870, the management in German firms took away the authority of foremen and passed it on to production chemists.[85] Heinrich Caro, as one of the leading figures in the early dye industry and one of its best historians, is well-equipped to pass judgment on Britain and Germany, having spent seven years (1859–66) in the

---

[84] See Biernacki (1995) for an excellent account of the differences in German and British shop floor practices from 1640 until 1914.

[85] Of course there was variation in the speed in which individual German firms put scientific chemists in charge of the production floor. Those firms that waited too long risked never being able to catch up with the early adopters of this labor practice.

British dye industry before joining BASF at Ludwigshafen for twenty-two years.[86] Already in his first major piece on the dye industry (1892), he put much emphasis on the differences in the social organization of production in the two countries. He credits the introduction of scientific knowledge onto the shop floor as an important factor in the ability of the German dye industry to produce dyes at lower cost and higher quality. Carl Duisberg, another leader of the German dye industry who worked for Bayer as one of the first research chemists, supports Caro's analysis in an article for the April 1904 *Popular Science Monthly*:

[M]ore and more the truth of Liebig's teaching became recognized, that agriculture and the industries would accomplish undreamed results if scientifically educated chemists were employed in all branches and were permitted to exercise control of all methods... [W]e now see that [large factories in Germany] are managed exclusively by scientific chemists. The practical man was forced to yield to the well-educated theoretical man (reprinted in Duisberg, 1923, pp. 273–4) [my translation].

As the number of dyes and dye intermediates proliferated, offering a full line of dyes gave firms a marketing advantage over their competitors who could offer only a small range of dyes. To render a full line of dyes an especially potent weapon, firms needed to figure out how to make the increasing number of intermediates and dyes in cost-saving ways. Here is where the trained production chemist comes in. Some dyes would be made only in small batches. Figuring out when to make what dye and what intermediate could yield very large cost advantages. Chandler (1990) has made this a basic point in his analysis of the rise of big business. Coordinating the production department with the marketing department for the sake of increasing the efficiency of the overall firm was, of course, much easier if academically trained chemists (who would typically feel closer to management than to workers) were in charge of the shop floor. Trying to explain the victory of the German dye firms over the British ones, Caro stresses the importance of tightly integrating the different functions of the firm to enhance the efficiency and rationality of the overall production system represented by the firm.

We see that the German factory owner wisely avoided the mistakes of foreign countries and, drawing on the treasure of accumulated experience, did not rely too much on his own power and genius as was the case in Britain, where a spirit of self-reliance was flourishing because of the early achievements and a distinct national character, or in France, where a sanguine carefreeness was pervading... [The German factory owner] created an entire production system where all members found a place to develop their powers, reminiscent of the German poetic line. "Always seek the whole, and if you cannot become a whole yourself, join a whole serving as a component" (1904, pp. 1358–9) [my translation].

Even Britain's most successful firms – Levinstein and Read Holliday – did not achieve a corporate culture before 1914 that saw it essential to integrate tightly the production floor with the other parts of the firm. As we shall see in the case study of Levinstein, the firms were steeped in the culture of a personal manager running the

---

[86] Caro married an English woman during his stay in Britain, leaving him not only with lifelong business ties but also with family ties to the island.

show. By not creating a production system that could deliver innovative low-cost and high-quality dyes, British firms over time found themselves uncompetitive compared to the strongest German firms.

Gradual Development of Winning Practices

It would be wrong to think that differences in shop floor practices between Germany and Britain were differences in kind. They were differences in degree that over time wielded profound influences in making British firms uncompetitive in comparison to German rivals. The taking control by scientists of German dye shop floors was truly an evolutionary process. It happened gradually and in some firms quicker than in others. But initial differences on the margin were sufficient to set off a process that led to the eventual control of the shop floor by management through the academically trained chemists. This allowed firms to constantly introduce new innovations in production processes. Combined with other factors, it led to worldwide domination by the German dye industry. As German dye firms erected new plants to expand production or manufacture new classes of dyes, they would set up these factories based on their accumulated experience and according to principles of efficiency. To take advantage fully of a superior research and training system, German firms had to hand over the control of the shop floor to academically trained scientists and engineers. To a considerable extent, they succeeded in this while British dye firms largely failed because the German national environment was permeated much more with scientific and technical values than the British one. This is why the education system is so important. When the larger portion of society has accepted science and technology as the way to guide business enterprise, it is much easier to push the spirit of rationality into every corner of the shop floor.

What about the United States?

Because American dye firms were such small players in the dye industry before 1914, we have almost no information on the social organization of their plants. Unlike the case of Britain, there is no good reason to believe that the social organization of plants would have been a problem if all the other elements that were necessary for success in the dye industry had been in place. Let me engage in some informed speculation based on what is known about the American workplace in the second half of the nineteenth century. Historians who have compared American and European labor during that period stress that because of its relative shortage, American labor was expensive and often much less skilled than British and German workers at the time (Nelson and Wright, 1994, pp. 131–41). This was clearly true in the chemical industry. American industry in general adapted to this shortage of skilled labor by creating a production system that would create a large output of standardized products that did not require handicraft skills (Hounshell, 1984). To dispense with highly skilled workers, American industry, like that of Germany, put engineers and scientists in control of the shop floor. The rise of Taylorism (Taylor, 1903) as a management philosophy is testimony of both the necessity to dispense with skilled labor and the spirit to organize the shop floor according to rational and not tradition-based principles.

American engineering expertise in heavy chemicals had certainly made great strides by the turn of the century. Haynes (1954, p. 265) notes that General Chemical, after being refused a license for BASF's new contact sulfuric acid process, designed a plant itself that was so much better than BASF's own process that the German firm felt compelled to license it. Already in his report on the U.S. chemical industry in 1893, Witt (1894) makes clear that as far as large-scale heavy chemical production facilities were concerned, American firms had no trouble competing with their European counterparts. Small-batch production techniques that characterized the dye industry at the time would have been more difficult for American engineers, but there is good reason to believe that the United States would have achieved a more efficient organization of the shop floor than Britain. However, because the United States lacked organic chemical knowledge when the dye industry started and later lacked cheap access to a large number of organic intermediate chemicals required for dye making, U.S. firms never came to the level where shop floor efficiencies would have been the decisive factor in the competition against German firms. In relation to Britain, U.S. firms clearly became more competitive over time – which may very well have to do with the fact that American firms pushed engineers onto the shop floor. But as I have said before, unfortunately, direct evidence is lacking.

What kind of products could be made on the shop floor was strongly influenced by the particular intellectual property right laws enforced in each the three countries. To understand why German, unlike British, firms were able to copy British innovations during the early years of the synthetic dye industry, we also need to examine how local patent laws affected the competitive position of each national dye industry.

Intellectual Property Right Regimes

I am of the opinion – an opinion which I arrive at from actual facts – that neither Prince Bismarck, nor any other German statesman, would ever think of introducing into Germany that complicated mystery called English patent laws...

—Signed by "A manufacturing chemist" in *Chemical Review* (1872, Nov., p. 24)

English brains created the color industry, English brains developed it, and English legislative folly has been the principle source of its decline.

—IVAN LEVINSTEIN, owner of the largest British dye firm, commenting on British patent laws in *Nature* (1903), as quoted in Wetzel (1991, p. 264)

A dye manufacturer (A) introduces an innovative dye that is highly valued in the market. A second manufacturer (B) sees the profit opportunities, copies the dye, and offers it for a lower price. B attracts many customers, which is, of course, bad news for A. What can A do to protect the value of his innovation? For the dye industry in the period from 1856 until 1914 the answer would depend largely on the geographical locations of the parties involved and the state of the patent laws at the particular moment in time. The patent laws and their applications changed in all three countries during this period.[87] The overview of patents statistics earlier in this chapter (see Relative Shares of Patents around 1877 and 1900) made it clear that the German dye industry dominated patenting across all important countries from the 1880s onward. Because patents in the strongest case confer a complete monopoly over a product, they have at least theoretically the power to confer important competitive advantages to the firm that is able to obtain a patent. In this section, I wish to establish four claims.

1. The rise of German dominance in the dye industry was aided by the nature of patent laws in Germany and in rival countries.
2. The long-term weakness of the British dye industry was related to the patent laws in Britain and in rival countries.
3. The existence of American patent laws introduced an important entry barrier for would-be start-up firms in the United States.
4. The patent laws, not in isolation but in combination with other factors, made a large difference in determining how the competitive positions of the three national dye industries would develop before 1914.

Because the argument I develop is complex, I want to summarize it at the outset. The German dye industry benefited from not being able to obtain patents in Germany before 1877 because the fierce competition in Germany forced German firms to build superior capabilities in the manufacturing and marketing of dyes. Once Germany had captured a dominant position in the global synthetic dye industry because its leading firms had developed the best organizational capabilities, the German dye industry benefited from the arrival of a German patent law in 1877. The leading firms could then cement their dominant position by developing systematic corporate R&D laboratories that kept them the most innovative firms in the world. I also want to offer right away a word of caution. The potency of using patents to protect investments in innovative products is often overestimated. Two surveys (Levin, Klevorick, Nelson, and Winter, 1987; Klevorick, Levin, Nelson, and Winter, 1995) indicate that in most industries today patents are insignificant for protecting R&D investments. But these surveys also make clear that in chemicals and pharmaceuticals, patents are important tools for extracting rents from innovations.[88] Redlich's (1914, p. 180) analysis reveals that this was also the case for the German dye industry before World War I.[89] To maintain a patent for the total full fifteen-year maximum lifetime, German patent holders had to pay an annual fee to keep the patent in force. Of all patents issued in Germany from 1877 to 1886, only 2.6 percent reached the fifteenth year of protection. In dyestuffs and related products (class 22), the corresponding figure was 15.9 percent,

---

[87] Unless otherwise specified, when I speak of patent laws I imply both the meaning of the written rules and their application by the relevant authorities.

[88] A recent study by Hall and Ham Ziedonis (2001) shows that a strengthening of U.S. patent protection in the 1980s had the effect that firms in the semiconductor industry patented more inventions to gain a bargaining chip for exchanging technologies with competitors but this did not increase the innovativeness of U.S. firms.

[89] Unfortunately I do not have comparable figures for Britain and the United States at the present time. But I have no reason to believe they would paint a different picture. German dye firms patented as heavily in those countries as at home.

making the class by far the leader in patent renewal frequencies.[90] (Photography was the runnerup with 7.5 percent.)

Even when patents offer significant protection, to profit from technological innovations, firms typically need to have several of additional assets (such as strong manufacturing and marketing capabilities) that give them sufficient reach into and power over the marketplace (Teece, 1986). Because a lot of critical knowledge would be attached to employees, dye firms always faced the threat that key individuals would look for a new employer who would pay them more.[91] An advertisement in the London-based *Chemical Review* makes it clear that individuals were not shy about openly peddling their expertise.

Important for Dye Manufacturers, Dyers, and Tar Distillers
A learned chemist, practically employed in the Tar and Tar-Colour Trade since the origin of these Trades, is willing to sell the best practically proved receipts for all the Colours collected in the first manufacturing places, and to give every instruction for manufacturing the same, as well by letter as practically.

Apply to T.C., Chemical Review Office, 131 Fleet Street, E.C.

—*Chemical Review*, 1874, vol. 3. no. 29, p. i

To avoid attributing too great a significance to patents alone, patent holdings should be judged in connection with other industry features that impinge on the firm's ability to profit from dye patents. Whether a firm would achieve a sustainable competitive advantage with patents depended not only on the nature of patent law in the key countries but also on the behavior of rival firms, the patent authorities, and individuals who had crucial competencies and connections.

Review of Patent Law Developments in the Three Countries

Patents played a role in the dye industry from day one. Perkin successfully patented the first synthetic dyestuff (aniline purple) and derived handsome profits from the monopoly on his innovation. In 1914, it was routine for the German industry leaders to patent the many new inventions coming out of their R&D laboratories in all of the major markets in which patents could be obtained.

Instead of giving a full exposition of the patent laws in the three countries from 1856 until 1914, I will focus on the differences among the three countries.[92] Only the

---

[90] Another statistic offered by Redlich (1914, p. 180) compares the number of patents issued in a given class during a fifteen-year window with the number of patents that were still valid at the end of this window. Taking the average of the fifteen-year windows ending from 1892 to 1900, the result was 26 percent for all classes. For dyes and related products, the corresponding figure was 63 percent, again testifying to the usefulness of maintaining patent protection for a dye invention.

[91] Evidence from the large German dye firms shows that they tried to protect their know-how by a variety of practices. One used, for example, by the Bayer and Oehler companies was to not allow workers and production chemists assigned to one factory to set foot into another factory of the firm (Homburg, 1992).

[92] For a short, general overview of the different national patent laws and their relationship to the dye industry, see Haber (1971, pp. 198–204).

differences must concern us here because only they can help explain why Germany established a virtual monopoly in dyes in this period.

The most crucial difference in the early period of the dye industry was that Germany, in contrast to Britain and the United States, had no unified patent law until 1877. Twenty-nine of the thirty-nine individual German states had offered some form of patent protection, but two factors made patents insignificant until the German Empire passed a patent law for the entire German territory in 1877. Prussia, by far the largest state, gave out patents very rarely because the powerful bureaucracy viewed patents as harmful for the development of the economy.[93] But even more importantly, a special article (an 1842 addition) in the Zollverein (customs union) agreement allowed the member states to grant patents in their own territories but forbade members to prevent producers in other member states from selling the product in all member states (Penrose, 1951, p. 14; Heggen, 1975). In effect, this meant that patents did not provide a monopoly of the kind they would confer in Britain and the United States at the time.

The all-German patent law of 1877 differed from the British one in significant ways. Germany instituted a rigorous examination by the patent office before it would grant a patent. The task of the patent office was to determine whether a patent application did indeed describe a novel product or process and to help demarcate the scope of the claim. Such a rigorous examination of every patent claim and the ability of third parties to file opposition during the application process made a patent legally more secure once it was granted.[94] It dramatically reduced the probability that a patent would later be declared void, and thus facilitated the creation of a market for patents where firms could buy inventions from inventors or other firms.[95] The United States had already instituted the examination of patent applications in 1836 (Lamoreaux and Sokoloff, 2001), but the examination in Germany appears to have been more intensive and rigorous. Another key difference between the United States and Germany was that U.S. courts could rule patents invalid, whereas in Germany only the patent office could do so. In both countries, courts would decide scope issues in patent suits. Because the British system lacked a rigorous examination of patent applications at least until 1905, courts basically had the role of deciding whether a patent claim was valid or not.[96] Hence any patent dispute in Britain would always involve a costly legal process.[97]

[93] Heggen (1975) gives an excellent overview of patent laws in Prussia from 1793 until 1877. He also provides comparative statistics that show how few patent applications were accepted by Prussia in comparison to those of the other German states, Britain, and the United States (pp. 78–9).

[94] Given the extensive examination and objection possibilities, two years typically passed in Germany before a patent applicant received a legal patent.

[95] For an account how a market for patents was created in the United States, see Lamoreaux and Sokoloff (2000, 2001).

[96] I have not been able to determine the precise date when Britain followed Germany and the United States in creating a rigorous examination about the patentability of an application before granting a patent, but surely it was not before 1905. Probably such an examination did not exist for the entire period studied here.

[97] The economic historian Aitken (1976, p. 204) concludes in his study of the early history of radio in Europe and the United States, "A British patent conveyed little more than the right to bring suit. When claims to property rights came into conflict, the courts would decide."

Furthermore, while it was possible to patent chemical products in Britain and the United States, German law allowed only the patenting of processes.[98] In addition, German law required that patents were worked (i.e., the product was manufactured or the process was in use) within the borders of the country.[99] This was not the case in the United States. In Britain such a clause had been on the books since 1883 but was seriously enforced only between 1908 and 1909.[100] German law recognized the first person to file as the legitimate patent holder, whereas U.S. law recognized the first person to invent as the legitimate patent holder.[101] Many commentators believe that the first-to-invent system gave rise to a greater number of long and costly patent fights than the first-to-file system because, under the former system, it was possible to have existing patents declared null and void by proving someone else had priority (Wertheimer, 1912, p. 164). Under the first-to-file system a patent holder could not be surprised by and lose the patent to someone who had already made the invention but did not file for a patent. Although not explicit in the law and therefore open to legal challenge, in Britain the first person to file would typically be awarded the patent.

Britain and the United States were among the founding members of the Union for the Protection of Industrial Property that became effective in 1884; Germany, in contrast, did not join the union until 1903 (Penrose, 1951, pp. 58–9).[102] The member

---

[98] Although German firms could not patent processes at home, they did apply with great alacrity for product patents in Britain and the United States. BASF, for example, was able to obtain a product patent that would cover any synthetic alizarin in the United States. In 1884, almost at the end of the patent duration, the U.S. Supreme Court voided the patent in response to a lawsuit brought by BASF's arch rival, the Bayer Company (Reimer, 1996, p. 108). We will return to this patent fight in the case study of the Bayer company.

[99] The working clause stipulated that the patent could be revoked after three years if the patent holder was not willing to license his or her invention when such licensing was in the interest of society at large. This had the effect that patent law clearly favored existing companies with large capital over the small inventor, giving large companies a strong bargaining chip in forcing the inventor to grant them a license (Heggen, 1975, p. 142). This was another factor that increased forces of concentration in the dye industry. At the turn of the century, however, there was a strong movement in Germany to eliminate the working clause altogether. A special patent treaty (1909) between the German and U.S. governments already did away with working requirements for American holders of German patents (Wertheimer, 1912, p. 465).

[100] In his commentary on the British Patents, Designs and Trade Marks Act of 1883, Daniel (1884, p. 143) points out: "These [working clause] provisions are quite new and mark a considerable change in the law. They are of the barest possible character, and afford no indication of the manner in which they are to be worked." Indeed, the wording of the clause was so vague that, in effect, foreign patent holders were almost not at risk of being forced to licence their patent if they did not work their patent in Britain. Only the Patent Reform Act of 1907 gave the working clause real teeth until a court struck it down two years later.

[101] In Germany, an inventor who did not file for patent protection was allowed to continue using the invention even if another party was granted a patent for the invention, eliminating many of the injustices that could occur under the first-to-file system.

[102] A plausible reason for Germany's delayed entry into the patent union is that the country in 1883 perceived itself as still more a technological borrower than exporter, giving the country a disincentive to recognize foreign patents. Twenty years later, the situation had more or less reversed itself. An official publication by the German patent office commemorating the fiftieth year of its existence in 1927 strongly supports this line of reasoning (Reichspatentamt, 1927, pp. 25–6).

states of the convention agreed to grant citizens of all other members the same legal status as their own citizens. Perhaps even more importantly, convention members would give successful patent applicants a twelve-month grace period during which they would enjoy patent priority in any of the member states (Machlup, 1958, p. 18). This made it easier for inventors – particularly large corporations – to obtain patent protection in many countries.

The German Patent Reform Act of 1891 had three provisions that were most important for the dye industry. First, it afforded a greater protection of dye patents by reversing the burden of proof in infringement suits (Fleischer, 1984). If the patent holder accused another manufacturer of infringing on his dye patent, the accused party now had to show that it produced the identical dye with indeed a different process. If the accused party could not, it would be found guilty of infringement, which was punishable by heavy fines and imprisonment. This made it much more difficult for firms to copy patented dyes, even by manufacturers who were based in foreign countries (Zimmermann, 1965). Second, it recognized to a greater extent the possibility of filing an addition to the original patent application (this is the so-called Zusatzpatent), extending the effective lifetime of a patent. Finally, it allowed oral arguments in front of the patent office, giving the dye firms an opportunity to meet in person and talk about many things that would concern the German industry.[103]

Although Germany made the most successful efforts to remove many of the difficulties of applying existing patent laws to synthetic dyes, the country also experienced enormous challenges in establishing patent laws and practices that would clearly delineate what was patentable and what not, what was the scope of a patent, what constituted an infringement, and what was novel enough to warrant a patent. Patents suits were rampant in all three countries throughout the period studied here. Often the large German dye firms would have patent fights with one another, not only at home but also in the United States.

Competitive Implications of Patent Law Developments in the Three Countries
Given that the period from 1857 to 1914 saw dramatic changes in the underlying science of dyes and in industry dynamics, it is convenient to analyze the competitive implications of the differences in national patent laws in terms of the three periods that were introduced in the performance overview earlier in this chapter.

Period 1, 1857–1865: Early Synthetic Dyes
The most significant patent-related event occurred in the very beginning of the dye industry. Early patents in Britain (e.g., Perkin's aniline purple and Medlock's magenta process) placed serious restrictions on entry into the British industry. In contrast, the absence of significant patent protection in the thirty-nine German states made it possible for a large number of firms to enter. Because Germany was endowed with a sizable number of chemists who were looking for employment (Borscheid, 1976) and because patent laws did not impose any significant restriction on entry, many

---

[103] In Chapter 4 I will discuss the significance of these opportunities for personal interaction among dye firms.

more firms entered in Germany than in Britain. This was clearly shown in Figure 5. Whereas in Germany, firms experienced a Darwinian kind of struggle that selected the strongest competitors, many British firms made high monopoly profits without developing strong competitive capabilities.

Because the British patent law of 1852 was formulated mainly to deal with mechanical devices and could not foresee the special nature of the new class of products represented by organic chemicals, the British patent law left open a large number of questions regarding what would constitute a valid dye patent. Given that the patent for magenta was of such great commercial value, a number of British firms found themselves in very expensive patent fights from 1861 to 1865. A large number of German firms produced magenta but, in Britain, the firm of Maule, Simpson, and Spiller (owners of the Medlock patent) was able to force other firms out of the market until the patent was declared void in 1865. By the time this important patent fight was over, two important developments had taken place. The surviving firms of the Darwinian struggle taking place in Germany had learned how to produce magenta much more cheaply and were ready to enter the British market where domestic firms had been sheltered from serious competition. Second, British capitalists had found the new science-based industry difficult to understand in the first place. The costly patent fights in Britain with their hard-to-predict outcomes did nothing but scare away capital from the industry even further (Travis, 1993, p. 131).[104]

Period 2, 1866–1885: The Rise of Scientific Theory in Dye Innovation
The German industry entered this second period with a meaningfully larger number of competitive firms than Britain. By the early 1870s, they had clearly overtaken their British competitors not only in terms of manufacturing prowess but also in terms of world market share. Just as scientific organic theory had made a dramatic step forward with the formulation of such tools as Kekulé's benzene ring theory in 1866, German firms shifted from being imitators of dyes to innovators of new products. BASF (German) and Perkin & Sons (British) developed at the same time the blockbuster synthetic alizarin dye. BASF was lucky enough to file one day earlier than Perkin for a British patent. Instead of fighting a patent battle in court, the two firms arrived at an agreement. But although competitors could be kept out of the market in Britain, the absence of patent protection in Germany again allowed a large number of firms to enter the alizarin field there quickly, further strengthening the firms that survived the shakeout in alizarin that soon occurred. BASF also filed for a patent in the United States, making it impossible for American firms to enter the alizarin dye field. Besides the other factors already mentioned, American firms would find it difficult in this period to enter the industry, not only because they would be late-comers but also

---

[104] This is not to imply that there was a capital shortage in Britain. British capitalists could have easily financed every single dye firm in the world. However, because the British financers did not have the ability to appraise the risk and opportunities afforded by synthetic dyes, patent fights could only hurt the dye industry's investment appeal in the eyes of the financial community. When bankers were involved in the financing of dye firms (BASF is an example), they would always go into business with chemists who had the relevant know-how to appraise risk and opportunities and to run firms accordingly. This suggests that a superior national education system can have important indirect advantages, for instance, allowing capital markets to function effectively in a new industry.

because dye patents of European firms in the United States restricted the dyes in which they could be active.

The timing of the all-German law in 1877 proved to be extremely fortuitous for the German dye industry. Scientific theories had become much better guides in searching successfully for new dyes. The German dye industry was populated by a sufficiently large number of firms with stronger marketing, manufacturing, and management capabilities than rivals in any other part of the world. A patent law at this point would not have the damaging effects it had in Britain in the beginning of the industry because competition between strong players would continue. Because of a key formulation in the all-German patent law that allowed only process and not product patents in dyes, firms had the incentive (in contrast to Britain and the United States) to search for every chemical route to a particular dye product to protect their R&D investments. True research laboratories whose only goal was to search for new dyes were created only after the passage of the German patent law in 1877. Between 1877 (BASF) and 1886 (Bayer), the seven largest dye firms in Germany set up laboratories devoted exclusively to research (Homburg, 1992). Without this change in the German patent environment, the German dye industry would not have been able to dominate the world market the way it did. This is not to say that the German industry would not have been strong. It probably would have held half of the world market share, but it would not have developed a virtual world monopoly that could be maintained over a long period of time without any patent protection at home.

Period 3, 1886–1914: The Age of Corporate R&D Laboratories

Given that German firms had already established strong capabilities in manufacturing and marketing, strong patent protection at home made it possible to pay for large R&D laboratories, thus allowing German firms to innovate British competitors out of the market or displace them into niches. In addition to unexploited technical opportunities in existing dye classes, the rise of azo dyes in the 1880s and their seemingly endless variations, as well as the technical challenges in developing a competitive indigo production process, gave a large R&D laboratory an enormous advantage over the "lone" inventor.[105] Patent statistics clearly reflect the shift to corporate patenting. In this period, the vast majority all of dye patents were corporate patents. From 1890 on, the big three German dye firms – BASF, Hoechst, and Bayer – owned between them 66 percent of all German-held U.S. chemical patents (Liebenau, 1988, p. 144). Thomson and Nelson (1997) confirm that large managerial firms (defined as those firms on Chandler's 1990 list of top 200 firms) took out around 66 percent of all chemical patents in all three countries. If the smaller German dye firms with R&D laboratories were also included, I suspect that the share of all dye patents issued to such firms would be around 90 percent.

Fueled by large profits on patented new dyes, the German dye firms had the money to invest heavily in R&D capabilities. By 1890, the big three German chemical firms employed about 350 (2.5 percent) academically trained chemists in a work force of around 14,000. In 1912 the number had risen to about 930 (3.1 percent) in a work

---

[105] In his case studies of the firms BASF and Hoechst, Reinhardt (1997) provides a very detailed account of how the importance of various classes of dyes in the R&D activities of the firms changed over time.

force of about 30,000 (Marsch, 1994). Although a majority of these chemists worked in production, the number of R&D chemists was sizable. Meyer-Thurow (1982, p. 371) reports that in 1897 Bayer allowed 15 percent, or 15 of its 99 chemists, to focus on research only. By 1912, 22 percent, or 57 of Bayer's 262 chemists, devoted their time to research. Reinhardt's (1997, pp. 286–7) investigations reveal that at least 71 chemists at Hoechst were research chemists in 1913 and that 28 of them worked in the main laboratory. Altogether, Hoechst employed 149 chemists in its various laboratories, some of whom clearly were also responsible for production and testing. BASF had 29 chemists alone in its main laboratory in 1914 (Reinhardt, 1997, p. 366). British and American firms were small mom-and-pop shops by comparison.[106]

German firms systematically patented everything that came out of their R&D laboratories in all countries that granted patents. This allowed them to turn patents into a formidable tool of corporate strategy (Liebenau, 1988). Among the large German firms, rivals often found ways around the patent of another firm because they created laboratories for Patentsachen (patent affairs), in which chemists systematically tried to resynthesize the patented dye processes of rivals and find alternative chemical pathways to the same products.[107] Amassing a huge patent portfolio allowed the strongest firms to force other firms to license some of their inventions. Because patents in Britain and the United States were often on a shaky legal foundation, possessing a large patent portfolio provided firms a strong bargaining tool in possible court battles, these firms being likely to find within their own product portfolio an area where the competitor was guilty of a patent infringement. Large patent portfolios also provided the large incumbent firms with an insurance policy against newcomers. German firms practiced what Bill Kingston (Personal communication, 1996) has called saturation patenting in foreign markets, filing patents in all possible areas of organic chemistry that could give rise to new dyes (Liebenau, 1988, p. 144). If competitors should discover a new dye field, the incumbent firms would often hold some patent in that area that would allow them to extract a cross-licensing agreement. Given their superior marketing capabilities, incumbent firms then typically would capture a large market share in these new markets.

A large patent portfolio coupled with strong organizational capabilities in manufacturing, marketing, management, and R&D were the tools that allowed the German dye industry to increase its world market share up to 75–90 percent and maintain it at that level. American and British firms year after year faced bigger and stronger German firms, making it ever more difficult to compete. And the large patent portfolios German firms amassed erected ever higher entry barriers for would-be start-ups in all three countries, but particularly in Britain and the United States, where synthetic organic talent was scarce in the first place.

---

[106] Donnelly (1987, p. 272) reports that in response to the dye shortage created by the outbreak of World War I, the largest British dye firm, Levinstein, employed Professor A. G. Green of Leeds University and placed him in charge of 13 researchers. This means that before the war, Levinstein certainly had fewer people than this employed in research, a tiny number compared to the R&D staff in the big three German dye-makers.

[107] Reinhardt's (1997) excellent study of the development of innovations at BASF and Hoechst also describes in detail how the two firms gradually developed full-fledged patent laboratories (particularly around pp. 155 and 286). Meyer-Thurow (1982) provides a similar analysis for the firm Bayer.

I now will move the analysis to the level of individual firms and examine how the performance of particular firms was shaped by the national context in which they found themselves. To understand why firms even in the same national context often differed dramatically in their level of performance, I try to shed some light on how some firms were more able than others to take advantage of their particular institutional environment.

3 Three Times Two Case Studies of Individual Firms

Plans were prepared and a site obtained at Greenford Green, near Harrow, and in June 1857 the building of the works commenced.

At this time, neither I nor my friends had seen the inside of a chemical works, and whatever knowledge I had was obtained from books. This, however, was not so serious a drawback as at first it might appear to be, as the kind of apparatus required and the character of the operations to be performed were so entirely different from any in use that there was but little to copy from.

In commencing this manufacture, it was absolutely necessary to proceed tentatively, as most of the operations required a new kinds of apparatus to be devised and tried before more could be ordered to carry out the work on any scale.

But the mechanical were not the only difficulties . . . No nitric acid sufficiently strong for the preparation of nitrobenzene could be obtained commercially, and, as we did not want to complicate our works by manufacturing the substance, experiments were made with a mixture of sodium nitrate and sulphuric acid, using the latter in rather larger proportions than necessary to give an acid sodium sulphate. This method was found to work on the small scale, but, when working with large quantities, special apparatus had to be devised and a great many precautions had to be taken to regulate the operation; however, very large quantities of nitrobenzene were made by it. Nitrobenzene had never been prepared in iron vessels before this time. . . .

Thus it will be seen that, in the case of this new colouring matter, not only had the difficulties incident to its manufacture to be grappled with, and the prejudices of the consumer overcome, but owing to the fact that it belonged to a new class of dyestuffs, a large amount of time had to be devoted to the study of its applications to dyeing, calico printing, etc. It was, in fact, all pioneering work – clearing the road, as it were, for the introduction of all the colouring matters which followed, all the processes worked out for dyeing silk, cotton, and wool, and also for calico printing, afterwards proving suitable for magenta, Hofmann violet, etc.

> —WILLIAM H. PERKIN (1896)[108] recounting in his
> Hofmann Memorial Lecture how the bold venture
> to launch the synthetic dye industry with his
> father and brother faced numerous obstacles
> before the manufacture of mauve could become a
> commercial success

In 1871, Professor Baeyer published the first of a series of papers on some new types of compounds which he had obtained by the condensation of phenols with phthalic anhydride and which he termed 'phthaleïns.' This ... was at first a piece of purely scientific work. Now, fortunately for that country, Germany had in one of her new colour factories a chemist whose services we in this country had lost – a man whose name will be indelibly stamped upon the history of the development of the coal-tar colour industry. I refer to my old friend Dr Heinrich Caro, of Mannheim. It was he who recognised the technological importance of Baeyer's work, and turned this "academic" chemical reaction into a manufacturing process by his discovery that substituted phthaleïns were possessed of great tinctorial value.

> —RAPHAEL MELDOLA (1910),[109] one of the leading
> British dye chemists who switched from academia
> to industry and back a number of times, in his
> Presidential Address to the Society of Dyers and
> Colourists

Nobody who was not in the dyemaking industry before 1914 has ever experienced the competition which existed then: no holds were barred. I sincerely hope that it will never be repeated. The German, the Swiss, and the much smaller British firms were in deadly cut-throat competition. There was no Dyestuffs Act, no dyestuffs cartel.

> —C. M. WHITTAKER (1956, p. 559), dye chemist from
> 1899 to 1950

---

[108] Pages 153–5 in a reprint of the lecture in Gardner (1915).
[109] Page 263 in a reprint of his Presidential Address in Gardner (1915).

Table 7. The Design of the Six Firm Case Studies

	Germany	Britain	United States
Relative success	Bayer	Levinstein	Schoellkopf
Relative failure	Jäger	Brooke, Simpson & Spiller	American Aniline

Purpose of the Matched Comparisons

In the previous chapter, I have argued that institutional differences in the three national environments can explain to a large extent why the German dye industry outperformed the British and American rival industries by a wide margin. Following the tradition of organizational ecologists (Hannan and Freeman, 1989; Carroll and Hannan, 1995b) and evolutionary economists (Klepper and Simons, 2000a, 2000b), I examined all the firms in each country to acquire a systematic understanding of the dynamics that shaped the industry. The firm entry and exit statistics for the three countries (Figures 5 and 6) showed that more firms failed in Germany than in Britain and the United States combined. In other words, favorable institutional environment was clearly not a sufficient condition for the success of an individual firm. To gain a deeper understanding of firm strategies and resulting performance outcomes that underlay the differences in national performance, let us look at specific firms in the three countries and investigate why they were successful. To avoid the all too common pitfall of inferring apparent success factors by looking at high-performance firms only, I will examine a relative success and a relative failure in each country (Table 7). Only those features of successful firms that are not present in poorly performing firms are likely to be causes of success. This carefully chosen study design will allow us to strengthen the tentative conclusions about why Bayer outperformed most other firms in the industry.

Looking first at the industry as a whole and then zooming in on a carefully chosen set of individual firms is, as far as I know, a novel research design.[110] The design has the advantage of making it easier to find support for the causal mechanisms that generated industrial leadership in the synthetic dye industry before World War I. Furthermore, it allows us to study the relationship between performance of the industry (macrobehavior) and the intentions of individual players (micromotives), a relationship that is far from obvious (Schelling, 1978). Although the chapter focuses on six firms, it draws comparisons to many other firms in Germany, Britain, and the United States to place the behavior of the six focal firms in the appropriate context. Because successful firms tend to become large and leave much more information behind than their more poorly performing competitors, I do not have equal amounts of data for all six firms. But in each case there is enough to allow fruitful comparisons. The point of the six case studies is not only to compare firms but also to present

---

[110] *Creating Modern Capitalism: How Entrepreneurs, Companies, and Countries Triumphed in Three Industrial Revolutions* (McCraw, 1997b) is similar to the present study in that it takes a historical and comparative approach, but differs in that it does not examine all firms in the same industry. *Big Business and the Wealth of Nations* (Chandler et al., 1997) also takes a historical comparative approach but differs from the present design in that it focuses only on large firms in different countries. Hence the present study is best viewed as a complementary methodology – the *industry-level analysis* – in the larger comparative historical business history project.

microlevel evidence on the processes that went on within dye firms. The marketing activities, for example, of the other leading German dye firms – BASF, Hoechst, AGFA – were very similar to those of Bayer; hence, Bayer often stands as a representative of the most successful firms in the industry.

Two sets of connected questions need to be pursued in the present context. The first one concerns an intracountry comparison. Why did Bayer, BASF, and Hoechst each hold almost 20 percent of the world market by 1914, whereas almost a hundred other German dye firms failed? Every one of these dye firms had very humble origins and only gradually did a few of them grow into large industrial enterprises. It is important to understand why one company grew and another did not. The second question concerns an intercountry comparison of firms. Why was Bayer in Germany much more successful than Levinstein in Great Britain and Schoellkopf Aniline in the United States? This second question will touch again on the national environment, but this time I will examine the national environment from the perspective of these individual firms. To put it a bit differently, in this chapter I will look at the competitive dynamics of the early dye industry at the level of individual strategy makers. The chapter provides a lot of descriptive information on how firms organized themselves and how they acted because I believe that the field of management needs more theoretically driven "thick" descriptions, à la Geertz (1973), of development of individual firms. The chapter is intended to provide the reader with descriptive material that helps explain how a successful firm such as Bayer organized itself. At its end, I will draw some conclusions about which factors and processes seem to have made particular firms more successful. Case studies can never prove propositions that are true for all firms in the industry, but carefully chosen ones can provide powerful clues about what is likely to be true about many firms.

The goal of this chapter, then, is to provide a detailed analysis of what appear to have been necessary elements of successful firm strategies during the various stages of development in the dye industry until 1914. The six case studies (two firms from each of the three countries) provide strong evidence that successful firms, besides making investments in Chandlerian organizational capabilities (in-house R&D, marketing, management, and manufacturing capabilities), gained international experience early and learned how to tap into the knowledge network of organic chemistry. Firms that were located at the periphery of this network (in Britain and the United States) had no choice but to connect with chemists who had links to the center of the network, if they were to enjoy some measure of success. In other words, to flourish, synthetic dye ventures had to acquire a knowledge gateway[III] that linked them to a center of discovery in organic chemistry. Furthermore, the high-performing firms in this sample were dominated by an entrepreneurial spirit. Because Bayer was able to maintain this spirit even when professional managers took over, the firm dramatically outperformed all but two rivals.

The Cast of Firms
When William H. Perkin launched the synthetic dye industry in 1857, the large multinational firms of today, which often enter a new line of business on a large scale,

---

[III] I owe this very apt metaphor to Rita McGrath.

did not exist. The early period of the dye industry was orchestrated by individuals who believed that the new field of synthetic dyes would be a magnificent business opportunity. Some were correct in their assessment about the possibilities of synthetic dyes. But many more were wrong, as is evident from the high number of business failures. The historical record also shows that few entrepreneurs set out on their own. They typically looked for business partners, often to secure financing and technical expertise, and they tended to start on a small scale.

The German Firms: Bayer and Jäger

When Carl Rumpf proposed to the founders of Bayer in 1871 that they should increase alizarin production to keep up with Hoechst and BASF by building a separate factory on an area that would cost six times as much as the existing factory grounds, they thought he was crazy. Rumpf then bought property himself and leased it back to the company . . .

When Carl Rumpf proposed in 1883 that Bayer should hire chemists whose sole task should be to make inventions, the management and board thought that such expenses were not justifiable. Rumpf then hired the first three research chemists, paying their salaries out of his own pocket [my translation].

—CARL VERG (1988), Bayer company historian[112]

Realizing . . . that Jäger's family firm was only viable if it did not walk on the main avenues of the coal-tar industry but if it moved on the little streets that would not be known by or would be too small for the large competitors, Dr. Carl began with the introduction of niche products [my translation].

—R. W. CARL (1926, p. 25), chemist and Jäger company historian in his reflections on corporate strategy

The Bayer company is as much a success story as Jäger is one of missed opportunities.[113] Bayer and Jäger are chosen for comparison because both started in the same town of Barmen. Selecting firms from the same geographic location allows us to hold environmental factors as constant as possible and thus to analyze with greater rigor how managerial actions shaped the path of each firm.

Jäger had already produced fuchsine by 1858. This made it one of the first firms in the world to enter the synthetic dye industry. Bayer was on the market with fuchsine five years later in 1863. Friedrich Bayer and Friedrich Weskott's first experiments with making fuchsine took place on a kitchen stove in their family homes (Beer, 1959, p. 73; Verg et al., 1988, p. 26). Two years elapsed before the two founders of the firm had worked out a production method that was economically viable.

---

[112] Pages 36 and 72 in Verg, Plumpe, and Schultheis (1988).

[113] The principal sources on Carl Jäger GmbH used here are Carl (1926), Scheinert (1988), and Henneking (1994); on Bayer, they are Anonymous (1895), the 50th, 100th, and 125th anniversary volumes (Farbenfabriken-Bayer, 1904; Bayer, 1963; and Verg et al., 1998, respectively) of the Bayer company, and Beer (1959).

If first mover (as opposed to early mover) advantages had been the only factor determining long-term success, Jäger should have outperformed Bayer by a large margin. But their roles were completely reversed. On the eve of World War I, Bayer, along with BASF and Hoechst, belonged to the trio of firms that accounted each for about 22 percent of the German dye production. Except for a severe financial crisis in the mid-1880s, which endangered the existence of the firm, Bayer was extremely profitable (see Table 8). Bayer trailed BASF and Hoechst in the 1880s but subsequently achieved greater growth rates than the two chief rivals, becoming fully equal in size by 1905. Jäger, in contrast, was no longer in the top ten German dye firms and belonged to the group of niche players, each of which probably had less than 1 percent of the market.[114] Unlike many of the German dye firms that went out of business in the early 1860s, Jäger initially was very successful, allowing Otto Jäger, the founder of the synthetic dye business, to retire from the business in 1869 (Carl, 1926, p. 19). The sizable profits from a highly successful natural dye (safflor carmine), sold not only in Germany but also in Paris and London, allowed the firm to invest in synthetic dyes (Carl, 1926, p. 10). Jäger was mentioned in Hofmann's (1863) report on the London exhibition both for its natural dyes as well as its aniline colors, and it appears that the firm did well throughout the 1860s. Because its management was reluctant to invest in more advanced production equipment, however, firms such as Bayer that put a large part of profits back into the business grew much faster than Jäger. In the end, Bayer bought Jäger as part of the restructuring of the German dye industry in 1916, leaving little doubt as to who had made the right and wrong moves in the struggle for market share over the previous five decades.

The firms of Friedrich Bayer and Carl Jäger had very similar origins. Carl Jäger organized a firm in 1823 to prepare and sell natural dyes and chemicals (Carl, 1926, p. 9). Similarly, Friedrich Bayer traded natural dyes at least since 1850. In 1863 the firm was renamed Friedrich Bayer & Co. to reflect the new partnership between Bayer and the dyer Friedrich Weskott. Bayer became the general manager while Weskott assumed the role of the technical director. Weskott knew everything about dyeing: He was already running a successful dyeing business employing twelve men (Beer, 1959, p. 73). To reduce their personal risk with the new enterprise, the two founders initially kept their successful old businesses along with the new one. With a practicing dyer as the technical director, Friedrich Bayer & Co. was more directly knowledgeable about the needs of dyers than the Jäger enterprise. Both Bayer and Jäger possessed a network of sales contacts because of their previous involvement in natural dyes. Friedrich Bayer, as a trader of natural dyes, had sales connections in many German cities as well as in Brussels, Amsterdam, Bradford (England), New York, and St. Petersburg (Verg et al., 1988, p. 24). Although Jäger's network may not have been as extensive as that of Bayer, Carl Jäger traveled annually to Paris and London (Carl, 1926, p. 11) and later Otto Jäger, the son of the founder, frequently traveled at least to Paris and perhaps to other centers of dyeing as well. On one

[114] In 1904 Carl Duisberg of Bayer prepared a memorandum for the leaders of the other German dye firms in which he set forth the advantages of a merger of all German dye firms into one company. Jäger is not enumerated on Duisberg's 1904 list of public and private coal-tar firms in Germany (1923, pp. 346–7), which means it fell into Duisberg's category of "some small firms."

Table 8. **Bayer Size Indicators and Return on Stock Capital**[a]

Year	Stock capital (in 000 marks)	Return on stock capital[b]	Total workforce	Number of chemists
1913	36,000	0.48	10,600	321
1912	36,000	0.44	10,002	
1911	36,000	0.39		
1910	36,000	0.35		
1909	36,000	0.36		
1908	36,000	0.32	7,833	203
1907	21,000	0.56	7,608	186
1906	21,000	0.52		171
1905	21,000	0.50		
1904	21,000	0.33	6,804	170
1903	14,000	0.43	6,723	163
1902	14,000	0.37		149
1901	14,000	0.29		150
1900	12,000	0.31		140
1899	12,000	0.29		109
1898	12,000	0.28		
1897	11,000	0.29		98
1896	11,000	0.28		102
1895	9,000	0.32		
1894	9,000	0.28		71
1893	9,000	0.27		52
1892	9,000	0.26		
1891	9,000	0.25		
1890	9,000	0.28		56
1889	9,000	0.25		60
1888	7,500	0.23	1,100	42
1887	7,500	0.17		
1886	7,500	0.11		
1885	7,500	No dividend		
1884	7,500	8% dividend	593	
1883	6,595	20% dividend		
1882	5,400	0.09	401	14

[a] The returns of Bayer may be a bit inflated when compared to figures of public corporations in the United States in the same period because of differences in accounting procedures. But clearly Bayer and the other successful German dye firms had exceptional returns. One source even claims that it was the industry with the highest returns in Germany.

[b] Return on stock capital is not the same thing as dividends paid out. Whereas Bayer in its first year as a stock company paid out 20 percent dividend (German investors at the time would demand high returns), it seems to have earned only a 9 percent return on the stock capital. In the few cases where return on stock capital figures are missing, dividend payments are listed in the table.

Source: Bayer annual reports and Homburg–Murmann database.

of his trips, Otto Jäger found out about fuchsine, the new brilliant red synthetic dye, shortly after it was introduced in Paris. Sensing a great business opportunity, he wasted no time in building a little production plant at the Wupper River back home.

The British Firms: Levinstein and Brooke, Simpson & Spiller

Throughout every aspect of the work, whether it was production, research, planning, construction, negotiation, purchasing or selling, "boss" Levinstein – perhaps in common with other Victorian masters – remained completely in charge. Within the business he was feared, but respected; his word was the law.

> —MAURICE FOX (1987, p. 13), leading historian of the British dye industry

For the well-being of our business, it is clearly necessary that all major ideas contained in this memorandum are examined closely by all those men in our firm who have many years of experience in chemical production and that ideas are sorted out in a free exchange of opinions [my translation].

> —CARL DUISBERG's final paragraph in his 1895 memorandum to the leadership of Bayer concerning the constructing of a large new plant in Leverkusen (1923, p. 409)

To ensure success, constant attendance at the works and close regular personal supervision by the principals of the conduct and management of the business are essential. Although this advice was given on many occasions, Brooke, Simpson & Spiller wilfully neglected the works and managed it carelessly and injudiciously. They seldom went over the works or remained on the premises more than two three or hours at a time, and for many weeks, none of the principals, with the exception of William Charles Barnes, visited the works for more than three or four days a week. Mr. Barnes was well-intentioned, but his limited knowledge of chemistry was a hindrance to competent judgement.

> —DIX PERKIN's (partner and brother of William H.) analysis of why Brooke, Simpson & Spiller failed with the alizarin plant that Perkin & Sons ran very successfully, as quoted in Fox (1987, p. 107)

By the standards of the British dye industry, the Levinstein company in its various legal incarnations was one of the best, perhaps the best, performer during the entire period from 1857 to 1914. Along with Read Holliday, Levinstein was the largest producer of dyestuffs in Great Britain from the 1880s until World War I. To finance the expansion of the work, Levinstein invested at least since 1895 every penny back into the firm. This allowed the firm to expand even though it did not offer lucrative financial returns to its share- and bondholders. The preferred shareholders (£30,000 at 6 percent) received no dividend between 1900 and 1914 (Reader, 1970, p. 263). Ordinary shareholders (£60,000) did not receive a dividend payment until the dye shortage in World War I changed the fortunes of the firm. In 1905 and in 1910, Levinstein had to ask debenture holders (£75,000) for permission to default on interest payments (Reader, 1970, p. 263). The holders must have had some confidence in the future of the firm since they granted the request. Particularly in 1910–11 the firm faced a financial crisis after German firms, starting in 1908, refused to buy dye intermediates from Levinstein because they were upset by Ivan Levinstein's strategic actions in connection to British patent law (Reader, 1970, p. 263). (See Chapter 4 for more details.)

By German standards Levinstein was hardly a success. Yet by British standards the firm looked very good, especially when compared to such failures as Brooke, Simpson & Spiller (BS&S). BS&S was formed in 1868 and was profitable until the mid-1880s (Fox, 1987, p. 106). From 1885 on, however, it went on a steady decline until finally in 1905, creditors forced the liquidation of the firm (Fox, 1987, p. 110). Very early the partners showed a remarkable inability to manage an existing dye business. The purchase of Perkin & Sons' highly profitable alizarin business in 1874 proved to be a complete financial disaster as the quote earlier has already suggested. Only two years later BS&S resold the alizarin plant, having incurred a great financial loss.[115] Levinstein eventually came into possession of BS&S's remaining plant when Levinstein in 1916 bought Claus & Co., which had acquired BS&S's Hackney Wick plant during liquidation (Fox, 1987, p. 104). Just as in the case of Jäger and Bayer, over time the lower performing firm came under control of the better performing one.

The origins of the two firms were quite different. Levinstein was formed in 1864 by three Levinstein brothers. In a letter Ivan Levinstein reports he already had started a small factory in Germany that produced synthetic dyes but he had decided to emigrate to England instead, where he erected a plant in partnership with his two brothers (Fox, 1987, Plate I). The Levinstein family came from Berlin, Germany, where Ivan Levinstein's father had won fame and fortune as a financial and political writer and a confidant of the rich and politically powerful.[116] All indications suggest that the father bankrolled the sons' venture into the British dye industry, just as happened in the case of Perkin's enterprise.

At least one of the Levinstein brothers had technical expertise. Before his seventeenth birthday, Ivan entered the University of Berlin to study chemistry and later moved to the famous Gewerbeinstitut[117] (home of Baeyer, Graebe, and Liebermann in the 1860s), where he became at age eighteen the assistant of Professor Weber in the applied chemistry laboratory. There he carried out work in coal-tar dyes. The Prussian patent Ivan obtained in 1863–64 for the improvement in the preparation of aldehyde green probably was worked out during his tenure at the Gewerbeinstitut (letter printed in Fox, 1987, Plate I).

The Levinsteins located their plant in the larger Manchester area, the heart of the British textile industry. Establishing close physical proximity to leading customers

---

[115] The subsequent owners of the alizarin plant (Burt, Bulton & Haywood and, after 1882, British Alizarine) generally operated it with profits (Fox, 1987, pp. 109–111, 117–19), underscoring the technical incompetence of BS&S's management.

[116] The present account of the origins of Levinstein relies mainly on Fox (1987).

[117] Fox (1987, p. 10) calls the school Gewerbe-akademie, the name it received after 1866 before it was renamed yet again and became the Technical University Berlin. To avoid confusion, I refer to the school as the Gewerbeinstitut before it became a Technical University.

may have been a key strategic decision, because by 1914 the London dye firms had lost their market position to Levinstein and its nearby rival in Huddersfield, Read Holliday.

The BS&S firm, in contrast, entered the dye industry by taking over the plants of one of the most important dye firms in the early 1860s, Simpson, Maule & Nicholson (SM&N).[118] During the mid 1860s, SM&N was widely reported to be the largest dye and intermediate plant in the world (Donnelly, 1987, p. 261; Fox, 1987, pp. 106–8). In 1874 the partnership BS&S also bought the alizarin plant of Perkin & Sons and thus became the heir to two of the early pioneers of the synthetic dye industry who were successful enough to retire from business with the sale of their firms.[119] Whereas Perkin & Sons and SM&N were characterized by their scientific and technically oriented leadership that had led to the first synthetic dyes and novel production processes, the partners in BS&S from the very beginning showed much less involvement in the technical and scientific affairs of the business.

The American Firms: Schoellkopf and American Aniline Works

Here was a business rooted in chemical science, and all the Schoellkopfs valued research realistically when most American chemical makers were just beginning to recognize the word... Their research made tangible contributions to dye technology..., fair notice that the German dye monopoly was not omnipotent.

—WILLIAMS HAYNES (1954, p. 309), leading historian
of the American chemical industry

Being quite ignorant of any color-making process, they advertised in English and German trade papers for formulas and directions. The English replies proved valueless and none came from Germany, for the publisher of their advertisement was promptly arrested, charged with aiding a surreptitious attempt to steal German trade secrets.

—WILLIAMS HAYNES (1954, p. 310) on the entry
strategy of American Aniline Works

A success story, by American standards, was the Schoellkopf Aniline & Chemical Company. Schoellkopf entered the American dye industry in 1879. Just as with

[118] All three founders of SM&N had been students at the Royal College of Chemistry under Hofmann. In fact, Edward Chambers Nicholson was in the first class that Hofmann taught on his arrival in 1845. Mr. Simpson in SM&N and Mr. Simpson in BS&S were brothers; otherwise, little connection existed between the two partnerships.

[119] It is interesting to see that Perkin's retirement from his dye business followed very much a script that August W. Hofmann (1863, p. 124) had publicly laid out for him many years earlier:

It is with sincere pleasure that the writer of these pages, who had the good fortune of guiding the chemical education of Mr. Perkin, congratulates his young friend on the splendid industrial result which he has achieved; expressing, at the same time, the hope that the commercial success of his enterprise, and the care and time involved in such an undertaking of such magnitude, may not divert him from the path of scientific inquiry, for which already he has proved himself eminently qualified.

In contrast to Perkin, Carl Alexander Martius, Hofmann's student, assistant, and long-time collaborator, ran his dye business until the end of his career and took on many public duties on behalf of German industry.

Levinstein in Britain, the firm was started as a family operation and remained a family-run business until its World War I merger into National Aniline. J. F. Schoellkopf, Jr., and C. P. Hugo Schoellkopf, two brothers who had studied chemistry in Germany, constituted the human capital of the firm; the father Jacob F. Schoellkopf, a successful entrepreneur in Buffalo, provided the financial capital.[120] By European standards, Schoellkopf was a latecomer in the dye industry, but it was one of the first firms to enter the American dye industry (number four, according to the Homburg–Murmann database). Undoubtedly, the U.S. Civil War (1861–65) was in part responsible for the delayed entry of American firms into the industry. Aside from the aforementioned differences in organic chemistry capabilities, would-be American dye entrepreneurs also faced very different incentives from those of their British, French, or German counterparts: At the start of the synthetic dye industry, American consumption of silk – the only fabric that initially could absorb Perkin's mauve – was not even 10 percent of what Britain, France, or Germany consumed (Federico, 1997).[121]

Because Schoellkopf never went public, not much of its financial data is available. The firm grew steadily, along with the expansion of the market for synthetic dyes. In its first year (1879) it had sales of $40,000. By 1893, sales reached $300,000. By 1900, 120 men were employed. And by the eve of the war, the firm had 250 employees and sold about 130 dyes. At this point, the entire U.S. synthetic dye industry employed 528 people (Steen, 1995, p. 528), whereas Bayer alone had 10,500 employees. Schoellkopf was clearly the largest American dye firm before the war (accounting for 50 percent of domestic production) and formed the keystone of the National Aniline & Chemical merger in 1917. The firm apparently was not profitable until 1895 (for sixteen years), but the elder Schoellkopf could afford to keep the firm alive (M. Feldman, unpublished). Given the enormous competition from German firms, this was no small achievement; most American dye entrepreneurs were not able to stay in business very long. Although the firm had become profitable before the war, it never came close to the profit level of Bayer.[122]

American Aniline Works represents a dramatic, albeit almost poetic, failure among the American dye firms before World War I. The third U.S. dye firm formed (according to Homburg–Murmann database), the firm existed only from 1875 to 1883. The disappearance of the American Aniline Works along with four others of the nine

---

[120] Jacob F. Schoellkopf, Jr., studied chemistry in Germany from 1873 until 1879 and entered the dye business directly after his return from Germany (Martin Feldman, unpublished).

[121] In the period 1859–63, Britain consumed 24,800 quintals of silk, France 33,050 quintals. Data for the United States begin only after the Civil War and show that U.S. consumption from 1865 to 1865 was only 2,010 quintals. German consumption for the period 1869–73 stood at 23,720 quintals (Federico, 1997, p. 213). The leading role of France in making silk textiles is also evident from trade statistics. In 1865 London traded 2,850 tons of silk, Lyons 2,900, and Milan 1,650, whereas New York (in 1867) traded only 200 tons (Federico, 1997, p. 153).

[122] According to Steen (1995, p. 55), Schoellkopf testified before the House Committee on Ways and Means in 1916 that the partly owned selling agency of Schoellkopf, the National Aniline Company, had a greater rate of profit than the manufacturing firm. Only a quarter to a third of the sales of National Aniline Company came from Schoellkopf's production; the remainder were dyes made by other firms. The profit margin of the National Aniline Company was 10 percent in 1913 and 1914. This figure leads us to conclude that the Schoellkopf manufacturing firm had less than 10 percent return just before the war, half of Bayer's margin.

existing American dye firms is typically blamed on the lowering of U.S. tariffs in 1883, but an unbiased appraisal of the firm's condition suggests that its exit was bound to take place even without the lowering of the tariffs. Many years later, one of the founders of the firm, the German-born Victor Bloede, openly conceded the complete economic failure of the firm: "It is hardly necessary to add the humiliating admission that the enterprise was not a profitable one. We simply carried it along because we did not want to give it up, our faith still being strong that somewhere along the line millions could be unearthed" (1924, p. 410). The concrete reason for the firm's closing came in the form of a natural disaster. The factory was sitting on the bank of the Ohio River. Exceptionally heavy rainfall had turned the typically placid river into a raging torrent that swept the dye plant away, "tinting the turbulent waters a beautiful raspberry shade for many miles, much to the amazement of the natives along the river shore" (Bloede, 1924, p. 411).

Organization of the Chapter

The competitive dynamics faced by synthetic dye firms changed dramatically over the period from 1857 to 1914. Because the strategies of the firms had to be adjusted substantially to meet novel competitive requirements, it is useful to break the analysis of this long period into three shorter intervals, as detailed before. Examining shorter periods allows for a more fine-grained discussion of the sources of a firm's success over the industry's development.

Period 1, 1857–65: Early synthetic dyes
Period 2, 1866–85: The rise of scientific theory in dye innovation
Period 3, 1886–1914: The age of corporate R&D laboratories

It is relatively straightforward to observe significant performance differences among the three pairs of firms. In 1914, an approximate ranking of the six firms would have looked like this:

1. Bayer (largest firm in world with BASF and Hoechst)
2. Levinstein (leading British firm)
3. Schoellkopf (leading American firm)
4. Jäger (German niche player)

- Brooke, Simpson & Spiller (dead in 1905)
- American Aniline (dead in 1883–84)

The real challenge lies in explaining why one firm in each country did so much better than a second firm as the dye industry took its course.

Given the scarcity of financial performance indicators for the four privately held companies, I use organization size (employees and output) as the chief measure of success to be explained in this chapter. To the extent that financial performance measures are available, they are used to support the arguments made about differences in growth rates. What, then, were the likely factors that created such disparate performance paths for the six firms?

The World of Pioneers (1857–1865)

The era up to 1865 was dominated by British and French firms. The precursors of BS&S – Perkin & Sons and SM&N – along with La Fuchsine in France were the leading dye firms in the world. Because the brilliant red fuchsine dye that appeared in 1858 was in very high demand (Caro, 1892, p. 1030) and because the technological requirements for "reverse engineering" the early aniline dyes were relatively low, many firms jumped on the fuchsine bandwagon. Jäger was successful mainly by imitating existing products, a strategy that was much more viable in Germany than in Britain because of the absence of significant patent laws in Germany. Bayer also entered the dye industry at the end of this first period by successfully copying the fuchsine dye. Although Levinstein in Britain began its commercial life by making a green dye, the firm also quickly took up production of the popular fuchsine dye when the British patent fell in 1865.

Two generic strategies seem to have worked in this first period. Given the availability of patent protection in Britain, product innovation was a successful strategy. Perkin & Sons and SM&N pioneered new products and related processes and profited handsomely. The absence of patent protection in Germany made it feasible to imitate the innovations made by other firms. Not surprisingly, Germany had more than twice as many fuchsine dye plants in 1864 than Britain (eleven versus five).[123]

Because the market for natural dyes had taken on an international character already before 1857, with firms like Bayer and Jäger shipping product to such dyeing centers as London and Paris, developing a customer base in foreign countries became an important strategic asset for grabbing market share from the very beginning of the synthetic dye industry.

Hindsight makes it clear that entering the synthetic dye industry early was to be of great competitive advantage, in terms of both gaining a strong position with dyers and printers and building up effective skills in the manufacture of dyes. No firm founded after 1870 became a world leader. Schoellkopf, which entered the industry in 1879, became a leader among U.S. domestic producers, but as we have seen, the firm was very small by world standards. Late entrants could not compete in the key synthetic dye markets with early entrants that had already accumulated significant organizational capabilities in production and marketing.

Product Strategies: Making or Buying Dye Inputs?

Besides the basic question of whether to enter the industry with an innovative dye or whether to simply copy an existing product, every entrepreneurial venture after Perkin cleared the path faced a host of other important decisions. Should the planned firm make all the dye intermediates and basic chemicals itself, or should it try to buy them from other firms and focus only on the actual dye production itself? When Perkin & Sons decided to make the first synthetic dye on a commercial scale, a market for basic and intermediate chemicals such as nitrobenzene and aniline did not exist (Perkin, 1896, pp. 153–5). To be able to put mauve on the market, Perkin & Sons had

---

[123] All figures on number of firms and plants come from the Homburg–Murmann database unless otherwise noted. They should always be interpreted as approximate figures because it is not possible to be certain that all small firms have been found.

to find an economical process for these early production steps of turning coal tar into intermediates and finally into finished dyes.

Jäger entered the industry a year later. At this point, the firm was already less constrained in its product strategy. Although no market for the aniline raw materials existed in Germany, Jäger could buy some aniline in Britain and France, where other firms such as SM&N had entered the production of aniline after Perkin showed the way. In 1861, driven by the desire to obtain a cheaper source of aniline, Otto Jäger offered to invest 90,000 German marks himself and persuaded his cousin Joseph Wilhelm (Anton) Weiler to start aniline production and provide Jäger with this necessary raw material (Scheinert, 1988, pp. 218–19).[124] Although Weiler's initial plan was to make nitrobenzene as well, the firm continued to buy nitrobenzene until 1867 from France and Britain, where SM&N, for example, had become a cheap producer of the chemical.

Comparing the backgrounds of firms with their product strategies makes evident that the choice of product strategies was strongly related to the previous activities of the firm (when it already existed) or of the founders of the new dye venture. The founders of BASF, for instance, came from the raw-material side (coal tar) and decided to manufacture all chemicals required to make fuchsine, starting with nitrobenzene, acids, and soda. Jäger and Bayer, which were previously engaged in selling natural dyes, concentrated on making aniline dyes and did not make basic and intermediate chemicals. Except for a few years at the turn of the century, Bayer always bought aniline in the market. BASF, on the other hand, also became the largest aniline producer in Germany for the entire period before World War I, largely because it was the largest synthetic dye firm for most of the period and made aniline in-house. Similarly, the previous experience of SM&N in fine chemicals gave the firm a skill base that made the move into the production of nitrobenzene and aniline less risky. Only after making these crucial intermediates did SM&N go further downstream and make synthetic dyes.

The more production steps a firm wanted to carry out, the greater the capital and knowledge requirement would be, and the greater the risk of losing a substantial sum of money in the highly competitive synthetic dye market. It is, therefore, not surprising that when new ventures were given the option to buy raw material in the market, most firms decided to concentrate on making direct precursors of dyes and dyes themselves and to leave the production of raw materials to other firms. Being the first firm in the industry, Perkin & Sons did not have the option and had to make basic raw materials initially. But when SM&N became the most efficient producer of nitrobenzene, even Perkin & Sons did not hesitate to buy a large portion of its nitrobenzene needs from SM&N (Perkin, 1885, p. 77). The early years of the synthetic dye industry reveal that product strategies were constrained by the degree to which markets for basic raw materials were developed. The very first firms, Perkin & Sons and Jäger, had to help bring about a market for raw materials. The later entrants could

---

[124] Weiler was bought in 1896 by the dye manufacturer ter-Meer. The firm "Chemische Fabriken vorm. Weiler-ter Meer" remained, after BASF, the largest producer of aniline in Germany. Later the firm merged into the I.G. Farben chemical conglomerate. Today the former Weiler-ter Meer aniline plants in Uerdingen belong to Bayer, which continues to be one of largest aniline producers in the world.

then rely on these emerging markets for raw materials (Stigler, 1963). After the 1880s, however, the market structure changed again. The independent aniline manufacturers largely disappeared.[125]

Organization of Production: Improvise and Improve

The retrospectives on the early days of the synthetic dye industry by such eminent participants as W. H. Perkin and H. Caro reveal that production equipment had to be devised from scratch. Specialized chemical apparatuses simply did not exist at the beginning of the dye industry. The earliest dye plants tried to scale up laboratory equipment by using vessels and ovens that were developed for other industrial purposes. Those firms that experimented a lot with different production arrangements, different equipment, and alternative chemicals had a very good chance of uncovering more efficient methods. Perkin & Sons found numerous ways to improve its production processes. But apparently SM&N, under the technical leadership of Nicholson himself, one of Hofmann's best students at the Royal College of Chemistry, was even better in developing more efficient production techniques.[126] The willingness to search for better manufacturing processes and SM&N's aggressive strategy of developing a portfolio of dyes with fuchsine and aniline blue (the latter licensed from the French pioneer Renard Frères & Franc) made it the largest producer of dyes and intermediates in the mid-1860s.

Whereas in Britain the market for fuchsine was largely controlled by SM&N, German dyers and printers had the option of choosing from several different firms producing fuchsine. For Bayer and Jäger to stay in business, given the strong rivalry between German fuchsine producers, they had to be more efficient than most of their competitors. By 1864, the price of aniline red had fallen to about 10 percent of the 1860 levels, which reflected both improved methods of large-scale production and the high level of competition (Morris and Travis, 1992, p. 65). To keep up with competitors, Bayer performed a large number of experiments that were primarily driven by empirical observation. Production workers and August Siller, the first "chemist"[127] Bayer hired only a year after the firm had started, fiddled around with different temperatures and ingredients, improving the yield of the fuchsine process substantially. Bayer was no different from other firms in this respect. No firm had a master plan of how it was going to operate in the new synthetic dye business. Rather, firms would be guided by the most pressing problems and opportunities – or what Cyert and March (1963; pp. 169–71, 1992 edition) have called problemistic search – proceeding largely by trial and error.

---

[125] The disappearance of the independent aniline producers had several reasons. (1) Some of the more successful firms internalized aniline production. For example, Hoechst started to build its own aniline plant in 1869, seven years after the firm was founded. (2) Vertical integration eliminated independent firms as in the case of the merger between Weiler (independent aniline producer) and ter Meer. (3) The aniline cartel of 1883 probably crushed the smaller producers. Consistent with these reasons, the Bayer firm gave up the production of fuchsine in 1889 because, according to Farbenfabriken-Bayer (1918, p. 193), the firm was not able to buy the necessary raw materials (aniline, toluidine) cheaply enough.

[126] Hofmann held Nicholson's talent in very high esteem. Hofmann would say about Nicholson: "[I]n him was united the genius of the manufacturer and the habits of a scientific investigator" (Fox, 1987, p. 105).

[127] Siller was not an academic chemist because he was trained at a local trade school and not at a university, where organic chemical research would have flourished.

Undoubtedly, the higher level of competition in the German environment forced Bayer and Jäger to pursue a simple strategy: Copy, improve, and make it cheap! Some evidence indicates that several German firms pressed by stronger local competition had become even more efficient than SM&N – the British leader in efficient production processes. When the British fuchsine patent fell in 1865, German firms could offer the dye at a lower price and quickly took a significant portion of the British fuchsine market. It is striking how technical education seems to have made leaders of firms more inclined to encourage experimentation on the shop floor. SM&N was the British firm with the greatest level of technical expertise and it became the leading firm. Germany possessed even more people who had received technical education in the 1860s and this allowed a larger number of firms to experiment with production technology just like SM&N. Not surprisingly, a few of them such as Bayer eventually would even do better than SM&N, which was more sheltered because of its monopoly profits. Of course, another reason why Bayer was able to experiment more with production processes for existing dyes is that, unlike its British competitors, Bayer and other German firms could make any dye in the color rainbow because Germany, unlike Britain, at the time did not have patents on dyes.

Marketing: Visit Your Customers and Win Medals

The pioneers of the synthetic dye industry faced an enormous marketing challenge. Given that dyers and printers had worked for thousands of years with the same natural dyes, in many regions of the world these trades were extremely conservative in their thinking and their ways of operating. The first challenge for Perkin & Sons, Jäger, and Bayer was to convince dyers to at least try the new synthetic products.

W. H. Perkin was very clever in how he went about marketing his new dye. Even before a plant was erected, Perkin sent samples of mauve-colored silk to Robert Pullar (head of the famous dye house J. Pullar & Son in Perth) and asked for advice on the commercial prospects of mauve. Pullar wrote back on June 12, 1856:

Sir, I am today favoured with your note with patterns of colours (sic) for which I am much obliged. If your discovery does not make the goods too expensive it is decidedly one of the most valuable that has come out for a very long time, this colour is one that has been very much wanted in all classes of goods and could not be had fast on Silk and only at great expense on cotton yarns. I inclose (sic) you pattern of the best Lilac we have in cotton . . . (as quoted in Fox, 1987, p. 95)

These were encouraging words. Perkin consulted another silk dyer, Thomas Keith of Bethnal Green, in early 1857 (Fox, 1987, p. 95). Keith conducted a series of trials and when he echoed Robert Pullar's optimism, Perkin had sufficient confidence to venture into the commercial production of mauve.[128] Finding customers who would order large quantities of mauve, however, was not that simple. Dyers in Britain were reluctant to try out the new dye. The real breakthrough of mauve first occurred in France. This was no accident because the technically most innovative – that is, the least conservative – dyers were in Lyon and Paris, the centers of the high fashion industry. Only after mauve became very popular in France did it receive a lot

---

[128] For more details on how Perkin commercialized his laboratory discovery, see Garfield (2001).

of free press in Britain, and British silk dyers became keen to put mauve on their wares.[129]

The success of German firms in the synthetic dye industry has often been ascribed to their focus on helping dyers and printers in applying the new synthetic dyes to the particular fabric used locally (Haber, 1958, p. 167; Beer, 1959, pp. 88–93). But careful study of Perkin & Sons reveals that W. H. Perkin's early success in the British industry, in fact, also hinged critically on his willingness to cooperate with dyers and printers in developing effective dyeing and printing techniques for mauve. According to Fox (1987, p. 96), "Records show that he carried out extensive 'technical service' work on factory floors in Glasgow, Bradford, Macclesfield and the London regions." Perkin was more than just the inventor of the first aniline dye. To market mauve successfully, Perkin experimented a great deal with a number of different application processes. He was clearly not the only one trying to push application technology forward. The French dyers and printers played a large role in developing improved application processes (Homburg, 1983; Travis, 1993). Even though collective innovations advanced the application processes of mauve, Perkin took a very proactive role in overcoming application problems. Although he benefited and learned substantially from the trials of other people, he actively worked on developing application processes in collaboration with individuals in the dyeing and printing trade.

The dyeing of cotton with aniline purple at first presented many difficulties... After some time Mr R Pullar and myself found a method for applying this colouring matter to cotton, which is based upon the insolubility of the compounds it forms with tannin ... This method of preparing cotton has been found suitable for nearly all aniline colours discovered since mauve, and is now almost universally employed in Great Britain for cotton dyeing. Other processes have been proposed but are not so generally employed as the one just described (Perkin, 1868, p. 39).

Perkin here appears to downplay the contributions of an extension of the process patented by Lloyd and Dale (English patent no. 701), which proved even more effective. In any case, collaborating with innovative dyers such as Keith and Pullar was a very effective marketing tool. Keith and Pullar were Perkin's first customers for dyeing silk with mauve before the French dyers made mauve popular in Britain.

The greatest technical challenge concerned the big market for calico printing. Perkin's writings reveal that besides calico printers in France he was actively involved in trying to extend the use of mauve to calico printing.

I distinctly remember, the first time I induced a calico-printer to make trails of this colour, that the only report I obtained was that it was too dear, and it was not until nearly two years

---

[129] Fox (1987, p. 96) reports:

Shortly after the introduction of the new aniline purple, French colourists boosted its popularity to the point of a craze. Enthusiasm for the new color was rife in the fashionable court of the Empress Eugénie, who seems to have been one of the first to wear it. It was, in fact, the French who first named the colour "mauve" because of its close resemblance to the flower of the wild mallow plant of that name. The dye enjoyed immense popularity throughout France and by 1859 an overwhelming mania for its colour spread throughout Great Britain. Satirists of the day described its extremely wide adoption as a "malady."

For additional interesting and funny details on the mauve craze, see Chapter 6 of Garfield (2001).

afterwards, when French printers put aniline purple into their patterns, that it began to interest British printers (Perkin, 1868, p. 15).

Being dissatisfied with this mechanical mode of applying aniline purple, in conjunction with Mr Grey I made a number of experiments with a view of obtaining some more chemical method of fixing this colouring matter, and at last succeeded...The process now nearly universally employed in the north [Manchester area] was discovered by M. Alexander Schultz and myself; it consists in printing the colouring matter with a mordant composed of a solution of arsenite of alumina in acetate of alumina (Perkin, 1868, p. 40)

Schultz, a Frenchman, and Perkin together obtained a British patent for this calico printing process in 1862 and thereby finally opened up for mauve (as well as other aniline dyes developed later) the large market of calico-printed fabrics. The ability of a technology developed for a particular market (in this case mauve applied to silk dyeing) to invade the territory of another technology (in this case natural dyes used to dye and print cotton) has recently been identified by Rosenbloom and Christensen (1994; Christensen and Rosenbloom, 1995) as a key feature of technical change.[130]

When Levinstein entered the market in 1864, Perkin and the other British pioneers such as SM&N had already developed a market for synthetic dyes.[131] The community of dyers, printers, and new entrepreneurs had made great progress in improving and extending the application of the new synthetic dyes to all different kinds of fibers. A series of application patents had been taken out by individuals from both the new synthetic dye firms and the traditional dyers and printers, indicating that a collective innovation process helped to make the industry a success. Some of the seventeen (yes, seventeen) Levinstein siblings had been active in London as traders of natural dyes and synthetic dyes at least since 1861. Apparently, Hugo Levinstein infringed Renard Frère's fuchsine patent and took up production of fuchsine on a small scale in London and Milan until Renard Frères took Hugo Levinstein to court in 1864. Hugo Levinstein and his brothers Gustav and Adolf ran an important dye trading house in London. In 1865 Levinstein & Co. presented itself in the London directory as "dyes manufacturer and export agents" with four offices in London; factories in London, Milan, and Manchester; and branches in Glasgow, Leicester, Huddersfield, Bradford, and New York. The firm claimed exports to China and the West Indies (Fox, 1987, p. 5). Even if this advertisement exaggerates the degree to which the Levinsteins operated in a variety of countries, the Levinsteins clearly had a strong international orientation and were serious players in the dye trade, which at this point remained largely that of natural dyes.

Before manufacturing was taken up under the direction of Ivan in the Manchester area, the Levinsteins were predominantly a sales and marketing organization.

[130] Christensen and Rosenbloom (1995; Rosenbloom and Christensen, 1994) have documented that incumbent firms in the disk drive industry were frequently replaced by other firms who had developed a new disk drive technology for a new user market and later were able to invade the markets of incumbent firms. The step by step invasion of new synthetic dye firms into the different markets for natural dyes is an example of the competitive strength of firms moving on a new technological trajectory.

[131] The firm was able to begin production of fuchsine relatively quickly because Ivan Levinstein appears to have experimented a great deal with this dye while he was assistant to Professor Weber in Berlin and because his brother Hugo had already gained some manufacturing know-how by producing the dye on a small scale in London (Fox, 1987, p. 11).

This marketing orientation remained a hallmark of the Levinstein enterprise. A one-page advertisement in the October 1871 issue of the *Chemical Review* shows the firm L. I. Levinstein & Sons as manufacturers of aniline dyes with works in Blackley and Middleton; two offices in London, one in Blackley, and one in Liverpool; and depots in Paris, Leipzig, Vienna, and Boston. Ivan Levinstein from the beginning assumed a very active role in sales. Fox (1987, p. 12) believes that the story of Ivan taking part of his fuchsine production to Scotland and returning to Hull to buy continental aniline, which he took home to make more fuchsine, was not an isolated occurrence. The Manchester synthetic dye business of the Levinsteins rested on the ability to find customers for fuchsine during a time when the prices for the dye were falling dramatically. Ivan Levinstein's decision to move production of synthetic dyes from Berlin to the heart of the British cotton textile industry in Lancashire itself may have been driven by marketing considerations.[132]

In one respect the situation of Bayer and Jäger in Germany differed substantially from that of Perkin & Sons and SM&N in Britain. Given that everyone was selling more or less the same unpatented product, competitive advantage could arise from two sources. Either a firm was able to make fuchsine and the other aniline dyes more cheaply, or it provided better service to the dyers than its competitors.

Bayer appears to have been a marketing-driven organization from the very beginning; it continued to develop its marketing muscle for the entire period before World War I. Friedrich R. Weskott, the son of one of the founders, who rose to leadership position at the firm, recalled in 1911:

Only through the personal engagement with and tedious instructions of the consumers were we able to make slow but steady progress. The task of the businessman was to win the customers over for this new field of synthetic dyes by constant enlightenment and hard work on the details; how much prejudice, outdated views, as well as open and hidden resistance had to be overcome is very difficult to fathom today (Bayer, 1918, p. 4) [my translation].

Bayer's initial marketing strategy was to sell the new synthetic dyes to their existing customer base from the traditional natural dye business. Bayer experienced the identical problems of Perkin & Sons in trying to sell to conservative dyers. Whereas Perkin collaborated with different dyers and printers, Bayer had this important learning alliance built into the firm from the very beginning, thanks to the partnership of a natural dye dealer, Friedrich Bayer, and a dyer, Friedrich Weskott. Just like William Perkin, Friedrich Bayer visited his customers frequently, who, in Bayer's case, were in the beginning located largely in Germany, Switzerland, and Austria (Bayer, 1963, p. 6). But Bayer already communicated with dye traders as far away as the United States, paving the ground for a potential expansion of the sales network in the second half of the 1860s (Farbenfabriken-Bayer, 1918, p. 4).

Jäger appears to have followed essentially the same strategy as Bayer in this period, and both firms appear to have been equally successful. Given that Weskott was a dyer, possibly Bayer was better at helping dyers learn how to use synthetic dyes.

[132] In his first British patent in 1865, he used the address "Ivan Levinstein of Berlin . . . Chemist" (Fox, 1987, p. 11). At this point, Ivan apparently still considered himself a Berliner, and may have not yet made a final decision about where he was going to concentrate his efforts. It turned out that Ivan would run the synthetic dye business from Great Britain for the rest of his life.

Unfortunately we do not have direct evidence of how Jäger went about the business of winning over customers. As we shall see, the big performance differences come later, when Bayer built a large marketing organization and Jäger failed to do so. In the early years of the synthetic dye industry, when relatively small, personally managed, firms competed with one another, Jäger possessed all the elements to compete successfully in the industry.

An important marketing vehicle for the synthetic dye pioneers was the international exhibitions. Until 1904 the exhibitions played a large role in advertising to the public and potential customers the new technologies that were springing up in the world of industry. Synthetic dyes were shown for the first time at the London exhibition in 1862. Because the public had never before seen such brilliant dyes, the display of these new dyes along with the still dominant natural dyes came as a great surprise to the millions of visitors and created a lot of excitement. Particularly until the mid-1870s, the international exhibitions could provide a dye firm with lots of free press, because one of the key features of these international exhibitions was the awarding of medals to firms that showed particularly good new pieces of technology. Reports on the world exhibitions were published in all major industrialized countries to spread the news about the latest advances in technology and industry, giving the public at large and dyers and printers a clear sense of the best producers of synthetic dyes. Hence winning a medal typically had direct consequences for the bottom line because it was the best advertisement firms could receive.

At the exhibition of 1862, August Wilhelm Hofmann was on the jury of technical experts that would decide what firm would receive gold medals and honorable mentions.[133] He also wrote a long report (Hofmann, 1863) on the state of natural dye and synthetic dye technology displayed at the exhibition. In his report he reveals who were the winners of medals and honorable mentions at the exhibition (1863, pp. 137–8). Among the British winners were, not surprisingly, the leading firms at the time: Perkin & Sons, SM&N, Read Holliday, and Dale & Roberts. Hugo Levinstein, for example, does not show up on the list, indicating that his fuchsine efforts were not commercially successful and that the Levinsteins became significant players in the synthetic dye business only after Ivan arrived in Manchester.

Many fewer German firms than British firms exhibited at the London exhibition, underlining the commercial superiority of the British dye industry at this point.[134] In fact, none of the German firms that would be the leading firms by 1914 were among the prize recipients in 1862. According to Caro (1892, p. 1035), Jäger was one of the five German synthetic firms that were represented at the London exhibition. Jäger received a medal for its red aniline dye as well as its famous safflor

[133] Because Hofmann became the leading academic expert on synthetic dyes in the 1860s, he continued to be asked to serve as a juror at later exhibitions. At the 1873 Vienna exhibition, members of the prize jury were accused of having favored firms with whom they were closely linked by consulting ties. See footnote 224 for more details about the alleged jury rigging in Vienna and the consequences for the accused academics.

[134] Ernst Homburg (personal communication, 2001) suggested an alternative explanation for why fewer German than British firms showed their products at the London exhibition in 1862. London was simply much further away for German firms than for British ones, which is why many more British firms appeared among the exhibitors.

carmine natural dye preparation (Carl, 1926, p. 11).[135] The second German firm that won a medal for aniline dyes was R. Knosp of Stuttgart, a firm that had close links to Perkin & Sons, as we will find out later.

Once Bayer entered the synthetic dye business, it quickly understood the marketing leverage these international exhibitions afforded. Bayer won a silver medal in Paris in 1867. The firm continued to exhibit its new dyes not only at international exhibitions but also at other trade fairs, which promised to provide the firm with favorable publicity. Among the many medals, it won a bronze medal in Philadelphia in 1876 and a gold medal for dye intermediates in Paris in 1900 (Bayer, 1963, pp. 20–1). To win these prizes, Bayer had to remain innovative; firms displayed their dyes only when they had a reasonable chance of receiving favorable press at the exhibition. The fact that not a single British firm even participated at the 1900 Paris exhibition indicates how far Levinstein and Read Holliday had fallen behind Bayer, BASF, and Hoechst in their innovative abilities.

Internationalization: Customers Are Everywhere in the World

The international exhibitions that were routinely held in the United States and Europe during the second half of the nineteenth century reflected the growing volume of international trade and rapid diffusion of new technology across countries.

Because dye centers in Europe were connected through a web of personal contacts (often colorists who would spread new technology from one firm to the next), information about new colors and dyeing processes traveled very quickly. The biographies of the leading colorists reveal that this network extended from Britain to Russia in the 1860s (and everywhere in between), but not to the United States. Furthermore, synthetic dyes were cheap to transport because of their high price/weight ratio (quite unlike sulfuric acid, for example), ensuring that few physical obstacles existed to the rapid internationalization of synthetic dye markets. It is striking how quickly the industry became international in scope. The swift demand in France prompted Perkin & Sons to sell mauve there. Given that mauve initially worked on silk but not on cotton, the silk industry in Lyon quickly became the largest customers of Perkin's dye. Perkin also did not wait long before he established a formal distribution agreement for continental Europe. Rudolph Knosp, a well-established natural dye dealer in Stuttgart, Germany, became the sole agent of Perkin & Sons' mauve for all of continental Europe on January 1, 1859 (Travis, 1993, p. 51).[136]

---

[135] Jäger had already received a prize at the 1855 Paris international exhibition for its safflor carmine natural dye preparation, and the success of this dye afforded the firm the resources to develop the synthetic dye business.

[136] The firm Rudolf Knosp was an important player in the early synthetic dye industry. Knosp later produced synthetic dye itself, then became the marketing firm for BASF, and later was absorbed into BASF itself as BASF felt compelled to developed its own marketing arm. Knosp's ability to take advantage of the new business opportunities in synthetic dyes was a result of the firm's position as an important natural dye dealer in Southern Germany. Knosp was at a structural location in the network of natural dye sellers, dyers, and printers where the information about new dyes was likely to land very early. As Burt's (1992) network theory would predict, this structural position allowed Knosp to sign an exclusive contract with Perkin & Sons to sell mauve in Germany, Prussia, Austria, Switzerland, France, Belgium, and The Netherlands for seven years starting January 1, 1859 (Caro, 1892, p. 1029).

There is no direct evidence that Perkin traveled to Europe to consult with dyers and printers to help them overcome the application problems. Although Perkin makes many references to his collaboration with British dyers and printers, we don't see him emphasize travelling to customers on the continent. His strategy seems to have been to focus on Britain and let Knosp deal with continental customers. Perkin undoubtedly welcomed European customers in London but he made no attempt to establish his own marketing operation in Europe.

It is a legitimate question to ask whether it would have made strategic sense for him to build up a marketing organization in continental Europe, given that natural dye traders such as Knosp, Bayer, and Jäger had already established contacts to customers. Because Bayer a few years later had difficulty convincing its existing customer base to switch from natural to synthetic dyes, Perkin would have had to invest a great deal of money to build up a continental marketing organization. Being located in the largest textile market in the world, the three Perkins may have felt that they had a large enough home market. In any case, the reluctance of Perkin & Sons to build up an international organization revealed itself very early on.

Possessing prior knowledge of the needs and psychological profiles of dyers and printers in different countries proved to be a critical competitive advantage. Bayer, Jäger, and Levinstein came to the synthetic dye industry with previous experience in the dye trade across a variety of countries. Their already existing contacts to the dyeing and printing trades gave the three firms an important advantage over other competitors who did not have such a foot in the door. Bayer seems to have been more aggressive in reaching international markets from the very beginning. This early orientation toward seeing the entire world as a possible market for the firm's dye production played an important role in its strategic actions. Bayer was directly represented on the British and American markets by the late 1860s, whereas Jäger seems to have focused on Europe.

The first synthetic dye firm in the world to build a factory outside the home country, in fact, was Read Holliday, an English firm that would become the second most successful company in Britain before World War I. In 1864 Read Holliday opened a branch factory in Brooklyn, NY, to serve the lucrative U.S. dye market. The plant made fuchsine as well as the organic intermediates needed for production of the dye. Read Holliday showed the industry that opening a manufacturing subsidiary abroad was feasible.

The strategy of gaining international experience early paid off handsomely for firms that had the resources, the courage, and the management talent to move into a foreign market. The decision of the Levinsteins to leave their native Germany and locate the headquarters of their various dye operations in Great Britain must be billed as one of the very first systematic international strategies. The aniline plant in Berlin, started in 1863, was given up when the Levinsteins perceived it to be more advantageous to manufacture in the largest textile market in the world.

R&D Strategy: Serendipity Is King

It would be wrong to assume that any firm had a systematic research strategy in the early stage of the synthetic dye industry. Strategies were unsystematic in two important ways. First, organic chemistry at the time provided very little guidance as to how one was to search for new dyes. Perkin discovered mauve by accident as he was trying to synthesize quinine, a natural drug for treating malaria. Over the next ten years, new dyes were developed by reacting aniline with every conceivable chemical. Many different groups of people were involved in experimenting with aniline and other promising organic materials. Most of these trials would lead nowhere; a few, such as fuchsine, turned out to be lucrative innovations. Perkin confirms the essentially empirical character of finding new dyes in the early 1860s.

> The commencement of the history of the azo colours in an industrial sense has little to do with the theoretical side of the question, the early products being the offspring of empirical observations, and in no way connected with the theory of the diazo compounds, a condition of things very different from that now existing (Perkin, 1885, p. 98).

After the synthetic industry had taken off, academic chemists such as Hofmann became heavily involved in trying to understand the chemical composition of the synthetic dyes made in industry. Perkin explains: "It was with products supplied by Mr. Nicholson that Dr. Hofmann made his first researches on [fuchsine]. He changed its name from roseine to rosaniline, and found that the base, when in combination with acids, had the formula $C_{20}H_{19}N_3$," (1885, p. 82). Being at the cutting edge of organic chemistry was not necessary to do well in the synthetic dye industry in the first decade. Having some general knowledge about chemistry helped, as is evident in the success of Perkin and Nicholson, but colorists were as well equipped as academic chemists to stumble onto a lucrative dye in this phase of the industry. The examples of Bayer and Jäger demonstrate that firms with no academic chemists could flourish in those early years. This is not to argue that having academic chemists hurt. Many British and German firms of the time were founded by academically trained chemists, but not Bayer. With August Siller, Bayer hired a "chemist" in its second year, 1864, but he had taken only a few classes at a local technical college and cannot be regarded at someone who would have been knowledgeable about the forefront of academic chemistry.[137] The success of Bayer in this early phase has to be attributed more to its marketing focus than to an ability in production innovation. Jäger did very well without, it appears, the help of any academic chemists.

Second, firms did not possess a systematic R&D strategy, in that they lacked formalized procedures for developing dyes on a routine basis. Once a new dye was created somewhere in the larger community of colorists, dyers, printers, or entrepreneurial and academic chemists, firms would scramble to get access to the new product by acquiring the patent (Britain) or by buying the information on how the dye was prepared. The story of fuchsine illustrates how easy it was to get access to knowledge about how to make this brilliant new dye first developed in France and then to imitate it successfully. Bayer, Jäger, Levinstein, and SM&N all were able to work out the manufacture of this new dye without having to do the original research. The key factors to success were process experimentation on the shop floor – bringing production costs down – and establishing a customer base that would provide revenue and profits that could finance investments in organizational capabilities. Both innovators (Perkin & Sons and SM&N) and imitators (Bayer and Jäger) did well as long as they found customers who would place a steady flow of orders. It was the firms without a solid

[137] August Siller became a partner in Bayer in 1872 and a member of the managing board when the firm was turned into a joint stock company (Farbenfabriken-Bayer, 1918, p. 4)

customer base that were simply pushed out of the market, accounting for many early failures in the industry.

Patent Strategy: Getting or Avoiding Them

Whether a firm could successfully adopt more of an innovator or imitator strategy depended in large measure on the legal environment in which they found themselves. Perkin & Sons and SM&N had more incentives to invest in original product and process innovation because the British legal system would afford the holders a degree of protection against unauthorized imitators. Not surprisingly, the two firms filed for patents whenever they thought they had a lucrative invention at hand. Perkin patented mauve and was able to remain the sole producer of the dye in Great Britain for its entire commercial life until 1868. Perkin also tried to obtain a patent for mauve in France, which would have given him another lucrative monopoly. In April 1858, Perkin travelled to Paris to claim a patent for mauve in France (Travis, 1993, p. 50). But his patent application was declared invalid because it was filed more than six months after the original patent application in Britain had been deposited. Fortunately for Perkin & Sons, the demand for mauve was growing very fast and the production problems were great enough that French industry entrants such as Alexandre Franc & Co and Monnet & Dury could not supply enough of the new dye, allowing Perkin & Sons to receive large orders from France (Travis, 1993, p. 51).

The high returns Perkin achieved with mauve and later SM&N with fuchsine were a direct consequence of the monopoly position they enjoyed in Britain. Simpson, Maule & Nicholson acquired a license from A. W. Hofmann in May 1863 to manufacture Hofmann violet, which reduced demand for Perkin's mauve considerably (Travis, 1993, p. 79). The firm also acquired a license for Girard and Laire aniline blue process under license from Renard Frères starting in July 1862 (Travis, 1993, p. 73), providing SM&N with a portfolio of most of the important synthetic dyes at the time. The strategy of assembling this portfolio of patented dyes allowed SM&N to become the largest manufacturer of dyes in the early 1860s.

Because the market for red dyes was so much larger than for purple (Caro, 1892, p. 1030), the incentives to infringe SM&N's fuchsine patent were much more powerful than for the mauve patent. Several firms did take up production of fuchsine, counting on the probability that the patent would not be enforced. During the 1860s, SM&N became embroiled in a series of patents fights, trying to enforce its legal monopoly.[138] In part the lack of a systematic examination of patent applications made these expensive trials possible. Given the administrative setup of the British patent system, dye inventors in Great Britain tended to file for any kind of invention they made and hope that the courts would uphold their claims. The various fuchsine trials that SM&N fought until 1865 cost considerable money for all parties involved – SM&N

---

[138] Perkin, who profited handsomely from his British patent for mauve, provides a revealing opinion about the fuchsine patent struggle:

This patent is notorious for the amount of litigation it has caused, showing that a patentee should not only be a discoverer but a lawyer, and even more, and able to discover precisely how much to claim and disclaim in his patent, and also to arrange his specification so that the intellects of the whole world may not be able to discover a single flaw in his description; and it is a misfortune common to inventors who wish to thoroughly protect themselves, to find that they have claimed too much (1868, p. 18).

alone spent £30,000 (Travis, 1993, p. 124) – and must have distracted the management from focusing their attention on constant innovation on the shop floor. To have a proper sense of magnitude of these costs, £30,000 in 1864 would have the purchasing power of £1,529,340 in 2001.[139] The trials were expensive because they dragged on for a long time and both sides called in numerous expert witnesses (see Travis, 1993, pp. 124–34). The most important trial was against the British firm Read Holliday, which produced fuchsine with the SM&N-patented arsenic process – the most efficient fuchsine process until another nitrobenzene process was invented by Coupier in 1866 (Caro, 1892, p. 1040).[140] The plaintiff (SM&N) called as expert witnesses E. C. Nicholson, A. W. Hofmann, and William Odling. The defendant (Holliday) recruited D. Campbell, W. A. Miller, Taylor, Letheby, and Wanklyn to testify that the patent by SM&N was not being infringed (Fox, 1987, p. 70). Although SM&N was able to win the early trials, by 1865 its fuchsine patent was declared invalid and the firm lost this source of enormous profits.

Jäger and Bayer could freely imitate the latest improvements in synthetic dye processes because they were located outside the jurisdiction of British patent law. To stay in business, therefore, Jäger and Bayer had to become as efficient as their competitors. Because Britain and France were larger dye markets, apparently part of the fuchsine production of German and Swiss firms were smuggled into Britain and France. Although there is no conclusive evidence that Jäger and Bayer were directly involved in bypassing the British patents by channelling their dyes into Great Britain, it is absolutely plausible that they were engaged in this activity, given how lucrative the British dye market was at the time. The moment the fuchsine patent fell in 1865, Bayer was "officially" on the British market with its fuchsine.

Relationship with Competitors: Let Die!

The quote in the beginning of this chapter testifies to the fierce competition in the synthetic dye industry in the decade before World War I, in contrast to the later period between the two world wars. Jäger and Bayer faced strong competition from the very beginning of the German dye industry. The strong rivalry among German dye firms manifested itself in rapidly falling prices and high exit rates. By 1863, seven firms had exited the synthetic dye industry in Germany in contrast to four firms in Britain (Homburg–Murmann database). To stay in business themselves, firms such as Bayer used all the marketing tricks they knew to push competitors out of the market.

The London-based *Chemical Review*, when it was under the editorship of Ivan Levinstein in the early 1870s, frequently complained about the apparently rampant business practices of giving the foreman in a dye and print works a kickback for choosing the dyes of a particular firm. The *Chemical Review* held German firms particularly responsible for introducing these aggressive marketing techniques into the trade. Although the *Chemical Review* may have put too much blame on German

---

[139] The calculation was made with the help of the EH.net webpage that compares the purchasing power of money in the Great Britain from 1264 to that of any other year including the present: *http://www.eh.net/hmit/ppowerbp/*.

[140] Coupier's process did not become widely adopted until the early 1870s.

firms, we have every reason to believe that Bayer left nothing untried to win customers in the early years of the German dye industry.[141] Having learned to sell in direct competition with other firms gave Bayer, of course, the ability to enter the British market successfully when the fuchsine patent fell there in 1865.

Perkin & Sons did not want competitors on the British market. Hence it filed for patents whenever possible. The firm also refused to grant SM&N a license for making mauve in 1858 because Perkin feared the competition. When SM&N obtained a patent for the arsenic process, they made it known publicly that they would take to court any firm that made fuchsine. As we have seen, SM&N had to make good on this promise several times until they finally lost their patent in 1865.

Let us recapitulate the most notable features of corporate strategies in this early period (1857–65). What amounted to successful firm strategies differed across countries. German firms could concentrate on copying British and French innovations, whereas British firms who wanted to follow Perkin & Sons into the industry had to produce dyes that were not already patented. Because of the absence of an effective patent protection in Germany, Bayer and Jäger entered the industry by manufacturing the lucrative fuchsine dye (aniline red) for which much more demand existed than for the first synthetic dye. Strong competition from other German manufacturers forced Bayer and Jäger to improve their fuchsine production efficiencies or go out of business. By contrast, Perkin & Sons and SM&N, sheltered behind their monopolies, did not experience the same pressure to constantly lower their production costs. Building on their existing international contacts in natural dye trading, Bayer and Jäger were able to ship their synthetic dyes to many places around the world from very early on. Perkin & Sons, on the other hand, which had no industrial experience before its dye venture and hence lacked the contacts to important dyeing centers around the world, was more dependent on foreign traders coming to them to obtain the first synthetic dyes. Already in this early period we see significant differences in how firms organized themselves.

---

[141] In his biography of Friedrich Engelhorn, one of the founders of BASF, Hans Schröter relates the following story, which has been picked up by many writers on the dye industry (see, for example, Reinhardt, 1997, p. 64) and appears to be quite plausible from what is known about the business practices at the time:

In 1867, Carl Clemm was sent to London by Engelhorn to obtain information on the latest production methods and production equipment. Clemm looked up an old friend, who happened to be the nephew of August Wilhelm Hofmann and worked in the latter's laboratory. There he apparently received a tip on how to get access to a London dye plant by bribing a worker there. He found a worker who was indeed willing to show him the plant in the evening. When the two stepped into the plant at night, it proved to be a trap. Clemm was beat up, then painted with tar and "dressed" with feathers. The half-dead Clemm finally had to pay a substantial sum of money before the men would bring him back to Hofmann's nephew. There his clothes were taken off and his body cleaned with benzene and spirit. August Hofmann apparently was very upset about the episode (Schröter, 1991, p. 126) [my translation].

Charles Tilly pointed out to me (personal communication, 1997) that tarring and feathering is a version of Rough Justice that arose among British seamen and spread widely in colonial America (Thompson, 1963). Tilly encountered the practice of Rough Justice frequently in his study of popular contention in Great Britain (Tilly, 1995).

Science Unbound (1866–1885)

Appearing on the scene in this second period were BS&S (1868), American Aniline (1875), and Schoellkopf (1879). Successful entry by this time had become much more difficult than in first decade because firms such as Perkin & Sons, Bayer, BASF, Hoechst, and SM&N had already accumulated significant experience.

Given the strength of existing firms and the willingness of the two British pioneers to sell out, the strategy of BS&S was to take over the existing businesses of Perkin & Sons and SM&N. In the less-technical hands of the new management, however, the existing competencies of the two predecessor firms were not used as a launching pad for growth, unlike the case with Bayer. In more competent hands, BS&S would have probably been well-positioned to remain the leader in Britain for a long time.

In place of BS&S, the Levinstein company – under the leadership of the German-trained chemist Ivan Levinstein – and Read Holliday became the largest firms in Britain. Levinstein achieved this success by pursuing a strategy similar to that of Bayer, namely, investing in new classes of dyes and building an international marketing presence. The development of new dyes increasingly required academic chemists, who were very scarce in Britain after Hofmann's departure from the Royal College of Chemistry in 1865 left Britain without a major center of dye research and teaching. Because the British education system did not produce enough qualified chemists, the only viable strategy to compensate for the advantage of German firms lay in looking for chemists in Switzerland and Germany. Levinstein recruited German and Swiss chemists on a larger scale than did such British rivals as BS&S and thereby seems to have become more successful.

The two start-ups in the United States apparently did not believe that entering the synthetic dye business twenty years later than Perkin would constitute a great obstacle. At this point, Bayer, its German rivals, and the Levinstein company had every intention of supplying the entire need of the U.S. synthetic dye market. When American Aniline and Schoellkopf entered the U.S. market, they found themselves in head to head competition with European firms. This put serious constraints on what firm strategies would be viable for these new entrants.

At the beginning of the 1870s, industrial leadership switched from Perkin & Sons and BS&S to BASF, Hoechst, and Bayer. According to William H. Perkin, serious competition from these and other German dye firms in the alizarin dye field came only around 1873 (Gardner, 1915, p. 250). But in the field of aniline dyes, German producers had become serious competitors a few years earlier. The relative decline of the British now proceeded in full swing because BS&S, as the successor of Perkin & Sons and SM&N, was not able to keep up with Bayer, BASF, and Hoechst.

Because over time theory in organic chemistry became better equipped to understand the chemical structure underlying dyes (one example is Kekulé's famous benzene ring model, widely used by 1880), the search for new colors during this second period could be guided to some extent by scientific theory. University researchers (such as Hofmann and Baeyer) and their students (such as Graebe, Liebermann, and Martius) became the dominant players in the quest for new synthetic dyes once the theoretical foundation for dye research had become more secure. Although process innovations in the manufacture of existing products still took place predominantly in industry, the vast majority of radical product innovations such as synthetic alizarin originated in university laboratories during this period. Chemical laymen could no longer compete with organic chemists in finding new dyes. Furthermore, the dramatically increased ability of chemists to determine the composition of dyes made it more difficult for individual firms to keep dye recipes secret and prevent competitors from imitating them quickly. The door was open for firms to make scientific and technical talent the chief weapon for competing in the marketplace.

Given this shift of innovative activity, the key strategic requirement for firms was to get close to the generators of new knowledge in universities. Being dominated by commercial people rather than scientists, Bayer was later than Hoechst and BASF to bring leading organic chemistry talent into the firm and forge strong ties to university researchers. This most likely is the reason why BASF and Hoechst grew faster than Bayer during this period. Compared with Jäger, however, Bayer took much greater risks when the firm ventured into synthetic alizarin, the hot new dye in the early 1870s. Taking greater risks rewarded the firm with much higher growth rates than Jäger. (Taking greater risks, of course, could also have had the opposite consequence and created greater losses for Bayer than for Jäger.)

As we shall see a bit later, one of the most important reasons why American Aniline went out of business and why Schoellkopf stayed in business was that Schoellkopf possessed superior knowledge of organic chemistry and of the conditions in the European dye industry. Jacob F. Schoellkopf had just returned from Munich with a chemical education (probably under Adolf Baeyer) and we can assume that he had much better access to the organic chemistry network than did Bloede of American Aniline. A strategy of imitating the simple aniline dyes that worked so well in the early period no longer had a high likelihood of success in this period, as the failure of American Aniline illustrates.

Product Strategies: Go after the Natural Dyes

Until the late 1860s, the production volume of synthetic dyes was far smaller than that of natural dyes. Madder and indigo were the two most important natural dyes and their production volume far exceeded that of any synthetic dye at the time.[142] Once the first synthetic dyes appeared, many people dreamed of making these two key colorants via a synthetic route and capturing a large profitable market. Yet throughout the first decade of the industry, this goal remained elusive.

The first significant breakthrough was not achieved by a dye firm, but rather by two academic chemists in Berlin, Carl Graebe and Carl Liebermann, who worked under Professor Baeyer at the Gewerbeinstitut. Having applied for a patent in Prussia, the two scientists looked for a company to exploit the patent commercially. Given that Prussia was unlikely to grant a strong patent, a race quickly began among dye firms in Germany, Britian, and France to bring alizarin onto the market. Because Graebe had worked at Hoechst before joining the laboratory of Baeyer (Wetzel, 1991, p. 325), it was natural for Graebe and Liebermann to offer Hoechst the commercial development of the alizarin patent. But Hoechst thought that, based on the previous practices of the Prussian patent office, a patent for alizarin was not worth much at all, because within a short while other firms would enter the business with either the same process

---

[142] The value of madder grown in Europe was around 60 million marks in the 1860s (Hückstädt, 1967, p. 385).

or a slight modification of it (Borscheid, 1976, pp. 130–1). Hoechst was interested in obtaining the scientific services of Graebe and Liebermann, but BASF beat Hoechst in acquiring the rights to the invention and the collaboration of the two scientists.

Many firms joined the race in Germany to develop a synthetic alizarin process that would make the synthetic product more cheaply than its natural counterpart. As first movers, Hoechst and BASF soon captured the largest market share, but many other firms followed them into this new market. By 1873, thirteen firms were making synthetic alizarin in Germany (Homburg–Murmann database), including Bayer but not Jäger. Alizarin required different raw materials and intermediates than the aniline dyes did. Jäger at this point displayed much less willingness to go after radical new production innovations that would require the firm to organize a competence in the new body of knowledge.

In Britain, a patent alliance between Perkin & Sons and BASF gave Perkin & Sons a monopoly and prevented Levinstein from entering the market even if it had wanted to. As we shall see later, a foreign producer acquired a product patent in the United States, making it impossible for the two U.S. start-ups to enter the synthetic alizarin market even if they had possessed the capabilities to do so. This restricted American Aniline and Schoellkopf to the aniline dye market and the novel azo dyes.

National context affected in very significant ways what strategies were possible for a firm to pursue. But because the leaders and the backgrounds of the two firms in each country were different, firms within a country displayed substantial variation in their product strategies. The management of Bayer viewed the entry of BASF and Hoechst into the lucrative alizarin market with great trepidation. Already the largest German dye producers, this foray of the two firms into alizarin production would promise to make them even bigger and give them more resources to invest in their organizational capabilities. Joining the race against these bigger firms would be risky, but not joining the race would probably condemn Bayer to remain small forever (Verg et al., 1988, p. 36). Although Jäger refused to enter into this competition, Bayer moved relatively quickly when the firm learned that one of its employees, Eduard Tust, had made a successful experiment with the manufacture of alizarin (Farbenfabriken-Bayer, 1918, p. 291).[143] Tust initially planned to create his own firm to commercialize his proccess, but Friedrich Bayer and Carl Rumpf were able to convince Tust to develop the business within the Bayer company. In 1872 Tust was made a formal partner in the firm, reflecting the importance of his services to the company (Verg et al., 1988, p. 38). He had worked his way up from a mere worker to a shareholder of Bayer (Farbenfabriken-Bayer, 1918, p. 5).

Bayer's intial alizarin process was not as efficient as those of BASF and Hoechst, most likely because unlike those firms it did not at this point have academic chemists with connections to the leading centers of organic chemistry. Perkin, with his academic knowledge and his previous process development experience, was able to replicate quickly the work of Graebe and Liebermann and find independently a better process

---

[143] Eduard Tust had worked at the madder factory of Gessert, first in eastern Germany and then in Elberfeld. Because of his striking talent, Gessert sent him to the local technical college in Elberfeld to obtain training in industrial chemistry (Anonymous, 1895, p. 5). Because the madder dye contained natural alizarine as its colorant, it is not surprising that he was very interested in the synthetic route of Graebe and Liebermann: It would constitute a direct competition for the madder business.

at the same time as the team of Caro (BASF) and Graebe and Liebermann. In 1872 Bayer was losing 120,000 marks with its alizarin plant because it did not have a process competitive with those of Hoechst and BASF.

But Bayer was saved from falling behind its German competitors by the strong entrepreneurial orientation of Carl Rumpf. Rumpf wanted to push the organization to dramatically increase the scale of production and develop a more efficient process. When the initial founders did not want to take the risk, Rumpf bought the plant himself and leased it back to the Bayer company (Verg et al., 1988, p. 36).

Jäger did not get into alizarin and missed an important growth opportunity. To look at it from another angle, Jäger did not take the same risks as Bayer. Instead, the firm continued to imitate well-established dyes. Because Hofmann's publication made public the chemical structure of the dye, Jäger in 1875 copied and started the manufacture of BASF's eosin dye (Henneking, 1994, p. 234). Even before Bayer, Jäger was interested in making its own fuming sulfuric acid in the early 1880s but could not acquire the technology and know-how to get this project off the ground (Carl, 1926, pp. 19–20). Hence it continued to rely on the market for heavy chemicals.

Levinstein, by contrast, was legally prevented from entering into the alizarin market. The firm continued to focus its attention on developing new aniline dyes. In 1869, Levinstein developed a highly successful aniline blue dye that was marketed under the name Blackley Blue and remained the main source of profits for many years.[144]

A Digression: The Short "Life" of American Aniline Works and Its Causes

American Aniline existed for only eight years, from 1875 to 1883. It is instructive to examine in some detail why American Aniline failed and Schoellkopf survived.[145] One obvious reason was the deeper pockets of Schoellkopf Sr., who could finance a long period of financial losses. But this was hardly the entire story. Even with more financial resources, American Aniline started with a considerable disadvantage compared to Schoellkopf.

Victor Bloede and his two partners in American Aniline came with a background in heavy chemicals. Bloede had received a chemical engineering degree from Cooper Union in 1849 at the age of eighteen (Haynes, 1954, p. 303). Chemical engineering at the time was exclusively concerned with heavy chemicals, giving Bloede no instruction in how to make organic chemicals. In 1873, two years before the formation of American Aniline, Bloede went to Pomery, OH, to manufacture bromine, a waste product of salt manufacture. Bloede (1924, p. 409) tells us that outside of medicine, his largest consumers were the German dye works. He joined the firm Oakes & Rathbone, which operated a small sulfuric acid plant and supplied acid to the bromine distillers in Ohio and West Virginia. When Oakes wanted to withdraw from the business, Bloede bought Oakes's share, and the firm, now operating as Bloede & Rathbone, extended its product line into sulfate of iron, nitrate of iron, salts of tin, stannate

---

[144] By 1885, 1,000 tons had been produced, representing £1,000,000. To complement its dye portfolio, BASF bought this dye from Levinstein. It continued to appear under the name as late as 1914, indicating an unusual longevity for this dye (Fox, 1987, p. 13).

[145] The analysis of American Aniline is based on the information provided in Bloede (1924) and Haynes (1954).

of soda, and other products used by the textile industry (Bloede, 1924, p. 409). As a supplier of various chemicals to the textile industry, Bloede and his partner got the idea of making aniline for synthetic dyes.

About that time, having secured a foothold in the dye and textile industries, the idea suggested itself that our firm might make millions by taking up the manufacture of aniline dyes, and we at once proceeded to develop this project (Bloede, 1924, p. 409).

Because neither Bloede nor Rathbone had any knowledge about distilling hydrocarbons, they recruited James A. Moffett as a third partner.[146] Moffett at the time operated the Camden branch of the Standard Oil Company and had both wide knowledge of the distillation and refining of crude petroleum and money to invest into the aniline venture. All three partners had no prior knowledge in the manufacture of aniline or related chemicals. Victor Bloede would later recall:

Not one of us, of course, had any practical knowledge of any branch of this complicated art, so we all began to read everything we could find on the subject of coal tar and its derivates, including those wonderful German books of technology with titles something like "The Entire Art of Aniline Color Manufacturing in a Nutshell," "Every Man His Own Aniline Color Maker," "Simplified Manual of Producing Aniline Dyes," etc. (Bloede, 1924, p. 409).

Bloede recounts that their reading of the German literature convinced the three partners "the Germans are an utterly impractical people, and that by bringing genius into the business we could re-invent the art and reduce it to a simpler form . . . " (p. 409). Undoubtedly, the three partners were influenced by the American industrial practice prevailing at the time of building as large-scale a plant as possible. Moffett, who would have seen the quest for larger large-scale plants in the American oil industry, insisted that, contrary the German plants described in the text books, American Aniline had to build a large-scale plant to be successful. Drawing heavily on the junk pile of the Standard Oil company, the three partners managed put together a 1,000-gallon reactor (ten times larger than the German textbook designs). After considerable difficulties, American Aniline was able to convert benzene into nitrobenzene, something that Perkin had achieved almost 20 years earlier. Converting nitrobenzene into aniline proved considerably more difficult. According to Bloede (1924, p. 410), their converter never worked properly.

When the three partners had the first aniline on the market, they experienced a rude awakening.

We had started this branch of the business with the intention – after clearing up a fortune in making and selling aniline – of erecting a plant to convert our output into the far higher priced and more profitable colors; and right here came our first disappointment, for we soon discovered that there was practically no market for aniline oil in the United States and certainly not at prices that would enable us to compete with the German product (Bloede, 1924, p. 409).

Given that their initial product strategy of selling aniline did not work at all, the partners decided to convert their aniline into finished dyes and rescue their venture

---

[146] The failure of American Aniline did not stop Moffett from carving out a very successful career for himself. He later became one of the high executives at the Standard Oil headquarters in New York, a position he held until his death (Bloede, 1924, p. 409).

by changing their strategy and moving from intermediate products into the synthetic dye market. Studying the many books that had been written by 1875 on how to make aniline dyes was not sufficient to learn the necessary skills to manufacture even a simple aniline dye. "We could not simply evolve these intricate processes from our inner consciousness, less yet from the various German 'every man his own aniline color maker' type of literature," Bloede recalls (1924, p. 410).

Faced with this problem, the three partners then came up with the idea of finding a chemist in Britain and Germany who would give them instructions via correspondence on how to make aniline dyes. No responses came from Germany. One of the British chemists who replied to their advertisement in trade journals claimed to have been assistant manager at BS&S. But his instructions and formulas proved to be completely useless, leading Bloede to conclude that "there must have been a reason why Brooke, Simpson & Spiller dispensed with his services" (1924, p. 410).

Unlike the two Schoellkopf brothers, who seem to have hired a German-trained chemist to help them start their venture in the synthetic dye industry (Merz, 1944, p. 1277), the leaders of American Aniline failed to attract European talent to their venture. Now they had to reinvent the art of making magenta as best they could. They were fortunate to find Frank Schuman, a young man working at a grocery store, who turned out to have an immense talent for making inventions.[147] Schuman read widely and studied the literature on dye making. He was able to help American Aniline produce fuchsine according to the old arsenic process. The new Coupier process, however, was beyond the technical skills of the self-taught Schuman. But the attempts of American Aniline to convert fuchsine into aniline blue dyes proved again an utter failure. The firm simply lacked technical expertise. After producing about 20,000 pounds of fuchsine, experiencing consistent losses, and having their plant destroyed, the owners of American Aniline realized they did not have the capabilities to compete with the German, British, and Swiss firms. Like countless other firms, American Aniline was swept away from the dye industry by the forces of competition, leaving hardly any trail of its existence. Let us now return to our five other firms and try to understand better why they were more successful than American Aniline.

Organization of Production: Getting Killed on the Shop Floor by Chemists

To remain competitive in the 1860s, it was sufficient to have clever workers and artisans in charge of production. But when firms such as BASF, under the technical leadership of Heinrich Caro, began systematic experiments to improve production technologies, Bayer also had to move or be left behind. New production technologies developed side by side with the dye industry and gradually specialized equipment was designed for the industry (Caro, 1892, pp. 966–7). One of the first developments was to introduce mechanical stirring in the dye vessels (Farbenfabriken-Bayer, 1918, p. 248). This innovation, originated at BS&S, diffused throughout the industry.[148]

---

[147] Frank Schuman later not only became famous as an engineer and inventor but also became wealthy (Bloede, 1924, p. 411).

[148] The development of production technology in the dye industry is consistent with Nelson and Winter's (1982) general idea of "natural trajectories." Nelson and Winter use the language of natural trajectories to describe the pattern in which technologies typically evolve by exploiting latent economies of scale and the potential for increased mechanization of operations previously done by hand.

Bayer implemented steam engines in more and more stages of production in the late 1860s and 1870s to achieve higher production efficiencies. Because the chemical reactions leading to different dyes would often require different vessel designs, the particular firm that was able to figure out how to increase significantly the yield with alternative production arrangements would develop an enormous advantage. Bayer experimented a great deal with ways to mechanize production. In 1872, for example, Friedrich Bayer and Weskott brought a pump from a local pub to be used as an air pump in the production of alizarin. When Bayer heard about a manufacturer of air pumps in the town of Kalk, they ordered one to improve the production process (Farbenfabriken-Bayer, 1918, p. 291).

One of the greatest challenges for Bayer in further increasing the productivity levels in its plants was to break the Meister System ("master system") that had taken root very quickly after the firm entered the synthetic dye business. The master system has been interpreted by observers such as Beer (1959, p. 74) as similar to the foreman system in Britain. A closer look, however, reveals important differences. The master system in Germany was carried over from the time of guilds because of Germany's much later industrialization compared to Britain.[149] The master system implied highly skilled artisans who were the teachers and unskilled workers who were under the supervision and control of the masters.[150] The foreman system in Britain, in contrast, implied control but not necessarily greater skills on the part of the foreman. At Bayer, the masters had full control of the shop floor, including hiring and firing in the 1860s. The masters were the highest paid employees of Bayer until the early 1870s, making more than lawyers and other professionally trained men (Beer, 1959, p. 74).

Although the master system was able to bring about production innovations in the era of simple aniline dyes in the 1860s, it was increasingly putting Bayer at a competitive disadvantage compared to such rivals as BASF. The production workers of the aniline blue plant, for instance, insisted that they would improve the quality of the dye by adding the whites of 48 eggs to the chemical reactions.[151] The masters and workers in the plant of course did not have the chemical training to test whether egg white was indeed helping the reaction. When the prices for alizarin tumbled in 1873, it became apparent that Bayer's alizarin plant was not nearly as efficient as that of BASF or Hoechst. Carl Rumpf asked the newly hired chemist in the aniline plant, Dr. Schaal, to assess the production methods in the alizarin plant. Dr. Schaal's judgement was devastating: "With this plant you are not going to make any money" (Hückstädt, 1967, p. 387). Rumpf then put a chemist instead of the master in charge of the production, and an extensive rationalization program was carried out. Three months later, 6,000 pounds, instead of the earlier 600 pounds of higher quality alizarin were produced daily (Hückstädt, 1967, p. 387). Bayer escaped the fate of many other

---

[149] Kieser (1989; 1994) provides a good English-language introduction to the German guilds.

[150] Dr. Rose, the later head of the alizarin plant, reports about the plant employees in the early 1870s: "There were no foremen, only master and workers" (Farbenfabriken-Bayer, 1918, p. 292).

[151] Bayer lore has it that the yolks of the eggs were first used by the workmen to make pancakes in the oven for dyestuffs experimentation and later sold to the nearby baker (Farbenfabriken-Bayer, 1918, p. 248).

alizarin producers in its Elberfeld[152] vicinity, who could not compete as alizarin prices tumbled further and further.

Being an efficient producer of one dye did not imply that Bayer was also an efficient producer of all the other dyes it offered. For instance, over the years other firms produced fuchsine (Bayer's first synthetic dye) more efficiently than Bayer. When Bayer could no longer produce a dye at competitive costs, it would typically give up production, as it did in the case of fuchsine (Farbenfabriken-Bayer, 1918, p. 249).

Unfortunately, no information of how Jäger tried to compete on the shop floor has survived. Because the firm did not grow while Bayer's sales shot up, we can assume that Jäger probably was not in the forefront of efficient production. Jäger nowhere shows up in the 1870s as having played a significant role in developing efficient new processes or as having put a great deal of competitive pressure on other firms.

As soon as Graebe and Liebermann published their invention of synthetic alizarin, Perkin started developing a commercial process for this highly lucrative synthetic dye. Perkin worked out a process as quickly as the team of Caro (BASF), Graebe, and Liebermann, filing for a patent in Britain only one day after Caro. The reason why Perkin was able to enter the field of alizarin so rapidly was that as a student at the Royal College of Chemistry, he had investigated in detail the starting material for Graebe and Liebermann's process. Previous experience with the compound was key in catching up with the German team. Perkin was also adept in increasing the yield in running the alizarin plant: In 1870 and 1871 Perkin & Sons produced more than BASF. Because of their cross-licensing agreement, BASF learned much from Perkin about how to construct efficient alizarin plants. Yet when BASF and the other German alizarin makers scaled up production volumes in 1872 and 1873, Perkin was faced with the strategic necessity of expanding his plant dramatically as well. The competition from Germany was becoming intense because firms such as BASF already operated much more according to principles of professional management than as a personally controlled firm. Caro was not an owner, but he was in charge of the technical side of running the business, whereas in the case of Perkin & Sons, Perkin and his brother were running the show. Just as Nicholson had done five years earlier, Perkin decided to sell out at this point. The value of Perkin & Sons was high enough that he could afford to retire to the countryside and devote himself to private chemical investigation, like Nicholson.[153] Perkin first offered his business to BASF in 1873 (which declined) and then sold the business to BS&S. Heinrich Caro recalled in 1908 the circumstances under which the Perkins sold out in a letter to the British chemistry professor, Raphael Meldola:

The German manufacturers had done good scientific work and recognised the conditions by which the three constituents of artificial Alizarin, viz. Alizarin, Flavorpurpurin and Anthrapurpurin could be obtained at will from the corresponding mono- and disulpho acid of the Anthraquinone process and from Dichloranthracene, whilst Perkin, fatally prejudiced in favour of his Dichloranthracene process, had almost lost sight of his original Anthraquinone process

[152] When the towns of Barmen and Elberfeld merged into one city on January 25, 1930, the name of the city was changed to Wuppertal. Elberfeld and Barmen today are two of the seven quarters that make up the city.

[153] Perkin's enthusiasm for scientific research remained so strong that he infected both his sons, who later became professors of chemistry. One of them studied under Baeyer in Munich.

and had in turn become unable to satisfy the demand for Alizarin and Flavopurpurin. The brothers Perkin felt, therefore, in 1873 the urgent necessity not only of enlarging, but more so of entirely reforming and re-modelling their manufacture in order to match at the head of their trade. But they must have also foreseen that their works had not only to be trebled or more and thoroughly changed, but altogether removed from Greenford Green and rebuilt in another more suitable place (as quoted in Fox, 1987, p. 99).

Caro makes clear that the German producers, among them Bayer, had worked out better processes in 1872 and 1873. When Perkin & Sons could not satisfy demand or when prices of alizarin on the continent were much lower than what Perkin & Sons would charge based on its monopoly in Britain, a great deal of smuggling of the dye into Britain would take place. Perkin was well aware of this problem. To keep up with the German competitors, Perkin would have to change his manufacturing processes and increase the plant to a size where professional managers would have to be hired to help manage business. Perkin was unwilling to embark on this path.[154]

Perkin & Sons made money with their alizarin plant until they sold it to BS&S for £105,000 (Fox, 1987, p. 107). BS&S, in contrast, were much less successful with the alizarin plant. The new owners failed to supervise the plant, as was evident from the court proceedings of a suit which BS&S brought (and lost) against Perkin for inflating the value of the business (Fox, 1987, p. 107). BS&S had neither the know-how nor the intention to pay as much attention to the running of the actual production process as did Perkin earlier and the ever-more aggressive German producers of alizarin. Losing money with the plant from the very beginning, BS&S sold the plant to Burt, Bulton & Haywood in September 1876. Within a few months, Burt, Bulton & Haywood built a new plant adjacent to their existing works in Silverton and made a profit with the new alizarin works (Fox, 1987, p. 110), underlining how incompetent BS&S had been in managing the dye plant.

Marketing: Replacing Commission Agents with Employee Representatives

Already before the era of synthetic dyes, Otto Jäger and Friedrich Bayer travelled abroad to their customers. The leaders of both firms continued this tradition when they made the first synthetic dyes. From the mid-1860s onward, however, Bayer became much more aggressive in building up an international presence. In 1872, for example, Bayer had a permanent representative in Rouen, France (Hückstädt, 1967, p. 387). Initially Bayer relied on agents, but starting in the late 1870s Bayer tried to build up its own sales force. Bayer began to replace agents, who would often sell the dyes of many different producers, with representatives, who would be employees of Bayer, selling exclusively the firm's dyes (Farbenfabriken-Bayer, 1918, p. 5). When Bayer's sales agent in Glasgow went bankrupt in 1873 because of dramatically falling alizarin prices, Carl Rumpf joined forces with one of the employees and created with his own money, independently of the Bayer company, a firm to sell Bayer's product in England.

---

[154] Garfield (2001, p. 109) also suggests as a reason for Perkin's sale that Perkin believed there were too few qualified English scientists and he would have a hard time recruiting from Germany. I have not found a direct statement to this effect by Perkin or by anyone else who would have talked to Perkin about his reasons. It seems to me that by far the larger issue was that he would have to find competent management and that the Germans at this point were ahead in creating professionally managed firms.

The sales company was very successful, and it soon had branches in Manchester and Bradford (Hückstädt, 1967, p. 387).

The trouble with sales agents carrying the dyes of multiple firms was that Bayer could not count on steady orders. Because most dyes would be offered by several firms, dyers and printers had a choice between competing producers. Often loyalty of customers appears to have been achieved by bribing the foreman of the particular dyeing and printing house who was in charge of buying dyes. Bayer also resorted to these kickback schemes so as not to fall behind competitors.

The strategy of replacing agents with an employee representative was implemented incrementally over the next 30 years. It proceeded at an uneven pace, depending on the existing contracts with agents, the local business practices, and the economic viability of having a company-paid representative. Bayer wanted to achieve more control over the way its dyes were sold, in part because a closer integration of the sales function would provide the firm with better information on market developments, which agents were unlikely to pass along, or if they did, they would provide the information to other firms they represented as well.

There is no evidence that Perkin built a large marketing organization. Nowhere in his writings does he emphasize any strategic actions that were designed to build up a strong marketing organization. As an individual entrepreneur, he was very attuned to the need of working with customers. We saw him diligently seeking advice about the prospects of his mauve. But it seems that Perkin & Sons always relied on agents instead of building a strong in-house marketing organization. When W. H. Perkin and his brother sold their synthetic dye business to the partnership of BS&S (their father had died by then), few organizational routines had been created that would have allowed the buyer of the works to continue the tradition of success.

Very little is known about the marketing side of the Levinstein business either. The quote at the beginning of this chapter brings into focus that Ivan Levinstein controlled every aspect of the firm once his brothers stepped aside and he became the sole leader of the firm. This was reflected by the name change to I. Levinstein & Co. in 1879. The name remained in force until the firm was made a limited liability company in 1890. Ivan Levinstein, by all accounts, was a very strong-willed autocratic personality. The London journal he created, the *Chemical Review*, featured full-page ads of the Levinstein company in the first couple of years when he controlled the editorial process. As mentioned earlier in the 1871 advertisement, the firm had two offices in London, one in Blackley, and one in Liverpool and depots in Paris, Leipzig, Vienna, and Boston. Because of the increased competition from German firms in the mid-1870s, Levinstein found it more challenging to sell dyes. The London office, especially, came under pressure.

Internationalization: Planting Foreign Factories
Friedrich Bayer appears to have been a founder of one of the very first dye ventures in the United States. According to Hückstädt (1967, p. 390), Carl Rumpf and Friedrich Bayer invested in the Albany Aniline works in 1865. Even if their joint involvement took place only in 1868, it is clear that Friedrich Bayer ventured into international markets very early, showing a strong international orientation from the beginning of his activity in the synthetic dye industry.

Carl Rumpf, who became the entrepreneurial spirit behind the Bayer company between 1872 and 1889, started out as a traveling salesman for aniline dyes for the firm Töpke & Leithoff. In 1862, at age twenty-four, he first went to the United States to sell dyes for Töpke & Leithoff (Hückstädt, 1967, p. 390). By 1864 he already had his own import–export business and then became a prime mover behind the Albany Aniline venture. Around 1868, Friedrich Bayer seems to have convinced Carl Rumpf to join Bayer's sales representative Louis Lutz in New York. There is some evidence that Lutz, who had been a traveling salesman for Bayer in Germany, went to the United States between 1866 and 1868 with the specific purpose of selling Bayer dyes in the large U.S. market (Anonymous, 1895, p. 3). While working with Lutz in New York, Carl Rumpf must have had a chance to interact with Friedrich Bayer on a personal level, because in 1871 Rumpf married Bayer's daughter Clara and returned to Germany to work with his father-in law.[155]

Rumpf's business acumen quickly impressed Friedrich Bayer and Friedrich Weskott. In 1872 Rumpf, along with the first production chemist of Bayer, August Siller, and the extremely talented former worker, Eduard Tust, were admitted as partners into the firm, expanding the owners beyond the families of the founders. (Jäger did not make a nonfamily member owner until 1899.) With Carl Rumpf, Bayer now had a top manager and owner who came with excellent connections to the United States and significant experience in the international marketing of dyes.

Otto Jäger, who pushed the Jäger family business into synthetic dyes in 1858, had also spent a couple of years in the United States after 1848 (Carl, 1926, p. 12). Unlike Rumpf, however, he worked on a farm and most likely had no connection to the U.S. dye business. This may offer some explanation as to why Jäger was much less aggressive in pushing its products into overseas markets than Bayer.

Although Bayer had a definite strategy to sell its dyes all over the world from very early on, its manufacturing strategy was to do all the production in Germany unless patent legislation or high duties forced the firm to carry dye production to a foreign location. In 1881, Bayer sold its stake in its first foreign investment in the Albany plant. But already a year later, probably to hedge bets about what was going to happen with U.S. tariffs on dyes, the sales agent of Bayer in the United States, E. Sehlbach, invested $10,000 into a new U.S. dye firm, the Hudson River Color Works in Albany, obtaining a 25 percent ownership stake (Haynes, 1954, p. 308). In Europe, however, Bayer chose in the 1880s to open up its own production plants. First, Bayer started (1882–83) a plant in Flers, France, to make dyes that were patented there. French patent laws required the patent holder to work the patent within France or lose the patent. In 1884, Bayer started a production site in Butirki, near Moscow, to avoid the high Russian tariff on finished dyes. To take advantage of scale and scope economies, however, Bayer shipped most of the chemical intermediates (which had much lower duties) out of its German plants. The same strategy was employed by BASF and Hoechst. German firms clearly preferred to produce all dyes at home. Only tariffs or patent legislation pushed them to produce abroad.

Jäger never came close to being forced to manufacture abroad. It did not have in its product portfolio any significant newly patented dyes that would have made it

---

[155] The New York sales partnership of Rumpf and Lutz was dissolved in January 1, 1875 (Reimer, 1996, p. 56).

strategically necessary to manufacture in France and Russia. Once Bayer was ahead in putting new dyes on the market and capturing a larger world market share than Jäger, the lead tended to be self-reinforcing: Bayer was making much larger profits than Jäger, which allowed Bayer to make investments that Jäger could simply not afford. Over time, one firm became a relative giant, the other a relative dwarf.

R&D Strategy: First Steps toward Routine R&D

None of our five firms that already existed by 1877 had a systematic R&D strategy before that date. Most innovations that were achieved in terms of both new products and new processes involved a community that spanned researchers at universities, dyers, freelancing tinkerers, and production chemists.[156] Firms tended to act opportunistically, moving when they heard about a new product or process from their customers or competitors. In the 1870s and early 1880s, the most important dye innovations came out of university laboratories. At this point Bayer was clearly behind BASF, Hoechst, and AGFA in developing new dyes and the associated chemical processes, in part because the firm had no significant connection to university researchers and employed no research chemists. When Graebe and Liebermann published their alizarin synthesis, Hoechst instructed one of their chemists, Ferdinand Riese, to develop a commercial process, even though Hoechst was just in the middle of negotiating with Graebe and Liebermann about rights to their patent and their services. Whereas BASF was competing with Hoechst for access to the expertise of Graebe and Liebermann, Bayer was not an attractive partner for Graebe and Liebermann because the firm did not possess significant R&D capabilities. Bayer at this point had not broken into the first league of dye firms that were able to compete for a close relationship with the leading organic chemists such as Adolf Baeyer.

Carl Rumpf realized by 1883 that the times where pure imitation would be sufficient for the success of the firm were gone. BASF and Hoechst had become the leading dye firms in the world by investing in new product development. Competition in the alizarin market was cutting deeply into the profits of Bayer. Not being able to convince the other owners of Bayer to hire chemists whose sole purpose it would be to develop new dyes, Rumpf hired the first three research chemists with his own money. One of them was Dr. Carl Duisberg, who had just spent some time in the laboratory of Baeyer in Munich while doing his military service.[157] Rumpf devised a scheme in which the three chemists were to spend six months at the laboratory of a university professor while paid by Rumpf.[158] Duisberg was sent to the University of Strasbourg to work under Professor Fittig, who had been a student of the famous chemist Wöhler. Rumpf gave Duisberg the gigantic task that was occupying all leading dye firms at the time, to find an economical route to synthetic indigo. When Duisberg returned to Elberfeld after six months, he had not, of course, found such a synthesis. But he was able to show that a route from inatin, for which Bayer had bought the patent, would

---

[156] A number of researchers have highlighted the concept that progress in a technology often involves a community of actors rather than a single firm. See, for example, Allen (1983) and more recently Storper (1996).

[157] The others were Dr. Hinsberg and Dr. Herzberg, who were sent to the chemical institutes of the Universities of Freiburg and Munich, respectively (Flechtner, 1959, p. 66).

[158] For the names of the other early research chemists, see Duisberg (1933, pp. 57–61).

never be economically viable in competition with natural indigo. Duisberg's stay in Strasbourg was extended for another six months, during which Rumpf gave him the task of finding a blue azo dye that perhaps could compete with natural indigo (Verg et al., 1988, p. 72).

The impetus behind this second assignment came from a new discovery. It is worth tracing the details about how this innovation came about because they reveal the significance of the social network of organic chemists in conferring competitive advantages to some players and not others. Peter Griess had found certain compounds that would dye cotton without the use of mordants. Henry Böttinger, one of the top managers of Bayer and the son-of-law of Friedrich Bayer, in 1883 visited his place of birth, Burton-upon-Trent, where Peter Griess had taken up the position of chemist at the famous Allsop brewery.[159] Böttinger's father, a student of Liebig, had previously held that position (Bayer, 1963, p. 9). Henry Böttinger and Griess were old friends and so it was natural that Böttinger would pay Griess a visit (Verg et al., 1988, p. 74). Griess showed him a sample of cotton dyed with a blue color without using a mordant. Böttinger took the sample of this radical production innovation back to Bayer's headquarters in Elberfeld. Bayer's management saw a great product opportunity, deciding to buy Griess's patent for this innovation and directing its chemists to develop a suitable commercial process (Bayer, 1963, p. 14). Seidler was first put in charge of the effort, then Duisberg also became involved during his second six months in Strassburg. But it turned out that Bayer could not overcome the technical difficulties involved in creating an efficient process, even though Griess was consulted a number of times.

In the meantime, another Bayer chemist, Dr. Paul Böttiger, had left the firm and shortly afterward filed for a patent for a red azo dyestuff that would color cotton without a chemical binder. Whether Böttiger had already developed the process while he was employed at Bayer is not clear. Realizing that Bayer might get very upset if he offered the patent to a rival firm, Böttiger approached Bayer about its interest in exploiting the patent. Bayer declined, concluding that the dye would not experience much demand because it faded when coming into contact with acid. BASF and Hoechst also declined the offer. Initially AGFA was also disposed to reject the patent, but a dyer in Berlin strongly urged the firm to buy the patent, believing that the brilliance of the dye would make the dye attractive to dyers despite its weak resistance to acid. He was right. As we shall see a little later, AGFA had struck a gold mine. The episode illustrates that Bayer made mistakes. But since it made fewer mistakes than such competitors as Jäger or BS&S, Bayer stayed ahead of most competitors.[160]

---

[159] Johann Peter Griess had received his university education in under Kolbe in Marburg. There he did his first work on the diazo reaction. He then moved to the Royal College of Chemistry where, according to Perkin (in Gardner, 1915, p. 167), he was not one of Hofmann's pupils although he clearly would have had direct contact with Hofmann. He married an Englishwoman and was one of the few German dye pioneers who did not return to Germany, despite lucrative offers from German dye firms (Travis, 1993, p. 265).

[160] The episode also shows that BASF and Hoechst made mistakes. Caro of BASF already had a strong relationship with Peter Griess in the mid-1870s, having jointly developed one of the first azo dyes. Caro would have clearly had the first option to buy Griess's radical innovation of an azo dye without a mordant. But Caro did not appraise the commercial possibilities of this new class of dyes accurately because it required a different dyeing process. This was how Bayer could get Griess's patent in the first place.

Even more importantly, Bayer was able to change direction once it became clear that a wrong decision had been taken. We will see this more concretely later in the context of a large product failure.

The R&D laboratory at Bayer did not come into existence full blown – nor at any other firm. Rather, the formal R&D laboratory was developed incrementally, first by giving production chemists some time for research, and then by hiring research chemists such as Duisberg. When Duisberg returned from Strasbourg, he was given a little room adjacent to the azo dye production floor, behind the bathroom of the director of the plant, Dr. Frank (Duisberg, 1933, p. 28). This room with a tiny window, access to gas and water, and a lead table served as Duisberg's "R&D lab." From these modest quarters the R&D activities expanded to a point where Bayer created a separate building and organizational structure for the firm's R&D efforts. As we will see later (in the section, "The Age of Bayer"), Bayer built upon these efforts that could be regarded as an embryonic form of R&D laboratory, when a patent by Carl Duisberg pulled the firm out of its financial crises in 1886, convincing all top managers at Bayer that investments in R&D would be the road to success.

In setting up a program of routine and systematic research, Carl Rumpf had created a systematic problem for firms such as Jäger that were not willing to play according to the new rules of the game. Jäger never went beyond the sporadic hiring of chemists, which made it impossible for the firm to compete head on with such firms as Bayer. In 1868 Jäger hired the chemist Dr. Benjamin Sieber. He married the youngest sister of Otto Jäger, but after a few years Sieber left the firm and moved to Switzerland (Carl, 1926, p. 19). The firm was then able to recruit Mr. Bulk, a teacher at one of the local technical colleges providing excellent education in the fields of industry that were active in the area of Barmen and Elberfeld.[161] Both chemists developed new dyes for the firm. But when Bulk died at a very young age, Jäger seems to have stopped recruiting new nonfamily chemists. Otto Jäger sent his son Emil to study chemistry with Adolf Baeyer between 1872 and 1875. Emil received his doctorate and was active for 10 years in the dye business until illness forced him into early retirement (Carl, 1926, p. 23.). At this point the firm seems to have stopped hiring a sufficient number of chemists who could have developed innovative dyes. Jäger clearly failed to keep up with Bayer, Hoechst, and BASF. For the next twenty-five years the firm retreated into niche markets. Only in 1899 did Jäger hire another academic chemist, R. W. Carl, who was made partner in the firm, and try to get the firm back into innovative dyes for the textile industry.

The Beginning of Systematic Patent Strategies
When Germany passed a unified patent law in 1877, the strategic options available to German dye firms changed dramatically. It was now possible to put money into product innovation and make money on these innovations because the state would grant a fifteen-year monopoly. Because the German patent law would grant only process and not product patents, Bayer was forced to search every conceivable route to a new dye it had invented to prevent other firms from making the same dye by using a slightly different process. Given that Jäger did not invest in R&D the same

---

[161] August Stiller, Bayer's first chemist, was also trained at a local college (Verg et al., 1988, p. 28). Similarly, Carl Duisberg spent one year at the College for Chemistry in Elberfeld before he went to university, first in Göttingen and then in Jena (Duisberg, 1933, pp. 13–19).

way that Bayer already had begun on a small scale, Jäger simply was not faced with the task of deciding on a patent strategy. There is no evidence that Jäger obtained any significant patents during this period.[162]

In his autobiography, Carl Duisberg, who later became the chief executive of Bayer, writes (1933, p. 36) that by 1885 it was Bayer's policy to patent all the new reactions developed by the Bayer chemists to prevent a rival from claiming a patent for a promising new dye area.

On March 17, 1885, we filed a patent for all dyestuffs based on tetrazo-bonds of the isomers of tolidine... Given the prevailing patent laws, it was necessary to be the first one to file. We could not waste any time. It was possible that AGFA had also found these reactions in the meantime and filed for a patent. For this reason is was standard procedure when one discovered a new reaction to write it down with all its theoretical possibilities in the form of a patent application and mail it the same day for submission to the patent office in Berlin [my translation].

From a later statement in his autobiography, it is clear that Duisberg misstates here a bit how early all new inventions were systematically patented at Bayer. A close look at the records reveals that in the late 1880s, it was still the case that Bayer would not patent all new inventions. Sometimes the firm still opted to keep a process secret rather than trying to obtain a patent. But after losing much revenue because Primulin had already been patented (1888) by BASF and Dahl & Co., Bayer adopted the policy of patenting all new inventions (Duisberg, 1933, p. 62).

Duisberg also gives us a picture of how he administered Bayer's patents when Tust handed him the responsibility of dealing with patent matters in 1885:

Besides [my duties of inventing and developing new dyes], I only had time at night and on Sundays both to do all the different written work such as the drafting of domestic and foreign patents, patent challenges and responses to patent challenges, and to keep abreast of the scientific and patent literatures (1933, p. 57) [my translation].

From a drawer of Tust's desk in the sales purchasing department (Flechtner, 1959, p. 80), all patent files were carried over to Duisberg's laboratory. Only later did Duisberg realize that an explosion in the laboratory could have destroyed all of Bayer's patents, and subsequently the patent files were put in a safer place. All of this shows that patent matters were handled for the first ten years after the passage of the German patent law as a side job, first by Tust and then by Duisberg. Only when the work became too much for a single person did Duisberg start to build a patent division and create formal administrative procedures.

See You in Court: Bayer versus BASF in the United States
As was true for British firms in the 1860s, German firms were suing each other in courts to prevent another firm from obtaining a patent on a very lucrative dye. Patenting in foreign countries occurred very early in the dye industry and became a hallmark of the

---

[162] It is possible that Jäger did *not* possess a single patent in this period. In Thomson and Nelson's (1997) survey of chemical patenting in Germany, the firm is not listed. (For details about the survey, see the appendix of their 1997 paper.) After Dr. Carl joined Jäger in 1902, the firm obtained a few patents in Germany (Carl, 1926, p. 25). Because the firm did not have an R&D laboratory like Bayer, BASF, and Hoechst, Jäger did not amass a significant patent portfolio that would have allowed the firm to remain among the leaders in the industry.

business. The Frenchman Cherpin immediately took out a patent in Britain, France, and the United States for aldehyde green, a color he discovered in 1862 (Beer, 1959, p. 62). BASF also filed a patent for the 1869 Caro, Graebe, and Liebermann synthetic alizarin process in Prussia, Britain, France, and the United States. Although Prussia did not grant a patent, the other three countries did and provided BASF with a very lucrative monopoly. Because BASF, based on its U.S. patent, was the only supplier of alizarin in the States, the firm made especially large profits there. When prices tumbled dramatically in Europe in the mid-1870s, Bayer and Hoechst became eager to sell alizarin in the United States as well. Because the United States in this period did not conduct a rigorous examination of patent claims before a patent was granted, Bayer pursued the strategy of having the patent declared invalid. In 1871 BASF had been granted a reissue of its U.S. patent to cover any synthetic alizarin until 1885. Although BASF and Bayer were part of the alizarin convention in Europe, Bayer did not hold back from going after BASF in the United States. Bayer's lawyer argued that the reissue was invalid and that therefore the patent should be declared null and void (Reimer, 1996, p. 105). Bayer was turned down twice, once at a lower and then higher court, because the courts refused to question the Patent Office's decision. Bayer's directors finally appealed to the U.S. Supreme Court. In 1884, one year before the patent would have run out, the court ruled the patent void (Reimer, 1996, p. 106). The U.S. alizarin market had been forced open by Bayer and the firm started to export the dye without delay.

Levinstein versus BASF

Although Ivan Levinstein showed a propensity to patent his dyes during the first couple of years in the dye industry, Levinstein filed no British patent between 1866 and 1875.[163] Levinstein did not patent Blackley Blue, a dye that turned out to be a resounding success and the mainstay of the firm for many years to come. It is possible that the process for Blackley Blue was too closely related to the blue dyes patented by Nicholson (B. P. 1,857) in 1863. But it is also possible that Levinstein at the time thought the best protection of the dye investments was to keep the process secret. The court proceedings in the 1880s make clear that he surely was not willing to share his processes with competitors. During the next eight years (1876–83), Levinstein received six British patents both for dyes and intermediates. This suggests that during this second period, unlike later, Levinstein did not have a consistent patent strategy. Sometimes the firm would opt to patent, sometimes not.

Levinstein did not try, for example, to patent a red azo dye (Roccelline, also later known as Blackley Red) the firm put on the market at the end of 1880, probably because he got the idea for it based on a French dye. It is also possible – something he later denied vigorously in court – that the dye was too close to a patent held by BASF (Zimmermann, 1965, 74–7; Fox, 1987, pp. 18–19). BASF promptly filed a suit against Levinstein in 1881, and the biggest dye patent battle in Britain during the 1880s commenced. The case dragged on for six years, at great cost like the British cases in the early 1860s. To understand why BASF would go after Levinstein even though every one knew about the costs and the risk involved in patent litigation from the 1860s cases,

---

[163] All of the patents received by Ivan Levinstein or his firm in its various legal incarnations as well as those of the other important British dye firms are listed in Fox (1987, p. 228 ff.).

one must keep in mind that production volumes had reached a level where a patent to an important dye had very large financial value. Hence BASF was sparing no expense to force Levinstein to give up production of his so-called Blackley Red. Levinstein employed the now standard tactic of countersuing BASF, asking the court to declare BASF's patent invalid. The legal battle was waged all the way from the High Court, to the Court of Appeal, and finally to the House of Lords.[164] Many chemists were called as expert witnesses by both parties. For BASF, they were Johann Peter Griess, James Dewar, Henry E. Amstrong, and Dr. Odling. For Levinstein, they were Dr. Adler and Dr. Carnelly and Ivan Levinstein (Fox, 1987, p. 18). Professor Henry Roscoe seems to have been a neutral participant, who conducted experiments on behalf of the court. Peter Griess, who at this point was regarded the highest authority on diazo dyes, delivered a devastating testimony against Levinstein's claim that BASF's patent was not valid:

In 1864, I distinctly state that by the combination of diazobenzol and phenol dye was obtained, and if I had been a little cleverer, analogy would have induced me to prepare this very dye which is now under consideration. But analogy did not lead me to do that; analogy does not go a long way in chemistry (as quoted in Zimmermann, 1965, p. 76).

In the end, Ivan Levinstein lost the case and was left with a large legal bill. He complained bitterly about the unfairness of the British patent system but also retained, according to Fox (1987, p. 19), an even greater determination to make it in the business.

One reason why Levinstein lost may have been related to his weaker cast of expert witnesses. Caro at BASF had lined up all the heavy hitters in dye chemistry, including his friend and business partner Peter Griess. Dye chemistry and the interpretation of patent laws at this point were still in a state in which reasonable people could disagree on what should count as an infringement of existing patent and what should not. The party that would be able to recruit more prestigious expert witnesses was likely to prevail in court cases such as this. And BASF, perhaps because Caro was better connected among the British academic dye elite than Levinstein was, assembled the more renowned experts. Ivan Levinstein may have overestimated how much weight his own testimony would carry in court.

Losing high-profile court cases against the largest German dye firm was not a good way to find investors for Levinstein's big expansion plans. From then on, Ivan had to get very creative in raising money; how he went about solving these financial problems we will see a little later.

For the moment, let us return to Blackley Red and Levinstein's immediate response. Emblematic of Ivan Levinstein's more pronounced entrepreneurial spirit in comparison to the owners of BS&S and his hard-nosed business sense, he simply arranged for the manufacture of his Blackley Red in The Netherlands, which had abolished any patent protection in 1869. Ivan Levinstein arranged for cloth worth several million pounds sterling to be shipped from Manchester to the dye houses of Leiden and Tilburg (Fox, 1987, p. 20).

The court cases from the very beginning of the industry had the unintended effect that academic chemists and dye firms were brought together, providing an opportunity for striking friendship or hatred depending on what side of the case the

---

[164] Much of the information about this case comes from an edited official report sixty-six pages long that served Fox (1987) as his main source.

individuals would find themselves. The court cases, of course, also offered nice fees to the dye chemists who were asked to serve as expert witnesses.

Relationship with Competitors: Make Them Fail, Then Buy Them Up

Because the area around the home of Bayer was traditionally a center of turkey red dying (using madder that contained natural alizarin), entrepreneurs started production of synthetic alizarin even before the Bayer company did. By 1874, competition had become very fierce, in part because Carl Rumpf of Bayer decided to increase production to a level greater than demand (Farbenfabriken-Bayer, 1918, p. 292; Bayer, 1963, p. 8). Competition between the German dye firms was threatening the existence of many a player, prompting individual firms to adopt very aggressive tactics to get hold of technical know-how that another firm might possess. Dr. Rose of Bayer gives this vivid account of how Bayer tried to stay ahead in this competitive game. "To keep the competition off our backs, we worked with rigged thermometers, every one showing 100 degrees too much. The competition tried to woo away our workers and paid 90 marks a week" (Farbenfabriken-Bayer, 1918, p. 292; my translation). To put this statement in proper perspective, Bayer itself hired talent from other firms, as in the case of Eduard Tust, who had been employed by the Gessert company (Bayer, 1963, p. 8). When Bayer worked out an alizarin production process that made Hoechst's process uncompetitive, Dr. Schaal, who was responsible for the new alizarin process, encountered much interest for his services:

As soon as the improved and pure alizarin came on the market, the then all-powerful firm Meister, Lucius, & Brüning (i.e. Hoechst) was almost completely displaced, similarly Brönner and the Brothers Gessert. This made Mr. Brüning himself come to Elberfeld and search in every corner of the town [for] a chemist who was knowledgeable about this new process (Farbenfabriken-Bayer, 1918, p. 292) [my translation].[165]

Because of the cutthroat competition in the alizarin market, five firms around Barmen and Elberfeld were forced out of the market by 1874 (Homburg–Murmann database), and the managers of BASF expected that Bayer would also have to go out of business that year (Farbenfabriken-Bayer, 1918, p. 292). Defying these expectations, however, Bayer survived and actually bought up one of its alizarin competitors, the failing firm Gessert.

When many of the alizarin dye producers were no longer making any money in 1881, the ten (nine German and one British) surviving firms of the alizarin market shakeout formed a convention that would fix prices. The agreement broke down by 1885 and fierce competition ensued, just as in all the other fields of synthetic dyes that were not protected by patents. At this point Bayer was again in a precarious situation. The firm was not able to pay any dividends in 1885. BASF and Hoechst were far larger than Bayer. Unlike BASF and AGFA, the firm played no role in the formation of the German chemical industry association. But times were about to change: The hiring of research chemists such as Duisberg was going to change the firm forever.

[165] Duisberg reports that Brüning even advertised in the local paper for a chemist who knew the details of the new alizarin process. Brüning must have been successful in obtaining a sufficient amount of information about Bayer's more efficient new process because Hoechst remained a successful producer of alizarin for many years to come.

Let us recapitulate the key developments in this second period (1866–85). One significant factor that differentiated successful firms (Bayer, Levinstein, Schoellkopf) from not so successful ones (Jäger, BS&S, American Aniline) in this phase was access to knowledge in organic chemistry, which was now predominantly located in Germany. The more successful firms secured better access to the new techniques and knowledge in organic chemistry by maintaining contacts with professors, by hiring students, or by obtaining chemical training themselves. Bayer pulled ahead of Jäger in this period partly because the firm brought into its management ranks nonfamily members having particular talents. The marketing expert Carl Rumpf, the production chemist August Siller, and the talented production worker Eduard Tust were asked to become partners by the original founders of the firm. By transforming itself into a public stock company and hiring professional managers into the firm, Bayer in contrast to Jäger created the opportunity to grow more rapidly. In the person of Carl Rumpf, the Bayer founders brought a new entrepreneurial spirit to the firm that was lacking at Jäger in the early 1870s. Bayer also gradually put chemists in charge of the shop floor, which allowed the firm to become more efficient and survive in the highly competitive alizarin market. The two most successful firms during this period – Bayer and Levinstein – continued to build their positions in international markets by obtaining more control over the distribution of its products. Finally, the failure of American Aniline underlines how readily entrepreneurs underestimated the capabilities required to successfully enter an industry at a later state.

The Age of Bayer (1886–1914)

The period from the mid-1880s until the beginning of World War I can be called "the Age of Bayer"; during this time, the firm caught up with its larger rivals BASF and Hoechst in Germany and left Levinstein, BS&S, and Jäger far behind. Building on the firm's existing position and the science capabilities of the German social environment, the managers of Bayer pursued the strategy of aggressively investing in all functions of the corporation, although particular investments continued to be made on an ad hoc basis. Especially by investing heavily in R&D, the firm pushed dye technology to unprecedented levels of sophistication and rendered many existing dyes obsolete. Bayer's R&D laboratories turned out new dyes at a rate that had never been seen before (Meyer-Thurow, 1982). To finance large R&D expenditures, the firm had to grow its sales volumes significantly, an approach that required the expansion of both plants and sales force. Bayer's strategy was to become one of the few large players with powerful economies of scale and scope on their side and to knock out competitors. Not making the same kind of investments, Jäger was pushed into niche markets; BS&S went out of business altogether[166]; and Levinstein and Schoellkopf could not match Bayer's fast expansion.

---

[166] When bankruptcy proceedings were started against BS&S in 1907, the firm put out a curious press release:

> The conditions for success [in the dye industry] are the employment of the best scientific knowledge, constant research and the adoption of modern and economical plant and process, and working on these lines it is predicted that the regenerated concern will be successful, though all the English firms are handicapped by our patent laws, which do not give British inventions and British brains a fair chance (as quoted in Fox, 1987, p. 110).

The growth of Bayer was not automatic, as the case of Jäger shows. Bayer's leaders had to make a clear choice to bring in new talent and let professionals rather than family members carry out the management of the sprawling firm. Whereas Bayer made the transition to a managerially controlled firm, Levinstein remained a personally controlled firm. Carl Duisberg's remarks in a speech on the occasion of the Perkin Jubilee in London in 1906 suggest that the Levinstein company suffered from not building up a large managerial hierarchy, which left it unable to exploit business opportunities.

One of the largest colour manufactories in England [Levinstein] had about ten years ago the licence for exploiting all the English patents of two of the largest German color works [Bayer and AGFA], which at the time represented the value of many millions of marks. It did, however, in no way avail itself of this advantage, although the English firm [Levinstein] had no restrictions and *were* no worse off than the German ones, as *they* merely had to pay for this licence a very small portion of their net profits to the patentees for the working of the respective patents (Duisberg, 1923, p. 379) [my inserts in brackets].[167]

Even after the sale of its alizarine interests in 1876, BS&S was the largest firm and was regarded as the premiere dye-making company in Britain (Fox, 1987, p. 108). Nonetheless, Levinstein, under the technically competent leadership of Ivan Levinstein, and Read Holliday overtook BS&S handily in this period. Critical examination makes clear, however, that Ivan's hands-on management style, while allowing the firm to surpass BS&S, was at the same time a powerful shortcoming: It prevented the firm from developing a professional management that would have enabled it to compete successfully with Bayer and the other large German firms.

Several observers of the dye industry at the turn of the century (e.g., Beer, 1959) believe that Bayer and its German peers easily could have driven the remaining British firms out of the market, had they wanted. The empirical evidence about the strength of such firms as Bayer indicates may indeed have been the case. But Bayer and its German peers understood very well that small British firms were a much better scenario for them than were nonexistent British firms. Under the latter scenario, British public policy makers most certainly would have taken steps against the German dye firms if all British firms were destroyed.

Product Strategies: Exploiting the Azo Gold Mine

A. W. Hofmann was the first academic researcher to articulate the enormous practical implications of the diazo reaction invented by Johann Peter Griess. Hofmann realized that Griess's method opened a vast domain for the synthetic dye industry, promising seemingly endless possibilities for new dyes (Van den Belt and Rip, 1987, pp. 148–9).

This public statement is testimony to a widespread problem in firms: Frequently firms don't have much trouble understanding intellectually what would be a sound strategy for their business at a particular point in time. But they often lack the abilities to implement strategies which have been found appropriate for the business context. Failing to implement the strategy outlined in their statement, BS&S was eliminated from the market.

[167] The grammar of the sentence is awkward for contemporary ears. I italicized the words that today would have been in the singular. Because Singer (1910, as reprinted in Gardner, 1915, pp. 289–90) in quoting Duisberg left the phrase as it was, we have reason to believe that this was not simply a grammatical mistake on the part of the German Duisberg in trying to compose an English speech.

With the development of Congo Red and Benzopurpurin 4B,[168] azo dyes had been catapulted to the forefront of synthetic dye technology. Benzopurpurin 4B rescued Bayer's profitability and put the firm back on solid financial footing.

Its success with Benzopurpurin 4B led Bayer to pursue an active strategy of harnessing this azo gold mine. By World War I, the largest number of dyes sold in the market fell into the class of azo dyes.[169] Having had no success with trying to invent synthetic indigo (BASF would eventually synthesize the king of all dyestuffs in 1887 after 17 years of intermittent R&D and spending substantial resources on the project[170]), Bayer concentrated its efforts on developing a blue azo dyestuff, and instructed its R&D department to comb systematically through azo molecules to create a rainbow of high-quality dyes.

In contrast to BS&S, the Levinstein company joined the azo dye race very quickly, trying to put many different colors on the market. A public index of dyes made by all producers in Great Britain shows that in 1914 Levinstein made more than 80 dyes, whereas Read Holliday, the second largest firm, produced slightly more than 50 (Fox, 1987, p. 37).[171] The Levinstein company had many more azo dyes on the market than either Read Holliday or BS&S, focusing particularly on the very lucrative direct cotton and acid wool dyes (Fox, 1987, p. 37). Still, not being backed by the same marketing or research muscle, Levinstein put far fewer new dyes on the market than the 1,800 dyes Bayer produced in 1913 (Farbenfabriken-Bayer, 1918, p. 4).[172]

Because of the fierce competition coming from German firms in finished dyes, Levinstein, more than any other dye-making company since the dyes of SM&N, focused on making intermediates for other dye firms. Levinstein increased its production of intermediates dramatically in this period (Miall, 1931, p. 76). The firm developed a reputation for producing high-grade intermediates from naphthalenes and, starting in the mid-1880s, developed a sizable export trade to German dye manufacturers such as Bayer (Fox, 1987, p. 17). Levinstein could build here on a traditional British strength of processing coal tar. Although firms such as Levinstein and Bayer would make most of their intermediates for the various stages of dye production themselves, both firms would also buy from the market because it was not economical to make every intermediate in-house. Bayer would buy, for example, the intermediate for making its blockbuster Benzopurpurin 4B dye from Wülfing Dahl in Barmen, and later also from Levinstein in Manchester (Farbenfabriken-Bayer, 1918, p. 177)

By the turn of the century, Levinstein had developed a particular stronghold in basic and sulfur dyes (Haber, 1958, p. 166), once again moving quickly when this new technological opportunity arose. The new class of sulfur dyes also offered Jäger the opportunity to get back into developing textile dyes because here the technological

---

[168] See Appendix I for chemical structures of Congo Red and Benzopurpurin 4B.

[169] See Appendix I for details on the relative frequency of dyes in different classes.

[170] Reinhardt (1997, pp. 196–212) provides an excellent account of how BASF interacted with university professors in developing a commercially viable synthetic indigo process and notes how many wrong turns were taken before truly competitive processes were developed.

[171] For a list of Levinstein's major sulfur dyes, see Fox (1987, p. 39).

[172] The number of dyes produced should be read as approximate figures for all firms (see discussion in Appendix I).

entry barriers were much lower than in the azo field, where the large firms such as Bayer had systematically combed through potential dye molecules. The aggressive marketing techniques of firms such as Bayer and its peers until then had forced Jäger into such niche markets as leather chemicals.

New sulfur dyes provided the opportunity for many of the smaller firms to put innovative products on the market once again. Schoellkopf, for instance, introduced its first sulfur dye in 1906 (Morris and Travis, 1992, p. 83). A few years earlier, at the turn of the century, Schoellkopf directed its research efforts to direct black dyes and, on the basis of two patents, offered very competitive black dyes in the American market, taking away market share from foreign firms in the black dye segment. To a much greater extent than Levinstein, Schoellkopf bought intermediates from Germany, being unable to manufacture many chemical intermediates at a cost that was competitive with German firms, who had more experience and greater economies of scale and scope.

As the dye companies were increasing their size, the more successful firms tended to integrate backward into making basic inorganic chemicals from which dyestuffs were made, such as sulfuric and nitric acid. Levinstein erected a sulfuric acid plant designed by the famous George E. Davis[173] in the early 1890s with a capacity of 250 tons per month. Levinstein also created the first nitric acid plant in England with the capacity of 100 tons per month (Fox, 1987, p. 21). In contrast, Jäger did not integrate backward into inorganic chemicals (Homburg–Murmann database) because its internal demand was not great enough to warrant such a move. Schoellkopf decided to produce sulfuric acid through a subsidiary, the Contact Process Company; by 1900, it had invested $1,000,000 in the sulfuric acid plant. Bayer was consuming more and more sulfuric acid but unlike its most important rivals, BASF and Hoechst, was not making its own basic inorganic chemicals until the 1890s. Intent on forcing the German cartel from which it bought its sulfuric acid to lower its price, the Bayer management decided to build its own sulfuric acid plant in Leverkusen after the cartel would not agree to lower terms (Duisberg, 1933, pp. 78–81).

As it turned out, however, Bayer grossly underestimated the know-how required to run a sulfuric acid plant at competitive cost (Verg et al., 1988, p. 106). Coming onstream in December 1893, sulfuric acid cost Bayer more than it would have had to pay in buying from the cartel. Bayer then called in the leading expert on inorganic chemistry, Georg Lunge, a university professor in Zurich, to help the firm create an efficient plant. After a painful remodeling effort, the plant finally worked, but the whole effort had cost Bayer a substantial amount of money, its management having misjudged how different inorganic production would be from the firm's existing competency base in organic chemistry. Once Bayer had a foothold in making inorganic chemicals, it decided also to make in-house the other two important acids, nitric and hydrochloric, starting in 1895. The growing internal demand for these acids was later satisfied by building additional plants. In 1897 the first plant working according to the new contact process was erected in Leverkusen, producing sulfuric acid side-by-side with the old lead chamber process (Verg et al., 1988, p. 107). Bayer had evolved into

---

[173] Davis wrote the first textbook on chemical engineering in the English-speaking countries. See Rosenberg (1998) for appraisal of Davis's role in shaping the field of chemical engineering in Britain and the United States.

a large inorganic producer, products it would continue to make in large quantities until the present.

Except for Schoellkopf, all of our five firms that still existed in this period before World War I seem to have pursued a strategy of product diversification. But they differed considerably in the scope of their diversification and how successfully they implemented it. The individual moves can be classified along two dimensions: whether the moves were motivated more by offensive or defensive considerations, and whether the new products were related or unrelated to the existing capabilities of the firm. When Benzopurpurin 4B gave Bayer large profits again, Bayer also found other new uses for its organic chemistry know-how, starting in 1888 by converting coal-tar intermediates into pharmaceuticals (Verg et al., 1988, p. 90). This diversification, based on existing production know-how, proved to provide a large growth market for Bayer.

Jäger did not follow Bayer into the lucrative pharmaceutical business. Jäger simply did not seem to have had the technical or management capabilities to leverage its dye know-how into a new area such as pharmaceuticals. Being on the defensive in its traditional textile dye market, Jäger first entered such niche markets as dyes for printing inks, shoe polish, flowers, soaps, greases, candles, paints and varnishes, and marking pens (Carl, 1926, pp. 25–6). It was relatively easy to enter these markets, and competition was much less intense than in the main market for dyes, textiles. After the firm had a foothold in paint products, it also developed drying substances. As a general strategy, the firm seems to have avoided direct competition with Bayer and the larger rivals by developing speciality applications for small markets. These niche strategies kept the firm alive but did not allow it to grow in the fashion of a Bayer.

Levinstein also often diversified for defensive reasons, many times making moves that were more unrelated to the existing competency base than did Jäger. When the competition from German rivals squeezed the Levinstein Co.'s profit margins, Ivan Levinstein seems to have felt compelled to look for other business opportunities. Between 1883 and 1894, Ivan Levinstein and Robert Ferdinand Graeser[174] founded and ran the Wrexham Lager Beer Brewery (Fox, 1987, p. 33). This venture to bring the German lager beer to Britain failed, and after considerable financial losses, the firm was liquidated. It did not escape Ivan Levinstein's notice that another immigrant from Germany, Alfred Mond, was making good profits with the new ammonia process for producing soda. In 1893 Ivan Levinstein became the principal shareholder and chairman of the Murgatroyd Co., Ltd. at Middlewich, Cheshire, a firm that produced soda according to the new ammonia process. In 1895, Ivan Levinstein sold the firm to Brunner Mond for reasons I have not been able to ascertain. Perhaps Levinstein wanted to concentrate his capital in his dyes firm, which was doing better again after he had gotten access to the best German technology.

When German firms abruptly stopped buying intermediates from Levinstein in 1908, the prospects of the firm once again looked particularly bleak (Fox, 1987, p. 37). Ivan Levinstein at this point ventured a second time into the more stable alkali business, where British firms were still the largest producers in the world. This time he founded the Ammonia Soda Co., Ltd. of Plumley, Cheshire (Fox, 1987, p. 34). Brunner Mond was again interested in buying up this venture to avoid having a British competitor.

---

[174] Like Ivan Levinstein, Graeser had come to Manchester at age nineteen to make a career as a chemist (Fox, 1987, p. 33).

Levinstein tried to keep the firm going independently, but in 1916, the year Ivan died, the firm was liquidated, because it could not get its waste disposal under control. In part, Brunner Mond was instrumental in making the firm fail because Brunner Mond held all the surrounding land and was not willing to sell it to a competitor. Just as in the case of Bayer's move into heavy chemicals, Levinstein underestimated the difficulty of managing an unrelated chemical business such as soda.

Having lost orders for dye intermediates and being unable to pay the bondholders, Levinstein desperately looked for other activities that could keep the firm going. The company now ventured into tannery chemicals and successfully developed fat-liquoring compounds and sulfonated oils. According to Fox (1987, p. 37), the famous Kromoline Whitcol and Turkey Red Oil series became commercially successful and allowed the firm to stay alive in the seven years before World War I. In the intermediates and dyes markets, the large German firms left hardly any space for the Levinstein company until World War I came along. Once hostilities started, Levinstein was back in business as a major producer of dyes and intermediates.

The BS&S firm diversified into nontextile dyes as a defensive move to stay in business while the German and Swiss firms were taking away its customers. During the last years of its existence, the firm made dyes for boot polishes, leather staining, color lakes, inorganic pigments, and printing inks (Fox, 1987, p. 110). But moving into the niches could not prevent the firm from going out of business in 1905. The big money was in textile dyes, and that is where the firm no longer was able to compete against Bayer and the other large German firms.

Organization of Production: The Advantage of Large Integrated Factories

One characteristic of the Age of Bayer was large-scale production that would lower the cost of making a particular dye. To go from manufacturing 100 dyes in 1878 to 1,800 dyes in 1913 (Farbenfabriken-Bayer, 1918, p. 4), Bayer had to expand dramatically the scale and scope of its production facilities. Since the very beginning of the synthetic dye industry, Bayer had faced a rapid decline in dye prices. The firm survived only by keeping up with the productivity levels of competitors. The key goal for Bayer was to improve productivity faster than prices were falling. As long as Bayer could decrease its cost more quickly than prices for dyes declined, it could maintain profit levels that would allow the firm to make larger investments in organizational capabilities than most rivals could.

Bayer achieved these critical cost reductions in a variety of ways. Over the years it increased the size of the production reactors several-fold. For example, in 1868 Bayer used autoclaves with a capacity of 30 liters; by 1905 they had reached 2,000 liters (Farbenfabriken-Bayer, 1918, pp. 251–2). In the beginning of the azo dye era, reactors were at most between 1,000 and 2,000 liters (Farbenfabriken-Bayer, 1918, p. 182). By 1907 a reactor to make azo dye was now 20,000 liters (Farbenfabriken-Bayer, 1918, p. 182).

Bayer's radical push for efficiency came in the 1890s. The main plant at Elberfeld had grown over the previous decades like a patchwork with very little rational planning. When the demand for a particular dye increased, Bayer set up a new production line. Over time, given the space constraints in Elberfeld, production steps that belonged together became located all over the site (Farbenfabriken-Bayer, 1918, p. 18), thereby introducing considerable inefficiencies.

"The Most Beautiful Chemical Plant in the World"

Even before Bayer decided to build its own basic inorganic chemicals plants, it was running out of space in Elberfeld and had to look for a new production site. A competitor in the alizarin dye business desired to get out of the business, offering for sale a very large site next to the Rhine River with lots of space for growth. The only drawback was that the site was out in the middle of nowhere, making it difficult at first to find workers. But Bayer needed more space badly. Because of the ideal shipping location of the terrain, Bayer acquired it in 1881 (Duisberg, 1933, p. 76). The new plant in Leverkusen also was not developed in a very systematic manner during the first few years, although the situation was somewhat better than Elberfeld. Typically, as a plant for a particular dye or intermediate line was running out of space in Elberfeld, the management of Bayer simply decided to move the plant to Leverkusen. Carl Duisberg began to be concerned that if the Leverkusen plant was to be built without a master plan, it would sooner or later constitute the similar inefficient patchwork as Elberfeld did in 1890.

Having broken his foot, Duisberg used the forced idleness when he could not leave his house to draft a long-term plan for the building of the Leverkusen site that he submitted to the top management of Bayer in January of 1895. This twenty-four-page "Memorandum on the Building and Organization of the Dye Works at Leverkusen" provides a unique insight into the thinking that subsequently governed the expansion of Bayer's production facilities. It would be quite appropriate to rename the memorandum "The Cost Manifesto" for its radical focus on creating the most efficient production plant possible. The memo lays out in minute detail how Bayer should make a transition from relatively unsystematic, ad hoc expansion to one based on systematic industrial planning for scale and scope economies. A few excerpts from the memo (reprinted in Duisberg, 1923) document this transition [my translation]:

As a matter of principle, we must avoid building sewers across the new terrain where later new buildings are to be erected. This will prevent [on the Leverkusen site] those annoying and very costly relocations that are now necessary in Elberfeld almost daily (p. 388).

We are convinced that it is absolutely necessary to change our current way of producing intermediates along with dyes in every single plant. To control quality, to simplify production, and to save costs it is necessary to centralize the production of intermediates in one single plant (p. 389).

It is absolutely imperative to avoid, as it is often the case now in Elberfeld, that dyes of a different class such as azo dyes, azine, induline, thiazine, etc., are produced in the same plant (p. 390).

The head of each [of the seven] production divisions must be an energetic person who has mastered the entire scientific and technical field [relevant to the division]. He is responsible toward top management that everything runs according to rules within the division, as well as that the plants are operated in the most cost-efficient and rational way, and that only the best and cheapest methods and the most appropriate apparatuses are used to make the different products.[. . .] Based on experience, we know that nothing is more productive for each plant than when the head of the division is in daily communication with each plant about their tasks and when the head informs the leaders of the plant about all the new improvements in technology in general and in particular those relevant for the specific plant. The leader of each plant in turn is responsible toward top management for the plant under his authority. Through constant work in the laboratory, he has to monitor the production and try everything to find more rational, better, and cheaper methods for making the various products (pp. 393–4).

All buildings of each plant are to be built in a way that it will be easy to expand them at least into one direction, better still into two. For these expandable sides, only half-timbered walls are to be used, which can be quickly removed for an expansion (p. 398).

As far as the arrangements within the plants are concerned, it is foremost the job of the chief engineers, the engineers, the architects to start discussing now how to set standard measures and sizes for all the apparatuses used in our industry. These standards are to be used throughout the entire [Leverkusen] factory and will allow uniform planning and calculations everywhere in the factory. By all means, we should introduce as quickly as possible standard measures for all pipes, taps, valves, slides, threads, screws, boilers, tubs, basins, etc. (p. 400).

With all new plants and plant relocations, it should be tried whenever possible to save human power and replace it with machine power (p. 400).

Drums made out of hard rubber did not work very well in the Elberfeld plant...The so-called screw-stirring devices proved to be most effective and they should be used wherever possible (p. 401).

We should erect an experimental plant where we will make all new products before it is clear that a new plant should be constructed. This experimental plant in due course will contain all apparatuses of the entire Leverkusen factory on a small scale so that it will be possible to make very quickly any new product, without having to build special equipment for the fabrication (p. 408).

Duisberg was able to implement this blueprint for creating efficient production because, although he was only the head of R&D at Bayer, he had full control over the construction of the new site in Leverkusen after 1895.[175] Duisberg could state: "I personally direct the construction of Leverkusen; no stone is set there without my permission" (Verg et al., 1988, p. 114).

Emil Fischer,[176] a student of Adolf Baeyer and the leading organic chemist in Germany at the turn of the century, visited Bayer's new plant in 1907 and remarked: "Undoubtedly this is the most beautiful chemical plant that I have ever seen" (Verg et al., 1988, p. 117). The plant may have been beautiful in the eyes of the Nobel laureate Fischer, but it must have been a nightmare for such firms as Jäger, BS&S, and Levinstein. By building a large, integrated plant, Bayer implemented efficient production that raised the requirements for being a successful player in the industry. The British and American firms could not keep up with Bayer's advances in efficient production, and this allowed Bayer to grow at a much faster rate.

A Look at the Plants of Bayer's Competitors

To get a proper sense of the proportion of Bayer's expansion, it is useful to look at the production facilities of some of the other firms. Read Holliday, roughly the same size

---

[175] For an account of Duisberg's role in the planning and construction of the Leverkusen factory, see also Duisberg (1933, pp. 74–87) and Flechtner (1959, pp. 141–8).

[176] We will encounter Emil Fischer again in Chapter 4, where he plays an interesting role vis-à-vis the dye industry and writes a revealing letter.

as Levinstein, had a total of 446 employees in 1907 (Homburg–Murmann database). Bayer's total work force at this point stood at 7,608 employees. Employment in its Leverkusen plant had risen to more than 4,000 in the previous year (Verg et al., 1988, p. 117).[177] Schoellkopf had a total of only 250 employees on the eve of World War I versus 10,600 at Bayer, 7,900 of which were now working at the Leverkusen plant (Verg et al., 1988, p. 198).

This raises, of course, the question of why Bayer's foreign competitors did not expand their plants as fast as Bayer did at Leverkusen. Several reasons present themselves, many of which appear to constitute a web of relationships that, taken together, made it difficult to keep up with Bayer. Probably the most important ones relate to the fact that these firms had neither a sufficient amount of profits nor enough new products in the pipeline that would have given them the resources to expand their production capacities. Whereas the firms from which BS&S derived had been clear leaders in process innovation, BS&S lost its innovative ability. As Fox (1987, p. 106) observed, "old products and processes continued to be worked when they were long outdated." According to Ernest Hickson, who was a chemist at BS&S for some time, the firm's failure to keep up with German competition had been hastened by the fact that the owners were taking too large a proportion of the profits out of the business (Fox, 1987, p. 110). By not reinvesting enough money, the firm lacked enough innovative products and processes that would have provided sufficient profits in the future, profits which in turn could have paid for an expansion similar to that of Bayer. Levinstein, being more innovative than BS&S during this period, did build a larger factory, but nothing on the scale of Leverkusen. Levinstein had great difficulty financing this planned expansion in the late 1880s because the firm lacked adequate returns to easily lure investors into the business.

Another reason as to why the two British firms and Schoellkopf in the United States did not expand their facilities as much as Bayer is related to the cost of building and running a dye plant in these three countries at the turn of the century. It was simply cheaper to build such a plant in Germany, which increased the returns from such an investment. With the rise of the German dye industry, the most advanced equipment makers more and more came to be located in Germany. Fox (1987, p. 40) describes that in this period Levinstein had to use German-built autoclaves for operations at higher temperatures, indicating that British production technology, unlike its position in the early years of the dye industry, was no longer at the cutting edge.

The most detailed evidence that building and running a dye plant was cheaper in Germany comes from an investigation in the United States. In 1908 Schoellkopf conducted a study (for the purpose of a congressional hearing on dye tariffs) that offers a unique perspective on the comparative costs of producing dyes and intermediates in the United States and Germany. The survey compared the relative cost of constructing and operating a dye plant in the United States and in Germany. Overall, the cost of building and running an aniline plant with 3,000,000 pounds of yearly capacity was 44 percent less in Germany than in the United States at that point (as quoted in Pfitzner, 1916, pp. 33–4). Breaking down costs into three categories – construction, labor costs for operation, and raw materials – gives more detailed figures. Building such a plant would have cost $104,000 in the United States and $70,000 in Germany.

[177] By 1988 the Leverkusen plant employed 36,500 people (Verg et al., 1988, p. 117).

Wages would have been $116,236 in the United States versus $61,493 for Germany. Finally, the expenses for all materials required in the production of 3,000,000 pounds of dyes would have been $443,000 in the United States but only $317,000 in Germany. Given these economics, it is not surprising that Bayer would expand much faster than Schoellkopf even without all the other factors that favored Bayer.

Marketing: The Triumph of the Sales Empire

Bayer outperformed all of the five other companies by developing a marketing organization that reached into every corner of the world. Along with Hoechst and BASF, it was engaged in a race to become the biggest dye firm in the world by systematically developing capabilities to serve very diverse customers. At the turn of the century, Bayer had sales subsidiaries in all the major textile centers of the world: Manchester, London, Milan, Barcelona, Brussels, Athens, Shanghai, Kobe, Saloniki, Bombay, Tokyo, Moscow (Bayer, 1963, pp. 30, 450–1), Paris (Farbenfabriken-Bayer, 1918, p. 361), and New York (Verg et al., 1988, p. 36). Between 1890 and 1902, the number of customers annually served by Bayer increased from 10,000 to 25,000 (Beer, 1959, p. 96). In 1913 Bayer had 44 sales subsidiaries and 123 sales agents (Verg et al., 1988, p. 198). These sales subsidiaries in foreign countries were at the same time the outposts of an enormous intelligence apparatus that periodically informed headquarters of the particular habits, preferences, and practices of local dyers and printers, as well as how these habits, preferences, and practices were changing as synthetic dyes became increasingly popular.

Bayer was perhaps the most marketing-driven organization in the entire dye industry. The others had to play catch-up with Bayer's organizational innovations. Among the several marketing innovations Bayer introduced was the idea of the travelling technician, who would help dyers and printers to apply Bayer dyes onto their fabrics. Given that dyers around the world worked with fabrics of varied compositions, such travelling technicians could make the difference in convincing dyers to adopt the Bayer products. In 1892 Bayer employed six people as travelling technicians; by 1894 this had grown to sixteen people (Verg et al., 1988, p. 86). As was the case with most organizational innovations, the travelling technical program started out on a small scale. When the program met with success, the Bayer management expanded it. The extent to which Bayer could run such programs depended on the local availability of chemists. When Bayer did not find enough chemists in the United States, its U.S. branch also began to sell patented dyes through competitors (Reimer, 1996, p. 133). Wherever possible, Bayer hired local technicians in the different countries because management had found that local technicians would be better able to understand the needs of the local customers. Hence, except perhaps for the general manager of the foreign subsidiary, employees tended to come from the native country and not Germany.

A similarly successful marketing tool that only Bayer and not the other five firms developed was designed to create purchasing loyalty by offering customers year-long technical training courses at the German headquarters in the art of dyeing and the new developments therein. On this "volunteer" program that started around the turn of the century, Bayer instructed young men who tended to be the sons of mill owners or were about to enter the management of a cloth-dyeing firm, for a year in leading-edge dyeing processes (Beer, 1959, pp. 92–3). The "volunteers" would see and become familiar with dye material they had never seen before and learn about innovative dyeing techniques that had been developed at Bayer. The program had a straightforward marketing motivation: The participants who learned how to dye with Bayer products would later be more inclined to order Bayer products because they already knew how to use them. Firms such as Levinstein and BS&S simply did not have the size to afford an in-house application development department that could have trained such volunteers.

Programs of this kind were also developed by the other major German dye firms. But to achieve some loyalty of the volunteers, Bayer and its strongest rivals such as BASF and Hoechst required that participants not participate in the program of a competitor for a year. For volunteers this was hardly a taxing requirement. They learned a lot and received free room and board for the entire year. The host firm in return learned about the most pressing technical concerns of their customers and could direct its R&D departments to find a solution for them.

Bayer figured out another extremely effective marketing technique. Given the wide variety in cultural experiences of dyers and printers around the world, Bayer customized its sales material for all major markets. Bayer translated catalogs and dye instructions into different languages and designed the jackets of the boxes in which dyes were sold in a way that would evoke identification of local dyers and printers with the product.[178] For countries who prided themselves on elephants, Bayer painted elephants on can jackets; other labels showed a tiger, a rickshaw driver, or even beautiful women.[179] One particular jacket exposing one breast of a beautiful woman provoked an angry letter from a textile producer to its dye sales house: "We cannot refrain from telling you how shocked we are that Bayer continuously violates common decency by putting half-naked women on the jackets of dye cans. We are really tired of continually removing this indecent picture. We strongly urge you to make Bayer use jackets that meet the standards of propriety" (as reprinted in Bayer, 1963, p. 80) [my translation]. Bayer, of course, had put that jacket on for good reason: It would make its dye stand out. A few complaints like the one we just heard did not matter. There is no evidence that BS&S or Levinstein was nearly as responsive to the differences in cultural traditions among dyers and printers in the various parts of the world. This is another reason why Bayer leaped far ahead of these competitors.

Over time, Bayer developed a marketing machinery that provided value for customers in a way that small players who did not cater to specific niche markets could not match. Jäger for one was forced to retreat to such niche markets as dyes for leather. But it would be wrong to portray Bayer as a "perfect company." Bayer did

---

[178] Alfred Marshall picked up the strong marketing focus of many German firms in his *Industry and Trade* (1923):

> The German's excel in the sedulous adaptation of their manufactures to local needs, high and low. They are quick to take account of differences in climate, of taste and custom, even superstition. They make cheap things for people of impulsive temperament; who prefer a brilliant gala dress, to one made of solid durable material. And with equal patience they get to know enough of the business affairs of individual traders to be able to sell with relatively small risk on long credit, where Englishmen sometimes demand prompt payment: in all this they are much aided by their industry in acquiring the languages of Eastern Europe, Asia, and South America. Even in markets where English is spoken they push their way by taking trouble in small things to which the Englishman will not bend himself (p. 136).

[179] For examples of Bayer's jackets, see Bayer (1963, pp. 80–1).

make mistakes and placed wrong bets. But the firm was better than all the British and American companies, and this was sufficient to leave behind all other firms except BASF and Hoechst, which quickly developed similar marketing machineries. Because Levinstein replicated on a small scale Bayer's international marketing orientation, this firm was more successful than BS&S. Levinstein, for instance, expanded its U.S. marketing organization after taking the U.S. sales into its own hands in 1906. Just as in many other British firms at the time, Ivan Levinstein put his son Edgar in charge of the American subsidiary. Edgar opened up sales offices in Chelsea (near Boston), Chicago, Philadelphia, and Farmington, as well as Montreal and Toronto, Canada (Fox, 1987, p. 42).

For Bayer, kickbacks were a hard habit to break. The use of kickbacks was especially pronounced in the United States. Reimer's (1996, pp. 137–42) detailed investigation shows that Bayer's kickbacks in the United States increased from 10 percent of receipts, or $250,000, in 1902 to 18 percent of receipts, or $700,000, in 1912. Although only in two states (Massachusetts and New York) was offering a commercial bribe considered a crime at the time, these kickbacks were dangerous in the context of a much more active anti-trust enforcement in the United States. But Bayer had a hard time weaning itself of the kickback schemes because that would have involved losing, at least temporarily, market share to rivals.

Internationalization of Efforts: Foothold Strategies

A direct result of Bayer's more aggressive sales efforts on the American market was that Levinstein's share diminished. Levinstein supplied 4.2 percent of American dye imports in 1902. But by 1913, all British firms together accounted only for 2.8 percent of American imports (Reimer, 1996, p. 135). At the turn of the century the United States was already Bayer's single most important market, and Bayer continued to develop its business there. In 1903 Friedrich Bayer Jr., Carl Duisberg, and Bayer's chief engineer traveled to the United States to look for a site where Bayer could run a plant as an insurance policy, in case the United States should raise tariffs on imported dyes (Verg et al., 1988, p. 156). Bayer was able to buy on very favorable terms the Hudson River Aniline and Color Works as well as the American Color & Chemical Color Works, both in Albany, NY. Because the plant in Albany was an insurance policy, Bayer employed only 84 people there by 1913, most of whom were used for the production of aspirin. Only a few workers ran a small dye production in Albany, in keeping with Bayer's goal of preserving its economies of scale and scope at its home plant in Leverkusen, Germany.

As we will see a little later, in 1890 Bayer, with AGFA, also acquired the majority stake in one of the largest British dye firms to establish a presence in the British Isles in case the political environment should make such a presence necessary for success in the local market. Although this involvement lasted only until 1897, Bayer was forced to produce within Britain's borders in 1908 when a change in the patent law made local production an economic necessity. Bayer first considered buying the Clayton Aniline company (Fox, 1987, p. 128), but then decided to build its own British plant in 1908, together with BASF and AGFA.

Only Bayer developed a sizable manufacturing presence in several other countries. It had production subsidiaries in five foreign countries by 1913 (Verg et al., 1988, p. 198). Jäger was too small at this point to be able to afford foreign plants; BS&S was gradually heading toward bankruptcy; and Schoellkopf was fully occupied by battling the powerful foreign firms in its U.S. home market. To take advantage of the large U.S. market, Levinstein in this period established small manufacturing plants along with its sales offices in Chelsea, Chicago, Philadelphia, and Farmington (Fox, 1987, p. 42). It is not clear how many of these plants actually made dyes, rather than Levinstein's other products. The plants also were supervised by Edgar Levinstein. Both the sales and manufacturing efforts were now organized through an American subsidiary, first I. Levinstein & Company (1906) and after 1910 I. Levinstein & Company, Inc. (Fox, 1987, p. 42).

R&D Strategy: The Industrialization of Innovation

During the first four years of Duisberg's tenure at Bayer (1883–1887), he and his assistants created twenty-one new dyes and dye intermediates (Flechtner, 1959, p. 91). By 1890, Duisberg had eighteen research chemists working under him alone (Flechtner, 1959, p. 100). And this trend continued: At the turn of the century Bayer had 140 chemists in its employ, whereas Levinstein had only 20 (Homburg–Murmann database; Haber, 1958, p. 166). By 1914 the ratio was even more unfavorable for Levinstein. Bayer had acquired an army of organic chemists who were searching for new dyes. Although BS&S engaged in R&D from an early date, it never developed a large formal R&D organization. In 1902, three years before it went out of business, BS&S's staff consisted only of five chemists, a dyer, a chief engineer, a manager of the printing ink department, and the company's secretary (Fox, 1987, p. 110). As Steven Klepper (1996) has emphasized, the R&D cost per unit goes down as the output of the firm increases, providing a big advantage to firms that are able to increase output more quickly. As we have seen earlier, Bayer was one of the firms that increased output more quickly than most rivals because its development was faster and more effective, making it possible to start production earlier and expand more easily to a large scale. This in turn gave Bayer sufficient sales to invest large sums into research.

Sophisticated R&D laboratories like that of Bayer were a killer weapon against small firms. For the few firms that could afford a large R&D laboratory, having a plethora of chemists working only on new dye technologies meant that the firm was much more able to find ways around a radical new product such as synthetic indigo. In response to BASF's synthetic indigo, for example, Bayer developed a whole new set of blue dyes (Verg et al., 1988, pp. 170–5). Through their large investments in R&D, firms such as Bayer changed the rate and direction along which dye technology would develop. The natural indigo trajectory on which farmers tried to find better ways to plant and grow indigo relatively quickly came to a dead end when BASF and later Hoechst flooded world markets with synthetic indigo. The R&D capabilities created by such firms as Bayer were responsible for an unprecedented acceleration of the rate of innovation. It is no exaggeration to declare that the evolution of dye technology from the late 1880s onward cannot be understood without coming to grips with the concomitant evolution of the R&D laboratory, a new organizational form in the history of business. Developing gradually out of early research activities of Perkin & Sons and the French firm La Fuchsine, its evolution later culminated in the creation of separate R&D laboratories at such firms as Levinstein and Bayer (Homburg, 1992). Compared to BASF, Hoechst, and AGFA, Bayer had come late to the research game, but once it experienced success with hiring research chemists, it also built a formidable research organization.

Building a "Factory" for Innovation

Propelled by his own success and that of other research chemists working for Bayer, Duisberg in 1889 became the motor behind building a new central R&D laboratory. He proposed to the top management of Bayer that it should build a laboratory for half a million marks, a gigantic investment at the time (Flechtner, 1959, p. 118). Duisberg himself took active part in the design of the Elberfeld-based laboratory, planned to provide ideal working conditions for research chemists. One of the key architectural innovations in the new laboratory was to have twelve chemists work in one open room. Every chemist was assigned his own workspace with all necessary equipment, but because there were no walls, the design stimulated interaction between chemists.[180] The laboratories there became better equipped than those of universities for carrying out organic chemistry research. The British chemist Henry E. Amstrong visited the Elberfeld laboratory and wrote in praise:[181]

... If, at the present time, it were desired to fit up a research laboratory for chemical purposes in London, we could not do better than take these plans [for the new Bayer laboratory] and reproduce them in their entirety, and that we should then, I believed, have reason to congratulate ourselves on possessing the best-appointed public research laboratory in the world (1893, p. 30).

Bayer started to provide its research chemists with a library of books and journals that would allow chemists to find out about all the developments in chemistry and science. By 1897 the library already contained 4,000 books. In that year same Friedrich August Kekulé died, and Carl Duisberg bought Kekulé's private library of 7,000 books (Verg et al., 1988, p. 124), making Bayer's library one of the very best science libraries in the world. Unlike Jäger, the two British firms, and Schoellkopf, who employed many fewer research chemists, Bayer had created a true "factory" for innovations. By 1896, Bayer's organic chemists synthesized 2,378 compounds (Meyer-Thurow, 1982, p. 378) trying to find a few dyes that would be commercially viable.

The Testing and Application Development Departments

But the laboratory for research chemists was only one component of Bayer's R&D organization. Equally important for the commercialization of dyes were the testing and the application development departments. The impetus for both was a clear failure on Bayer's part to appraise properly the value of the Congo Red patent when it was offered to the firm for purchase and an embarrassing disaster with a new azo blue dyestuff (benzoazurine). After this latter dye was put on the market, buyers found it would fade rapidly under the influence of sunshine (Duisberg, 1933, pp. 52–6). In response to this debacle, Bayer began in 1887 to systematically test all new dyestuffs (Verg et al., 1988, pp. 85–6). From now on, no dye would be put on the market that

[180] The *Chemiker Zeitung* widely reported in minute detail the architectural features of this new laboratory (Bayer, 1963, pp. 300–1). For a drawing of the ground floor, see Verg et al. (1988, p. 100).

[181] Amstrong held the position of Professor of Chemistry at the City & Guilds of London Institute and was a leading dye chemist in Britain at the turn of the century. Amstrong also had appeared as an expert witness in the fight between Levinstein and BASF in the 1880s (Zimmermann, 1965, p. 75). More details about this fight were given in the section, "Levinstein versus BASF."

had not undergone elaborate testing at Bayer. Once again, Bayer incorporated into the organization a function that was previously performed by the community of dyers, printers, and tinkerers of all kinds. In 1906, Meyer-Thurow (1982) reports, 2,656 new chemical compounds were synthesized in Bayer's research laboratories. Sixty of those were tested on a larger scale after first screening, and only thirty-six ever reached the market.[182] Some evidence shows that Levinstein did this testing on a very small scale (Fox, 1987, p. 40), but the firm's efforts could not compare with those of Bayer.

The dyeing and printing laboratories were another true organizational innovation. The effectiveness of these laboratories flowed from a marriage of scientific and practical experts (van den Belt and Rip, 1987). Organic chemists could develop new compounds, but only the trained dyer and colorist could evaluate whether the dye would work well with the different fabrics in use all over the world (Beer, 1959, p. 89).

Academic Alliance with Professors: Jockeying for Access to the Best and Brightest

After the development of its sophisticated in-house R&D laboratory, Bayer was less dependent on university researchers to provide the dye innovations that would keep the firm at the forefront of the industry, as had been the case with alizarin. Nonetheless, it remained important to keep a close relationship with academics for the purpose of recruiting new scientific and technical talent. Carl Duisberg explained to an American audience in 1896:

In our works in Elberfeld and Leverkusen, in which, for our special object, we choose almost exclusively young chemists from universities, we always give preference to those, who after passing their examinations, have worked one or two years with one of the professors with whom we are associated (reprinted in Duisberg, 1923, p. 146).

There was competition among the German dye firms for the best university talent. To go from 102 chemists in 1896 to 321 in 1913, Bayer had a lot of hiring to do. Just as firms wanted to hire the brightest young chemists, the new graduates themselves preferred to work for the firm that offered them the best laboratory equipment and support staff, as well as a lucrative profit-sharing agreement for new inventions. Joining Bayer on these counts was a much more lucrative proposition for any aspiring young chemist than joining a small firm such as Jäger or a foreign competitor, who could not match Bayer's profit opportunities.

Getting Access to the Network of Chemists from Abroad

Because neither Britain nor the United States educated organic chemists with qualifications comparable to those gained at German and Swiss universities, Levinstein and Schoellkopf pursued the strategy of hiring talent from abroad.[183] In contrast, BS&S

---

[182] Another of Bayer's biggest rivals (besides BASF) developed a similar testing organization. In 1900 Hoechst tested 3,500 of its new colors or combinations of old colors. Only eighteen reached the market. A few years later, 29 of 8,000 dyes were marketed (Beer, 1959, p. 89). For additional statistics on the efforts of BASF and Hoechst, see Reinhardt (1997, pp. 290, 317).

[183] For the names of many of the chemists that were employed at the Levinstein before World War I, see Fox (1987, p. 14). Unfortunately, much less documentation is available on Schoellkopf. Reinhardt's (1997, pp. 350, 363) short biographies of many of BASF's research chemists reveal that Schoellkopf hired away from BASF at least two chemists – Friedrich Köhler in the mid-1880s and Leonhard Wacker in 1903.

did not systematically recruit German and Swiss talent, possibly in part because its principals, unlike Ivan Levinstein, were not familiar with German culture. This could easily be the key reason why the innovative ability of BS&S declined and customers switched to producers with more innovative dyes.[184]

Because of Ivan Levinstein's autocratic personality, many foreign chemists did not stay very long with the firm. Nonetheless, given a recurring oversupply of chemists in Germany, Levinstein always found new individuals who could not obtain a job in Germany. They often had some experience with one of the smaller continental dye firms (Fox, 1987, p. 14). The various foreign chemists that passed through the Levinstein company called themselves the "Club of Former Levinsteiners," a title that is both funny and serious. At Bayer, academically trained chemists found themselves in a professional environment; at Levinstein, they were subjected to the rule of one man. Chemists in Britain were paid on average significantly less than in Germany (Reader, 1970, p. 261)[185] because they had on average much less academic training and were less qualified (Haber, 1958, pp. 186–98; van den Belt et al., 1984, pp. 127–30).[186] It is safe to assume, however, that British firms who wanted to recruit German *research chemists* had to pay more rather than less in comparison to German firms if they wanted to attract talent at the same level of quality. From the beginning of the industry, there existed a market for talent, and firms routinely tried to lure talent from competitor firms. Chemists would frequently move to a firm that bid up the price of their services. But apparently Levinstein would not pay his research chemists enough to "bribe" them into submitting themselves to his autocratic leadership style for long. Levinstein also had the problem that first-rate talent was getting more expensive when

[184] For a biography of the most important BS&S chemists, Raphael Meldola and Arthur Green, see Fox (1987, pp. 108–9).

[185] Read Holliday, Levinstein's only serious British rival at the turn of the century, apparently did not pay their chemists good salaries. Whittaker, the author of the quote at the beginning of the present chapter, started his career as a chemist at Read Holliday in 1899 without pay, then went to the University of Berlin for a year at his father's expense, before receiving a regular salary at Read Holliday (Whittaker, 1956).

[186] Homburg (van den Belt et al., 1984, pp. 127–30) found that the term "chemist" was more poorly defined in Britain than in Germany. British "chemists" displayed a far greater range of salaries and qualifications. Many "chemists" in Britain did earn less than in Germany, but according to the evidence seen by Homburg, these were not highly trained academic chemists. Homburg concluded there is no reason to believe that excellent research chemists in Britain were paid less than in Germany. One example of a well-paid German research chemist in Britain is Peter Griess, who earned £700 in Britain in 1870, a sum far higher than the salary of the typical German company chemist. (£700 in 1870 had the same purchasing power as £34,545 in 2001.)

Before the formal development of its R&D department, Bayer recruited most of its chemists from other firms. Meyer-Thurow (1982, p. 366) reports that "so far as can be determined, six of the eight chemists hired during 1863–1871 and five of the six during 1874–1878 were recruited from other companies." Turnover among those chemists was very high. When the formal R&D laboratories emerged, Bayer, BASF, and Hoechst changed their practices and recruited most chemists directly from universities. At Bayer, all research chemists after the mid-1880s had to sign a noncompetition clause stipulating that they would not work at another dye firm or share their production knowledge for three years after leaving Bayer (Meyer-Thurow, 1982, p. 373). Because the largest firms provided the best chemical talent with the best working conditions and because they forced research chemists to sign noncompetition clauses, they lost relatively few chemists after 1885 compared to the turnover in earlier periods. Reinhardt's (1997, pp. 335–64) biographies of research chemists at BASF show that the firm was very similar to Bayer in this respect.

Table 9. **Financial Incentives for Bayer Research Chemists (in Marks)**[a]

| | 1902 | | 1906 | | 1912 | |
| | Annual | | Annual | | Annual | |
Chemist	salary	Royalties	salary	Royalties	salary	Royalties
I	7,500	19,041	9,500	28,685	20,000	51,727
2	5,400	14,084	6,000	22,095	6,750	39,878
3	4,800	3,993	6,250	7,655	7,750	13,214
4	4,800	744	6,000	1,058	7,750	3,785
5	4,000	651	4,600	5,766	6,800	9,227
6	3,600	559	5,500	462	8,000	3,050
7	3,000	—	4,300	575	6,600	1,377

[a] The table reports salaries for all chemists in the main research laboratory, one of the multiple laboratories that Bayer maintained in the period. Meyer-Thurow (1982) assembled the salary data from chemists' personnel files. Chemist I was the head of the department. Royalties came from two different sources. Bayer's board of directors offered prizes and premiums for the solution of specific research problems defined by management. Research chemists also received a fixed percentage of the net profits that the firms made from patented inventions (Meyer-Thurow, 1982, p. 373).
Source: Meyer-Thurow (1982, p. 374).

the leading German firms figured out how to incorporate formal research into their corporate strategies. Because the sales and the profits of Bayer became so much larger than that of Levinstein, Bayer could afford to pay their research chemists more than such competitors as Levinstein, who had to distribute research cost over a smaller output.

As the figures in Table 9 illustrate, the income of academic chemists at Bayer increased substantially as the firm figured out how to use chemists as continuous generators of new products and profits. One example is Carl Duisberg, who joined Bayer as one of the three initial research chemists. His compensation increased dramatically after a couple of years because he received a percentage of the profits made from Benzopurpurin 4B, the patented dye he developed.[187] In 1885 Bayer increased his salary from 2,700 to 6,000 marks, and he received 2.5 percent of the net profit Bayer made from his discoveries. In the first year of Benzopurpurin 4B production this gave him an additional 9,000 marks, which he invested in Bayer stock (Duisberg, 1933, p. 40). By the time Duisberg retired, he was a millionaire just like Heinrich Caro of BASF, who also was not among the founders of his firm but rose into a leading position because of his innovative abilities. Both men probably belong to the best paid research chemists during their tenure in the dye industry.

More systematic evidence on how chemists' salaries compare to that of other employees is available for BASF. Chemists received by far the highest salaries at BASF in the period from 1890 to 1914, earning on average four times more than workers, and almost twice as much as commercial employees (Borscheid, 1976, p. 137). This was only their regular salary, which they could improve dramatically by sharing profits

[187] The chemical formula of this enormously successful dye is shown in Appendix I.

from their inventions. From 1874 on, H. Caro, the technical director of BASF, received besides salary and money for an apartment 2 percent of all profits of BASF; F. Riese who developed an alizarin process for Hoechst received 7 percent of all profits made from the product (Borscheid, 1976, pp. 131–2). There is no reason to believe that pay scales were significantly different at Bayer.

The literature on the chemical and dye industries at the turn of the twentieth century is filled with accounts that the average British chemist was poorly paid. Richardson, for example (1962, p. 113), reported: "In this country the value of chemists and of their research to industry was grossly underrated. Even 18 months after the outbreak of the First World War the Government was advertising for chemists of university training at a pay of 45 shillings per week – little more than an unskilled worker's wage." Simply blaming individual British entrepreneurs for a lack of enlightenment about the benefits of employing academic chemists misses important economic constraints under which lagging firms operate. British dye firms simply did not have the scale and profit margins of the successful Germans firms that would have allowed them to pay premium salaries. This created a vicious cycle. The foreign talent hired at Levinstein would not be the best chemists but rather the second-rate students who were not hired by the big German firms. This essentially meant that once Bayer had a significant lead, it was very difficult for Levinstein to catch up.

The Patent Strategies: Making the Courtroom the Battlefield

With the rise of azo dyes, Bayer adopted the strategy of patenting every new compound that showed some commercial potential, not only in Germany but also in the United States, Britain, France, and other countries that granted patents. By 1913, Bayer had amassed 8,000 domestic and foreign patents.[188] To make its patent strategy work, Bayer had to be prepared to sue other firms that would not respect Bayer's patent monopoly. Because patent laws as applied to organic chemicals were still sufficiently imprecise in the beginning of this period, whether or not a chemical process or product would meet the requirements of novelty was often a subject on which reasonable people could disagree. Not surprisingly, firms pursued two strategies: first, to file very broad patent claims, and second, to start manufacturing a new dye while hoping that the courts would eventually rule that the firm did not infringe an existing patent.

To be able to prevent rivals from filing broad patents, Bayer in 1886 began systematically to analyze patents of competitors (Verg et al., 1988, p. 120). As the number of patent filings and patent objections increased, Duisberg created a permanent staff to handle all patent matters. By 1896 the volume of this activity had become so large that Duisberg established an independent patent department (Verg et al., 1988, p. 118). This created a formal organizational structure through which Bayer tried to implement its patent strategy.

To protect the value of its patent portfolio, Bayer actively sued not only in Germany but also in all other national markets where patents were granted. Reimer (1996) documents some of the U.S. patent fights in this third period, which were directed against both local American firms such as Albany Aniline Company and

---

[188] In the second half of the 1880s, Carl Rumpf was voted into the patent commission of the German Chemical Industry Association (Ungewitter, 1927, p. 302), indicating Bayer's increased standing among the German dye firms.

German competitors. Bayer was not the only firm suing. Most firms were involved in patent fights because the economic value attached to some new dyes such as Congo Red was extremely high. For instance, Schoellkopf sued Levinstein and Read Holliday in the United States for infringing its black dyes in 1911 (Reimer, 1996, p. 136). As a general rule, lucrative dyes such as Congo Red and Benzopurpurin 4B would entice competitors to try to get away with infringing the patent or to have courts declare the patent invalid. Hence the one feature that remained relatively constant over the entire development of the synthetic dye industry before 1914 was frequent battles in court. Sometimes the stakes were particularly high for the firms involved, as in the case of the Congo Red patent, which challenged the very foundation of the R&D strategy Bayer had adopted since its success with Benzopurpurin 4B.

The Congo Red Case: Bayer versus AGFA, Then Bayer and AGFA versus Ewer & Pick
When Bayer filed a patent for Duisberg's Benzopurpurin 4B dye, AGFA's first reaction was to officially ask the patent office not to grant Bayer a patent because it would infringe on AGFA's Congo Red patent (Duisberg, 1933, p. 42). Bayer took the offensive and filed a suit to have the Congo Red patent declared void (Flechtner, 1959, p. 80). But the management of both firms realized that these lawsuits were fraught with risks for both parties. As a result, AGFA and Bayer agreed in the offices of the Deutsche Bank in Berlin not to challenge the Congo Red (AGFA) or the Benzopurpurin 4B (Bayer) patents, because it was not clear in whose favor the courts would eventually rule (Flechtner, 1959, p. 80). Instead, the firms formed an alliance to exploit both patents. The Benzopurpurin 4B patent was transferred to AGFA, and the two firms agreed to commercialize both dyes.

This extremely profitable market-sharing agreement was challenged, however, by a small company, Ewer & Pick, which put both Congo Red and Benzopurpurin 4B on the market, having made them by slightly different proceses. Based on the Bayer–AGFA arrangement, AGFA was the legal owner of the Congo Red and Benzopurpurin 4B patents, and it had to file the infringement suit. Ewer & Pick opted for the standard response, to file a countersuit claiming that the Congo Red and its Benzopurpurin addition should be declared void. The most important German dye patent case had started and, as we shall see, the outcome was far from certain.[189]

By 1889, the case had reached the highest court in Leipzig. The final day in court was to take place on March 20. AGFA's head of R&D, Dr. Gustav Schultz, who later became the editor of the famous dye tables, had already been in Leipzig for weeks, instructing AGFA's lawyer on the technical details behind the Congo Red and Benzopurpurin 4B patents. Bayer's management wanted Carl Duisberg to experience a trial at the highest patent court and thus sent Duisberg to Leipzig to watch the proceedings. Duisberg was going to meet the "Who's Who" of dye chemistry. In addition to Schultz, Heinrich Caro of BASF, the leading German dye firm at this point, appeared in person as the court's neutral expert witness. Besides Caro, Professors Adolf Baeyer and Johannes Wislicenus had already provided a written expert testimony. AGFA's lawyer, Reuling, had received word before the day in court

---

[189] The main sources on the Congo Red patent case are Duisberg (1933, pp. 42–8); van den Belt and Rip (1987, pp. 153–5); Flechtner (1959, pp. 102–7), who largely relies on Duisberg; and Verg et al. (1988, pp. 118–23).

that the two renowned chemists had recommended in their written statements that the Congo Red patent should be declared void under the current German patent law (Verg et al., 1988, p. 120). Reuling was thus aware that the case was going to be an uphill battle, and he was very nervous and agitated from the very beginning of the procedures.

The lawyer of Ewer & Pick started with a brilliant motion, asking the courts to allow only legal representatives of the firms to participate in the court proceedings. The courts granted the request, which forced Dr. Gustav Schultz, who had come prepared with dye samples and elaborate documentation to prove that AGFA and Bayer indeed had made a new innovation, to leave the courtroom. Because Carl Duisberg already had the commercial power of attorney for Bayer, he was able to stay. Before leaving, Schultz gave Duisberg all his material, hoping that it could still be of help even in his absence. AGFA and Bayer were now deprived of their technical expert, who had spent weeks preparing for the patent fight.

After the two lawyers for the opposing firms stated their case, the court called Dr. Heinrich Caro. By all accounts, Caro gave a brilliant ninety-minute speech in which he laid out the history of azo dyes and at the end concluded that the Congo Red patent did not meet the requirement of novelty as he interpreted the 1877 German patent law. His main contention was that because his laboratory boy could easily make Congo Red if Caro would simply give him the title of the Congo Red patent, the dye did not qualify as a new invention. As had Baeyer and Wislicenus, Caro recommended that the patent be declared null and void. AGFA's lawyer, sensing imminent defeat, frequently interrupted the proceedings and became very aggressive even toward the court. After another interruption, the court gave Reuling a final warning or he would be removed from the room. Reuling had tried to scare the court by telling the judges that they were about to make the same mistake as a few years earlier, when the court had ruled in his favor and later found that they had made an error. The judges were not going to tolerate such tactics and were ready to throw Reuling out of the courtroom.

Carl Duisberg realized at this point that AGFA and Bayer were about to lose their case, and with it Bayer would be robbed of the recent prosperity brought by its blockbuster azo dyes.

My entire efforts and work in the area of azo dye chemistry seemed to be in vain. In the case that the Congo patent should have been declared null and void and that all other azo dyes should be destroyed, Bayer would have again lost its solid economic footing and its very promising recent development. My own future was also largely dependent on the outcome of this important trial (Duisberg, 1933, p. 45) [my translation].

Duisberg became agitated and without premeditation asked the court to let him speak on the technical background on the Congo Red–Benzopurpurin 4B patents. He now gave a detailed account of how he developed the Benzopurpurin 4B dyestuff, using the dye samples and documentation that Schultz had left behind on the table. In direct response to Caro, Duisberg stated that he could also give his laboratory boy the name of BASF's patented dyes and the boy would be able to make the dyes. Duisberg tried to make clear for the court that if it was going to invalidate the Congo Red patent, all other azo dye patents (the main source of new dye innovations) had to be declared null and void as well.

After Pick of Ewer & Pick, the main plaintiff, was given the opportunity to speak, the judges retreated into their chambers to deliberate about their verdict. When they came out, they made a ruling that became the landmark decision for the field of dye chemistry. The judges decided that the Congo Red patent was valid because it represented a new technical effect. This doctrine of "new technical effect" subsequently governed how the patent office and courts would evaluate the merits of a patent application. The wording of the law had not changed, but the way the law was going to be interpreted henceforth had. Duisberg would later recall his reaction to the final ruling in the Congo Red case: "I was never as happy and glad as in the evening of this exciting[190] and eventful day" (1933, p. 46).

Patent Strategies of the Other Firms

The management of BS&S showed little interest in developing a large R&D laboratory or in patenting the dyes developed by the few chemists the firm employed. By British standards, the firm had probably the best native talent, Raphael Meldola, from 1875 to 1885, and then after him, Arthur Green from 1885 to 1894 (Fox, 1987, p. 109). These two men who successively occupied the position of the research chemist, a tradition that seems to have been taken over from the predecessor firms, made brilliant discoveries, for example, the Meldola Blue and Primuline by Green. But because BS&S's management with few exceptions did not care to patent the two chemists' discoveries or prevent the two chemists from publishing their research findings, rival firms, in particular those in Germany and Switzerland, exploited their inventions at the expense of BS&S (Fox, 1987, p. 109).

As Levinstein increased its research and development efforts, the company pursued the strategy of patenting as much as possible, exploiting the azo gold mine just as the leading German firms did (Fox, 1987, p. 17). This strategy gave the firm many more patents than in the previous period. Between 1888 and 1914, the firm obtained sixty-seven British patents (Fox, 1987, pp. 228–30), whereas from 1864 to 1887, it received only eight patents, four of which were obtained in the 1880s. Levinstein sued and was sued frequently in this period. Because of his close relationship with Bayer and AGFA, which will be described a bit later, Ivan Levinstein also fought patent suits against other British firms on behalf of his German partners between 1890 and 1895.[191]

Fox reports that Levinstein was also taken to court in 1910 by Henri Raymond Vidal because the latter claimed that Levinstein had infringed Vidal's sulfur patent (B. P. 16,449; granted in 1896). In the first decade of the new century, sulfur dyes had become very lucrative products; hence, it is not surprising that litigation also started in this field about who held the rights to the most important innovations. After more than a year of litigation, Levinstein successfully defended itself in this case, but the firm could not recoup the legal cost because the Vidal group soon was bankrupt. In 1912, Levinstein was also taken to court by AGFA for infringements on one of its sulfur black patents (Fox, 1987, p. 39). The case dragged on for a long time because the World War interrupted proceedings, but finally in 1921 the German firm lost its case.

---

[190] The German adjective *aufregend* in this context also has the meaning of agitating. The experience was not solely pleasant.

[191] A particularly important case involved Benzopurpurin 4B, for which Levinstein had received a license from Bayer. Carl Duisberg travelled to the court proceedings in 1891 and participated as an expert witness, helping to win the case for Levinstein (Duisberg, 1933, p. 46).

Schoellkopf played on a small scale the same game Bayer was playing, namely, profiting as much as possible from patent monopolies. The firm amassed seventeen U.S. patents (Steen, 1995, p. 54) and about eighty worldwide patents (Homburg estimate, personal communication, 2001), compared with 8,000 worldwide patents held by Bayer (Verg et al., 1988, p. 198). Just like Bayer, Schoellkopf patented in foreign countries, but on a much smaller scale. It filed for a patent (DRP No. 40571) in Germany in 1885 (Duisberg, 1933, p. 33) and a year later received a German patent for the creation of alpha-naphtholmonosulfonic acid and naphtholmono- and-disulfonic acid (Farberfabriken-Bayer, 1918, p. 113). This gave Schoellkopf an important dye intermediate patent (Caro, 1892, p. 1096). Because of Duisberg's great interest in the potential of the intermediates for making dyes, Bayer bought a license for this intermediate from Schoellkopf in 1888 (Duisberg, 1933, pp. 33–4; Reimer, 1996, p. 129).[192]

Relationship with Competitors: The Taming of Competition
Theft of Firm Secrets Continues
In the 1890s the practice of paying people for revealing the secrets of other companies continued. J. W. Kumpf was one of the few people who actually got caught and put in jail for bribing employees at BASF to obtain crucial details about the indigo synthesis and then selling his information to Binschedler of Basel (Haber, 1958, p. 176). Ivan Levinstein also came into the possession of some secret information about BASF's indigo process, suggesting that Ivan kept his ears open for any significant information about the secrets of rivals. If anyone had offered a firm competitively relevant information, none of the six firms would have objected, given the prevailing business norms at the time.

Ivan the Great or Ivan the Terrible?
In 1890, the Levinstein company entered into a relationship with Bayer and AGFA that Reader (1970, p. 262) has called a very curious episode. Because of the difficulty of raising capital in Great Britain for the expansion of his factory, Ivan Levinstein sold two-thirds of his company, one-third to Bayer and the other third to AGFA. To facilitate this ownership arrangement, the Levinstein firm was converted into a limited liability company and given the name of I. Levinstein & Company, Ltd. By this act, the firm essentially became an outpost of the German synthetic dye empire. Besides obtaining capital to build a new factory, Ivan Levinstein received additional assistance from his former rivals. Bayer and AGFA not only shipped a great deal of their technical talent to Manchester but also licensed all their patents for the very lucrative direct cotton dyes to the Levinstein Co. in return for a fixed share of profit from their sales in Britain (Reader, 1970, p. 262).

After five years into this "marriage," Ivan Levinstein and his German bosses turned out to be unsuitable bedfellows. By temperament, Ivan was not well equipped

---

[192] Bayer and Schoellkopf developed a relatively friendly relationship by the standards of the very competitive dye industry, starting with this licensing deal. Hugo Schoellkopf visited Bayer's new Leverkusen plant in 1899 with his son and sales manager and, according to Reimer (1996, p. 130), "received a grand tour through the works, including parts normally off-limits to competitors." Duisberg wrote to Bayer's U.S. sales manager, "Yes, he is a competitor, but not a dangerous one" (quoted in Reimer, 1996, p. 130). In 1911 Bayer loaned its U.S. corporate counsel, Anthony Gref, and its patent expert, Hugo Schweitzer, to Schoellkopf for its suit against Levinstein and Read Holliday (Reimer, 1996, p. 136).

to take direction and orders from his German partners, who now owned 66 percent of the firm. From his study of Ivan Levinstein's leadership practices, Reader[193] (1970, p. 261) concluded that "he ran his business as an autocracy tinged with favoritism." When the ownership agreement among AGFA, Bayer, and Ivan Levinstein was up for renewal in 1895, AGFA under the leadership of Martius decided to withdraw immediately from involvement with Levinstein. Once again a new legal entity was created, Levinstein, Ltd.; von Böttinger of Bayer remained on the board for another two years, before he too bailed out of the relationship with Levinstein.

Why would the Germans have invested Levinstein in the first place and why did they withdraw after a few years? The most plausible interpretation is that the two German firms were afraid that British patent laws would change, requiring them to work their patents in Britian. Fox (1987, p. 22) speculates that Ivan Levinstein "had deliberately sewn the seed of worry in the minds of the Germans on the score of impending patent reform." After the British patent laws remained unchanged for five years, the leadership of Bayer and AGFA probably concluded that a change in British patent law was not going to occur any time soon. Because Bayer needed a lot of capital for the construction of its large Leverkusen plant (Bayer had to resort to bonds), the firm probably concluded that its money was better invested at home than in the British Levinstein enterprise.

Building Cartels

Once the United States became the largest single market for Bayer's dyes, Carl Duisberg as one of the top managers at the time visited the States to look after Bayer's business. Seeing the giant sulfuric acid plants and the large trusts that at the time were organizing entire industries, he became convinced that the German dye industry would prosper in the future only if the intense competition between the large dye firms was tamed. In a memorandum to all important German dye firms, Duisberg proposed a full merger of the industry into a single firm.[194] He argued that such a merger would be much easier to pull off successfully during a time when profits were still excellent (Bayer was then running at a 33 percent rate of return on stock capital and the other large firms were all above 20 percent; Haber, 1958, p. 178) than if they waited a future date, when the industry's fortunes would probably be worse because of the mounting cost of finding new dyes and supporting large sales forces.

In the past, attempts to create cartels and trusts in the German dye industry proved very unsuccessful. But times had changed. The large firms were now responsible for most innovations. The top three firms accounted for more than 60 percent of German dye production. A new alizarin convention had been running with success since 1901. And the recent years had provided more opportunities to develop trust during meetings of the German chemical industry association.[195] Although the individual dye firms were too proud of their own identities to merge into one firm,

---

[193] Reader is well-qualified to pass judgement because of his access to the ICI archives; this gave him also access to all the private documents still available on Levinstein Co., which became part of ICI in 1926.

[194] Duisberg's memorandum is reprinted in the 1923 collection of his writings (pp. 343–68).

[195] As Bayer was moving into the first tier of German dye firms, its managers began seeking influence in the industry association. Dr. von Böttinger was deputy director of the chemical industry association in 1896 (Ungewitter, 1927, p. 26). He joined the board of the association sometime after 1886 (p. 31) and left in 1916.

Bayer formed a triple alliance with BASF and AGFA in 1905, after Hoechst formed an alliance and exchanged stock with Cassella. The much smaller firm Kalle joined the Hoechst alliance in 1907. Although competition within each alliance was not completely eliminated, particularly not in foreign markets, which were more difficult to control from the home office, competition was clearly reduced, allowing the German dye firms to continue making large profits until World War I.

Even Schoellkopf, although not formally a part of a cartel for black dyes in the United States, aligned its price policies with the cartel after a fierce price war. The firm had entered black dyes in 1900 (Reimer, 1996, p. 129), threatening the market share of the existing producers, among them Bayer. In 1908 Schoellkopf asked Bayer, with whom it had had a relatively good relationship since the days when Bayer licensed one of Schoellkopf's patents in 1888, to sponsor Schoellkopf's membership in the direct black convention (Reimer, 1996, p. 131). Schoellkopf was not admitted into the convention, but to create a truce between itself and European dye makers, Schoellkopf agreed on January 14, 1910, to sell direct black dyes at the same price as the cartel.

Did Managerial Action Make a Difference?

I want to emphasize that the invention of Benzopurpurin 4B was not a heroic deed based on a flash of genius but, while founded on a very sharp ability for observation, essentially due to luck.

> —CARL DUISBERG (1933, p. 48), on how he invented the dye that brought Bayer back to profitability in the mid-1880s [my translation]

We don't know what we're doing most of the time. We're making it up.

> —ROBERT SHAPIRO, CEO of Monsanto, commenting on the firm's strategy of leaving the chemical business and focusing on biotechnology, as quoted in *The Economist* (April 26, 1997, p. 66)[196]

Robert Shapiro's contemporary remark might just as well have been uttered more than 100 years ago by the leaders of such firms as Jäger, Bayer, and Levinstein, who wanted to switch their operation from natural dyes to new synthetic dyes. There were a great many unknowns in this switch: What would be the potential of the new technology in comparison to natural dyes? Who would buy the new dyes? How was it possible to sell at the same time to the high-fashion houses in Lyon and Paris and the traditional dyers in India and China?

For science-based industries in the early phases of their development, it is particularly difficult to predict what kinds of products will come from the scientific

---

[196] The quote comes at the end of a paragraph that gives more detail about Monsanto's current strategy: "Integrating so many disparate businesses – while at the same time sloughing off an old part of the firm – would test the mettle of any boss. But these acquisitions are based on little more than an intelligent guess about where the money is to be made in such a new industry. As Mr. Shapiro points out, there are no books on how to sell genetically modified seeds in places like China and India."

and technical breakthroughs. When success is produced by the interaction of many variables, decision makers face an enormous challenge in devising and implementing strategies. Given that managers 100 years ago, just as today, operated in a business world marked by enormous complexity, it is quite appropriate to ask whether firm managers are, in fact, able to enact strategies that will be consistent with a continuously changing competitive landscape. Perhaps firm success is due to the sheer luck of having picked the right strategy from many possible ones, rather than a rational evaluation of the environmental requirements and the strategies that may be consistent with these requirements. The challenge for the analyst of firm behavior is to find evidence that the work of decision makers did in fact have something to do with the success of the firm. Do the six case studies lend some support for the notion that managers made a difference for the performance outcome of individual firms?

A close look at the fates of individual firms suggests that they do, but managers are clearly not complete masters of their fate. Tracing the development of the six firms shows that some elements of success have to be attributed to luck and other elements can be linked to the purposive action of individual managers. Perkin's discovery of mauve was luck: He was looking for quinine. The commercial development of the dye with all the problems that had to be overcome was not pure luck: Consulting silk dyers such as Pullar and Keith before building a plant was a clever strategy to reduce risk. Similarly, Perkin's close interaction with users in developing application technology was an intentional strategy that paid off handsomely. Perkin made the carefully deliberated decision to sell out and devote himself to private scientific research. Instead, he could have decided to spend his entire energy on putting together a firm that would have pioneered a managerial firm in British industry.

Levinstein and Schoellkopf did better than their local rivals because they actively went out of their way to overcome the lack of scientific talent in their local environment and recruit it from Germany and Switzerland. The firm of BS&S could have done the same, but instead relied almost exclusively on British talent. The failure of American Aniline was to a large extent predictable: Bloede and his partner did not take the trouble to survey the market and their prospective rivals; they could have easily found there was not a market for aniline in the United States. A systematic evaluation of the strengths and weaknesses of their start-up operation in comparison to European dye firms would have also revealed that they would not stand a chance.

Levinstein could have tried to build a managerial hierarchy. As a one-man operation, Levinstein was as good as any of the other dye pioneers. He was cunning, sly, and driven to succeed. But his unwillingness to delegate important decisions to managers prevented Levinstein from building an organization that could compete with Bayer's economies of scale and scope. Although the British social context undoubtedly made it more difficult to create a managerial firm than in Germany, Chandler (1990) has shown that managerial firms were possible to create even in Britain, although it happened very infrequently. In the case of Levinstein, his personality was probably as much an obstacle to moving away from the personal firm as the British social context was.

Jäger and Bayer faced essentially the same external environment, being located in the same town and coming from the natural dye business. Both firms were lucky in the sense of being located in a national environment that was capable of providing local scientific and technical talent to a degree not available in Britain and the United

States. But what made Bayer a gigantic success by 1914 and Jäger a relative failure was the entrepreneurial spirit that came to Bayer in the person of Carl Rumpf and later Carl Duisberg. Rumpf pushed the firm into becoming a large alizarin producer, a move that had the potential to kill the firm, but in the end left it with stronger competitive skills than most German and foreign rivals. Bayer, like Jäger, was initially slow to develop connections to academic scientists when BASF, Hoechst, and AGFA shifted the competitive rules by making innovation a necessary component of any successful growth strategy. Rumpf paid for the first research chemists out of his own pocket when his organization did not want to move in this innovative direction, again making an intentional choice that was not replicated by the leaders of Jäger.

Carl Duisberg was hired for his chemical talents. Bayer was lucky that this academic chemist proved to be such a good manager as well. Under his leadership, Bayer systematically developed its R&D capability and invested in a new plant that had been designed in a systematic manner, not in the haphazard ways that Bayer previously expanded its plant facilities. By building up an organization that was constantly in search of new products and different ways of delivering the product to diverse customers, Bayer became one of the top three firms of the German dye industry.

New market or technological opportunities were often not predictable. But luck rewarded those who were persistent and prepared for these uncertainties as much as possible. To play on Pasteur's famous quote, "Chance favors the prepared mind," the experience of the synthetic dye industry shows that chance favors the prepared organization. By building large R&D laboratories, a firm such as Bayer was able to tame chance to a considerable extent. For those firms that could afford them, R&D laboratories were something of an insurance policy against the innovations that would almost invariably eventually destroy the value of existing dye products. Even when a competitor introduced a radical new dye, Bayer after the 1890s was typically able to develop other dyes that would preserve its position because it had access to sufficient capital and a large reservoir of know-how.

Those firms that had missed the boat of building research laboratories and in-house development departments when the first movers started to exploit this new organizational tool were simply left behind. Jäger, for instance, failed to make these investments and was reduced to an insignificant player in the dye industry.

When Bayer became a leading firm in the dye industry, it did not need nearly as much luck as it did earlier to be successful. Rivals that had fallen behind (e.g., Jäger) could not afford to make similar investments into organizational capabilities. Success became self-reinforcing. The divergence of the paths such as Bayer and Jäger suggests a powerful principle characterizing a world of increasing returns in which getting ahead in the beginning determines to a large extent who will win in the end: Success breeds more success, and failure breeds more failure. As we shall see in the next chapter, German firms also engaged collectively in actions that would limit the amount of luck necessary to prevail against their foreign rivals.

4 The Coevolution of National Industries and Institutions

> *While in former times industry has primarily profited from the advance of science, now the wonderful rise of industry provides the means for further advances in science* [my translation].
>
> —A. W. HOFMANN in his speech to the constituting gathering of the German Chemical Society in 1867, as quoted in Johnson (1992, p. 171)

> *[T]he active interest and support of business was a precondition for the setting up of most of the civic universities after 1850.*
>
> —MICHAEL SANDERSON in *The Universities and British Industry 1850–1970* (1972, p. 61)

> *The future of American industry is bound up with the future of American science. The schools of mines, engineering, and chemistry . . . are anxious and ready to undertake with great energy some of those specific tasks which will aid American industry to improve its products, to decrease its wastage, to coordinate processes and to multiply its resources for dealing satisfactorily with the many-sided human problems which industrial relationships and industrial enterprise of necessity involve.*
>
> —NICHOLAS MURRAY BUTLER, president of Columbia University, announcing in 1916 plans for a great industrial-research center at Columbia as quoted in Noble (1977, p. 145)

Overview of Collective Strategies

In many ways, this chapter is the most important contribution of the present work to the field of strategic management and its progress. In Chapter 2, I provided evidence that national institutions helped German dye firms to achieve their dominant position in the world. I essentially argued that the line of causation ran from the institutional environment to firms. Now I will argue that the causation also ran in the reverse direction as the industry developed. Institutions were not just a given and thus beyond the control of individual firms. They were also shaped and built by purposeful actions of firms (Pfeffer and Salancik, 1978).

This chapter develops empirical support for the argument that in the long run the firms in Germany were more successful than their British or American counterparts because they were more effective in collectively shaping their selection environment after the industry had taken off. Once German firms were ahead of their British and American rivals, superior economic performance and bigger size provided German firms with the resources and visibility to collectively influence their selection environment in a way that was not possible for the less successful British and American firms. A more favorable selection environment then set in motion powerful feedback processes that allowed German dye firms to extend their lead and eventually dominate the industry.

Here I will focus my analysis on how national university systems and patent laws were shaped by firms' actions, these institutions being the most visible locations of collective action. I will also briefly touch on trade policies because they provide an opportunity to bring into view other industries that competed with the dye industry for political support.

Once the German dye industry got started and expanded at a rapid pace, it became active in ensuring that the German academic system would turn out large numbers of highly trained organic chemists. The network of ties that were created between academic researchers and industrialists provided the tool to shape the institutional environment so that university science and dye firms would benefit even more. German dye firms were able to outperform rivals in other countries because a coalition between academic scientists, industrialists, and government officials allowed them to build an ever stronger system of research and training, on which the dye industry depended. Lacking this necessary economic clout or political muscle, British and American dye firms were not able to stimulate the development of a science capability in organic chemistry that was competitive with the German one.

Similarly, the changes in German patent laws concerning chemicals were not exogenous events but, to a large extent, were brought about by the collective body of the German chemical industry in alliance with the association of chemists. The social network that connected individual players was an important instrument in shaping German patent laws. Because British firms failed to bring about changes in British patent law that would have favored domestic firms, the evolution of patent laws constitutes another powerful example of how collections of national firms were sometimes able and sometimes unable to change their selection environment.

Forging a National Science Capability

We saw earlier (in Chapter 2) that enrollments in science and engineering grew much faster in Germany than in Britain. Germany trained the vast majority of organic chemists in the world before World War I. At the turn of the century, Prussia, the largest of the German states, spent almost 20 times more on universities than did all of Britain. Although trying to catch up with Germany's superior research and training system, Britain was still far behind Germany in 1914. Contemporary observers such as the great economist Alfred Marshall took notice of Germany's superior university system.

Calling it "the industrial leadership of Germany: science in the service of industry," Marshall devoted an entire chapter of his book *Industry and Trade* (1923) to analyzing the supportive role of the German university system in the development of industry. But Marshall had very little to say about the process by which some branches of German industry came to enjoy better support from universities than was the case in Britain.

A look behind the scenes of how research and training systems were funded reveals that in all three countries the size and quality of the university system were in part a result of industrial leaders taking actions. The three countries, however, differed enormously in the degree to which dye industry leaders became involved and were successful in building a strong research and training system. I already argued in Chapter 2 that the academic–industrial network played an important role in producing winners and losers in the dye industry. However, I did not feature one of the most important roles of the network in the earlier discussion, namely, its use as a tool for shaping the research and training system in each country. Because state authorities would have something to do with the provision of, or at least regulation of, education, government officials should be included in the analysis, for they were significant players who could either block or promote efforts to upgrade educational facilities. I will begin with Germany and then present the British case. Finally, I will feature the United States as a powerful *indirect* confirmation for a coevolutionary process.

Germany: A Triple Alliance

The expansion of the research and teaching system required large sums of money. Unlike the United States, where many private universities existed, German universities and research institutes were public entities, funded almost entirely by public monies. This meant that increased contributions to universities had to pass through the political process. Even though the German economy was expanding at unprecedented speed from 1857 to 1914, making it economically feasible to spend more on education, government officials and parliaments still had to be convinced to spend more money on education than on other politically popular programs.

Because the individual German states and not the central government were responsible for the provision of education (one exception was the newly formed University of Strasbourg, created in 1872 as an Imperial University after Alsace was annexed from France in 1871), individual state governments had to agree to spend more money on universities if the system was to expand. The academic–industrial network alone could not expand the university system; it had to work through parliaments, dukes, kings, the emperor, and, most importantly, government officials in charge of higher educational affairs. What forms did this process take?

Instead of examining the process in every single German state, I will restrict myself to the case of Prussia. Because it was the largest state, but even more importantly, because it was a laggard in its support for science and technical education (on a per capita basis) compared to such states as Baden and Bavaria (Borscheid, 1976), Prussia presents the most appropriate site for examining why spending on universities and Technische Hochschulen (technical universities) increased rapidly in the period from 1857 to 1914. More or less the same processes took place in the other states; the only difference was the cast of characters inside these governments. Hence it is much more useful to examine Prussia in detail rather than all of the states on a more superficial level.

Inside the Bureaucracy: "The System Althoff"[197]

To influence the direction of academic chemistry, the dye industry used several strategies. These strategies can be properly understood only after having developed some sense of how Prussian universities were administered. Let us take a quick look into section IIa of the Ministry of Religious, Educational and Medical Affairs (formed in 1817), which was in charge of administering Prussian higher education. Between 1882 and 1907 Friedrich Althoff was the bureaucrat who all handled professorial appointments at Prussian universities and Technische Hochschulen, serving under five successive ministers. Although he was never minister of education himself, not even the second in command, he became the most influential official in higher education in Germany by fashioning excellent connections to the parliament (in charge of the purse strings), the finance ministry (the dispenser of the money), the King of Prussia, concurrently Emperor of Germany (the actor with the highest prestige and discretion), industry (the source of support for his expansion plans), and the seats of power within academe (the important gatekeepers).

Not an uncontroversial figure inside and outside of higher education, he curtailed dramatically the autonomy of universities in appointing their teaching staff. He was able to do so by fashioning a very close network of relationships to all key constituencies in the educational policy arena. His power became so large that at times he was able to push through professorial appointments against the wish of university faculties. For instance, he forced the appointments of Emil Bering (1901 Nobelist in Medicine), Robert Koch (1905 Nobelist in Medicine), and Paul Ehrlich (1908 Nobelist in Medicine), who became the world's leading medical scientists of their generation (Brocke, 1980, pp. 93, 111). Furthermore, he decided to create centers of excellence at Prussian universities (e.g., Mathematics and Physics at Göttingen, Chemistry at Berlin) rather than trying to endow every university with high-quality talent in all fields. Critics saw his autocratic actions as evidence that Prussian universities suffered under his rule; supporters, in contrast, thought that he was the chief guarantor of quality by ensuring that the best people rather than friends and proteges of incumbent professors would be appointed.

The enormous expansion of universities, Technische Hochschulen, and the many research institutes formed after the 1880s was orchestrated from his desk. Althoff was the chief promoter behind expanding Emil Fischer's chemical institute in Berlin, which trained large numbers of organic chemists who later joined industry. Because he shared the vision that broad scientific and technological research and education would be of immense benefit to society, he was a key ally in the efforts of the dye industry to expand educational facilities. Furthermore, given his unique control over the direction of the Prussian university system and Prussia's trendsetting role for other German states, the dye industry would have to form an alliance with him if they wanted to be successful at all during his long tenure.

[197] I am relying chiefly on Brocke's (1980) superb essay *Hochschul- und Wissenschaftspolitik in Preußen und im Deutschen Kaiserreich 1882–1907: Das "System Althoff"* for my account of the internal organization of Prussia's higher education bureaucracy. See also Schmeiser's (1994) *Akademischer Harsard: Das Berufs-schicksal des Professors und das Schicksal der deutschen Universität 1870–1920* for an excellent study of the development of the German university system and the prospects of young academic talent.

Strategy One: Using Collective Organizations to Mobilize Support
Although individual contacts between firm leaders in some instances played a role, for example, the close personal relationship between Böttinger (Bayer) and Althoff (Brocke, 1980, p. 77), collective bodies were the main tools through which the dye industry marshaled the necessary political support for expanding the training of chemists and chemical technologists that were so crucial for their business. Carl Duisberg's (Bayer) draft of a petition, written in the name of the Association of German Chemists, to convince Prussian authorities to appoint more professors in chemistry is a good example of how dye firms engaged in collective action.

Concerns
Request of the *Verein deutscher Chemiker* [Association of German Chemists] for the creation of *Extraordinariaten* [Assistant Professorships] for general chemistry and technical chemistry in particular.

To the
Royal State Minister and
Minister of Religious, Educational and Medical
Affairs[198]
Mr. Dr. Bosse
Excellency
Berlin.

The German chemical industry, a source of our national wealth, has, thanks to the joint efforts of science and technology and thanks to the continuous support of the Imperial and state governments, reached a height that aroused envy in all nations that compete with us on the world market and stimulated those nations to take more initiatives than previously in improving their chemical industry and their chemical science...

It would be a crime against our nation,[199] if we should rest here and not do everything possible to keep, in the competition of peoples, always our leading position in the chemical sector...

While most *Technische Hochschulen* possess the professorships in the different specialities that are necessary for the education of chemists, the universities, which are preferred by many industrialists for some branches of chemical technology, lack a sufficient number of qualified and experienced teachers, particularly representatives and teachers of technical chemistry. Only the University of Berlin has a professorship in technical chemistry besides an institute...

[198] The adjective "religious" strikes me as a better translation of the German word *geistliche* than the more literal translation "spiritual."
[199] The German phrase is "Es hieße unserer Nation Frevel begehen." The word *Frevel* could also be translated as "sin."

We present your Excellency therefore with our devoted request to appoint qualified teachers, particularly at universities close to the centers of the chemical industry, and make available those small sums required for the purpose. Those academics also will be better qualified to serve as experts in all governmental and legal questions.

> Your Excellency's devoted
> Chairman of the Association of German Chemists
>
> Petition of 1897, as reprinted in Duisberg (1923, pp. 153–4) [my translation]

How effective and necessary the actions of the dye industry's collective bodies were in expanding research and teaching facilities is also evident from the testimonies of academics. Professor Emil Fischer, for example, who had already received the Nobel Prize in Chemistry in 1902, sent the following letter to the German Chemical Industry Association after having received well-wishes from the association on the occasion of his sixtieth birthday, October 9, 1912.

Recognizing that scientific and industrial work must go hand in hand, your association cultivated from its very beginning friendly and close relations with the teachers of chemistry at universities. I still particularly remember with great thankfulness the very effective help that your association gave me 15 years ago, when it lobbied the Prussian finance ministry with the weight of its reputation for the construction of new buildings for the Chemical Institute of the University of Berlin . . . I hope that the chemical industry and chemical science will maintain their friendly[200] relations for their mutual benefit, and I remain

> with high respect
> your very devoted
> Emil Fischer
>
> Letter reprinted in Ungewitter (1927, p. 40) [my translation]

Strategy Two: Working on the Parliament Directly
When Henry Böttinger (one of Bayer's directors) won a seat in the Prussian parliament as a member of the National-Liberal Party, he used this public platform to advance the educational goals of the dye industry directly (Duisberg, 1923, p. 181). Because he was a very close friend of Althoff (Brocke, 1980, p. 17) and the Prussian finance minister, Baron Georg von Rheinhaben (Johnson, 1992, p. 79), he could coordinate

---

[200] The German word here is *freundschaftliche*. It could also be translated as "close."

his parliamentary proposals with the key players inside the Prussian government to increase educational spending.

Strategy Three: Creating Private–Public Academic Partnerships

Böttinger and Althoff worked together on numerous projects to upgrade German science and engineering education. At the turn of the century, they created a new organizational form in the German research and teaching landscape, a public and private partnership to sponsor industrially relevant applied research. The Göttinger Vereinigung zur Förderung der angewandten Physik (Göttinger Association for the Advancement of Applied Physics) was financed in large part by private firms (Burchardt, 1992, p. 20). The success of this partnership paved the way for a large effort that began in 1905 to improve chemical research in Germany.

The Alliance in Action: The Formation of the Kaiser Wilhelm Institute for Chemistry

The collective efforts that lay behind the formation of a German Research Institute in Chemistry are also very instructive about the collective processes that made the growth of the German research and teaching system possible.[201] In the first years of the twentieth century, several academics and chemical firms increasingly felt that German universities did not satisfy industry's need for basic research that could lead to industrial applications. Searching for ways to remedy this problem, the industry formed an alliance with German academics and government officials to form special research institutes.[202]

Following the tireless efforts of the industrialist Werner Siemens (head of the Siemens electric firm), the German government had already agreed in 1887 to finance the Imperial Institute for Physics and Technology. Initially, the plan was to create a similar Imperial Research Institute for Chemistry, also financed by the central government. The organizing effort started in 1905 when three academic chemists, Emil Fischer, Walter Nernst, and Wilhelm Ostwald, sent a memorandum outlining the plans for a chemical research institute to some forty academics and industrialists (Johnson, 1992, p. 48). Before mailing out the letter inviting representatives from industry and academe to join the efforts to form such an institute, Emil Fischer had discussed the plans with Althoff. Althoff agreed to give the director of the planned institute a full professorship at the University of Berlin, providing prestige and financial support for the position. Otto Witt (at this point Professor at the Technische Hochschule and editor of the journal of the Chemical Industry Association) used his excellent ties to the Prussian government (already in 1893 the minister of education, Bosse, had sent him to report on the International Exhibition in Chicago; see Witt, 1894),

---

[201] Jeffrey Johnson's excellent monograph *The Kaiser's Chemists* (1990) provides a very detailed study of how industry, academia, and the German government cooperated to form the first basic research institutes in chemistry.

[202] German industrial leaders had increasingly begun to see the United States and not Britain as their true industrial rival. By all accounts, visiting German industrialists were awed by the enormous size of American plants and their productivity (Duisberg, 1933). One of the motivations for creating more fundamental research capabilities was the fear that the newly formed and richly endowed Rockefeller and Mellon research institutes would jeopardize German leadership in science-based industries (Johnson, 1990).

academe, and industry to enlist all important dye industry representatives for the effort.[203]

Because the social insurance schemes and the military buildup put large new demands on the Imperial budget, the Imperial government was reluctant to provide the funding. To help garner both financial and political support for their plans, academics and industrialists welcomed the idea of recruiting the emperor to lend his name to a new scientific association, the Kaiser Wilhelm Society for the Advancement of Sciences, to be financed largely by private and corporate philanthropy.[204]

Under its wings three chemical research institutes were created between 1911 and 1914. Dye-industry representatives formed the largest contingent of industrialists on the board of directors of the Kaiser Wilhelm Institute for Chemistry and made substantial financial contributions. Every large dye firm was involved: von Brünning (Hoechst), Oppenheim (AGFA), von Böttinger (Bayer), von Brunck (BASF), Duisberg (Bayer), and ter Meer (ter Meer) joined leading academics such as Emil Fischer and Carl Liebermann as well as government officials on the board (Ungewitter, 1927, p. 436; Johnson, 1992, pp. 99–101). Emil Fischer could rely on Althoff's and Böttinger's help in getting the state government of Prussia to donate the land upon which the first two institutes (The Kaiser Wilhelm Institutes for Chemistry and Physical Chemistry) were to be built in Berlin-Dahlem (Ungewitter, 1927, p. 434).

A third Kaiser Wilhelm Institute was dedicated to coal research and opened in Mühlheim on the Ruhr River just before the war. This third institute received even more funds directly from industry: The giant coal corporations of the Ruhr shouldered large portions of the yearly costs of running the institute, which was led by high caliber chemists who were given the money to work on projects that were too large to be financed with the moneys available to university research laboratories (Johnson, 1990).

When the Alliance Breaks Down

It would be wrong to think that industry had full control over how universities would develop. The close alliance between academics and industrialists did break down at times, as the case of the chemical education reform movement shows. First a group led by Carl Alexander Martius (AGFA) attempted to use the Chemical Industry Association for the purpose of persuading the government to institute a state examination for chemists at the end of their university studies analogous to the practice for lawyers (Scholz, 1992, p. 223). The industrialists hoped that such an examination would force universities to create students who would be better prepared for industry. The examination would have tested students on a broad range of chemistry topics instead of allowing them to gain a university degree by simply writing a dissertation, typically on a very narrow subject that fell into the research agenda of the dissertation adviser.

---

[203] See Johnson (1990, pp. 55–8) for a full list of the members of the select and general Committee for the Founding of an Imperial Chemical Institute.

[204] Since 1948, the Kaiser Wilhelm Society for the Advancement of Sciences has operated under the name "Max Planck Society," supporting more than thirty-five research institutes scattered throughout Germany. I finished this book while I was visiting one of them, the Max Planck Institute for Research into Economic Systems in Jena (http://www.mpiew-jena.mpg.de/), for seven months in 2002.

The first attempt did not go far because neither the Prussian Ministry of Education nor the university professors thought this was a good idea.

In 1896 Carl Duisberg and Henry Böttinger, the leaders of the Bayer corporation, made a second organized attempt, enlisting this time the Association of German Chemists and starting a large public campaign.[205] The strength of the movement at that point prompted the German chemistry professors under the leadership of Wilhelm Ostwald and Adolf von Baeyer to form an association of all laboratory directors (Verband der Laboratoriumsvorstände an Deutschen Hochschulen), the purpose of which was to defeat the movements by industry and the Association of German Chemists (Scholz, 1992, p. 224). A state examination would have dramatically curtailed the chemistry professors' autonomy in running their laboratories and would have made it more difficult to attract students, because it would have become possible to receive a university degree without taking a doctorate. To take away the momentum of the pro-state examination lobby, the university teachers agreed voluntarily to introduce an examination for chemists (Verbandsexamen) after the basic courses had been taken. But professors, not the state, would design and administer it.

At this point, the consensus among dye firms fell apart during the general meeting of the Chemical Industry Association in 1897. Only the representatives of Bayer were still eager to force a state examination; the other dye firms thought that professors would be well-equipped to design their own exam (Scholz, 1992, p. 224).

The episode illustrates that industrialists had a great deal of influence over what would happen at universities. Still, when their interests clashed with university teachers, industrialists could at best achieve only part of their agenda in shaping education.

Britain: Under the Curse of Having Been the Leader

As in Germany, industrialists actively shaped the research and training system in Britain.[206] A coalition between academicians and leaders of firms was successful in expanding research and training opportunities, but not nearly to the same extent as in Germany. A survey held in 1902 by the British Association for the Advancement of Science found that in a sample of 502 chemists employed in the British chemical industry, only 59 were graduates of schools of higher education (Morrell, 1993, p. 108). This means that, unlike in Germany, even by 1902 only a small fraction of British chemists were trained at institutions that were at the forefront of research in chemistry. The remainder continued to be educated by polytechnics, local colleges, evening classes, and the like.

Several factors were responsible for the British inability to catch up with Germany. Most importantly, a strong bureaucracy championing higher education was missing (Wrigley, 1987, p. 163). The alliance between civically minded industrialists and academics was dramatically weakened by not having this third element that made the German lobbying alliance so successful. Because the British industry had been the world leader for many decades, the awareness of the link between education

---

[205] The campaign for the state examination for chemists left a long paper trail. See, for example, the writings of Carl Duisberg (1923, pp. 189–93, 196–209), who was one of the main protagonists in the phase around the turn of the century.

[206] Sanderson's *The British Universities and British Industry, 1850–1970* (1972) remains the most valuable book on the subject of how business participated in creating and upgrading universities in Britain.

and industrial progress was much weaker in British society and its ruling classes than in Germany.[207] This made it more difficult to bring society's spending up to the same level as in Germany. Furthermore, as we already have seen, the British dye industry was collectively not as organized as the German industry.[208] Because the dye industry fell far behind that of Germany in terms of size, the British alliance between industrialists and academics did not enjoy nearly as many resources and as much political clout as the German one.

In examining the influence of industry on the development of universities in Britain, it is necessary to make a distinction between Oxford and Cambridge and the other English universities.[209] Because Oxford and Cambridge until 1900 were not receptive to the idea of training large numbers of students in science and technology, industrial interests were largely behind the creating of new universities in the industrial cities of England (Sanderson, 1972). As I mentioned before, the Royal College of Chemistry was initially (in 1845) founded and funded by private individuals. When some of the donors become disappointed with the "practical returns" to their investments and lost interest in the project, the government chose to step in and absorb the Royal College of Chemistry into the Royal School of Mines (Bud and Roberts, 1984).

Manchester

Particularly close was the relationship between industry and civic universities in the North of England, especially in Manchester. The local Owens College was created in 1846 when the successful businessman John Owens left £100,000 to set up a college to "teach such learning and sciences as were unusual in universities" (Sanderson, 1972, p. 62). But the college became a success in chemical education only when Henry E. Roscoe (who received part of his education under Bunsen in Heidelberg, Germany) was appointed professor in 1857. Roscoe restructured the curriculum into a four-year program that became very popular with students. During his long tenure from 1857 to 1885 (Nye, 1993, p. 38), he managed to turn the poor finances of the

---

[207] But as I argued in Chapter 2, there was clearly some awareness in Britain of the link between education and industrial progress. The various Parliamentary Commissions in the second half of the nineteenth century served as a forum to air the view that British industries would suffer by falling behind Germany in technical education. See Cardwell (1957), Bud and Roberts (1984), and Alter (1987) for details.

[208] I have not seen as strong a coalition between British industrialists and academics for influencing a national institution such as higher education or patent laws. This may be a sample selection bias because I know the German literature on the dye industry somewhat better than I do the British. Clearly, professors, industrialists, and civil servants met sporadically within the framework of the various Parliamentary Commissions. I have, however, many reasons to believe that Levinstein, Playfair, Roscoe, Schorlemmer, Holliday, and the other players never formed as strong a coalition for advancing education as their German counterparts did. They acted more as individuals: Levinstein writing editorials and giving speeches (e.g., 1886) in which he warned Britain that Germany would surpass all British industries that were based on science and technology, Playfair heading government committees and writing reports (e.g., 1868) in which he gave the same prescient warnings as Levinstein. But I have not seen British academics and industrialists work for longer periods of time on the same national committee toward a common goal as the Germans did frequently. Such collective bodies as the Association of German Chemists or the Chemical Industry Association were missing on the British scene, making it much more difficult to coordinate efforts of industrialists and academics.

[209] Given that the dye industry was centered around London and Manchester, I will restrict my analysis to English universities and not discuss Scottish, Welsh, and Irish institutions.

institution around by recruiting leading manufacturers to support the college.[210] In 1866, for example, Roscoe persuaded the cotton manufacturer Thomas Ashton (a fellow Heidelberg student) to help him enlist other manufacturers for support. This effort raised £200,000 that allowed the college to move to new quarters in 1873. From his detailed studies of the new civic universities in England, Sanderson concludes that Manchester became the best endowed of all modern universities in England.

Because chemical knowledge was becoming more important in the dyeing and printing industries that played such a large role in the economy of Manchester and its environs, a chair in organic chemistry was created at Owens in 1874. The first holder was Carl Schorlemmer, also a chemist with German connections. In 1885 Julius Cohen, an Adolf Baeyer student, was made a demonstrator for Schorlemmer. Cohen introduced practical organic chemistry at Owens College (Morrell, 1993, p. 107). When Schorlemmer died in 1892, he was succeeded by W. H. Perkin Jr., who also had received part of his education under Baeyer in Munich. Perkin managed to build Manchester into the leading British school of organic chemistry before World War I (Morrell, 1993, p. 110).

Ivan Levinstein, the owner of the largest British dye works between 1875 and 1914, actively championed the improvement of technical education in Manchester. On the governing board of Owens College for many years (Fox, 1987, p. 28), he hoped that his efforts would lead to chemists and engineers being locally trained so that his firm would no longer have to hire German and Swiss talent. He financially supported a second chemical laboratory at Owens that "was not to instruct dyers and printers but to train graduates for leading positions in industry, especially dye works, via technical organic research, especially the synthesis of new dyes in quantities sufficient for industrial purposes" (Morrell, 1993, p. 109). Levinstein's action makes clear that until that date the more successful industries around Manchester, namely, printing and dyeing, were the ones that had induced Owens College to teach subjects that would be of use to their firms. Economic interests in every nation were powerful forces in pushing schools of higher education to offer a curriculum that would coincide with the needs of local businesses.

Technical Education in Leeds, Bradford, and Huddersfield

The local textile, dyeing, and printing industries in Leeds, Bradford, and Huddersfield tried to improve the technical schools in their vicinity with the clear purpose of improving their own competitiveness versus foreign firms. In all three towns, courses in color chemistry were made available (Travis, 1992, p. 218). Leeds had particularly strong support from the textile industry (Sanderson, 1972, p. 80). Together with Manchester, Leeds probably had the best dyeing school in the world. According to Sanderson (1972, p. 23), its dye school was clearly better than what Berlin could offer at the time. Such notable dye chemists as A. G. Green and then A. G. Perkin (another son of W. H. Perkin)

---

[210] Sir Henry Roscoe left a very large literary estate. Sanderson reports (1972, p. 83) that his letter books (Letter Books of Sir Henry Roscoe 1866–1878; 1878–1883. Manchester University Library MSS. CHR107, 108) "display a remarkable range of advisory work" for firms around Manchester. They would allow a very valuable case study of the science–industry interface in the British chemical industry during the second half of the nineteenth century.

held the chair in color chemistry at the Yorkshire College, which was later upgraded to the University of Leeds. In 1890, for example, Yorkshire College at Leeds set out to improve its organic chemistry capabilities by hiring Julius Cohen away from Manchester (Morrell, 1993, p. 107). The *Yorkshire Daily Post* could report on September 19, 1894:

When one compares the character of the trade of Leeds and the district of two decades ago with what it is at the present day and considers that many of the most important mills in the locality are supervised by Yorkshire College men, it becomes evident that the instruction imparted in that institution has in no small degree benefited the weaving industries of the city and the neighborhood (quoted in Sanderson, 1972, p. 86).

Although such dye-making firms as Read Holliday and Dan Dawson in Huddersfield benefited from the improvements in local schools, the schools were primarily designed to assist the very successful printing and dyeing industries of the area.

But let us return once more to the role of Roscoe in organizing the science–industry interface. Roscoe undoubtedly was to Britain what Hofmann was to Germany, with the only, and perhaps crucial, difference that Hofmann was an organic chemist who ventured fully into dye chemistry, whereas Roscoe was a general chemist. (For the German dye industry it was clearly an advantage to have an organic dye chemist at the center of the link between science and industry.) Sanderson observes that "it is quite impossible to do justice to or exaggerate the importance of Roscoe as the new model of the English industrially oriented scientific professor, as a conceiver of the idea of a civic university serving local industry, and as a founder of modern chemical education in this country" (1972, p. 84). As the leading professor–consultant in the British chemical industry, Roscoe organized with Ludwig Mond and George Davis the Society of Chemical Industry and served as the first president of the society. Furthermore, he helped turn Owens College in Manchester into a full-fledged university with a Royal Charter. Roscoe also became a member of Parliament, helping to pass the Technical Education Act (Cardwell, 1957, p. 127).

Imperial College, London

Roscoe was also one of the leading promoters behind the formation of the Imperial College in London. It was organized in 1907 as a merger of the Royal School of Mines, the Royal College of Science, and the City and Guilds College. The intention was to create a British institution that would close the gap in higher education with Germany. The institution was consciously modeled after the Technische Hochschule in Berlin. Unlike other London schools, Imperial College had quite lavish private support from rich bankers who had taken seriously the warning of imminent loss of British industrial leadership by Lyon Playfair, Ivan Levinstein, and others. But unlike the civic universities in the North, Imperial College was not supported by local industry (Sanderson, 1972, p. 116). William Ramsay (1904 Nobel Laureate in Chemistry), who in recognition of his long service to various branches of industry was elected President of the Society of Chemical Industry, complained in 1902 that although the university could continue to turn out excellent chemists "yet the demand for such men is not keeping up with the supply. Manufacturers are not as yet sufficiently alive to the necessity of employing chemists" (as quoted in Sanderson, 1972, p. 117).

Still, a lack of demand by London firms did not prevent a dye firm in northern England, the Huddersfield firm Read Holliday, from working closely on the new technology of sulfide dyes with Professors G. T. Morgan and Frances Micklewait of the chemical department of the college. Dyes and gas were the two industrial linkages Imperial College had before World War I (Sanderson, 1972, p. 108). Indeed, Imperial College here started to serve the function of catching up with Germany in the science of dyes, as the promoters had intended.

Coevolutionary Dynamics

An industry that was falling behind its foreign competitors, an industry in which some of the most important leaders were retiring early, and one that did not systematically lobby for better educational facilities (e.g., Perkin and Nicholson) was not such fertile ground for stimulating the buildup of a strong scientific and technological base that would support the industry. Between 1857 and 1914, scientific and technical training programs expanded significantly in Britain but not at the same rate as in Germany. A chief cause lay in the resistance of British firms to hiring many university graduates at the time that German firms were staffing large R&D laboratories with many chemists and hiring engineers to build efficient production processes. This underlines how coming relatively late into the era of industry was a blessing for Germany because firm managers were not encumbered by an outdated model that saw university graduates as an inappropriate tool for improving the efficiency of production (Wrigley, 1987, pp. 173–5). A relatively small domestic demand for organic chemists did not allow British universities to build up large research and teaching programs in organic chemistry.

This created a vicious cycle. When progressive firms (i.e., Levinstein) wanted to hire academic organic chemists and production engineers, they typically had to import German and Swiss talent before 1900 because British universities did not produce the same quality of graduates. Unless British firms paid these foreigners more than they would make at home, they would not be able to hire the best talent away from Germany and Switzerland. Either paying more or having lesser talent would put them at a competitive disadvantage with German firms. When British industry then lost more and more market share to the German firms, it did not have the resources to support universities and lobby to expand the system to the same degree as in Germany. Whereas in Germany success bred the resources for more success, in Britain the relative decline caused a lack of resources that led to further decline. In Germany's case the process of expanding universities was self-multiplying; in the British case it was self-limiting.[211]

Between 1895 and 1914 even the largest British firms (Levinstein and Read Holliday) were in danger of going out of business. British universities and technical colleges have often been blamed for having been the source of British industrial decline. But studying the management practices of British firms makes it evident that the greater unwillingness of British firms to hire scientists and engineers before

---

[211] Consider the counterfactual scenario of Britain training more chemists than jobs available before the rise of the dye industry. Under these circumstances many chemists would have been "forced to become entrepreneurs" as in the case of Germany. In this scenario it would have been less difficult to expand educational offerings because more firms would have been around to hire graduates. Instead of such a positive cycle, however, Britain was caught in the reverse process. The fact that educational facilities expanded at all is testimony of the persistent efforts by progressive industrialists and typically German-trained scientists.

1914 was intimately connected with the problem. Given the analytical difficulty of separating demand and supply dynamics here, it is necessary to consider both to understand why British universities did not catch up with their German counterparts.

United States: The Land of Unlimited Practical Opportunities

David Noble's *America by Design: Science, Technology and the Rise of Corporate Capitalism* (1977) documents in rich detail how educational programs at both private and public American universities were shaped by industrial players. A comparative reading of the American history of higher education suggests that the influence of industrialists was even stronger than in Germany (see in particular Flexner, 1930; Brubacher and Rody, 1958; and Ben-David, 1971). In Germany high-quality universities preceded the age of large-scale industry; in the United States universities and industry developed more concurrently. Because of the practical orientation of American culture and industrialists, universities were under stronger pressure than in Germany to turn out students with useful skills.

Because the United States did not possess a significant domestic dye industry, dye firms had very little clout to induce the rapidly growing state universities to create programs in organic chemistry and dye chemistry in particular or even to collect large, private donations to establish such programs. The case of the United States illustrates once again the strong mutual dependency between economic and academic development. In those sectors where American firms were strong, academic strength would develop rather quickly. The oil and steel industries (besides agriculture) were the sectors that first made use of academic chemists. Skolnick and Reese (1976, p. 2) report that "in 1855, Benjamin Silliman, Jr., professor of chemistry at Yale College, had completed the first scientific analysis of petroleum. Petroleum refining was booming by the early 1880s when Standard Oil Co. hired George Saybolt, probably the first full-time chemist in the industry." The American oil industry dominated the world market in the second half of the nineteenth century because of its efficient production methods. Skolnick and Reese also cite Andrew Carnegie as being the first industrialist to hire trained scientists to do full-time research on the problems in steelmaking (1976, p. 2). Of such problems Carnegie would say later, "Nine-tenths of the uncertainties were dispelled under the burning sun of chemical knowledge" (Skolnick and Reese, 1976, p. 2).

Andrew Carnegie represented the avant-garde of American industrialists. Most firms were only interested in hiring university graduates who could help them with their practical production processes. The large paper, glass, oil-refining, and electrical firms worked very hard to ensure that the expanding universities and colleges would teach students how to solve industrial problems. The academic discipline of chemical engineering, which Nathan Rosenberg (1998) has appropriately called a "distinctly American achievement," in my view reflects the power of industrialist interests to influence the research agenda and curriculum at American universities.[212] At the time

---

[212] For an account of the development of chemical engineering in Britain and Germany, see the excellent papers by Rosenberg (1998) and Landau (1997). Servos (1980) focuses on the pioneering role of MIT in chemical engineering. Two volumes edited by Furter (1980, 1982) provide a wealth of information on the history of chemical engineering the world over. A paper by Guédon in Furter (1980) places the American achievements in chemical engineering in proper perspective against those of Britain and Germany.

when American academics (chiefly at the Massachusetts Institute of Technology [MIT]) developed the unit operations paradigm that abstracted what elementary chemical production processes were common across all chemical process industries, inorganic and physical chemistry had already developed the theory of thermodynamics, which would later in the 1950s deliver the key concepts for chemical engineering (Buchholz, 1979). But because American industry in the nineteenth and early twentieth century would not have supported the abstract and mathematical science that chemical engineering developed into after World War II, the entire rise of chemical engineering in the United States took place on the basis of a curriculum that had enormous practical value for American industry (Buchholz, 1979, p. 54). Fundamental scientific research as practiced at German universities and Technische Hochschulen was rare in the United States before World War I (see especially Landau, 1997, on the difference between Germany and the United States as reflected in the curricula for chemistry and chemical engineering).

Given the weakness of the American dye industry and the ability of American dye firms to hire British, German, and Swiss chemists, American universities had neither a strong incentive nor the necessary support to upgrade their capabilities in organic chemistry the way they did in inorganic chemistry and chemical engineering. Arthur D. Little, the pioneer of industrial research in chemistry and chief promoter of chemical engineering at MIT, rightly pointed out that American industrialists faced much better investment opportunities than those offered by synthetic dyes, which had been dominated by the Germans since the 1870s[213]:

We should first of all review our own almost boundless natural resources and especially should we consider our gigantic and shameful waste. They offer opportunity for the ultimate development of a score of industries, each of a magnitude comparable to the color industry of Germany, and for the almost immediate upbuilding of hundreds of smaller enterprises no less profitable (1915, p. 239).

The situation changed only during and after World War I, when the buildup of an organic chemicals industry became a national concern. Firms like Du Pont then became active in helping to create a strong U.S. research and teaching base in organic chemicals.

---

[213] Given Arthur D. Little's expertise and eminent position at the interface between science and industry in the United States, it is interesting to hear what he had to say about why the United States did not build a strong dye industry:

The plain underlying reason why we have been unable during thirty years of tariff protection to develop in this country an independent and self-contained coal-tar industry while during the same period the Germans have magnificently succeeded is to be found in the failure of our manufacturers and capitalists to realize the creative power and earning capacity of industrial research. This power and this capacity have been recognized by Germany and on them as corner-stones her industries are based. As a result the German color plants are now quite capable of meeting the demands of the whole world when peace is once restored. Why, then, should we duplicate them only to plunge into an industrial warfare against the most strongly fortified industrial position in the world. Let us rather console ourselves with a few reflections and then see how otherwise we might spend our money to our better advantage (1915, p. 239).

Lobbying for a Supportive Patent System

> *The time of secrecy is over. Those who want to present their peers in the profession with a chemical puzzle in the last quarter of the 19th century must expect that the puzzle will be solved sooner or later* [my translation].
>
> —A. W. HOFMANN (1877, p. 390), defending himself against the charge (by Heinrich Caro and others) that he was not justified in publishing the chemical formula of a new BASF dye

> *The disappearance of company secrets was an unexpected blessing for the development of the [German] dye industry* [my translation].
>
> —HEINRICH CARO (1892, p. 959)

Even if there had been no patent protection in any of the three countries, Germany would have outperformed the British and American dye industries.[214] But without patents in Germany and in other large dye markets, the German dye industry would not have been able to acquire a virtual monopoly. Earlier in Chapter 2, I argued that the differences in the intellectual property right regimes across the three countries during the period from 1857 to 1914 were in part responsible for Germany's dominance. The patent laws were presented in that section as if they were simply given in the social environment. Now I will show that dye firms in Britain and Germany, in fact, tried very hard to influence the nature of the patent laws but had differing success. I will explore in detail the mechanisms that made German firms more successful than their British rivals in obtaining a domestic patent system that provided a competitive advantage. Two factors stand out. German dye firms and their industry association were more effective in organizing themselves and their lobbying efforts than was the British industry. Furthermore, just as in the case of the lobbying efforts in education, the bigger size and larger profits of the German industry gave it more resources and clout than its British rival industry had.

The Shaping of German Patent Law
Episode One: The Exception
The creation of the all-German patent law in 1877 can be illuminated by examining it through the conceptual lenses of the social movement perspective. Davis and Thompson (1994, p. 152) explain that "[t]he political process model of social movements emphasizes the role of opportunities provided by the *political climate*, particularly major *disruptions* in the political status quo, and the role of insurgent consciousness flowing out of a *shared interpretation* that a political system has lost legitimacy and is vulnerable to new demands for rights from the *aggrieved population*" [my italics].

The formation of the German Empire in 1871 under Prussian leadership constituted a major *political disruption*. Attempts to harmonize patent laws had been tried and had failed since the 1840s. The polities in the thirty-nine states were not willing to give up their own patent rules. But suddenly the formation of the empire largely

---

[214] The statement, of course, assumes that all other conditions remained the same.

eliminated the power of individual states to block an all-German patent law because the right to pass patent law now rested with the national government.

The dye industry was clearly not the driving force behind the German patent law. The *aggrieved population* was German engineers, who had felt for a long time that they did not possess the status within German society they deserved, given their professional achievements. In 1856 German engineers had formed a professional organization, Verein deutscher Ingenieure (Association of German Engineers), to press their cause.[215] This organization took as one of the central items on its agenda in the 1860s the need to create a strong patent protection in all German states (Zimmermann, 1965, p. 22). However, the Association did not succeed because the forces against patent protection were stronger.[216]

Only a change in the *political climate* gave the propatent forces the upper hand. In 1873 the German economy plunged into a recession, strengthening the protectionist forces in Germany. Because propatent forces were able to convince a broad audience of the argument that patents, like tariffs, would protect domestic producers, they were able to achieve a level of political support within parliament they had never enjoyed before (Machlup, 1958, p. 5; Heggen, 1975, p. 125). Furthermore, the formation of the empire increased nationalist sentiments in Germany, sentiments that also penetrated the economic sphere (Stern, 1977, p. 184). An all-German patent system could be conveniently "marketed" as a timely act to affirm the nation.

A strong social movement needs an organization. Davis and Thompson (1994, p. 152) also explain:

Incentives are neither necessary nor sufficient for collective action. Instead, movement activity flows from effective social organizing among actors, typically drawing on preexisting social structures.[217]

Stimulated by the 1873 international patent congress in Vienna,[218] Werner von Siemens (of Siemens electric) relied on his existing contacts in the propatent

---

[215] Heinrich Caro, at the time only 22 years old, was one of the founders of the association (Zimmermann, 1965, p. 22)

[216] A strong movement to eliminate patents altogether developed in the North German Union of States, which was created after Prussia's victory over Austria in 1866. Chancellor Bismarck was advised by the finance ministry in 1868 to propose to parliament the complete abolition of the patent system. Prussia's bureaucracy was supported in its plans by the association of German economists, which had declared in 1863 that patents are harmful for economic growth (Zimmermann, 1965, p. 16). Propatent forces barely marshalled enough clout to make Bismarck delay the abolition drive in parliament (Heggen, 1975, p. 102). One of the organizations involved in stopping the abolition move was the newly formed German Chemical Society. As its president, A. W. Hofmann wrote a petition to parliament emphasizing that patent protection was an important public policy for stimulating economic growth (Heggen, 1975, p. 104). This marked Hofmann's entry into patent lobbying in Germany.

[217] Tilly's *From Mobilization to Revolution* (1978, particularly Chapter 3) and McAdam, McCarthy, and Zald's *Comparative Perspectives on Social Movements* (1996, particularly the introduction) provide a good overview of the organizational requirements of successful collective action.

[218] To get American manufacturers to display their products at the 1873 International Exhibition in Vienna, the Austrian government had to provide transitory patent protection. The propatent forces around Werner von Siemens used the occasion of the American boycott threat to convince the chief organizer of the exhibition, Baron von Schwar-Senborn, to hold an international patent congress of propatent forces with delegates from all major industrialized countries. One of the resolutions of the congress was to form national organizations in every country that could press the cause of a strong patent protection (Heggen, 1975, pp. 111–16).

movement – especially on the membership and the organization of the Associa-tion of German Engineers, of which he was a prominent member – to form the Deutscher Patentschutzverein (German Association for Patent Protection) in 1874 (Wetzel, 1991, p. 253).[219] Siemens became its chairman. Carl Alexander von Martius and his old teacher August Wilhelm Hofmann were among the few members who had a background in organic chemicals (Ungewitter, 1927, p. 285).[220]

The German Association for Patent Protection was very successful in exploiting the change in political climate and putting a patent law on the legislative agenda. By spring 1877, the German national parliament was debating the passage of the first all-German patent law. The proposed law formulated by the Imperial government would have granted product patents for chemicals and pharmaceuticals. Only at this point did the chemical community become an important force in the shaping of the patent law. Realizing that nothing could have stopped a patent law now, the chemical community at best could try to affect changes in formulation of the patent law that would further its own interests.

The dye industry was far from unified on the questions of patents in the years before an all-German patent law became imminent. Although Martius, the cofounder of AGFA, promoted the creation of an all-German patent system in any way possible, Heinrich Brüning of Hoechst (who happened to be on the government commission in charge of preparing the patent law) was strongly against any patent protection in the chemical industry (Wetzel, 1991, p. 253). After all, the German firms had become successful by copying British and French innovations. And there was the example of France, where a sweeping product patent had in the minds of many dye industry leaders destroyed the French dye industry. Furthermore, some firms such as BASF had been burnt by the Prussian patent-granting practices, which took a very narrow approach to inventor rights (Zimmermann, 1965, p. 20; Wetzel, 1991, p. 253).[221]

Because a chemical industry association was not yet in existence, the German Chemical Society was the organization that could perhaps broker an agreement be-tween academic chemists and dye firms on the issue of what kind of patents should be given for chemicals and pharmaceuticals and also speak with an authoritative voice for all chemists. On the basis of a proposal by Carl Alexander von Martius, the German Chemical Society formed a special commission in 1876 to deal with the status of chemical patents in the new law. Martius and Hofmann wanted to make sure that chemicals and pharmaceuticals were not going to be eliminated from the patent law.

To get more members of the German Chemical Society and the dye industry behind his patent plans, Hofmann strategically published the formulas of dyestuffs

---

[219] Siemens had written an essay in 1863 on the advantages of the patent system that became the point of reference for the subsequent patent discussion. Many of Siemens's electricity-related patent applications had been rejected by the Prussian authorities, making him a fierce advocate of patent reform (Heggen, 1975, p. 92).

[220] Hofmann and Martius were, in fact, members of the Board of Directors of the German Association for Patent Protection (Johnson, 1992, p. 175; Meinel, 1992, p. 45).

[221] In 1869 BASF had filed two alizarin process patent applications in Prussia. The second one represented an improvement over the first one. It was rejected because, according to the patent examiners, it did not contain a new thought. The first patent application was subsequently rejected because BASF had not worked the original patent within six months. This left the firm without any protection (Zimmermann, 1965, p. 20). Within a short while, twelve firms had started production in Germany (Borscheid, 1976, p. 131), pushing prices down.

that firms had tried to keep secret to maintain their competitive advantage. In 1874 he published the structure of the eosin dye that Caro (BASF) and Baeyer had developed together. In 1876 Hofmann published a paper on the chrysoidine dye that Otto Witt had developed for a British firm and Caro for BASF (Johnson, 1992, p. 175). Production of the dye had just started at BASF (Zimmermann, 1965, p. 21). Witt and Caro were quite upset about Hofmann's publication because other firms could now much more readily copy the dye. Witt complained to Hofmann that the latter had not acknowledged Witt's announcement of the dye in a small exhibition catalog. The quote at the beginning of the section was Hofmann's official reply to a public criticism by Peter Griess (who worked with Witt and Caro) of Hofmann's practice of publishing the formulas of new commercial dyes (Borscheid, 1976, p. 149). Hofmann's goal, of course, was to convince his fellow chemists and the German dye firms that patents would be a much better protection of an invention than secrecy.

Martius and Hofmann achieved enough of an agreement within the German Chemical Society that the board of directors of the organization could send a petition to parliament in the name of the entire association.[222] The petition came at the last minute, on March 16, 1877 (Wetzel, 1991, p. 253). Exactly a month later, the patent commission accepted the key points in the petition by a large majority, and the entire German parliament passed the law on May 25.

What was in the petition? It asked to change the proposed patent law in one key way: An exception was to be made for chemicals and related products. Instead of a product patent for chemicals (as was the practice in France, Britain, and the United States), the petition urged parliament to rewrite the patent law proposal and allow only process patents. By not allowing product patents, the petition argued that the search for and use of better processes would not be blocked (Ungewitter, 1927, p. 286). This was a compromise between the forces within the chemical community that feared to repeat the mistakes of France and the people who had campaigned for the strongest possible patent protection of chemicals. The success of the lobbying effort of the chemical community can be witnessed by reading the very beginning of the printed patent law (my translation):

German Patent Law, May 25, 1877

§ 1 Patents are issued for new inventions that allow a commercial application.

Excepted are:

1. Inventions whose application would violate laws and common decency.
2. Inventions of food products, pharmaceuticals, as well as products that are created by a chemical reaction, *except when these inventions concern the process by which these products are created.*

The very first paragraph reflects the wishes of the German Chemical Society.

---

[222] Johnson (1992, p. 176) reports that apparently the leadership did not submit the petition for a general vote of all society members. Because there was no rebellion by the rank and file after the petition and because I have not seen that Caro or others complained about what the leadership did, apparently

The association also convinced parliament to write into the law that the patent office had to seek expert advice at every stage of the patent process (Johnson, 1992, p. 176). By now it hardly comes as a surprise that Hofmann and Martius were among the four members of the German Chemical Society who were appointed as official experts by the patent office (Ungewitter, 1927, p. 286; Johnson, 1992, p. 176).

This first episode is clearly not a story about full control over the patent environment by the chemical community. For obvious historical reasons, the dye industry as a collective entity came late to the patent lobbying efforts. Pushed by Hofmann and Martius, the chemical community that included the representative from the dye firms arrived at collective agreement just in time to influence the patent law in a direction that was in the interest of the majority. At best, the property right regimes for chemicals remained a work in progress. The efforts came late enough that many questions about how the new patent law was going to be handled in practice remained wide open.

Episode Two: Keeping the Swiss Out
Eight months after the passage of the patent law, the chairman of the patent office urged industry to help the new governmental agency develop adequate procedures for handling all aspects of the patent process (Ungewitter, 1927, p. 286). The leaders of BASF, having had painful experiences with the actual patenting process in the late 1860s and early 1870s, took the initiative to press for further clarification and development of the patent law in regard to chemicals. Heinrich Caro, with the backing of the BASF management team, composed a memorandum on February 25, 1879, for the newly formed Chemical Industry Association in which he urged the formation of a permanent patent commission within the association.[223] The memorandum was cosigned by such leading members of the association as Martius and Schering.

The factors responsible for the formation of the German Chemical Industry Association in November 1877 are quite relevant for understanding its effectiveness. The idea for the creation of the association was born during the 1876 International Exhibition in Philadelphia. Martius and Holz (of the pharmaceuticals firm Schering) had been impressed by the U.S. trade association for chemicals (Manufacturing Chemists' Association) and became eager to create a similar lobbying association in Germany (Ungewitter, 1927, p. 4). Martius's initial idea was to form the Chemical Industry Association as a subsection of the German Chemical Society, but Hofmann was strongly against this plan after having been embroiled in somewhat of a scandal in which he was accused of having compromised his position as a scientist to advance the material gain of his friends in the dye industry (Johnson, 1992, p. 176).[224]

Martius and Hofmann had brokered a compromise with the "process patent clause" that the key players in the dye industry could live with.

223 The importance of patent law for the dye industry is evident in the biographies of many of its leaders. Caro (BASF), Martius (AGFA), Duisberg (Bayer), and Levinstein (Levinstein) became experts in patent laws of the key industrial countries.

224 Hofmann was appointed to serve as a juror for the dye section at the 1873 International Exhibition in Vienna. Apparently he voted to give the prizes to those dye firms with which he was connected through consulting or friendship ties. His fellow jurors (largely distinguished chemists) were incensed about Hofmann's overt favoritism and caused a scandal in the chemical community (Borscheid, 1976, pp. 124–5; see also Vaupel, 1992, pp. 194–6). Hofmann was painfully made aware that overt profiteering did not mesh well with the ideal of the German university as articulated by Humboldt. From then on, Hofmann refused to associate himself publicly with a corporation (he had been a silent partner in

The late lobbying efforts of the German Chemical Society in the fall of 1876 had not left enough time for industrial firms to work out in detail how the new patent system was supposed to work in practice. This convinced many participants in the dye industry that a trade association was urgently needed that would be in the position to influence early on (not when it was almost too late, as in the case of the 1877 patent law) all legislation that would affect their industry. As the invitation that was sent by Martius, Caro, and thirty other industrialists to chemical manufacturers stressed, "many important tasks that impinge upon the industry can only be achieved when chemical manufacturers find an agreement among themselves" (Ungewitter, 1927, p. 5). All important dye firms joined the association, and the dye manufacturer Fritz Kalle was elected chairman of the association. Caro, Martius, and Hofmann's nephew, P. W. Hofmann, a small dye manufacturer located next door to BASF in Ludwigshafen, were among the fourteen elected board members (Ungewitter, 1927, p. 7).

In this second episode, the Chemical Industry Association became a key instrument for shaping patent law and practice. Caro's proposal to form a permanent patent commission was approved with great enthusiasm by the members of the Association. The first meeting was to be held at the general gathering of the Association on September 19 and 20, 1879, in Baden-Baden. This meeting was perhaps the most important one until World War I because it was the first time the dye firms had a chance to air the views and concerns about the patent law, which had been by then in existence for two years (Ungewitter, 1927, pp. 290–300). The meeting laid out most of the important patent issues that would concern the dye industry before World War I. Two leading professors in patent law (Klosterman and Koehler) were invited to help the commission set up the design of its internal organization and arrive at principles the patent office should employ in the examination and the granting of chemical patents.[225]

The key issues raised by dye firm leaders had to do with the interpretation of what constitutes *novelty* (as required by the first article of the law) in a chemical process and to what extent the *product* that is created by a patented chemical *process* is protected according to the law of 1877.[226] Several dye firms complained that their German patents could not prevent the Swiss from selling the same dyestuffs in Germany because it was impossible to establish infringement when plants (i.e., the manufacturing process) were not located on German soil.

Over the next twelve years, the issue of Swiss firms copying German dyes remained central in the work of the patent commission. In the mid-1880s the commission voted to recommend to the Chancellor of the German Empire to seek an emergency law that would prevent the Swiss from selling copied dyes in Germany. But the Swiss were able to mollify German dye firms once more by promising that they would pass their own patent law for chemicals (although they did not do so until 1907).

AGFA) and tried to present the German Chemical Society as a purely scientific organization, which it was not, given the membership of many industrialists.

[225] Professor Klostermann and the lawyer Bürger were elected as members of the Assocation's patent commission in March of 1880 to provide it with adequate legal advice (Ungewitter, 1927, p. 30).

[226] Apparently very detailed notes were taken during the meetings of the patent commission of the German Chemical Industry Association. Ungewitter (1927, pp. 284–322) describes in detail the different positions taken by individual members of the patent commission in their meetings from 1879 to 1891, which led to the important change in the patent law in 1891.

In the meantime, the patent commission of the chemical industry actively shaped the way the patent office would interpret chemical patents.[227] The majority of the members in the patent commission preferred to change the administrative rules and procedures of the patent office rather than press for a revision of the patent law so soon after it had been passed. But in 1884 the Association of German Engineers started drafting a petition to change the existing patent law. Not to be late again, the patent commission of the German Chemical Industry Association became active right away to draft a revision that would reflect its own interests.

The new patent law that became effective on November 1, 1891, contained a provision that German dye manufactures wanted very much because the Swiss dye firms were becoming their only serious competitors in the 1880s. By reversing the burden of proof in a patent infringement suit (the party accused of the infringement now had to show that it was using a different process in making the same dye), Swiss dye firms no longer could simply copy German inventions and sell them with impunity in Germany. Furthermore, the new law allowed for oral arguments before the patent office. The hope was that this would shorten the time it would take for patents to be issued and at the same time help avoid lengthy and costly patent litigation. One consequence was that dye firm representatives would meet more frequently than just at the regular meetings of the Chemical Industry Association. This may have made it easier to create relationships that allowed the formation of the two big alliances: in 1904, the "Dreibund" (Union of Three) of Bayer, BASF, and AGFA, and in 1905–7 the "Dreiverband" (Association of Three) of Hoechst, Cassella, and Kalle.

Students of the historical development of German patent law tend to agree that the dye industry generally got the kind of patent law it wanted (Borscheid, 1976, p. 146; Fleischer, 1984).[228] One reason why the dye industry was so successful in shaping German patent had to do with the effectiveness of the Chemical Industry Association. Key disagreements among dye firms were ironed out within the Association, which meant the Association spoke collectively for all of the chemical industry when it lobbied the patent office or other units of government. Furthermore, the chemical industry grew faster than the economy as a whole during most years before 1914. The spectacular success of the German dye industry provided it with prestige among industrial and governmental circles. But even more importantly, firms were highly profitable, which allowed them to finance the work of a permanent patent commission that had lawyers on its staff. Collective organization was the key to success in shaping patent laws.

British Patent Politics: Incentives Are Not Enough
Episode One: A Working Clause without Bite
The British case is both similar to and different from the German one. In Britain, business also influenced the patent law, but the British dye industry was much less

---

[227] The German Chemical Industry Association also tried to shape the behavior of its members. Based on a proposal of Carl Rumpf (Bayer), the association strongly urged its members to use mediators in patent fights rather than go to court (Ungewitter, 1927, p. 302).

[228] A membership survey by the German Chemical Industry Association in 1884 showed that dye firm members were by far the ones most interested in shaping the patent laws (Ungewitter, 1927, p. 302).

successful in getting its patent proposals enacted. A year and a half after the passage of the all-German patent law, the following "call to arms" appeared in the *Chemical Review*.

Patent Law Reform

In one respect, and one only, the present Patent Laws sin by excess of liberality. But the liberality in this case is merely a specimen of that one-sided reciprocity for which, as a nation, we have made ourselves so notorious. A foreigner of any nationality can obtain a patent for the United Kingdom, and, provided he pays the usual duties, he can retain it for the full term, whether he works it on British ground or not. This is not the case in foreign countries. An Englishman may, for instance, obtain a patent for the Austrian Empire, but unless he works that patent in the Austrian dominions, within a certain time and on a commercial scale, his patent lapses. We should, therefore, propose that every alien obtaining a patent for the United Kingdom should be bound to work it within the United Kingdom, or to grant licenses for its use on reasonable terms before the expiry of twelve months from the date of its being brought into operation in any other country. At present foreigners obtain English patents merely to prevent any one from working their inventions here, and refuse to grant licenses. Thus the public who wish to obtain articles made under any such patent are compelled to import them from abroad. . . .

If Government had felt the pressing need of such a measure, they would have introduced it officially. Not having done so, and finding the matter taken up by well-known opponents, they will doubtless show the Bill little favor – as we have, in fact, been already informed.

We must, therefore, beg our readers to take the question up earnestly. Let every one write to his Parliamentary representative, Conservative and Liberal alike, urging the claims of this measure upon their favourable attention. Let every one seek to get resolutions in favour adopted by local and municipal bodies, and forwarded in forms of petitions. Above all, seek to secure the support of the local press. If any of our correspondents is willing to co-operate heartily with us in this matter, we shall be happy to give him further information in private as to how he may serve this most important cause.

—Unsigned Editorial in *Chemical Review* (January 1879, pp. 49–50)

The reader browsing through the first fourteen years (1871–84) of the Levinstein-founded *Chemical Review* is struck by the frequency with which patent issues are discussed. After education, patents were clearly perceived by the editors of the trade journal as the second most important public policy issue to affect the chemical industry. And unlike education, patent laws could be improved with a stroke of a pen.

As the movement to reform the British patent system gained momentum, the Society of Chemical Industry (see Chapter 2 for a description of the role of the society) took a very strong position on forcing patent holders to operate their patents within Britain.

> ### The Coming Patent Law
>
> The Society of Chemical Industry has through its council resolved upon certain recommendations....
>
> If a patent is not in operation on a large scale by the fourth year it is to become void.
>
> We are simply petrified at such a proposal from such a quarter. Unless an inventor is himself a capitalist or a very able negotiator and man of business, he finds it in the rule impossible to get his process adopted as early as the fourth year.
>
> —Unsigned editorial in *Chemical Review* (November 1882, pp. 9–10)

The *Chemical Review* was evidently more concerned about the interests of the small inventor than was the Society of Chemical Industry. But on the question of instituting a working clause requirement, the chemical industry was fairly unified. Opposition did not come so much within the chemical community as from outside. Particularly, traders were against the change in the patent laws because they would only lose business if foreign production was to be moved to Great Britain. In 1883, a new patent law passed that changed procedures and fees for obtaining patents (Daniel, 1884). On the issue of the working clause, however, the chemical industry had achieved a victory only in words, not in practice. The *Chemical Review* predicted correctly that the working clause as phrased in the new law was virtually unenforceable.

> ### The New Patent Act
>
> We are glad to find that the Board of Trade may order a patentee to grant licenses to work his patent, provided it can be shown, among other things, that the patent is not being worked in the United Kingdom. This seems to be an attempt, at least to do away with a serious abuse, – the taking out of patent in the United Kingdom in order to prevent any process from being worked therein. Whether this provision will have the desired effect, or whether it will prove to be rendered unworkable by some blunder or oversight, will have to be proved....
>
> In short, we are not without fear that this salutary provision may prove a mere scarecrow.
>
> —Unsigned editorial in *Chemical Review* (October 1883, pp. 283–4)

The dye industry and the chemical industry in general did not have the necessary political strength to get a working clause requirement that would have forced German dye firms either to work their patents in Britain, or even better, to grant British dye firms licenses to the new dye innovations that were starting to come out of the R&D laboratories. Given the general political climate in which free trade supporters were still in the clear majority, the opponents of the working clause were strong enough to make the wording of the clause sufficiently vague and throw large hurdles in the way of anyone who wanted to force a foreign patent holder to grant a license.

German dye firms continued to obtain the vast majority of British dye patents without manufacturing an ounce of dyestuff on British soil.

Episode Two: A Short-Lived Victory[229]

Some background information is necessary to understand the second attempt to change British patent practice and the role the dye industry played in this movement. Ivan Levinstein was the chief protagonist in this second episode because his dye firm and Read Holliday were the two main players in Britain during this period. When their partnership agreement was up for renewal in 1895, Bayer and AGFA sold back their two-thirds stake in the largest British dye firm, I. Levinstein & Company, Ltd. As part of the equity arrangement, Bayer and AGFA had given I. Levinstein & Company, Ltd., access to their very valuable direct cotton dyes (Reader, 1970, p. 262). In the late 1890s Levinstein (the man) stepped up his campaign for a reform of the British patent law, most likely because he no longer had the same access to licenses for valuable new inventions coming out of the Bayer and AGFA research laboratories. Although Levinstein had been an active advocate for patent reform at least since he lost the big patent case against BASF in 1887, his most organized push appeared as it was becoming more and more difficult to compete with incessantly expanding German dye firms and as his firms experienced real economic difficulties.

After the failure in 1883, Levinstein was well aware that he needed allies, as many as possible, and organizational support to bring about a change in the working clause requirement (Section 22 of the 1883 law). The British market was being invaded more and more by American and German products, which gave protectionist forces a much larger audience than ever before. The Manchester Chamber of Commerce (once leader of the free trade movement and the originator of the anti-corn law league) had turned protectionist and became one of the key organizations Levinstein joined forces with in his fight for a change in the law (Zimmermann, 1965, p. 78). After the Manchester Chamber of Commerce secured support from other associations, Levinstein organized a deputation of twenty-two individuals who were members of Parliament, trade associations, and chambers of commerce to appear before the Board of Trade in 1898 to complain about the ineffectiveness of the working clause requirement in the 1883 law. Levinstein told the board that of the 600 coal-tar patents issued to foreigners from 1890 to 1895, not a single one had been worked in Britain (Zimmermann, 1965, p. 80). The deputation then demanded that the patent law be rewritten to make the working clause effective. The board, however, countered that it could not recommend a revision of the patent law before cases had been brought and it had been demonstrated that the clauses were not working as intended. At the end of the meeting, the deputation and the Board of Trade came to the agreement that test cases had to be brought.

Levinstein was the one who then chose the test cases. He selected two patents by BASF and two patents by Hoechst that concerned a chemical precursor the Levinstein firm needed to produce its azo dyes. The patents would appear very weak because the two Hoechst patents had been declared invalid in Germany, one during the application process, and the second one during a revocation suit. But the German firms countered and challenged Levinstein's own patents in court. The stakes and the costs of the case

[229] I am relying mainly on Zimmermann's (1965, pp. 78–128) excellent detailed account of the patent reform movement that led to the 1907 revision of the patent law and its subsequent defeat.

were becoming higher and higher for both parties. If the German firms were to lose the patent fight, they still would have had the option of taking the case to higher courts. In the end, the Board of Trade forced BASF and Hoechst to grant a license at reasonable terms without making a judgement about the validity of any of the patents. But the case was far from a complete victory for Levinstein. It also showed that obtaining a forced license via a lawsuit was very expensive and risky. With patents that had a stronger legal footing, BASF and Hoechst might have taken the case all the way to the highest court and perhaps won. Despite the victory, Levinstein and his confederates recognized that only a change in the law would make it simple to force German firms to grant licenses to British dye firms or work their patent on British soil.

The agenda for Levinstein and his allies was fairly straightforward: Put patent law reform on the legislative agenda, write a very strict working clause requirement that would be to the advantage of British industry and procedurally easy to invoke, and get it passed by Parliament. To avoid the same defeat as in 1883, Levinstein and his associates needed the widest possible support. Although the opposition was not as strong as in 1883, large numbers of people still thought that creating a strong working clause requirement was exactly the wrong way to proceed at this point in time, given that a worldwide push to eliminate working clause requirements was taking shape in all member states of the patent union.[230] To harness the dynamics and strength of a social movement, Levinstein and his confederates enlisted the support ranging from industrialists to workers and as many associations they could find.

> In the meantime Manchester[231] had secured the support of more than a quarter million of working men, represented by their trades unions, of a considerable number of the largest manufacturing concerns in the country, and of practically every interested Chamber of Commerce, of many powerful associations and societies, amongst these the Incorporated Law Society; and finally, they had with them a large number of influential members of Parliament.
>
> —Ivan Levinstein, looking back around 1902 (as quoted in Zimmermann, 1965, p. 92)

If we interpret Levinstein's prime motive to help the fortunes of his dye firm, the events that followed suggest that he lost control of the efforts to change patent law to help his position in relation to the German dye firms.[232] By the end of 1901, the

---

[230] For more details on the patent union see the discussion in Chapter 2.

[231] Levinstein means the Manchester movement for patent reform.

[232] Two interpretations can explain Levinstein's patent reform actions. (1) He may have been truly concerned with the welfare of his adopted nation rather than his firm. A strict working clause requirement would have forced German firms to operate their British patents in Britain, and that meant employ British workers. If German firms were to build plants on British soil, the British dye industry would have grown, but the firm Levinstein probably would have done less well because of increased competition from the new plants. His biography shows a strong streak of British nationalism, making this interpretation a plausible one. (2) He was chiefly concerned with the welfare of his firm. A strong working clause requirement would have given him a strong hand in asking German firms to grant him a license for making the patented dye in Great Britain. He would have been able to point out that giving him a license would satisfy the working clause requirement without the need for

organizing drive of the Manchester Chamber of Commerce led to a resolution by the Associated Chambers that called for the elimination of forced licenses altogether in favor of patent nullification:

> A patent may be revoked if it be proved that the article patented, is worked abroad, and not in the United Kingdom, the onus of proof that the patent is worked bona fide in this country, resting with the patentee or licensee (quoted in Zimmermann, 1965, p. 92).

Only forced licensing would have helped the Levinstein dye business because the threat of patent revocation would have simply prompted German firms to build plants in Britain as they had done in France and Russia. In 1902 a temporary law was written that allowed the revocation of patents. However, the opponents of the working clause were able to keep it weak enough, and it remained very difficult to win a patent revocation suit.

The Manchester movement was hardly satisfied with the outcome and continued to press for a stronger version of the bill. At this point an unexpected ally with great political power and connections appeared on the scene. David Lloyd George, who became Prime Minister during World War I, was made Minister of the Board of Trade with the change of government in 1905. He viewed the patent movement as a very expedient issue for rallying voters behind his causes. In 1907 he introduced into Parliament a bill that he marketed as the "Poor Man's Patent Bill." It was designed to stop large foreign companies and syndicates from exporting jobs from Great Britain by taking out patents in Britain but producing abroad. Given the political climate at the time, the bill found much support in Parliament, and when it was passed, a working clause with real teeth had been put on the books for the first time.

> **Excerpt of Section 27 in the 1907 Patent Act**
>
> Any time not less than four years after the date of a patent, any person may apply to the Comptroller for the revocation of the patent on the ground that the patented article or process is manufactured or carried on exclusively or mainly outside the United Kingdom (quoted in Zimmermann, 1965, p. 95).

As soon as the new British patent law with a strict wording of the working clause requirement became law in 1907, the large German dye firms started to build dye plants in Great Britain to preserve their patents. (This was probably not what Levinstein had hoped for.) The Dreibund alliance of Bayer, BASF, and AGFA built a plant at the Mersey river in the Liverpool area and the Dreiverband alliance led by Hoechst built a plant in Ellesmere Port (also in the Liverpool area). The latter plant was to manufacture in particular synthetic indigo, which was at the time the most valuable patent in Hoechst's portfolio.[233] To be as much as possible in line with the

---

German firms to build a plant in Great Britain. Both motives may actually have governed Levinstein's actions, one being sometimes stronger than the other.

[233] As the German dye firms were setting up their factories in England, they discovered that wages for chemical workers had become lower in Britain than Germany (Duisberg, 1923, p. 663), a dramatic

new law, BASF transferred its patent portfolio to a British subsidiary formed under the name of Mersey Chemical Company.[234]

But after only about nineteen months, Justice Parker of the British High Court took the teeth out of the law. By 1909, sixty-nine applications for revocation had been made and fifteen had already been granted. The occasion of Justice Parker's action was case against the "eternit" asbestos patent. The Comptroller General heard the case and revoked the patent as the law instructed. The patent holder then filed for an appeal at the High Court. Justice Parker agreed with the Comptroller General's decision because the product of the patent was manufactured only on the continent. But the Justice took the occasion of the case to lay down rules for all future patent revocation cases, handing down a ruling that would make it virtually impossible to bring a successful patent revocation suit. His decision essentially reversed the burden of proof by stipulating that the applicant for a patent revocation had to show first that the patent holder was abusing his monopoly position by not working the patent in Britain. This of course was extremely difficult to prove, and with one ruling, the working clause of the new act was rendered once again ineffective.

The working clause movement did not have the strength to force through Parliament another revision of the patent law that would have superseded Justice Parker's ruling.[235] Given that Levinstein had been such an active figure in the patent revision movement, German firms retaliated against him by refusing to buy intermediates from his firm (Haber, 1971, p. 148). Although the two German alliances kept their plants in Britain, they dramatically scaled back their production plans and continued to manufacture most of their dyes in Germany.

In the end, the British dye industry once again did not get the patent system it wanted. Although the much smaller size and much lower profitability of the British dye industry can explain to some extent why the industry never got a patent regime that would have helped it compete with the German dye firms, differences in the penetration of education throughout society had much to do with the kind of patent regimes that would develop in the two countries. Not only were the differences in the quality of education largely responsible for allowing the German dye industry to overtake the British pioneers in the first place, they were also responsible for making it easier in Germany and more difficult in Britain to obtain a patent regime that would help the dye industry. As we have seen in the case of Germany, engineers, scientists, and the creators of large industrial firms like Siemens and the German dye pioneers were forces behind the creation of a patent system that they thought would help the

---

reversal from the early days of the dye industry. Earlier, German wages were much lower, but the dramatic expansion of the German economy resulted in workers in Germany catching up with British wage levels.

[234] Within the German industry, there were debates right away as to whether the Imperial Government should be asked to retaliate against the new British law (see Duisberg, 1923, pp. 663–7).

[235] The anti-working-clause forces at this point had gained strong allies across the Atlantic. American firms like the American Shoe Company and Yale Lock Co. were very unhappy with the working clause requirement of 1907, given that no such requirement existed for British firms in the United States. A bill introduced in Congress to impose the same requirement in the United States was intended to force countries like Britain to repeal the working clause requirements (Zimmermann, 1965, pp. 123–4). By rendering the working clause requirement ineffective, Justice Parker's ruling spared the British government another imminent battle over patent law.

cause of Germany industry. Britain had far fewer scientists and engineers who could have pushed for a more adequate patent system.

Thus the backward education system was not only connected to the much lower ability of British industry to create large firms that could exploit economies of scale and scope as described by Chandler (1990) but also intimately related to the inability of the British dye industry to get a patent system that enhanced their competitive position. The German dye industry could always count on being able to form an alliance with scientists and engineers in other industries as well as to work with a state bureaucracy that was infused with the values of science and scholarship.

The case of patent law illustrates once more that the relative failure of the British dye industry and the stunning success of its German counterpart cannot be explained without understanding the profound differences in the institutional environments firms faced in the two nations. Because I have not encountered any evidence that American dye firms tried to influence American patent law, I have not discussed here the shaping of U.S. patent laws. The dye industry in America probably was too weak to have had any impact. Noble (1977), however, has shown that industries tried to shape American patent law in their favor, supporting the general argument put forward in this chapter.

Influencing Tariff Laws

Why did Germany have no tariffs on dyes but tariffs on many other chemical products? Why did Britain not enact a tariff on German dyestuffs when domestic firms were clearly falling behind their German rival in the 1870s? Why did the relatively high tariffs that were imposed on dyes in the United States in the 1860s gradually go down despite efforts by dye manufacturers to increase the tariffs? The answers to all three questions have to do with the relative strength of different industries within the respective national economy. The key industries in this context were coal-tar distillers, dye makers, and dye users. Because the interests of the last two sectors in particular often would not coincide, whether or not the dye industry was able to marshal more political support than the dye users had important consequences on the tariffs that would be imposed. Knowing how to create coalitions within the machinery of government was an important strategic asset for any industry association. An industry association that possessed such capabilities was often able to achieve important competitive advantages for its member firms.

When the synthetic dye industry started in 1857, Britain and the United States had a much larger textile industry than Germany. In Germany, therefore, a growing synthetic dye industry would appear much larger in relation to the domestic textile industry than in Britain or the United States. Consequently, the German dye industry had relatively more political clout than its British or American counterpart. This meant that the German industry was much better able to protect its tariff interests than were its rivals in Britain or the United States. Let us briefly examine how the three national dye industries fared in regards to tariff legislation.

The prolonged economic crisis that followed the boom years of 1872 and 1873 helped the protectionist forces in Germany. Led by the politically powerful agricultural interests, the German government was ready to enact tariffs on a wide variety of products. Because the fledgling German soda manufacturers were eager to receive protection against the efficient British producers, tariffs for chemicals were also on the agenda. In 1879 and 1882 higher tariffs for soda were enacted, but the German dye industry was able to keep coal tar and dyes free of tariffs (Eichengreen, 1998). Given that it was the largest exporter of dyes in the world, the German dye industry had to fear that dye tariffs in Germany would only lead to retaliation by other countries. The Germany dye industry was successful in getting a tariff regime it desired because it had much political clout. By holding a key position in the chemical industry trade association, it was able to prevent tariffs from being enacted on all chemicals.

British manufacturers were eager to receive tariff protection from their government to weaken the competitive advantage of German firms. But British dye-makers were not at all successful in persuading the government to impose dye tariffs. Partly this had to do with the fact that the pro-free-trade forces were in the clear majority before World War I. Even more immediately, the British textile industry, which was 100 times bigger than the dye industry, did not want to lose access to cheap and high-quality German dyes. Although dyes represented only between 1 percent and 2.5 percent of the cost of a finished textile, they were critical for marketing, and British textile interests would hurt their own business by allowing German dyes to become more expensive. Given that British coal-tar distillers and the British dyers and colorists had both formed strong trade associations, the relatively unorganized British dye-makers faced an uphill battle for protection. When the dye firms battled the coal-tar distillers and dyers for political support, the dye firms lost every time.

American dye firms were even more eager than their British counterparts to receive trade protection. In the United States, unlike Great Britain, protectionist forces had gained the upper hand in the second half of the nineteenth century. Tariffs on imported synthetic dyes had existed since 1864, but they were gradually reduced until 1894. Haynes (1954, p. 312) holds that the removal of the 50 cents per pound specific duty (on top of an ad valorem duty) in 1883 was responsible for the failure of five American dye firms, half of the entire population of dye manufacturers. Just as in Britain, the powerful textile industry of the United States was able to prevent, with one exception (in 1897), the enactment of higher tariffs (Haynes, 1954, p. 311).[236] It also managed to get some dyes, for example, synthetic indigo, completely free of tariffs.

The tariff history of all three countries shows that the relative powers of supplier, producer, and user industries had important consequences for an industry's ability to bring about favorable tariff regimes. The quality of an industry's collective organization, not just its economic size, was a determinant of political influence. German firms were more successful in getting a tariff regime they desired not only because they were much bigger than their British rivals, but also because, through the network of contacts that linked firms and other centers of power, the German dye industry had the tools to engage in more successful collective action.

[236] Hesse (1915) provides a very detailed account of the battle for dye tariffs from the 1860s until 1914. See also Steen (1995) for data on how the tariff levels changed from 1864 to 1914.

5 Toward an Institutional Theory of Competitive Advantage

> *[Cournot] taught that it is necessary to face the difficulty of regarding the various elements of an economic problem, – not as determining one another in a chain of causation, A determining B, B determining C, and so on – but as all mutually determining one another. Nature's action is complex: and nothing is gained in the long run pretending that it is simple, and trying to describe it in a series of elementary propositions.*
>
> —ALFRED MARSHALL in *Principles of Economics*
> (Preface to the first edition, 1890, pp. xv–xvi)

In this final chapter I assess the adequacy of existing theories in accounting for Germany's long dominance of the synthetic dye industry; I then develop a coevolutionary model to explain how Germany moved from a laggard to an uncontested leader in this industry. I argue that although academic disciplines from economics to strategic management have provided a variety of theories to account for industrial success and failure, no one theory can adequately explain why and how Germany dominated the synthetic dye industry for so long and why firms within Germany differed so dramatically in their fortunes. Although international economics can explain quite well the success of the German industry as a whole, it cannot deal with the vast differences in performances of firms within the same national environment. By contrast, a theory such as the resource-based view of the firm developed by management scholars has difficulty explaining why most of the successful players cluster in a particular national environment, rather than being spread out evenly across countries. Both kinds of theories, moreover, have difficulty explaining the dynamics of how competitive advantages change over time. The shortcomings in current theoretical arguments provide the starting point for the second part of Chapter 5, in which I develop an institutional theory of competitive advantage that deals with the national industry and firm level at the same time.

To make coevolutionary arguments persuasive and not a catchall label for the analysis of organizational and environmental change, we need to know the specific mechanisms that characterize coevolution. After showing that the industry, technology, and institutions all evolved, I articulate a more detailed coevolutionary model of industry development than I sketched in the introductory chapter. Besides highlighting the three abstract causal mechanisms of evolutionary explanations (variation, selection, and retention), I identify the *exchange of personnel*, the *formation of commercial ties*, and *lobbying on behalf of the other social sphere* as the more specific causal mechanisms that connected the evolution of national populations of firms with the evolution of national populations of universities. Having articulated my coevolutionary model, I move on to discuss the implications of the present study for evolutionary economics, management, and business history. Because scholars from these different domains are all interested in the study of industrial change, in the last section of the book I propose future research that should be carried out in the fertile triangle of evolutionary economics, management, and business history.

Theoretical Gaps

Economists, sociologists, and management scholars have developed a variety of theoretical approaches for explaining competitive advantage.[237] Some theories locate the causal origin of better economic performance strictly in the environment of the firm, whereas others see the firm and the discretionary behavior of its managers as the true source of superior performance (Nelson, 1995a, 1996a). In this section I will examine how well some of these approaches can explain the dramatic differences in economic performance experienced by firms and national industries in the synthetic dye industry before World War I.

Mainline economic theory locates the sources of competitive advantages as residing clearly outside the boundary of the firm. For most economists, competitive advantages accrue either on the country or the industry level. A firm enjoys competitive advantage in mainline economics simply because it happens to be located either in a country that enjoys advantages or in an industry that has a more favorable structure. Theorizing in this tradition typically traces the origins of competitive advantages to such national variables as climate, natural resources, capital–labor ratios, relative prices of the factors of production, or such industry structure variables as concentration ratios, entry barriers, and the like.

Let us examine how well mainline economic theories can explain the decline of the British and the rise of the German dye industry. Britain clearly had a better natural resource endowment (coal tar) than Germany for the first three decades of operation of this industry. German firms bought most of their coal tar from Britain until a change in the process for making illuminating gas reduced the amount of coal tar created as a waste product of British illuminating gas factories. This forced German firms to locate other supplies of coal tar, which they found at steel mills that created coal tar as a by-product. Rather than natural resources, educational institutions constituted the chief national advantage that accounted for why German and not British or American firms dominated the industry. One can, of course, extend the language of input factor

---

[237] The literature in strategic management typically uses the term "competitive advantage" to refer to advantages that one firm has over the next. At the time of Adam Smith (1776), economists also applied the term competitive advantage to two nations. Ever since David Ricardo (1817) pointed out almost 200 years ago that although one nation may have an absolute advantage in all industries over a second nation, under such circumstances the two nations would still be better off by focusing their efforts on those industries in which they had the greatest relative advantage or smallest disadvantage, economists have adopted the language of comparative advantage to discuss the relative competitive strength of two countries in a particular industry. In the present work, I am using the language of competitive advantages both at the firm and industry level to refer to absolute competitive advantages.

advantages of international trade theory to include skilled labor (chemists, engineers, and managers) as "factor" advantages, and economists have done so. But education is qualitatively a very different kind of "good." Natural resources are used up in the production process, whereas skills are reusable and often are even enhanced through their use (Lamoreaux, Raff, and Temin, 1999; Winter and Szulanski, 2001). Even more importantly, countries cannot change their natural resource endowments but they can improve the skill and motivations of their workforce through public policies or collective actions of firms.[238]

The broad theoretical literature in economics recognizes that the availability of skilled labor often accounts for why one nation has an advantage over a second. But it typically does not acknowledge that strong national industries often tend to be supported by highly specialized supplier industries and supporting institutions (Porter, 1990; Nelson, 1996a). In Germany, financial organizations that had the skills to appraise the risks inherent in the industry developed side-by-side with such science-based industries as synthetic dyes (Da Rin, 1998). Similarly, specialized equipment manufacturers became stronger in Germany than in Britain and the United States, making it possible for the German dye industry firms to improve their production technologies more readily than either British or American firms. Supporting institutions such as universities that produce skilled labor are not created instantaneously and often require significant interaction with parties outside a particular industry. For this reason, British and American companies could not quickly catch up with German firms after the latter had developed a significant lead in the 1880s.

Whereas mainline economic theories can give a fairly good explanation for why Germany was able to dominate the synthetic dye industry before World War I, they are entirely silent on why, within a particular national context, some synthetic dye firms became very rich while many more went out of business, often with substantial financial losses. The dominant perspectives on comparative advantage formulated by David Ricardo (1817, p. 83 in the 1911 edition), or more recently by Heckscher-Ohlin,[239] simply do not address the question of why specific firms in one country would do so much better than other firms in the same country. The firm itself is typically not seen as an independent generator of advantages. Its active role in creating industrial strength is repressed in the analysis. The examples of Bayer or Levinstein in contrast to Jäger or BS&S suggest, however, that individual firms did to some extent influence their fate, particularly by making timely investments in organizational capabilities and creating strong ties to key players in the institutional environment. The study of the synthetic dye industry has demonstrated in a variety of ways that the national environment makes it easier or harder to succeed but it does not fully determine the economic success of firms located within its boundaries. A comprehensive theory of competitive advantage would explain why one firm can perform so much better than another firm, even when they find themselves in the same national environment.

Mainline economic theories, moreover, often lack a clear dynamic account of how competitive advantages change over time. The industry structure in Britain in the early period was less competitive than Germany's because patent laws created

---

[238] Countries can, of course, change their ability to exploit their natural resources by developing the technological skills to do so. See Rosenberg (1998) for an elaboration of this point.

[239] See Krugman and Obstfeld (1997) for an introduction to the Heckscher-Ohlin theory.

entry barriers that were absent in Germany. But over time, the German dye industry became more concentrated as entry barriers rose, partly as the result of changes in technology and partly because of collective actions of German firms. Until the recent developments in strategic trade theory (Krugman, 1991), mainline economic theories tended to focus on differences in industrial leadership at a particular point in time, but left out an account that would explain how German firms over time surpassed British firms and subsequently were able to transform their leadership position into a domination of global markets. Strategic trade theory highlights the possibility that increasing returns may be a key mechanism that can lead to dominance of a nation in a particular industry. It also makes clear that a dynamic analysis is required to understand why the performance path of two national industries may be quite similar initially but later diverge in dramatic ways.

Several sociological theories, such as organizational ecology, also focus on the environment as the principal source of competitive advantages. The dynamics of the first period in the dye industry are broadly consistent with organizational ecology as formulated by Hannan and Freeman (1977). Their version of ecology, however, cannot deal with nor account for the fact that firms successfully shaped their selection environment and that many of them changed their internal structures. German dye firms were not, as early Hannan and Freeman argue, passive entities born with either appropriate or inappropriate features for their environment. Rather, firms actively shaped their selection environment, allowing their features to become better suited for global competition in the synthetic dye industry. German firms to a large extent were able to outperform their British and American rivals because of their greater success in bringing about educational institutions, patent laws, and tariff policies that made their social environment more hospitable to a synthetic dye business. Population and organizational ecologists have acknowledged in more recent years that firms are not completely inert entities (Hannan and Freeman, 1984, 1989; Barnett and Carroll, 1995), but empirical work in this tradition has not focused on how firms can change their environment through collective action.

Scholars in business schools often have set their analytical eyes only on firms themselves as sources of competitive advantage. Those researchers who have studied industries in which technical change is a defining characteristic have emphasized differences in firm competencies as the key source of competitive advantage (Winter, 1990; Teece and Pisano, 1994; Teece, Rummelt, Dosi, and Winter, 1994). By focusing exclusively on firms, these researchers have typically omitted the larger social environment from the analysis of firm strength. This is not the place to enumerate and compare the variety of managerial perspectives formulated by management scholars. Instead I will focus on recent developments in the field of strategy that were set in motion by the popularization of the resource-based theory of the firm and the reactions against this view (Penrose, 1959; Wernerfeld, 1984; Barney, 1991; Conner, 1991). Greater competence, rather than location in an industry with structural impediments to competitive forces, lies at the heart of the explanatory logic in the resource-based view (McGrath, Gunther, MacMillan, and Venkataraman, 1995).

Several strategy scholars extended the resource-based theory of the firm and begun to focus on the ability of firms to adapt continuously to changing environmental requirements as the key source of competitive advantages. The writings of Porter (1990, 1991), Teece, Pisano, and Shuen (1997), and Kogut and Zander (1996) point to the notion of dynamic firm capabilities as a key building block of a theory of sustained competitive advantage. Winter and Szulanski (2001, p. 734) define dynamic capabilities as "the partly routinized activities that are carried on to expand or change the capabilities that directly affect revenue generation." By putting the analytical emphasis on the ability to reconfigure the activities of the firm, the dynamic capabilities view enriches the theoretical approaches in mainline economics and organizational ecology.

Yet by focusing to date mainly on the internal features of the firm, the dynamic capabilities view, as articulated by Teece, Pisano, and Shuen (1997), for example, has neglected that often the particular institutional environment in which firms are embedded constitutes an important cause for superior firm performance.[240] Of course it is important to focus on the actual skills of a firm and not just the level of competition in a particular industry or the relative factor endowment of the environment, yet a perspective that sees firm capabilities as being largely a result of the firm's own doing cannot account for the fact that all leading synthetic dye firms after the 1880s came from Germany. If better management alone, or at the other extreme, mere luck was the decisive factor, leading firms should also have appeared in other countries. The analytical lens of the dynamic capabilities view needs to be broadened if the theory is to explain the clustering of firms in particular institutional environments. It needs to recognize that firms don't create all their capabilities themselves but rather that they draw on raw capabilities in their national environments.

Firms in the synthetic dye industry not only benefited from advantageous institutions such as education or intellectual property rights but also helped to upgrade those institutions.[241] The German dye firms were clearly successful in creating and upgrading supporting institutions that would confer considerable competitive advantages on local firms. If one can assume that the synthetic dye industry is representative of a large number of industries, a comprehensive theory of competitive advantage must be able to incorporate the interaction of firms and their institutional environment.

Except for Porter (1990, 1991), Nelson (1995a, 1995c, 1996a), and Hall and Soskice (2001), there has been little effort until now to integrate the existing theories that emphasize either environmental or firm-level factors into a comprehensive framework. Such a framework undoubtedly would provide a useful conceptual tool for analyzing firm strategy in an increasingly global market environment. In contrast to his earlier work (1980), Porter more recently (1990, 1991) argues that successful firms have to analyze and manage both their external environment and the internal organizational system of activities. Following this line of reasoning, the scholar of strategic management needs to include both environmental as well as firm-level variables in the analytical picture. Porter observes that "[t]his style of research nudges strategy research, and indeed industrial economics, into the world of the historian" (1991, p. 116). Nelson (1996a) similarly fears that if we neglect the ways in which firm and environmental factors interact, we will not make much progress in research on

---

[240] My argument that the institutional environment of firms is an important source of comparative advantage is also supported by the recent study, *Varieties of Capitalism: The Institutional Foundations of Comparative Advantage* (Hall and Soskice, 2001).

[241] The proposition can also be stated in negative terms: British and American firms in the synthetic dye industry not only suffered from inferior institutions such as education or intellectual property rights, but also failed to upgrade those institutions.

industrial leadership. A key challenge for strategy research, then, is to develop a better understanding of to what extent the larger environment rather than actions by the firm are the true sources of competitive advantages (Porter, 1991, p. 115).

In this chapter, I will begin to formulate an institutional theory of strategy that brings together the idea of dynamic firm capabilities (à la Teece et al., 1997) and the larger institutional environment in which the firm is embedded (à la Granovetter, 1985). The goal is to bring both the firm and the environment into one analytic picture. My approach is congenial to institutional analyses such as those of Meyer and Rowan (1977), Fligstein (1990), Powell and DiMaggio (1991), and Dobbin (1994) but focuses more on an evolutionary logic like that of Nelson and Winter (1982) in explaining industrial change. Before formulating the outlines of such an institutional theory of competitive advantage, let us review through the lens of an evolutionary theory the key dynamics in the development of the synthetic dye industry and its institutional environment.

Recall for this purpose that a sound evolutionary explanation occurs at the level of the population, not the individual, and has to meet the following requirements: First, to introduce novelty into the economic system, a mechanism must exist that creates variants of the existing structures. Without a constant source of novelty, a selection process cannot create new economic structures that may be better adapted to the economic requirements of society. Second, selection pressures need to be consistent, or more precisely, new variants must be created more frequently than new selection criteria because otherwise the evolutionary process cannot act as a "blind watchmaker" that brings about through trial and error structures that are better adapted. The evolutionary system would degenerate into a random walk that on average could not be expected to lead to structures that are better adapted to their environment. Third, a retention mechanism must be present that transmits economic structures from the present into the future. Without such a retention mechanism, new developments could not build on previous adaptive achievements but would have to start from scratch; complex nonrandom structures would not be possible.

This articulation of evolutionary theory is much more general than the Darwinian formulation for biology. The biological case has the special features that variations are completely random and *not* guided by previous experience. In sociocultural evolution, by contrast, the process that creates variants is not entirely independent of the process that selects variants. It is also useful to keep in mind that evolutionary explanations are neither necessary nor compelling in contexts where agents have perfect knowledge about the environment and can create the optimal variant on the drawing board. But for all those situations in which agents do not understand their environment well and many different trials are needed before well-adapted variants emerge, an evolutionary explanation can account for how better adapted structures emerge over time without anyone having anticipated which variant would prove effective in the particular context.

Evolutionary Interpretation of the Key Findings
Evolution of Technology

The first synthetic dye appeared in 1856 not because someone had a conscious plan to create such a product; rather, Perkin was searching for a synthetic route to a medicine and serendipitously discovered a purple substance. What made him different from other organic chemists who had seen colored materials in their test tubes was that he pondered its possible commercial value and set out to investigate whether the purple material would work as a dye for textiles. Once Perkin acquired some positive feedback from silk dyers, his family decided to invest funds into a production plant. Conceptualize the existing natural and semisynthetic dyes as a population. In this framework, Perkin's initially serendipitous discovery led to the introduction of a new type of dye into the population of existing natural and semisynthetic dyes. Let us call natural dyes *Type A*, semisynthetic dyes *Type B*, and synthetic dyes *Type C*.

Before Perkin could sell his aniline purple dye, he had to engage in significantly more trial-and-error learning about how to produce the dye cheaply enough to make it competitive with natural dyes. At the very beginning of the new industry, nobody had a sense that within a few decades synthetic dyes would replace virtually all natural and semisynthetic dyes in the market place. To put this in formal evolutionary language, nobody had the foresight that the frequency of Type C dyes in the population of all colors that were applied to textiles would increase to almost 100 percent by World War I. Clearly, an evolutionary mechanism drove this change: The transformation did not come about because individual natural dyes "metamorphosed" themselves into synthetic dyes but rather because natural dyes were selected against, dropping out of the population, and synthetic dyes were selected for, increasing their share in the population.

Corporate dye portfolios also evolved through variation and selective retention processes.[242] The at least 900 different distinct dye molecules manufactured in 1914 had been selected from thousands of synthesized molecules. The number of molecules that chemists synthesized for each dye that reached the market place is staggering: Bayer's research laboratories, for example, synthesized 2,656 new chemical compounds in 1906 (Meyer-Thurow, 1982), of which 60 were tested on a larger scale after a first screening, and only 36 ever reached the market. A few years earlier, Hoechst had tested 3,500 color molecules but introduced only 18 into the market (Beer, 1959, p. 89).

This description of how the dye population changed over time highlights the operation of at least two distinct levels of selection. The first winnowing process occurred inside firms, with companies testing dyes for perceived suitability. Of all the molecules a firm synthesized, only a few received the development and marketing funds necessary to introduce them into the market. The marketplace in turn selected from this reduced set an even smaller number of dyes. The dye that flourished in the market survived for some time until still better (i.e., higher quality or lower cost) synthetic dyes became available and replaced earlier ones. It is useful to conceptualize the relationship between these multiple selection processes as a nested hierarchy. At a lower level of selection, each firm had its own internal selection criteria for deciding which of the many molecules synthesized by its chemists would receive a full-fledged market introduction. The selection criterion could have been how well a particular

---

[242] If one conceptualizes bodies of knowledge as populations of ideas from which individuals select a subset, these trial-and-error processes of individual dye developers had the consequence that the body of knowledge surrounding the manufacture and application of the physical artifact evolved as well. Discoveries introduced new ideas into the existing population. As other practitioners learned about these ideas, certain ideas became less widely used and other ideas became more frequently subscribed to. Consequently, the composition of the entire idea population changed.

dye performed in internal tests. Alternatively, the management of the firm could have had a preference for dyes of a particular color or a particular technological class, or it could have been guided by some other personal predilection in deciding what dyes to introduce into the market. If, however, a firm used internal selection criteria that were inconsistent with the market selection criteria for too long, the firm would lose money and eventually go out of business (Langton, 1984; Burgelman, 1991). For instance, a company that used the internal selection criterion of focusing exclusively on aniline dyes when azo dyes became so popular would not have survived in the competitive German market. In contrast, those firms using internal selection criteria for dye molecules that were consistent with what the market wanted made profits that allowed them to increase their R&D budget and expand their production capacity. The retention mechanism in this process is easy to specify: Firms retain a successful dye in their product portfolios until the dye no longer finds enough customers.

For reasons of exposition, I presented the internal selection mechanism of firms as a one-level process. But the internal selection processes can certainly involve multiple levels. At the lowest level, a chemist may discard many molecules before even considering proposing some of them as dye molecules to the leader of the laboratory. Multiple echelons of approval may be necessary before a dye is given the firm's support for a full-fledged market introduction. Each level may have somewhat different criteria. It is important to recognize that what are selection criteria at one level are but trials of the criteria at the next higher, more fundamental, more encompassing, and less frequently invoked level (Campbell, 1974, p. 421). If we examine how dye molecules were selected, we find that they most frequently were selected out at the firm level and less frequently at the level of the marketplace. Lower-level selection criteria were eliminated by higher-level selection forces if the former yielded results that were inconsistent with the larger environment. A chemist, for example, who used selection criteria that were not leading to successful products in the eyes of his boss stood a good chance of being removed from his job. At a higher level, a firm whose selection criteria put dyes in the market that were not in demand would go out of business.

Kekulé's benzene ring theory, published in 1866, was an important development in organic chemistry because it gave chemists a better understanding of the chemical structure underlying dye molecules. In 1876, Otto Witt published the first theory of the relation between a compound's molecular structure and its color properties (Witt, 1876). As a result, starting in the mid-1870s, Kekulé's benzene ring theory and later theoretical advances in organic chemistry such as Witt's theory had a significant impact on the development of new dyes because the new structural understanding of molecules allowed chemists to reduce the search space for developing new dyes (Wilcox, 1966). Chemists still needed to synthesize a large number of molecules to find a useful dye, but they had a better grasp of what kind of molecule was more likely to work as a dye. This shortcut in developing new dyes – as we learn from Kekulé's autobiographical sketches – emerged itself from a trial-and-error process (Rocke, 1985).

Evolution of the Industry
The industrial dynamics that characterized the development of the dye industry are consistent with the key features of an evolutionary process. One of the most striking findings in this study of the synthetic dye industry before World War I concerned the

sources of industrial leadership: German dominance was built not only on a much larger number of firms that entered the industry but also on a much larger number of firms that failed. In Germany 91 of the 116 entrants into the dye industry before 1914 went out of business; for Britain 36 of 47 firms failed, and for the United States 25 of 35 firms did. The fact that the failure rate in the three countries was very similar (Germany 78.4 percent, Britain 76.5 percent, and the United States 71.4 percent) highlights the importance of the absolute numbers of entry and exit for understanding the competitiveness of an industry. Both the high numbers of turnover in all countries and the German dominance are consistent with the predictions of an evolutionary theory. Analyzing the underpinnings of creative thought, Campbell (1960, p. 395) pointed out:

The . . . variation-and-selection-retention model unequivocally implies that ceteris paribus, the greater the heterogeneity and volume of trials the greater the chance of a productive innovation. Doubling the number of efforts very nearly doubles the chance of a hit, particularly when trials are a small part of the total domain and the repetitiousness among trials is low . . . [U]nconventionality and no doubt numerosity [are] a necessary, if not sufficient condition of creativity.

A similar proposition follows from an evolutionary theory of industrial development. Having more start-ups, all other factors being equal, increases the odds that some firms will be successful. In the beginning of an industry, when uncertainty about the requirements for a successful product are particularly high, those countries with a larger number of start-ups have a greater probability of some firms trying a business model that, in hindsight, turns out to be well adapted to the new context.

Because of the absence of patent protection and the availability of abundant chemical talent, many more German than British firms quickly followed Perkin & Sons into the industry. The large number of German entrants triggered severe price competition in the early 1860s. By 1864, the price of fuchsine (aniline red) had fallen to about 10 percent of the 1860 amounts (Morris and Travis, 1992, p. 65), prompting an exit wave of the firms that could not compete under these market conditions. Evolutionary explanations about industry development are compelling precisely because it is possible to specify a consistent selection criterion in this context: *Firms are selected for their levels of profitability.* Only those firms that take in more money than they pay out can survive in the long run. Similarly, sources of variation are not difficult to identify for a population of industrial firms (Metcalfe, 1998). Given that entrepreneurs differ in their psychological profiles and their experience bases, they tend to introduce variety into this population even when they consciously try to imitate the model of another firm. A faithful replication of a business model typically requires organizational capabilities that are not readily discernible from the outside; hence imitation attempts often lead to imperfect replicas and frequently fail (Winter and Szulanski, 2001). The larger the number of entrepreneurs that start new firms, the more varied the population is likely to be. Without doubt, the diversity of retention mechanisms is greater in industrial evolution than in other evolutionary systems. Business models of successful firms are preserved because they are written down in organizational rules and passed on as an organizational culture that tells members who they are in the context of the organization and in general terms what they are supposed to do (see Witt, 1998, 2000, about the importance of business models as coordinating and motivation devices in firms).[243] In addition to such rules, however, individuals store in their memory their respective roles in the larger organizational structure. When an individual leaves the organization, the new person assigned to the role will learn the job either through elaborate instructions or by learning from the know-how of other people who carry out similar tasks.

If it had been clear at the very begining of the industry that synthetic dyes would almost completely replace natural and semisynthetic dyes by the time of World War I, we can assume that the development of the industry's structure would have proceeded quite differently. The number of firms entering the industry, the concentration ratio, the fraction of firms with R&D laboratories, and the share of investments by the top five firms, for example, would have developed along a different path. With foresight that output would increase between 1862 and 1913 by 3,800 percent in terms of value and that R&D laboratories eventually would be able to provide a continuous stream of new dyes, investment decisions would have been much less incremental than what is seen in the historical record. The record of the synthetic dye industry shows the following action pattern: When something worked, firms invested more. The R&D function of dye firms, for example, emerged gradually, starting with just one chemist who would be allowed to spend most of his time on research. When this strategy proved successful, firms hired more chemists to focus on R&D and gradually built up an organizational function that was separate from regular production. In hindsight it would have made sense early on for firms to make large investments in firm capabilities to capture a significant portion of this highly lucrative business. But actual investment decisions looked very different. By 1914 standards, entrepreneurs started on a small scale because at the beginning it was far from clear how large the synthetic dye market was likely to become. Under conditions of fundamental uncertainty, strategic analyses made after the event offer little guidance about how a firm should behave in real time. Firms simply could not see very far into the future. They made investments based on short-term forecasts of how the market was likely to develop. But even forecasts for the next few years were often inaccurate because firms did not know how other firms would act. When new classes of dyes emerged, several firms correctly anticipated sizable demand for the product. But when many firms that were hoping for monopoly profits entered the same market, they found that they were all chasing the same customers. As shown earlier in Figure 8, entry waves were typically followed after a short lag by exit waves because only the most effective firms survived such heightened competitive conditions. The structure of the industry evolved by allowing firms to grow that made the right decision or were simply lucky and by forcing firms that made a wrong move or simply had bad luck to exit the industry.

Evolution of National Institutions

Scholars who study the development of countries from a comparative perspective have discovered time and again that countries differ significantly in their social structures and practices (Skocpol, 1984; Ragin, 1987; Aoki, 2001). Contrary to what one

---

[243] In terms of Hull's (1989c, p. 96) concept of interactors and replicators in evolutionary change, the interactor in this context would be the business firm, whereas the replicator would be the business model.

might expect, little evidence suggests that the recent globalization of markets is causing a wholesale eradication of national differences (Guillén, 2001). For every instance of institutional convergence, scholars seem to find another instance indicating that countries are becoming more different in some other respect (Teubner, 2002). In the introductory chapter, I noted that the word "institution" is used in many different ways in the literature. I suspect that the key reason for this variety is that scholars chose a definition that is tailor-made for their research questions and analytical purposes. Because analytical purposes differ, many different concepts of institutions have emerged that resist repeated attempts to standardize the meaning of the concept. From a pragmatic point of view, multiple uses of the term "institution" are problematic only when one is not told in what sense the term is meant. To avoid such confusion, I have tried to make explicit my own definition in the present book. I use the term "institution" to denote actions, rules, social structures, and practices that persist over time and are features of social aggregates that are larger than a single organization – whether the single organization is a firm or a university. One dye firm, for example, with certain practices that remain moderately stable for many years I would *not* count as an institution. Only when a practice exists in the majority of dye firms operating in the same environment would it qualify as an institution by this definition. When at the end of the nineteenth century all major dye firms had established an R&D laboratory and the R&D function came to be regarded as a standard feature of large firms, one could talk about the corporate R&D laboratory as an institution. My definition is tailor-made to highlight the findings that in global markets firms often possess a competitive advantage because the national institutions that surround them are better suited for organizing industrial activity in their particular sector of the economy.

Providing a full-fledged evolutionary explanation of the development of institutions is much more challenging than for industries because it is harder to define consistent selection criteria such as profitability in the case of institutional evolution (Nelson, 1995b). But because explanations of institutions that are based purely on rational choice models (especially the extreme reductionist types that locate causality only in individual preferences and intentions) are difficult to reconcile with the historical record of how most institutions come about (Tilly, 1997, pp. 17–34), evolutionary metaphors appeal to many a scholar of social change. A long tradition of American legal writing, for example, sees common law as the outcome of competition between different rules (see Elliot, 1985, for an excellent survey of this literature). Drawing on an even earlier German group of legal scholars such as Friedrich Karl von Savigny (1831) and the British scholar Henry S. Maine (1861), Hayek (1973) emphasized that law has evolved because it would be impossible for any human mind to design from scratch as complex a system as the body of common law that governs social life in Britain and the United States. He rejects the notion that all complex social institutions that characterize large contemporary societies have been created by deliberate design. Building on the work of Bernard Mandeville (1715), David Hume (1741), Adam Ferguson (1767), and Carl Menger (1871), Hayek argues instead that through trial and error common law has developed into a complex system of rules that works quite well. Just like other writers on the evolution of law, Hayek explains how abstract legal ideas such as property have developed, but he does not articulate detailed mechanisms for how particular legal rules emerged. In Hayek's (1989) line of reasoning, societies that adopt rules of conduct allowing them to increase their population faster – via higher rates of procreation and via admitting immigrants – will increase their share of the world's population. Unlike natural selection arguments that work through the birth and death of individuals, in this process legal rules and not people decline in importance or go out of existence because they lose adherents.[244]

In my view, Hayek's argument can explain how entire bodies of law spread and how others retrench, but it cannot account for how individual legal rules emerge. The selection forces that allow one society to grow and another society to shrink causally work through bundles of laws and probably through many other features of these societies.[245] Hence it is very difficult to identify which features in such bundles are causally responsible for the success of a body of law. A particular area of law may be selected simply because it happens to be attached to other features of a society that together constitute a social structure capable of generating more material wealth and therefore is able to spread more successfully than alternative structures can. Whereas in connection with the development of patent laws in different countries we saw that individual rules often had to be reworked because they could not deal well with a new product class such as synthetic dyes, it is difficult to define a simple selection criterion for legal evolution. Some scholars argue that selection criteria in this domain have to do with how well a new legal rule fits into the existing body of law or codifies a society's sense of fairness; others see the interests of powerful constituencies as the key force shaping law; and still others hold that economic efficiency is the key driving force behind legal change. In the case of patent laws we saw that precedent, interests of various social groups, and experimentation with the application of legal rules played a role in shaping national patent practices. Clearly, however, we do not have a full-scale evolutionary theory of legal change that possesses the same analytical rigor as the theory of economic evolution. Nonetheless, scholars for more than 250 years have been drawn to an evolutionary metaphor in describing changes in law: Not only is today's law largely inherited from yesterday's law but also the law often appears to adapt to environmental changes through trial and error with different rules rather than through a single legislative act.

To analyze the development of university systems – populations of universities at the level of individual nations – through an evolutionary lens is much more straightforward because universities, like firms, require material resources to maintain themselves. This has been true since the first university was organized in 1088 in

---

[244] For a thoughtful discussion of how what appears to be a group selection argument in Hayek's work can be interpreted in terms of an individual selection process, see Vromen (1995, pp. 171–91).

[245] An extreme illustration is the recent collapse of the East German state in 1990. East Germany – because of the pressures of the masses – was absorbed into the West German institutional legal framework. From one day to the next, the East German legal codes were scuttled wholesale for the West German legal codes. In this process, clearly individual legal rules were not selected but rather the entire body of West German law. To be sure, the lack of familiarity of East Germans with many of the West German codes caused significant problems in the proper functioning of many laws for years. Imposing legal rules on a society whose microinteractions reflect a different tradition typically has the result that legal rules are interpreted and applied somewhat differently. American anti-trust laws that were imposed on Japan after World War II did not replicate the anti-trust practices in the United States.

Bologna, Italy. During the first centuries of the organization's existence, professors at the University of Bologna were paid directly by students.[246] Initially the university took the form of a cooperative because students had organized the meeting of lecturers and students. Until the sixteenth century, when the university became a state organization, students even served as rectors. The internal organization of the university was shaped to a large extent by a selection process that acted on the level of individual professors. Professors who did not attract enough fee-paying students could not pay their bills and would be forced to give up their lecturing, just as firms have to give up production when they pay out for long periods more money than they take in. The better professors could also charge higher fees and their subjects would flourish.[247] It is quite appropriate to describe the organization of the first university as a marketplace, where disciplines that could attract students would flourish at the expense of other disciplines that lost out in the competition for students. Most students in the beginning came to Bologna to learn law in a more systematic way. But by the fourteenth century the study of law ceased to be the main subject for which students signed up. Medicine, philosophy, arithmetic, astronomy, logic, rhetoric, and grammar had been added as subjects and became more central in the curriculum.

Over the last 1,000 years, various different funding and governance models for universities have been tried. But one can identify general processes that shaped the development of universities over the millennium. First, those universities that attracted financial support, first-rate scholars, and students would grow relative to other universities. Second, individual disciplines competed with other disciplines for resources. As Schmookler (1965) and others have demonstrated, the expansion of universities in the Western world was intimately tied to the utilitarian goals of the individual student and of society at large. Academic disciplines expanded to the extent to which they could convince students, benefactors, and later, governments, of the utility of their discipline for their individual careers or the advance of society.

Just as in the case of technological evolution, it is important to distinguish between different levels of analysis (Aldrich, 1999). Academic disciplines of national university systems evolved to some extent through the opening and closing of individual universities. Of the 1,990 four-year colleges founded in the United States between 1636 and 1973, 515 had gone out of existence by 1973 (Marshall, 1995). This 25 percent failure rate is clearly much less than the 71 percent to 78 percent failure rate we saw for the three national populations of dye firms, but it still amounts to a considerable turnover. A map of German universities in 1900 by Franz Eulenberg (1904) shows that a

---

[246] For a history of University of Bologna, see Rashdall, Emden, and Powicke (1936) and Cobban (1975). A short history is also available on the website: http://www.unibo.it/avl/english/story/nine.htm.

[247] Scottish universities were very different from English universities before the twentieth century, in that they took in students from a wide social range, including the lower and middle classes; here too, professors were funded mostly by student fees (Sanderson, 1972, p. 149). The larger the class size, the more money the professor would make. Scottish universities enrolled a much higher percentage of the population than did English or Welsh universities. Under these circumstances, it is not surprising that Adam Smith, who gave public lectures in Edinburgh under the patronage of Lord Kames on such topics as "The Progress of Opulence" and taught at the University of Glasgow from 1751 until 1763, produced such useful and readable books. He had to help his students figure out the economy; otherwise, they would have stayed away from his lectures.

number of German universities existed for some time and then were closed.[248] In terms of the birth of new universities, the second half the nineteenth century witnessed a significant number of new institutions in Britain, Germany, and the United States. One common reason for the formation of new universities in all three countries was that traditional universities were exhibiting substantial inertia in incorporating more science and engineering education into their curricula. In Britain no new university was formed between the University of Edinburgh in 1583 and the University of Durham in 1832, followed shortly afterward (1836) by the more significant University of London. In the sixty-four years before World War I, however, six English universities (Manchester, Birmingham, Leeds, Liverpool, Sheffield, Bristol) and one Welsh (The University of Wales) were chartered. All new universities were much more focused on science and engineering and thereby increased the frequency of appointments in these areas. Similarly, the population of German universities was greatly changed through the creation of technical universities. Altogether, eleven technical universities were organized between 1868 and 1910 (Munich, Aachen, Darmstadt, Brunswick, Hanover, Berlin, Karlsruhe, Stuttgart, Dresden, Danzig, Breslau) that focused on teaching science and engineering subjects. Some of the German technical universities were created from scratch. Others were formed out of existing polytechnics and local colleges. After a long political struggle with traditional universities, the German technical universities were given the right to grant doctorate degrees in 1901 and thereby could compete even more successfully for students.

Beginning with the Morrill Act of 1862, through which the U.S. Congress appropriated to each state funds from the sale of federal land, the United States began to build a very large system of higher education, creating many new campuses and upgrading existing ones (Rosenberg and Nelson, 1994). In 1860, the United States had approximately 750, often small, private colleges, but their teaching in the practical arts was extremely limited (Ferleger and Lazonick, 1994). The Morrill Act had the explicit goal of setting up "colleges for the benefit of agriculture and the mechanic arts" but left it up to each state legislature to determine specifically how the federal grants were to be spent and what courses were to be offered.[249] This provision made the existing colleges and the seventy-five newly created Land Grant schools very receptive to local educational needs. By 1872, the number of engineering colleges had increased from six to seventy. MIT, a private institution founded in 1861, for example, received after 1862 parts of the Land Grant money given by the federal government

[248] The abandoned universities are as follows ("?" indicates date is uncertain): Osnabrück 1680–1733?, Duisburg 1655–1816, Köln 1488?–1796, Trier 1473–1798, Mainz 1477–1797, Herborn 1384–1816, Paderborn 1615–1819, Kassel 1633–52, Stuttgart 1781–94, Rintel 1621–1804, Fulda 1732–1808?, Helmstedt 1516–1810, Erfurt 1302–1816, Bamberg 1648–1803, Altdorf 1522–1803, Ingolstadt 1472–1800, Dillingen 1554–1807, Landshut 1800–26, Salzburg 1622–1810, Olmütz 1376–1888, Wittenberg 1502–1817, Frankfurt (at the Oder River) 1306–1811.

[249] Section 4 of the Morrill Act articulates its focus on practical education:

... each State which may take and claim the benefit of this act, to the endowment, support, and maintenance of at least one college where the leading object shall be, without excluding other scientific and classical studies, and including military tactics, to teach such branches of learning as are related to agriculture and the mechanic arts, in such manner as the legislatures of the States may respectively prescribe, in order to promote the liberal and practical education of the industrial classes in the several pursuits and professions in life.

to the State of Massachusetts to offer engineering courses (Ferleger and Lazonick, 1994).

The more significant evolutionary transformation of national university systems took place, however, not through the birth and death of individual universities but rather through degree choices of students and faculty appointments of individual universities that tried to adapt to changing environmental conditions. Natural science disciplines such as chemistry and physics increased their share of students between 1850 and 1914 in all three countries, but in Germany and the United States this trend was much stronger than in Britain. Across Europe until the late eighteenth century, chemistry was taught as an ancilliary subject by faculty who had a chair in medicine, botany, or pharmacy (Meinel, 1988). In eighteenth century Germany, chemistry was also taught as an ancilliary subject connected with mining or the cameralist tradition. The initial German attempts to create separate chairs of chemistry in the philosophical faculty (Ingolstadt, 1773; Göttingen 1775; and Halle, 1788) sooner or later failed because not enough money was taken in the form of tuition and examination fees (Meinel, 1988, p. 104).[250] The first economically viable chair in chemistry was established in 1789 at the University of Jena, which at the time was the third largest university in Germany.

When most of the German states followed Bavaria (1808) and Prussia (1825) in requiring compulsory university training for apothecaries, the demand for chemistry faculty increased. Many of the private teaching laboratories were turned into regular teaching laboratories for chemistry and pharmacy as part of the philosophical faculties and not the medical faculties, thus providing a steady supply of students for future chemistry professors. Most German universities, beginning with Erlangen (1818), Jena (1820),[251] Bonn (1821), and Würzburg (1836), took the step of creating a dedicated chair for chemistry in the philosophical faculty during the nineteenth century (Meinel, 1988, p. 107). Chemical chairs also were created in the new technical universities in the later part of the nineteenth century, transforming the disciplinary organization of the German university system by changing the frequency of appointment in different fields of study.[252] In 1864 there were 13 chemistry faculty for every 100 faculty in the humanities. By 1890 the corresponding figures had risen to 23 and by 1910 to 33 chemistry faculty for every 100 faculty in the humanities.[253] Between 1850 and 1870 the transformation of American higher education was equally pronounced with science and engineering faculty being added in unprecedented numbers (Ben-David, 1977). Although Cambridge and Oxford were slow to incorporate laboratory science, the Cavendish Laboratory at Cambridge and the Clarendon Laboratory at Oxford, established in 1871 and 1880, respectively, marked important steps toward more science research and teaching at the two most prestigious universities in Britain (Haber, 1958, p. 76).

---

[250] Ernst Homburg (personal communication, 2002) pointed out that chemistry continued to be taught at the medical school of the University of Göttingen even after the attempt to create a chair in the philosophical faculty failed. Göttingen continued to be an important center of chemical research in early nineteenth century except during the years of the Napoleonic wars.

[251] To avoid confusion, note that the first economically viable chair dedicated to chemistry at Jena (1789) was not in the philosophical faculty.

[252] In the case of technical universities that were created based on existing institutions, chemical chairs were not created from scratch; their status was upgraded and they came to play a more important role in the system of higher education.

[253] These calculations are based on data provided in Johnson (1985, p. 507).

The change in the relative frequencies of enrollment in the different faculties (medicine, law, religion, philosophy) of the German universities during the nineteenth century also shows how the transformation of the German university system was brought about by students' choices. In the academic year 1830–31, 17.7 percent of all university students were enrolled in the philosophical faculty. By 1881–82, this had risen to 40.3 percent to a large extent because of the greater number of sciences students in the philosophical faculty. In 1841, 13.6 percent of students in the philosophical faculty studied science; by 1881, the percentage had risen to 37.1 percent (Cardwell, 1957, p. 134). The higher enrollments in science were brought about first by larger demand for science teachers in Germany's secondary schools and later by the demand for chemists in industry, as we saw in the case of synthetic dyes.

Analysis of the historical path of the three national university systems reveals key properties of an evolutionary process in their development. Each population of national universities was transformed to some extent through the creation and the failure of individual universities. Administrators and academic entrepreneurs frequently tried to adapt their university to changing environmental conditions. But they could foresee only imperfectly what actions would allow them to attract more resources to their organization and thereby enhance its viability. In the first unsuccessful attempts to create independent chairs in chemistry, there was considerable trial-and-error learning in the process of appointing professors for new subjects. Ultimately students, through their choices of what subjects to study and what professors to hear, acted as agents through which the relative importance of particular disciplines within the university system changed over time.

Having now demonstrated that the development of dye technology, the dye industry, and national institutions such as the university system all have features of an evolutionary transformation, I can articulate how these three developments can be interpreted as a coevolutionary process.

A Theory of Coevolution

One of the more important post-Aristotelian developments in evolutionary theory is the emphasis on endogenous environments, on the ways in which the convergence between an evolving unit and its environment is complicated by the fact that the environment is not only changing but changing partly as part of a process of coevolution. There is mutual adaptation *between the unit of evolution and the environment.*

—JAMES MARCH in *Evolutionary Dynamics of Organizations* (1994, p. 43)

Coevolutionary analysis has become more widely practiced in organization science over the last decade (Kieser, 1989; Yates, 1993; Baum and Singh, 1994; March, 1994; Levinthal and Myatt, 1995; Barnett and Hansen, 1996; Haveman and Rao, 1997; McKelvey, 1997, 1999; Coriat and Dosi, 1998; Koza and Lewin, 1998; Baum and McKelvey, 1999; Lewin et al., 1999; Lewin and Volberda, 1999; Van De Ven and Grazman, 1999; Eisenhardt and Galunic, 2000), in part because scholars have realized that it is almost impossible to understand the behavior and performance of organizations without examining how their environments change (Pfeffer and Salancik, 1978, p. 1).

Unfortunately, the term "coevolution" in this literature at present refers to a variety of different processes. Often the term is simply used to refer to the parallel development of two phenomena without specifying the precise nature of the causal relationship. To avoid unnecessary ambiguities and to allow more cumulative research, I want to provide a precise definition of how I use the term "coevolution": *Two evolving populations coevolve if and only if they both have a significant causal impact on each other's ability to persist.*[254]

Such causal influence between two populations can proceed through two avenues: by altering the selection criteria or by changing the replicative capacity of individuals in the population without necessarily altering the selection criteria. This means that a coevolutionary relationship can increase the average fitness of both populations (mutualism), decrease the average fitness of both (competition), or have a positive impact on the average fitness of one and a negative one on the other (predation and parasitism). Whether a coevolutionary process is beneficial or harmful for the parties involved depends on the particular causal relationship that links them and, therefore, that relationship needs to be specified in the empirical analysis. As shown in the previous section, taking one at a time, it is possible to give a compelling evolutionary explanation for the development of dye technology, the industry, and national institutions such as the university system. But to establish that these three phenomena coevolved, one has to show that causal processes linked industrial, technological, and institutional dynamics. As already indicated in Chapter 1, I use the prefix "co-" in "coevolution" not in the restricted sense of two things evolving together but in the broader sense of multiple things jointly evolving. Arthur Stinchcombe (2000) argues that we need to examine the "physiology" of the evolving social system to do a proper evolutionary analysis. By extension, a coevolutionary analysis should examine the physiology that links two or more evolving systems. Given that the task here is to understand the relative performance of the same industry in different countries, I will focus on articulating (1) how national populations of dye firms coevolved with the population of dyes in existence and (2) how national populations of dye firms coevolved with national populations of universities.

Coevolution of Industry and Technology

Before the advent of the first synthetic dye in 1856, approximately 2,800 firms in India alone extracted the coloring matter of the indigo plant (*Indigofera tinctoria*) to produce the natural version of the dyestuff. When the value of Indian indigo exports fell from £3,570,000 in 1896 to £225,000 in 1911, the livelihood of most of these firms was destroyed. Similarly, within a few years after synthetic alizarin came on the market in 1870, hundreds of French farmers had to give up planting madder, from which natural alizarin was derived (Redlich, 1914). The transition from natural dye technology (a population that consisted of 100 percent Type A dyes) to synthetic dye technology (a population of almost 100 percent Type C dyes) had a profound causal impact on the evolution of the industry's structure. Synthetic dye technology harbored the potential for much greater economies of scope and scale, dramatically reducing the number

---

[254] This definition of coevolution is very similar to Nitecki's (1983, p. 1) for whom "[c]oevolution occurs when the direct or indirect interaction of two or more evolving units produces an evolutionary response in each."

of firms that could make a living producing dyes. Before 1914, the global number of synthetic dye firms never exceeded eighty-five (Homburg–Murmann database). Compare this to the approximately 2,800 indigo firms in India in 1856. The top three producers in 1913 – Bayer, BASF, and Hoechst – each produced 20 percent of all synthetic dyes in the world. No natural dye producer ever came close to producing such a big share of the total demand. Changes in the nature of the technology clearly had a dramatic impact on the development of the industry structure and provide one of the necessary causal links in the coevolution of two populations.

But what is the causal link operating from the populations of firms to the populations of dyes? How did the changes in the industry structure affect the evolution of the dye population? Over time, firms that established in-house R&D laboratories to develop new products came to capture well more than 90 percent of the market share in dyes. The development of R&D laboratories as a routine function of dye firms made it possible to discover new kinds of synthetic dyes that would have never been developed by lone inventors or full-time production chemists. Synthetic indigo is an important example of how large-scale R&D efforts led to a dramatic turnover in the population of dyes. Only through organized activities of many people was it possible to create such dyes as synthetic indigo as well as many others that came out of the R&D laboratories of synthetic dye firms after 1877. Changes in industry structure thus had a direct influence on changes in dye technology.

Coevolution of Industry and the University System

Of all the features that characterized the institutional environment of the three national synthetic dye industries before 1914, the development path of the national university system had the greatest impact in determining why Britain lost its leadership position and Germany overtook the early leaders and cemented over time its dominant position with a market share of more than 75 percent. Germany had the strongest university capability in organic chemistry at the start of the synthetic dye industry.[255] By 1877, Germany and Switzerland together accounted for approximately 74.4 percent of all organic chemistry publications,[256] followed by France with 15.2 percent, Great Britain[257] with 5.9 percent, and the United States with 0.9 percent (Boig and Howerton, 1952, p. 30).[258] The strong cross-fertilization between the dye industry and the chemical research and teaching at German universities had the consequence

---

[255] In 1850, France was not too far behind Germany in terms of its organic chemistry capability, and clearly ahead of Britain and Switzerland. For more details on the French dye industry see Murmann and Homburg (2001).

[256] Ernst Homburg (personal communication, 2001), who independently counted abstracts in the *Jahresberichte der Chemie* (Annual Report of the Chemical Field), found that Germany had a share of 50–60 percent.

[257] Boig and Howerton (1952) use the designation "England" in their list of countries. But since they do not present Wales, Scotland, or Ireland in their list, one can reasonably assume they mean Great Britain.

[258] A study of the French literature in chemistry essentially paints the same picture. A breakdown of abstracts by "nationality" (referring to the journal's place of publication) has been done for 1890 and 1900. German articles – those written by German, Austrian, Swiss, Swedish, or Dutch authors – constituted 70 percent of the abstracts. In organic chemistry, which was most voluminous, the figure was 80 percent for 1870, 1880, 1890, and 70 percent for 1900, when more American, Italian, and British abstracts were featured (Fell, 1998, p. 33).

that in the second half of the nineteenth century, chemistry professors in traditional German universities focused almost exclusively on organic chemistry.[259] In contrast, the weak U.S. dye industry before World War I did not stimulate the development of a strong discipline of organic chemistry in the United States.[260] Instead, supported by American strength in the agriculture, mining, and oil-refining sectors, analytical and inorganic chemistry flourished in the United States during this period, at the expense of synthetic organic chemistry. From 1860 to 1914, only about 5 percent of all U.S. Ph.D.s in chemistry focused on organic chemistry (UMI U.S. Dissertation Database).[261] More specifically, there were three distinct bidirectional causal links between the national populations of firms and the national populations of universities that helped shape their development trajectories.

Exchange of Personnel
The most important causal flow linking industry and university was the exchange of personnel between these two social spheres. This exchange led to a flow of skills and knowledge beyond what was disseminated through the academic journals available across borders. Leading professors in the academic field trained students, many of whom later became leading chemists in industrial firms. Exchange also occurred in the opposite direction. Chemists working in firms were also recruited to join the faculty of universities. The flow of personnel between the two social spheres created a mutualistic relationship in which both sides benefited. The German dye industry overtook the British one in large measure because the much larger number of German organic chemists quickly led to a larger number of firm start-ups in Germany. The fierce competition that ensued among German firms forced them to acquire superior skills. Those German firms that survived this competition had acquired capabilities that allowed them, in turn, to beat their British rivals once the early dye patents of the British firms had expired and the German firms were free to enter the British market. Later an increasing number of university graduates often would join the staff of the growing corporate R&D laboratories. Over the entire period 1857–1914, the magnitude of the personnel flow between the German universities and the German dye industry was much larger than in Britain or the United States.

Formation of Commercial Ties
Academics who were responsible for the majority of the most important dye innovations before the development of corporate R&D laboratories in the late 1870s typically sold their innovations to firms. Because academics were closer in social space to the firms in their own national environment, they were more likely to enter into a commercial relationship with a domestic firm. The firms, in turn, provided academics with royalties as well as equipment and materials to conduct research. These commercial ties also led to the flow of knowledge from professor to firm and vice versa. They created

---

[259] The concurrent need for teaching in inorganic chemistry was met in the last part of the nineteenth century by professors of the newly organized technical universities who concentrated their teaching on inorganic chemistry and chemical engineering.

[260] In 1876 only three U.S. universities were carrying out laboratory work in organic chemistry. The University of Pennsylvania, the University of Virginia, and MIT at that time had altogether eleven students engaged in this task (Haber, 1958, p. 78).

[261] Bibliographic information on all U.S. dissertations since 1860 can be obtained at http://www.umi.com/hp/Products/Dissertations.html.

a second mutualistic relationship between the two social spheres. Professor August Wilhelm Hofmann was the first to recognize that entering into commercial relationships with his students at the Royal College of Chemistry and later at the University of Berlin was advantageous in both financial and academic terms. He provided a model for many other such relationships that followed.

Lobbying on Behalf of the Other Social Sphere

Industries compete with other industries for favorable regulation, tax treatment, and other forms of support from governments (Hirsch, 1975). Because science and education budgets are limited in every country, academic disciplines compete with other disciplines for resources. Given the possible joint benefits that can accrue to academic disciplines and their related industries, academics and industrialists have an incentive to lobby governments to increase support for their partner's social sphere, or they can form coalitions on issues that concern both. Forming such a coalition creates a mutualistic relationship between academic and industrial partners, but at the same time it can create a competitive relationship between different academic disciplines (or between different industries) by pitting them against one another. This kind of lobbying goes on in all countries and explains in part why national industries and academic disciplines differ substantially over time in their international performance. In the synthetic dye industry, successful industrialists lobbied the German states to build large laboratories for the German senior organic chemistry professors. This allowed the professors, who were the heads of these institutes and entitled to fees from each student, to become the highest paid group of academics in the university (Johnson, 1985, pp. 517, 521). Academics in turn lobbied on behalf of the industry to help change existing patent laws.

Direct Support from State Agencies

A final causal process that creates an indirect link between industries and academic disciplines is the state, which can take actions to strengthen both an industry and the relevant academic discipline. In this case, the causal relationship does not directly connect an industry and an academic discipline and hence does not qualify as coevolution. The actions of the state may play a significant role in determining whether an industry and its relevant academic disciplines will coevolve to become a leader or to become weak. Triggered by dye shortage and the crisis of World War I, the British government, for example, supported both the science of chemistry and the dye industry to overcome the country's dependency on German organic chemical technology.

The Explanatory Structure of a Coevolutionary Analysis

Evolutionary theory is a concatenation of three general causal processes (variation, selection, and retention) that can account for how well-designed social structures come into existence without an omniscient designer. To cover a wide variety of phenomena, the processes that link two populations to form a coevolutionary relationship (competition, mutualism, predation, parasitism) have been articulated on a very abstract level. To explain a change in a particular phenomenon as a coevolutionary process, it is therefore necessary to identify in more detail how two (or more) populations are causally linked to produce the observed outcome. The chief aim of solid social science research is to identify robust causal processes that explain how social outcomes are produced from a given set of social conditions (Tilly, 1998). To explain the coevolution of dye firms and universities in the period between 1857 and 1914, I identified the exchange of personnel, the formation of commercial ties, and lobbying on behalf of the other social sphere as the more specific causal mechanisms that connected the evolution of each population. Lobbying activity of industrial leaders changed the fitness landscape of organic chemistry professorships within each country. Similarly, the size of the flow of organic chemistry talent from universities to firms changed the fitness landscapes of firms that operated in the synthetic dye industry (see also Kauffman, 1993, on the idea of coupled fitness landscapes). In this analytical picture, the agents in one population (firms, for example) alter the success chances of the agents in a second population (professors in a particular discipline, for example). Because novelty enters populations as modifications of existing structures and not as new structures developed from scratch, the past constrains the path along which a population can evolve. In coevolution, the path of one population is influenced significantly by the characteristics of a second population. German firms flourished at the expense of British firms because the former could draw more readily on scientific talent that would allow them to create a stream of innovative products and lower their production costs.

Coevolutionary theory is an advance over existing theories because it focuses expressly on how competitive leadership positions are gained and lost over time. Unlike in a static theory, it is not necessary in such a dynamic account that a country, which at the end of a longer period possesses a large leadership in market share, starts out with a significant lead. Over time, relatively small differences in market share can amplify and develop into much larger differences, provided that self-reinforcing processes dominate self-limiting ones (Arthur, 1994). This is precisely what happened in the synthetic dye industry before World War I. Because of a significantly larger number of organic chemists in Germany and an absence of patent monopolies before 1877, more firms entered the synthetic dye industry in Germany than in Britain and the United States. Based on their product innovations and patent monopolies, British firms led the industry during the first eight years. But the fierce competition in Germany allowed to survive only the firms that had become more efficient and competent in producing and marketing dyes than the British firms. As a result, leading German firms were able to take world market share away from British firms, first in foreign markets and later also in the British market itself. This capturing of market share through cost reduction had a self-reinforcing property because the average cost of production would decline more for the firms that were ahead in scaling up their plants, product offerings, and marketing organizations. Until a limit was reached at which the cost of dye production could not be reduced any further by increasing scale and scope, firms with a larger output had the advantage that their per unit R&D and operating costs were lower than those of firms with a smaller output (Klepper, 1996). This allowed German firms to reduce their prices and still make profits on many dyes.

Because German firms in the 1870s also came out with innovative dyes that could fetch premium prices for some years, the large German dye firms experienced very high profit rates after 1885. As a few German firms became significantly more profitable than their British competitors, they could invest substantial resources into developing more sophisticated capabilities for inventing, making, and distributing synthetic dyes. These organizational investments were crucial to survive in an industry that constantly produced new products and processes because they allowed firms to add new skills to their accumulated knowledge base and raise the bar for their competitors. (See Dierickx and Cool, 1989, and O'Sullivan, 2000, for an excellent theoretical discussion of the need of continued investments in firm capabilities to sustain a competitive advantage.) Because British firms lacked the profits to invest in the same quality of organizational capabilities, the population of British firms was weakened by international standards and their market share reduced even further. In the case of the German industry, the gain in market share became self-reinforcing, whereas in Britain the loss in market share became self-reinforcing. Over time this led to a dramatic reversal of fortunes of the two national industries: Germany came to dominate the industry in a way similar to American firms' domination of the packaged software industry at the turn of the twenty-first century.

A second category of self-reinforcing processes is related to the institutional environment of the national firm populations (Young, 1928).[262] Before 1856, organic chemists in Germany were not trained in anticipation that they would be useful in creating and sustaining a flourishing national synthetic dye industry.[263] Germany, by a stroke of good luck, possessed in the beginning of the synthetic dye industry a larger capability in training organic chemists than Britain and the United States. This fortunate historical coincidence first led to a greater number of start-ups and later gave German firms superior access to new dye innovations and to the scientific and technological talent coming out of German universities. When the German synthetic dye industry overtook the British one and became very profitable, it used some of its profits to organize an industry trade organization that lobbied the government successfully for an increase in education spending and a more favorable patent regime. These developments, in turn, helped German firms cement their dominance of the world dye industry. In support of Pfeffer and Salancik's (1978) resource dependence theory of organizations, German firms collectively shaped their selection environment so that they would find it easier to expand and reduce the threat of serious competition from foreign firms. The British decline in world market share and profitability, in contrast, did not allow the British synthetic dye industry to lobby as effectively as its German counterpart. The British industry could neither win tariff struggles with the economically more powerful textile industry nor marshal enough political support to change the British patent laws in such a way as to aid British synthetic dye producers and hurt German firms. Similarly, the weak U.S. producers lost their tariff struggles against the large domestic textile industry. Nor were they able to stimulate the creation of a strong discipline in organic chemistry that would have provided the human capital that would have made it easier to catch up with their German competitors.

---

[262] Allyn Young (1928) long ago pointed out that when the size of the market for a particular product becomes significantly larger, an industry can use what he called "roundabout methods of production," namely, instead of labor, specialized machinery that is not economical when the market is relatively small. Because the overall German production of dyes was so much larger than in the United States, the German industry (not necessarily the firm) could afford a supporting infrastructure that would not have been cost-effective in the United States.

[263] As we saw at the beginning of Chapter 2, some academic chemists such as Justus von Liebig were already in the first half of the nineteenth century stating how useful chemists could be for industry. But no chemist was trained in anticipation of the coming of a synthetic dye industry before Perkin commercialized the first synthetic dye in 1857.

In contrast, the large and very successful agricultural sector in the United States successfully lobbied for the creation of university disciplines that would help advance its international positions.

On the basis of these comparative observations of industry developments, we can note more generally that the coevolutionary processes between industries and supporting institutional structures lead to a market economy that is to a considerable extent self-organizing. Resources are redirected to building institutional structures for the more important industries in the economy. Industries that are large and profitable today will fare better than those that are weak and unprofitable because of the self-reinforcing causal processes outlined above. Importantly, however, these self-organizing forces should not be interpreted as leading in any meaningful sense to an optimal allocation of resources in the economy. For a number of reasons coevolutionary processes cannot guarantee that the economy represents an optimal adaptation to needs, desires, and opportunities of society as a whole.

First, recall that evolutionary social processes cannot look far into the future.[264] Because they chiefly select on present outcomes, there is no assurance that the economy will allocate its resources toward building institutions that support those industries having the highest long-term economic potential. At the beginning of the synthetic dye industry, nobody knew that advances in organic chemistry would allow synthetic dyes to replace almost all natural dyes and that scientific advances would pave the way for many more products such as pharmaceuticals, rubbers, plastics, and the like. If British public policy makers and leaders of firms had known the vast growth and profit potential related to this science-based industry, in all likelihood they would not have waited until the crisis of World War I to create a more favorable institutional environment for British synthetic dye firms.

Second, evolutionary processes create the future out of existing structures. As a consequence what institutions can be devised are significantly constrained by present arrangements. Britain had built up institutional structures to support the economy of its empire, which included producing and trading natural dyes. Consistent with the general argument articulated here, British scientific disciplines before the birth of the synthetic dye industry had coevolved with industries important for a colonial empire, such as botany and geology. These existing institutional structures stood in the way of quickly erecting supporting institutions for the synthetic dye industry. One reason why the German states could respond more quickly to opportunities of building supporting institutions for industries of the second industrial revolution (e.g., synthetic dyes) is that they already had in place more extensive organizational structures than Britain or the United States dedicated toward administering efforts to develop the economy and run educational institutions. These structures made it easier to expand relatively quickly the educational offerings in line with industrial needs. We also must not underestimate the inertia that is built into coevolutionary processes. Large industries that are in decline have an incentive to use their remaining political clout to lobby for protection from competing products and technologies. British natural dye producers and traders had no interest in the emergence of institutions that would help synthetic dye producers because it would have only hastened

---

[264] In the biological realm, of course, evolutionary processes do not look into the future at all.

their own demise. For this reason coevolutionary processes can slow dramatically the pace at which the economy will adapt to new circumstances and thus can lead to a misallocation of resources. What is good for the development of a particular industry (here, natural dye producers) is often not beneficial for the development of the economy as a whole.

Third, if domestic industries face international competition, the specific historical moment during which a new industry emerges may have significant long-term consequences that are difficult to reverse because the development locks in on a particular path. Had the synthetic dye industry emerged during a period when Britain or the United States had a similar strength in organic chemistry and all three countries had possessed the same patent regimes, it would have been much less likely that Germany would have caught up with Britain and France relatively quickly and then developed an undisputed leadership position for four decades. To put it more generally, merely because the birth of an industry happened at one point in historical time and not at another, coevolutionary forces may lead one nation to create institutional structures and specialize in a set of industries that may have lower rates of return and growth opportunities than a second nation.[265]

In the synthetic dye industry, national university systems and patent laws were the key institutions that mattered for the relative success of national populations of firms. At other times or in other industries, tax laws, labor laws, employer–employee relations, financial institutions, or competition policies may play a decisive role in the long-term competitive success of firms.[266] We have good reason to believe that coevolutionary processes also shape these latter institutional structures. Of course, it was not the social environment that invented industrial-scale processes and manufactured dyes. Firms played a key role in translating institutional differences into competitive advantages. Among many other things, firms had to learn to take chemical processes from the laboratory and scale them up for industrial production. Given the central role of firms in the creation and production of new products and services (Lazonick, 1991), I want to formulate more generally what such an institutional view of competitive advantage means for the strategies of individual firms.

[265] Among the advanced countries, these differences in specialization may not lead to significant differences in living standards because each nation continues to create and absorb innovative products and processes developed elsewhere (Mokyr, 2002). Between the industrialized and the underdeveloped countries, however, these differences in specialization may make enormous differences over time because underdeveloped countries may lack the institutional and industrial infrastructure to absorb all the new knowledge and know-how that flows readily among the industrialized countries. Consistent with an evolutionary argument, North (1990) has pointed out that today's developed countries were quite lucky in ending up with institutions that supported economic growth. Underdeveloped countries in many cases find it very difficult to achieve institutions that support economic growth because a small segment of the population profits from the status quo and those people develop strategies and organizations to maintain the status quo.

[266] For a good comparative account of the role of financial institutions, see Lazonick and O'Sullivan (1997a, 1997b). Mowery and Nelson (1999), Arora, Landau, and Rosenberg (1998), and Dobbin (1994) provide very insightful comparative studies of the same industries in different countries. Scherer's (1996) nine industry case studies of grain farming, crude oil, petroleum refining and marketing, steel, semiconductors, computers, automobiles, pharmaceuticals, and beer show that industries in the same country differ in their institutional infrastructure. The studies also underscore that the institutional infrastructure of a particular industry changes over time.

Table 10. **Firm Capabilities as Causes of Firm Performance**	
Firm capabilities	Firm performance outcomes
Ability to create more efficient production methods	Leadership position in industry
Ability to discover new products	Quantity of goods and services made
Ability to enter new markets	Profits
Ability to reorganize the firm	Payment of high wages
and so on . . .	*and so on . . .*

Enriching the Firm Capabilities Theory

The case of the synthetic dye industry has shown that tracing the development of firm capabilities is a key aspect of understanding why some firms perform so well over time and others so poorly. Remember that the proximate cause for a firm's competitive advantage lies in its ability to offer a product or service at lower cost or higher quality than its rivals.[267] To achieve such a low-cost or high-quality position, a firm needs to acquire a variety of skills. Let us define firm capabilities as all those skills that allow a firm to deliver high-quality or low-cost products to customers. To avoid making an explanation of firm performance based on firm capabilities a tautology, we need to keep firm capabilities analytically distinct from performance outcomes. Table 10 provides examples of what qualifies as a firm capability and what constitutes a performance outcome indicator.

Because in many industries a large number of individual activities are required to deliver a product to customers at a competitive price, firms face the challenge of coordinating and integrating a variety of skills. This is especially true when the product, customers, and competitors are changing as rapidly as happened in the dye industry before 1914. In a rapidly changing environment, only firms that constantly reconfigure their activities to create innovative products, or firms that cut their production costs, will be able to sustain a competitive advantage. The central task of management is precisely to coordinate the diverse activities that occur within a firm and allocate its resources toward those activities that enjoy the greatest likelihood of success, given the capabilities the firm already possesses (Lazonick, 1992). As the synthetic dye industry evolved, firms had to coordinate a larger and increasingly *diverse set* of activities to deliver a competitive product in the market place. Those firms that did not build and coordinate superior capabilities in marketing, production, and new product discovery fell behind and lost in the race for industrial leadership. Firms that did not make the transition from proprietary organizations managed by individual owners to a staff of professional managers (for example, Jäger in Germany and Levinstein in Great Britain) did not possess the abilities to take advantage of the growth opportunities available in the market for synthetic dyes. The inventor of the first synthetic dye, William Perkin, saw this clearly. He realized after seventeen years in the business that

---

[267] Strictly speaking a firm could offer a product not only at higher quality or lower cost but also at higher quality and lower cost. To avoid having to write repeatedly the clumsy term "and/or," I am using "or" in this context to include the possibility of "and."

he could no longer compete with leading German firms without investing large sums of money in new organizational capabilities and hiring a professional management. Perkin opted not to build a managerial firm, but rather to sell out and retire on the fortune that he had made as the pioneer of the synthetic dye industry. The buyers of Perkin's plant did not make these investments either and later were eliminated from the market.

The central insight gained from the comparative analysis of the synthetic dye industry before World War I is that firms do not create their capabilities from scratch. As long as nations differ systematically in their institutional structures, national institutions can serve as the ultimate source of competitive advantage because they provide firms with raw capabilities that are not available elsewhere at the same cost and quality.[268] We already discussed in detail how universities provided German firms with superior organic chemistry talent. Over time, the supporting institutional and industrial structures also provided German firms with a clear cost advantage. At the turn of the twentieth century, the German firms Bayer, BASF, and Hoechst were able to set up the largest chemical plants in the world in part because the social and economic environment of Germany made it easier to do so than was the case in Britain or the United States. A study commissioned by the management of the American firm Schoellkopf in 1908 (as quoted in Pfitzner, 1916, pp. 33–4) showed that the overall cost of constructing and running an aniline plant with 3,000,000 pounds yearly capacity was 44 percent less in Germany than in the United States, in part because Germany had in place several supporting institutions and related industries that provided crucial cost advantages to German firms. Detailed accounting figures reveal that building such a plant would have cost $104,000 in the United States versus $70,000 in Germany. The expenses for all materials required for the production of 3,000,000 pounds of aniline would have run $443,000 in the United States but only $317,000 in Germany.

Besides providing raw capabilities for firms, the matrix of existing social, legal, and political institutions defines the "rules of the game" for engaging in a particular industrial activity (North, 1990). The absence of a unified German patent law, for example, allowed every interested German entrepreneur at the beginning of the synthetic dye industry to enter dye production by copying British and French innovations, whereas British patent law imposed serious restrictions on entry into the industry in Britain. The "rules of the game" provide entrepreneurs and managers with the incentives to concentrate their efforts on particular activities (Baumol, 1993). Because the rules of the game are often not the same across countries, *the same firm strategies can lead to very different outcomes in different national contexts.*

---

[268] Because we draw on the same intellectual heritage of Thorstein Veblen (1899, 1915), who defined institutions as widely common and predictable behavior often driven by habits, my view of institutions is congenial to Nelson and Sampat's (2001) approach. They also highlight that institutions influence the cost of carrying out particular industrial activities. For them "institutions influence, or define, the ways in which economic actors get things done, in contexts involving human interaction. They do this by making certain kinds of transactions, or interactions more generally, attractive or easy, and others difficult or costly" (p. 39). Nelson and Sampat's idea that institutions represent social technologies to get things done with low transaction costs is very close to my notion of "raw capabilities." I chose the term "raw capabilities" because, for the present purposes of understanding the differential success of firms, I wanted to highlight that firms develop many of their capabilities by drawing on and combining skill sets and action patterns that originate in the social environment.

Two important implications follow for designing business strategies of individual firms. First, firms need to evaluate carefully in which national context to locate particular activities because differences in national contexts may ultimately decide which firms will win the industrial game. Expanding on the existing formulations of the resource-based theory of the firm (Wernerfeld, 1984; Barney, 1991; Conner and Prahalad, 1996; Foss, 1997; Kraatz and Zajac, 2000), an institutional theory of competitive advantage underscores that national institutional structures often constitute the hard to imitate, replicate, and trade assets that have been highlighted as the sources of competitive advantages in the resource-based theory. To be able to evaluate the relative advantage of one national context over the next, firms need to develop intelligence capabilities that provide a good picture of how the institutional environment will influence a firm's ability to develop competitive capabilities. Hall and Soskice (2001) have provided intriguing contemporary evidence that there is a systematic property to the way in which national economic systems differ. The theory of coevolution I have outlined here provides the dynamic explanation of why institutional structures in a country become complementary over time: Those structures that support one another have a greater chance of growth and survival. Hall and Soskice (2001) argue, for example, that the institutional make-up of liberal market economies represented by the United States is more conducive to radical technological innovations, whereas the institutional make-up of coordinated market economies represented by Germany is more capable of the persistent incremental innovations that are key for success in many mainstay manufacturing industries such as automobiles. Hall and Soskice's work provides additional evidence for an institutional theory of competitive advantage that I formulated to account for the performance differences of firms in the synthetic dye industry. In appraising what national context is best suited for a particular industrial activity, firms may discover how to spread different functions of a business across countries. The successful British and American dye firms did not go all the way to setting up research laboratories in Germany, but because traveling and communication today are much cheaper, the most sophisticated firms may, for example, locate an important part of their R&D activities in one country and do the manufacturing in another.

Second, firms need to develop lobbying capabilities to shape the institutional environment in their favor. Obviously, institutions differ in how readily they can be changed by firm actions. Williamson (2000, p. 597) has proposed a useful four-level typology of institutions that utilizes as an organizing principle how frequently a particular institution changes.[269] Because firms can only change those institutions that

---

[269] Williamson (2000) calls level 1 "embeddedness" and it involves informal institutions, customs, traditions, norms, and religion. Institutions at this level change every 100 to 1,000 years. Level 2 in this scheme is the "institutional environment," composed of formal rules of the game – especially property (polity, judiciary, bureaucracy). Institutions at this level change every 10 to 100 years. Level 3 is the level of "corporate governance." Institutions at this level are the play of the game, especially contracts, aligning governance structures with transactions. Institutions at this level change every 1 to 10 years. Finally, the fourth level in this scheme concerns resource allocation and employment, which involves prices and quantities and incentive alignment; at level 4 changes occur continuously. Williamson further explains that level 1 is the domain of social theory; level 2 is the domain of the economics of property rights and positive political theory; level 3 is transaction cost economics; and level 4 is neoclassical economics and agency and agency theory. Williamson later in the article points out that a still earlier level of analysis (level 0) is concerned with biological evolution, in which the mechanisms of the mind take shape.

experience a change during the lifetime of an industry, the present coevolutionary theory is concerned chiefly with what Williamson identifies as the *institutional environment* (level 2) and the play of the game (level 3), where changes happen on a time scale between 10 to 100 and 1 to 10 years, respectively. Many industry-specific regulations can be changed much more readily and frequently than can features of the institutional environment, which apply to a wide variety of industries and are deeply embedded in the institutional infrastructure of a country. This means that firms need to organize their lobbying efforts so as to deal first with the institutional features that apply most directly to their industry and are not systematically connected to other parts of the institutional environment. To modify institutional features that apply to a wide variety of industries, firms need to form coalitions that span across industries. As Williamson (2000, p. 595) recently noted, "We are still very ignorant about institutions." Compared to our understanding of markets, we clearly are only at the beginning of our understanding of how institutions work and how they change.

Coevolutionary models were pioneered in biology (Futuyma and Slatkin, 1983; Nitecki, 1983; Thompson, 1994) and have already been applied with explanatory success by such anthropologists as Boyd and Richerson (1985) and Durham (1991) to the development of culture. Building on Nelson (1995a), Levinthal and Myatt (1995), Lewin et al. (1999), and others, I have taken steps toward outlining a coevolutionary theory of industrial development that has the promise of illuminating many of the central questions about economic change because it places institutions at the center of analytical attention. I reemphasize that the use of biological theory in the social sciences must proceed with care. Importing ideas that have been pioneered in other fields, the task of the analyst is to translate theoretical ideas so that they make sense in a new context and discard those aspects that apply only to the arena in which it was originally developed. In social evolution, variations are clearly not completely random, and the notion of generations that is so important in biology is peripheral in social change. A successful translation of a theory to another domain, moreover, requires that the analyst is intimately familiar with the terrain into which she or he is fitting the theory and makes necessary adjustments to the theory. Most good theories do not emerge fully developed but are articulated incrementally in interaction with the empirical data (Williamson, 2000, p. 607). For this reason, further development of coevolutionary theory requires that it be tested in the context of other industrial settings and refined to spell out with greater precision the causal mechanisms that drive change in a particular domain. In the two remaining sections, I want to discuss the implications, questions, and opportunities for future research that can be drawn from this study of the synthetic dye industry.

Implications for Industrial Organization Studies

An evolutionary model leads to several observations and questions about economic development that differ from those arising from other perspectives. The most immediate cause of why some nations are richer than others is that richer nations produce more goods and services by organizing their production processes in more efficient ways (Porter, 1990; Kogut, 1993). Technological, institutional, and organizational innovations have been identified as key drivers behind economic growth (North, 1990;

Nelson, 1996b; Arora et al., 1998). Because firms constitute the productive capabilities of a national economy, they play a central role in an evolutionary theory of economic change. From an evolutionary perspective, the creation of firms that provide the goods and services of the economy is not a trivial task because firms represent complex social organizations that operate in an even more complex economic environment. Firms such as Bayer, Intel, Citibank, Motorola, or Ford cannot be planned on the drawing board one afternoon and be in operation the next morning. As the carriers of productive knowledge, firms are extremely complex coordinating mechanisms that, from an evolutionary perspective, develop out of more simple structures. This process requires significant time. For every firm that manages to be successful, a very large number of firms will fail (Aldrich, 1999). Evolutionary processes are very inefficient in this sense because they require a large number of trials to create a few well-adapted results. To establish that an evolutionary process is the causal driver of economic development, the single most important task is to find evidence of failed variants, be they firms, policies, legal rules, or other institutional arrangements. Evolutionary explanations for the development of a particular industry work best when the number of individual firms in an industry is large. They do not work when one or a few firms constitute the entire industry because that number is too low for birth and failure processes at the industry level to achieve a greater adaptation to the economic environment. In the case when one firm constitutes the entire industry, evolutionary explanations can only be used to model the firm as a population of routines, groups, or business units that evolve according to selection criteria specified by management. (I will return to such internal selection processes a bit later.) But for an evolutionary argument to be sound at the level of the individual firm, one must document either many failed routines, or projects, or employee hires, or business units, and so forth. As a general investigative rule, it is useful to keep the following in mind: no failures, no evolutionary adaptation through selection.

In economics textbooks the creation of effective firms is for the most part conceived of as an incentive problem. Given the right incentives, for example, in the form of large expected profits that can be made from providing a particular good or service, managers or entrepreneurs are seen as being able to create firms without any trouble by choosing from a set of feasible production possibilities, given current market and technological constraints. From an evolutionary perspective, creating an effective firm is equally a problem of acquiring the relevant skills and capabilities (Dosi, Nelson, and Winter, 2000). Organizational change is a cumulative process. From this point of view, the future trajectory of a firm is not so much determined by external incentives as by internal capabilities. As long as a firm can obtain sufficient amounts of resources from the environment, it is much more likely to look for new opportunities in the vicinity of the existing activities than to enter markets that in theory offer the highest profit margins in the economy. When a firm makes negative profits for an extended period, it will not be able to obtain additional resources, and sooner or later it will die.[270] Whereas in neoclassical theory, firms are typically viewed as homogeneous and constrained only by technological and market

---

[270] Just because the market will force a firm out of existence does not of course mean that the firm's component capabilities will no longer exist in the economy. Those capabilities frequently are taken over by another firm.

conditions, firms in evolutionary theory are seen as diverse and constrained by their own administrative heritage (Nelson, 1991). Variation in the strategies and structures of firms is necessary for a selection process to be responsible for the transformation of an industry or the economy. Without heterogeneous firms, one cannot give an evolutionary explanation for the development of an industry (Metcalfe, 1998). An explanation of industrial transformation that relies on a selection process as the chief causal mechanism for cumulative change raises questions that can be asked at different levels of analysis. It is convenient to organize the discussion of these questions under three headings: an entire national economy,[271] an industry within a country, and an individual firm.

Level of a National Economy

Because an evolutionary view makes very different assumptions about economic agents, it is not surprising that a host of different public policy questions arise from this perspective. When two countries differ in their economic performance, evolutionary theory would predict that this is so either because one country does not generate enough novel variations out of its existing economic structures or because it has a very poor institutional infrastructure for generating new firms and selecting out inefficient ones. Economic progress cannot come about without trying out new technologies and new organizational arrangements, in the form of either new supporting institutions or new firm strategies and structures (Nelson, 1990; Rosenberg, 1992; Freeman and Louçã, 2001). From an evolutionary perspective, universities are particularly interesting organizations because their activities constitute one of the most important mechanisms for generating novelty in modern societies.

One of the key questions for the evolutionary perspective is, What kind of institutional structures are capable of generating a sufficient amount of novelty for progress in the economic system? When a particular country pulls ahead of all others in its economic performance for a number of years (recall, for example, Japan in the 1970s and 1980s or the United States in the 1990s), it typically does not take long before books appear that identify the leading country's economic institutions as economically superior and causally responsible for the economic "miracle." Over the last decade many an "expert" has recommended that countries around the world should adopt the American model of corporate governance to jumpstart their economies and permanently give them higher growth rates. From an evolutionary perspective, such recommendations appear naïve at best and dangerous at worst. A complex economy that is moderately effective cannot be designed without a great deal of trial and error by the economic agents (Hayek, 1973). The leading economies over the past centuries – Britain, the United States, Germany, and Japan – developed gradually by modifying their institutional structures piecemeal. Often changes are mistakenly labeled as "radical" because the observer does not measure all the things that remain in place. An evolutionary perspective would predict that there has not been a single country in world history that has revised its economic structures from the ground up without generating at least temporarily a decline in economic performance. Countries have

---

[271] Instead of framing questions at the level of an entire national economy, one could, of course, ask these questions at the level of the global economy. Because most public policy instruments today still operate only at the level of a country, I shall frame them at the country level.

often tried to imitate a seemingly successful foreign practice by adding it to their domestic institutional framework. However, unless the practice is *not* systematically connected to other practices, such importation attempts tend to transform the practice in question because it has to be fit into the overall institutional architecture of the importing nation.

When German universities became the leading institutions of higher learning in the second half of the nineteenth century, laggard countries all over the world tried to import the German model. The American attempt to import the German practice of advanced research and specialized teaching led to a very different type of university organization in the United States than in the German model. Instead of creating a population of free-standing graduate schools, as initially conceived by the founders of Johns Hopkins University, Americans superimposed the German model on the existing college organization; from this fusion emerged the American graduate school staffed with professors who also taught in the traditional college (Ben-David, 1977). One hundred and forty years later, the direction of importation has changed. German universities now are trying to import some of the practices that seemingly have made the American university the leading system of higher education in the world; as far as I can tell, however, they are trying to import individual practices without recognizing that they work in a larger context that may not be replicable in the German context without much more drastic changes in the funding, admission policies, and governance of German universities. Before trying to import practices from a different social context, one needs to compare the two contexts and ask whether they are similar enough to warrant the conclusion that such a transfer will lead to the desired result. Homegrown experimentation may be much more successful than imported forms. From an evolutionary perspective, societies are historically grown entities and exhibit a large amount of path dependence in their development. Where they can go tomorrow is significantly constrained by where they are today. For this reason it becomes vitally important to understand what institutional arrangements are functionally equivalent and therefore can equally well lead to good economic performance, and what institutions are decidedly inferior in their social consequences. Trying to replace the latter kind is smart public policy; trying to replace the former is a sign of ignorance with potentially tragic consequences.

Another important question at the level of a country is how much reform and institutional innovation can be implemented without leading to a collapse or at least serious decline of the level of economic development already achieved. Biological evolution has a tight constraint on the amount of novelty permitted in the genetic blueprint of a species. Biological evolution has created numerous repair mechanisms that keep the gene pool of a species relatively stable but at the same time allow for mutations and genetic recombination to lead to a better adapted species in the course of a large number of generations. The ability of a social system to absorb innovations in its foundational structures may be greater than in biological inheritance systems, but an evolutionary view suggests that too radical revisions in the institutional architecture will destabilize the system. As the recent experience of trying to convert Russia into a market economy reveals, too much novelty in the system may first lead to a prolonged economic decline rather than an improvement (Kogut and Spicer, 2002). In particular the Russian example shows that introducing markets before having in place the regulatory infrastructure necessary to make markets work as well as in advanced countries ignores the sequential nature of economic development and the danger of market failure (Stiglitz, 2002).

By no means does the market mechanism always constitute a very stringent selection environment that will allow efficient firms to replace inefficient ones quickly. One key contribution of this book has been to show that large firms are able to change selection criteria in their favor. As a first approximation, as long as actual or potential competition exists in a market, firms that lose money will not be able to survive over long periods. Markets are very powerful selection forces that lead to the transformation of an economy. One of the important questions of evolutionary economics is to understand better how stringent the selection forces have to be to bring about constructive economic transformation. From a public policy point of view, it is important to examine how low the number of firms in an industry can fall before the industry will seriously suffer from not having enough variation in its firms to possess insurance against new rivals in a foreign industry. As the experience of the United States and Great Britain in the early synthetic dye industry showed, having only few a firms not only hurts consumers in the short run because of high prices but also may have deleterious long-term effects because the industry may not be able to generate sufficient novelty to compete against foreign industries that are populated by many more firms.

The media have a tendency to cover massive layoffs and firm failures but rarely mention when firms hire a large number of people or when a surprisingly large number of new firms are being formed in particular months. From an evolutionary point of view, firm bankruptcies are undesirable only if they are not brought about by other firms that provide better products and services.[272] Joseph Schumpeter's (1942) characterization of capitalism as a *process of creative destruction* underlines the evolutionary view that better economic structures can only be achieved by allowing underperforming entities to be replaced by organizations that can make better use of their resources. Ideally, surviving firms should learn from the mistakes that the failed firms made. Thinking through how experience and knowledge can be disseminated from one firm to the next without paving the way for collusion is an important public policy issue. From an evolutionary perspective, the question of whether infant industries or temporarily underperforming firms should be protected and supported by governments needs to be evaluated in terms of more than short-term economic efficiency. New firms may represent important new organizational models that may become an important insurance policy against future changes in the economic environment. Existing firms have many advantages that give them the power to force a new rival out of the market. This means that from an evolutionary perspective, anti-trust authorities and other public policy makers and enforcers need to be concerned with protecting economic diversity and the mechanisms that generate novelty in the economic system (Metcalfe, 1998).

---

[272] In many countries governments try to preserve jobs in failing firms by providing a host of subsidies. From a societal point of view these subsidies often are poor investments; society would reap much higher returns by supporting education to stimulate the creation of new technologies and the formation of new firms. Bankruptcies, of course, involve individual hardships, and it is a noble motivation to want to reduce such hardship. But from a moral point of view, helping someone to keep a relatively unproductive job at the expense of helping unemployed people to find employment by supporting the creation of new firms is a highly dubious proposition.

Level of a National Industry

There is no such thing as a completely unregulated industry. Economic historians such as North (1990) have shown that successful economic development requires governments to set and enforce rules that provide economic players with the incentive to make productive investments rather than live off the fruits of others. When pirates dominated the seas, traders were reluctant to ship precious cargo to foreign lands. Large-scale trade across the sea happened only when governments systematically went after pirates and made sea trade relatively secure for investors. The perceived danger of large-scale piracy at the upper echelons of public corporations in the summer of 2002 has scared potential investors away from the stock markets, underscoring once again what was already recognized after the stock market crash of 1929: Regulatory oversight of the financial sector, for example, is crucial for investors to have confidence that they will not be misled, cheated, or expropriated. To curtail opportunities for economic actors to engage in strategies that are known to decrease the overall wealth of society, governments regulate all industries to some extent.[273]

Because governments interfere in the development of an industry in so many ways, it is important to articulate the questions that arise from an evolutionary perspective for the regulation of industries. Recall that German dominance in the synthetic dye industry before World War I was built on the much larger numbers of firms that entered the industry than in Britain and elsewhere but also on the much larger numbers of firms that failed. Biologists agree that small population size and geographic isolation are the best predictors for the death of a species (Sober, 1984, e.g., p. 25). The figures also emphasize that in an evolutionary perspective, firm failures are a necessary component of industrial success. Evolutionary processes are very inefficient, requiring a large number of trials and a great number of failures to find structures better adapted to their environment. This much we know. What we don't know is *how* inefficient they have to be. How many firm failures were necessary in Germany to lay the foundation for dominance of world markets? How can firms learn from one another so that new trials are not merely repetitions of unsuccessful experiments that other firms have already made? It is not a trivial task to learn the right lessons from both apparently successful and unsuccessful strategies of a competitor, because very frequently, causal ambiguity about what led to the success makes learning difficult (March, 1999). A host of mechanisms seem to be present to help diffuse knowledge throughout an industry. In the context of contemporary Germany, industry associations apparently help transfer good practice in regard to new technology (Hall and

---

[273] There is always the danger that governments go too far in regulating industries. From an evolutionary point of view, too much regulation may dramatically reduce the economic experiments in which the players in an industry will engage. Players may find solutions to economic problems that are novel and therefore not known to regulators. It is important to distinguish between regulation that aims to make markets work effectively and regulation that aims to undermine the working of market processes. The former is desirable; the latter tends to reduce economic performance. Above all, policy makers need to remember that different industries require very different regulation. One size does not fit all economic activities that occur in the economy. It would also be a gross misreading of economic history to believe that markets are always the most efficient form of organization. Effective economies possess a diversity of governance structures. Organizational hierarchies and various institutional structures, some of which I have documented in this study, complement markets and play an integral role in high-growth economies.

Soskice, 2001). In the United States, in contrast, the comparatively high migration rate of employees from one firm to the next seems to play a similar role. From this point of view, the lower levels of employee loyalty in the United States – which is undoubtedly sometimes detrimental to the performance of individual firms – may have a large net benefit for the economy as a whole because it leads to a dissemination of new knowledge and effective practice across firms. In light of the findings in this study of the synthetic dye industry, it is important to figure out to what extent academic institutions in general help diffuse knowledge across firms. What role do trade associations, patent documents, and legal court battles play in diffusing know-how from one firm to the next? To find answers to these questions, we need to study other industries and compare them with each other.

The database of synthetic dye plants collected by Ernst Homburg and myself reveals that many plants outlived the firms that built them. This suggests that when firms go bankrupt much of their productive capability may not be lost because another firm takes over their plants. Our data do not allow us to assess whether the new owners of the plant simply took over the physical hardware or whether some of the old practices of the plant were also absorbed. Perhaps new organizational practices can emerge from the recombination of practices from the newly acquired plant and the acquiring firm's existing plants. If so, the large number of failed firms in Germany may have provided a pool of plants that could supply important raw material for recombining existing organizational practices and for creating novel and sometimes more effective ways to organize dye production. Future research should examine the role of a population of plants rather than firms as an important carrier of productive knowledge and organizational practices.

The record of the dye industry before 1914 reveals that collective action on the part of German firms was very important in cementing their leadership position in the global industry. We need to study more industries to be able to answer more precisely these important questions: How much influence do political processes have on industry development? Can we measure the role of trade organizations? Under what circumstances can lobbying be more successful? When do lobbying campaigns help only particular industries but hurt the welfare of the entire society? Following the lead of Murtha, Spencer, and Lenway's (1996) revealing analysis of differences in the kind of technology policies that can be implemented in the context of U.S. and Japanese political institutions, we need to examine how lobbying organizations and collective strategies work in different countries. To understand the dynamic character of industry evolution, it is also very important to inquire whether specific moments exist in the development of a national industry when its long-term competitive position will be determined.

Level of an Individual Firm

On first glance, evolutionary theory seems to call into question the very notion that managers are capable of leading their firms to long-term competitive advantages. Because of its emphasis on selection processes, an evolutionary view of industry development would be skeptical that the intentions of the managers are sufficient to explain why particular organizations are successful. In his contribution to a symposium on *Evolutionary Thought in Management and Organization Theory at the Beginning of the New Millennium* (Murmann, Aldrich, Levinthal, and Winter, 2003), Sidney Winter argued that besides the action of making adequate investments in organizational capabilities, little evidence suggests that managerial wisdom lies behind sustained superior firm performance. To put it differently, among those firms that have made the necessary investments in organizational capabilities to be viable contenders for leadership in an industry, it is not clear that differences in managerial strategies lie behind differences in firm performance. In the same forum, Daniel Levinthal argued that managers might to some extent be able to engineer evolutionary processes. I want to probe a bit further into the question of what useful managerial lessons can be derived from an evolutionary perspective. Is there any other recommendation that one can make about managerial practice besides noting that managers need to make investments into capabilities that will allow the firm to become a serious player in a particular market?

Earlier in this chapter, I spelled out a theoretical perspective that conceptualizes technological change as a nested hierarchy of variation and selective retention mechanisms. Social change has a similar hierarchical structure (Simon, 1981). Starting at the microlevel are the actions and reactions of individual human beings (Weick, 1979) at the next higher level are work groups and teams in organizations, followed by business units within organizations, entire organizations, entire industries, communities of industries, the organization of national economies, and finally, at the most macrolevel, the world economy. Relatively few scholars have attempted to analyze empirically a firm as a population of practices that change in response to changed internal selection criteria. Notable exceptions are Langton (1984) and Burgelman (1991). The most forceful articulation as to why stability in organizational practices can be useful for firms was made in Hannan and Freeman's (1984) article "Structural inertia and organizational change." A selection-based argument requires considerable organizational inertia to make the argument work. Unfortunately, to my knowledge, no empirical study has submitted to a competitive test the early view of Hannan and Freeman (1977) and the various managerial perspectives on industrial change, such as those of Chandler (1962) and Nadler and Tushman (1988). Early on, Hannan and Freeman (1977) saw individual organizations as fundamentally incapable of change and regarded industrial transformation as proceeding almost exclusively at the population (industry) level, through the birth and death of inert organizations. Managerial perspectives, in contrast, view organizations as quite readily changeable through managerial actions. Evolutionary theory in the tradition of Nelson and Winter (1982) takes an intermediate position but sees clear limits in the ability of managers to understand the environment of firms and adapt their firms' strategies and structures to track with changes in environmental conditions. Given the limits on predicting and understanding future competitive environments as well as knowing the fine details of how one's own organization works, what positive recommendation can an evolutionary perspective make about managing an organization?

The answer, in my view, is to see the managerial role as one of establishing internal selection criteria for the goals and actions of all the individual and collective agents that work within the organization. Burgelman (1991), for example, examined organizational changes at Intel and showed that the firm's corporate strategy of exiting from the memory chips business and focusing on microprocessors resulted from an evolutionary process in which internal capital allocation rules acted as the selection environment. To date, so little empirical research has been done on internal selection environments that we have no systematic knowledge about what selection criteria are used in different firms. Are corporate vision statements important guides for processes of internal selection? Is the reason why most management consultants suggest that vision statements should not be changed more than once every five years precisely because otherwise not enough stability is available in the internal selection environment to allow a variation and selection retention process to design micro-structures in firms that will be consistent with where managers want the firm to go? Similar questions can be asked about corporate cultures. Do key organizational values act as selection criteria for employee initiatives?

Hayek (1973) drew a fundamental distinction between the self-organizing spontaneous order of the entire economy and the consciously designed order of individual organizations, such as industrial firms. I think Hayek was overly optimistic in terms of how much an organization can be designed by intentional action rather than through an evolutionary process; in the latter, the particular organizational arrangements are not planned but emerge through the interaction of the individuals in the organization. It seems to me that the arguments Hayek made for the economy as a whole can also be applied to some extent to individual organizations. Top managers cannot possess all the knowledge that the various individuals in an organization have about their task environment. For this reason it is probably most effective to specify goals and selection criteria but also to allow lower-level employees to find the best solution to their particular task.

Because large organizations are composed of many units – small groups, functional departments, production sites, divisions – another role of top managers is to make sure that the selection criteria used at these various levels of the organization are consistent with one another. Ulrich Witt's (1998, 2000) notion that top managers need to provide cognitive leadership – i.e., create a common frame of reference for key employees – to assure the growth of the organization can be interpreted through this selection framework. If top managers fail to do so, the different components will develop in different directions and the effectiveness of the overall organization will be impaired. Because organizations are made of individual human beings who often have different ideas about where the organization should be heading, the political fights among different factions tend to lead to an organizational truce (March and Simon, 1958; March, 1999), which is responsible for a great deal of the inertia that characterizes firms. Much of the literature on organizational change (Tushman and Romanelli, 1985) highlights that top managers need to force their organization to generate variations of their existing practices. In this view, a CEO should see him- or herself as the Chief Evolutionary Officer, responsible for ensuring that the firm engages in a sufficient amount of experimentation with products and organizational practices to increase the odds that it will be better aligned with the competitive environment. The key challenge from this perspective is to find the appropriate balance between experimentation and retaining existing practices. For the most part, managers seem to err on the side of not building enough experimentation into their firms to allow it to become an effective evolutionary system that is to a large extent self-organizing.

Opportunities for Future Research on Industrial Development

I return once more to the quotations that served as the preamble to Chapter 1. At the end of this comparative analysis of the synthetic dye industry from 1857 until 1914, it should be more evident why I selected quotations from Schumpeter, Keynes, Porter, Marshall, and DiMaggio to announce the themes of the present monograph. Even scholars who do not frame their work in formal evolutionary terms have discovered the importance of bringing history into the study of economic development. Both Porter (for the field of strategic management) and DiMaggio (for the field of organizational sociology) have called for more qualitative and historical studies of industry development because they found that large-sample cross-sectional studies are not adequate to understand how organizational structures change over time. The present study brought together the sampling methods pioneered by organizational ecologists (Hannan and Freeman, 1989; Carroll and Hannan, 1995b) and later employed by evolutionary economics (Klepper and Simons, 1996, 1997, 2000a) with business and economic history (Chandler, Amatori and Hikino, 1997; McCraw, 1997a; Landes, 1998). By examining the entire population of dye firms that existed from 1857 to 1914 – large firms and small firms, long-lived and short-lived, successes and failures – while at the same time conducting qualitative studies of the institutional environment of six firms, as well as of individuals in firms, academia, and government, we could identify with greater confidence causal mechanisms that produced the observed differences in economic performance. Case studies of individual firms have the advantage that one can observe causal processes at a much finer level of resolution. But such studies always run the risk that one may have picked a firm that is not representative of the majority of other firms in the industry. Studies of all firms in the industry, on the other hand, run the risk of mistaking a correlation (two things appearing jointly) for causation (one thing bringing about another thing) because they typically do not include sufficient knowledge about the context in which firms are operating.

A survey of the literatures associated with evolutionary economics, business and economic history, and strategic management reveals substantial overlap in the empirical concerns of the three groups. Evolutionary economists and organizational ecologists have conducted a series of studies examining the entry and exit of all firms over the entire life history of an industry. Organizational ecologists have studied populations of firms in such industries as newspapers (Carroll and Delacroix, 1982), brewing (Carroll and Swaminathan, 1991), automobile manufacturing (Carroll and Hannan, 1995a; Carroll, Bigelow, Seidel, and Tsai, 1996), banking (Ranger-Moore, Banaszak-Holl, and Hannan, 1991; Barnett and Hansen, 1996), savings and loans (Rao and Neilsen, 1992; Haveman, 1993) life insurance (Ranger-Moore, Banaszak-Holl, and Hannan, 1991), early telephone communication (Barnett and Carroll, 1987), hotels (Ingram and Inman, 1996; Ingram and Baum, 1997), and microprocessors (Wade, 1995). Except for the analyses of the automobile and newspaper industries, all aforementioned studies focused on the United States or regions within the United States. Evolutionary economists, in turn, have examined such U.S. industries as television sets (Klepper and Simons, 2000a), penicillin (Klepper and Simons, 1997; Klepper, 2002), automobiles (Klepper, 1997), tires (Klepper and Simons, 2000b), lasers (Klepper, 2001), aircraft (Frenken, 2000; Frenken and Leydesdorff, 2000), and helicopters, motorcycles, and microcomputers (Frenken, Saviotti, and Trommetter, 1999). Similar to the patterns we observed in Chapter 2, these studies collectively show that the odds of performing well change substantially across different periods in the life cycle of an industry. Many industries in this list experienced a dramatic decline in the number of producer firms relatively early in the industry. But all of these studies – with the notable exception of Carroll and Delacroix's (1982) work on newspapers in Argentina and Ireland and Carroll and Hannan's (1995a) investigations of automobile firms in the United States and Western Europe – have focused on the United States and hence could not see that the success chances of firms at the very same point of time in the development of an industry may differ substantially across national contexts (see Figure 7).

Understanding such national differences in the development of industries has been on the agenda of economic history for decades. David Landes' seminal study, *The Unbound Prometheus: Technological Change and Industrial Development in Western Europe from 1750 to the Present* (1969), and more recently Joel Mokyr's *The Lever of Riches: Technological Creativity and Economic Progress* (1990) place institutional reasons at the center of their explanations for why the industrial revolution first occurred in Western Europe and not in another region of the world. Although it is impossible to draw a sharp boundary between the two groups, a useful way to differentiate between economic and business historians is to note that the former are more concerned with the development of the economy as a whole, the latter with the development of business firms. In contrast to organizational ecologists who search for regularities of industry development across historical time and location, the underlying assumption in much of the work in business history is that one cannot understand managerial actions divorced from their setting in time and place. Some historians highlight that differences in historically specific business cultures shape managerial actions (Lipartito, 1995). Others highlight technological opportunities and constraints inherent in the development stage of an economy as the key forces shaping managerial action (see John, 1997, for an excellent survey). Although early business history focused on firms within particular countries, since the mid-1970s scholars around Mira Wilkins[274] and Alfred Chandler have started to produce cross-country comparative work in monographs and journals such as the *Business History Review, Business and Economic History* (now called *Enterprise & Society)*, and *Business History* (based in London). Similarly, Japanese business historians around Keiichir Nakagawa were early advocates of comparative business history (Nakagawa, 1975). They started in the 1970s an annual business history conference with an expressed comparative focus. For twenty years (1975–94), the proceedings of these so-called Fuji conferences were published annually in book form by the University of Tokyo Press. Comparative business history has also been practiced in two excellent recent volumes, one by McCraw (1997b), *Creating Modern Capitalism*, and a second one edited by Chandler, Franco Amatori, and Takashi Hikino (1997), *Big Business and the Wealth of Nations*. Outside the field of business history, a comparative methodology has been adopted by economists such as Lazonick (1990, 1991, 1992), Best (1990),

---

[274] Mira Wilkins must be regarded as the pioneer in comparing systematically the business activities of firms in different countries. Throughout her career, she examined the historical development of multinational companies across many countries. See, for example, Wilkins (1970, 1974, 1989) and Wilkins and Schröter (1998). Working in the Wilkins tradition, Geoffrey Jones (1996) compared the history of multinational firms worldwide.

Langlois (1992; Langlois and Robertson, 1995), and Mowery (1984, 1996; Mowery and Nelson, 1999), who have all used comparative historical analyses to better understand the role of firms in creating differences in economic performance. In a recent study of the paper industry, Magee (1997) found it also analytically essential to compare the respective national environments of Britain and the United States to be able to understand the development of the British industry.

Under the influence of mainstream economics and sociology, management and corporate strategy scholars have devoted substantial effort over the last three decades to developing universalistic theories of management that would be true for all places and times. Thompson's (1967) *Organizations in Action* represents one of the most persuasive examples of the program that seeks to discover Newtonian-type covering laws in the social sciences. Large literatures have developed, for example, on top management teams (Hambrick and Mason, 1984) and their decision behaviors (Bourgeois and Eisenhardt, 1988; Eisenhardt and Bourgeois, 1988; Eisenhardt, 1989b); on organizational demography, a body of work that seeks to trace the behavior of organizations to their demographic characteristics (Pfeffer, 1983); and on technological determinants of organizational and industrial change (Tushman and Anderson, 1986; Henderson and Clark, 1990; Utterback, 1994; Christensen and Rosenbloom, 1995; Mitchell and Singh, 1996). Undoubtedly, the quest for invariant social laws that seek to explain individual instances of behavior by invoking a general law according to which behavior unfolds in a regular fashion had a very positive result: Management scholars more frequently would test their theories with large samples as would be required to support universal claims. But this universalist quest also distracted analysts from developing robust causal explanations (Abbott, 1998) and from doing justice to the fact that time and place have a dramatic impact on how managers and firms behave (Hodgson, 2001). Researchers in international management have documented extensively how prevalent failures are when managers and firms leave their national context for the first time. Evolutionary thought in management and organizational theory (Tushman and Romanelli, 1985; Burgelman, 1991; Aldrich, 1999; Van De Ven and Grazman, 1999) has taken hold precisely because evolutionary explanations are sensitive to time and place (Blute, 1997). They offer causal mechanisms that are cumulative and hence lead to different outcomes over time. In evolutionary explanations what remains constant are not behaviors but the causal mechanisms that produce behaviors. In different contexts the same causal mechanisms lead to different behaviors. Because contexts are never exactly the same when causation is cumulative, social science has not produced any significant covering laws (Tilly, 1997). To explain particular actions of managers and firms, it is therefore imperative to specify the particulars about time and place. This is precisely the working assumption of much of business history. With these methodological considerations in mind it becomes apparent why a growing number of management scholars and evolutionary economists interested in the development of firms (Nelson and Winter, 1982; Winter, 1995; Dosi, 2000; Dosi, Nelson, and Winter, 2000) have found it particularly useful to draw upon business historians such as Alfred Chandler (1962, 1990), who analyzed in detail the development of the large firm in the economy: Business history provides the important details for explaining economic change.

As this short and necessarily incomplete literature survey of evolutionary economics, business and economic history, and management shows, all three groups of scholars are deeply concerned with the development of firms and industries. There is also a growing recognition among leading scholars in all three groups that research on industrial change would benefit from an even closer collaboration between historians and social scientists. The benefits of such interactions have become apparent in such volumes as *Inside the Business Enterprise: Historical Perspectives on the Use of Information* (Temin, 1991), *Coordination and Information: Historical Perspectives on the Organization of Enterprise* (Lamoreaux, Raff, and Temin, 1995), and *Learning by Doing in Markets, Firms, and Countries* (Lamoreaux, Raff, and Temin, 1999). The present study has demonstrated that the methods used by the three groups are complementary rather than mutually exclusive. Their theoretical approaches sometimes differ markedly (especially in regard to the explanatory role attributed to the intentions of the actors), but these differences should be regarded as a productive and welcome challenge because they invite scholars to consider alternative explanations for the same phenomenon and to design studies that subject the explanations to a competitive test.

Seen from this perspective, the study of firm and industry development is a fertile triangle in which scholars from three groups can work together in building more powerful models and providing greater understanding of the microfoundation of economic activity. The variation and selective retention logic of evolutionary explanations provide an abstract framework into which additional pieces of explanation have to be added to explain a particular social outcome at a particular point in time. Knowledge about the context of a developing population such as an industry is essential to explaining its behavior and performance. We should, therefore, now readily understand why economic and business histories constitute necessary inputs for a productive program in evolutionary economics. By the same token, research in management, business, and economic history would benefit from absorbing some of the conceptual and empirical results of evolutionary economics, which would allow the analyst to formulate more penetrating questions about the development of firms and industries.

Earlier I spelled out some research questions that follow from the present study for the evolutionary research program. I now want to raise some additional questions of particular interest for management scholars and business and economic historians. We saw in the synthetic dye industry before World War I that changes in the industry organization took place through both the birth and death of organizations and through the transformation of individual organizations. In the early formal models of industry evolution (Nelson and Winter, 1982), routines were treated as fully inert during the periods in which selection forces operated to transform an industry. Recognizing, of course, that organizations, besides following rules, sometimes deliberate about new rules, Nelson and Winter (1982) introduced a hierarchy of decision rules (routines) in which higher-level, less frequently invoked rules control lower-level, more frequently invoked rules. Moving up the hierarchy, one finds that decision rules become less and less routine-like and deterministic of action. In the early formal selection models, however, deliberation about low-level operational routines ceased before selection forces became active (see Vromen, 1995, for an excellent exposition of these models). Unlike the early organizational ecologists, Nelson and Winter (1982) from the beginning recognized that firms learn to adapt to some extent to their environment. The past two decades have seen considerable progress in understanding in more detail how routines come about, how they persist, and how they change. Dosi, Nelson, and Winter (2000); the Special Issue of the *Strategic Management Journal* (2000) on *The Evolution of Firm Capabilities*, edited by Constance Helfat; and Murmann, Aldrich, Levinthal, and Winter (2003) provide excellent overviews.

As these surveys make apparent, however, we need to know much more about the nature of routines in organizations. Management scholars and business historians are in the position to carry out in-depth case studies of individual firms to provide more detailed answers to these questions: Do those routines that govern most fundamentally the behavior of an organization form at the beginning of the organization, as Stinchcombe (1965) argued in his imprinting hypothesis? Or do routines become more inert as firms practice them for longer periods of time? Are there any systematic strategies managers can use to change the fundamental routines of organizations, even though this may be very difficult to do and seldom leads to success? Many proponents of the dynamic view of firm capabilities, such as Sidney Winter, are committed to the notion of higher-level decision rules that allow firms to change their lower-level operational rules.[275] Levinthal and March (1993) have argued that successful learning in organizations can take place only if the different levels in the hierarchy of routines do not change concurrently. If Levinthal and March's view is correct, we should see that firms having dynamic capabilities possess them precisely because they do not change the higher-level routines while revising the lower-level operational routines. In contrast, firms that change all their routines at the same time should lose their capabilities to adapt successfully to new environmental conditions because the populations of routines making up the organization would never display sufficient consistency and coherence to constitute effective enterprises.[276]

It would be extremely useful for management scholars and business historians to trace systematically how the population of rules representing a particular organization changes over long periods of time. In this regard March, Schulz, and Chou's (2000) study of changes in the formal rules over the life history of a university is a pioneering effort. One can only hope that it will be followed by many other studies of individual organizations and enriched with more qualitative approaches. Particularly promising candidates for such studies are firms for which detailed descriptions of their vision, their business model, and their organizational routines are available from the early days of their operation. I have recently discovered the bylaws of the foundation that owned the famous optical instruments company Carl Zeiss in Jena, starting in the late eighteenth century (Abbe, 1896). The 140-page document describes in detail the vision for the company and its key organizational routines.[277] By tracing carefully how the Zeiss companies have developed

---

[275] See also the contribution of Sidney Winter in Cohen, Burkhart, Dosi, Edigi, Marengo, Warglien, and Winter (1996).

[276] For an articulation of the notion of corporate coherence, see Teece, Rumelt, Dosi, and Winter (1994).

[277] There remain rich opportunities for business historians to analyze in detail the vast amount of primary materials that are available in the Zeiss archives on development of this important company. Unfortunately, most of the existing literature on Zeiss (e.g., Mühlfriedel, Edith, and Walter, 1996) is in German. For a brief overview of some of the key milestones in Ziess's development, see Hagen (1999) and Kogut and Zander (2000).

over the past 100 years, one should be able to shed important light on the processes underlying the persistence and change of organizational routines. Similarly, I am confident that business historians will be able to find many other promising case studies to trace how populations of routines change within companies. When scholars have collected a significant number of such case studies across different countries, they should even be able to investigate which routines can be set up in any country and which ones are quite specific to a particular national context. Such studies would considerably further our understanding of the institutional nature of competitive advantage.

I have not presented a mathematical model of coevolution in this book because I believe that such models need to be based on a solid empirical footing; that has to be developed first. Mathematical models are very useful for testing whether our empirically grounded causal explanations presented as verbal accounts can be recreated in a dynamic model. Human beings are excellent pattern recognizers, but not so good in making sequential logical inferences. Thinking through the logical implications of causal reasoning that involves more than one variable or multiple iterations is especially challenging. Take, for instance, the very revealing cognitive challenges of correctly identifying the logical implications of folding a single sheet of paper forty times. How thick does a single a sheet of paper (original thickness, 0.35 mm) become after folding it forty times onto itself? If you have never worked with mathematical models, you probably will be surprised by the answer. The paper folded forty times will be as thick as the distance between the earth and the moon (385,000 km, or 3.8×10^8 mm).

Why do we at first assume that the thickness of the folded paper must be quite small? Without the assistance of paper and pencil or an electronic calculator, we don't walk through every step in the calculation that doubles the thickness of the paper forty times. We may do it a few times and conclude that when we fold the paper once onto itself, the paper at 50 percent of its original length and width has twice the thickness of the original sheet of paper, namely, 0.7 mm, which does not amount to very much at all. We overlook, however, that next time we fold the paper it is already four times as thick, after the third fold it is eight times as thick, and after the fourth fold sixteen times as thick. When we continue this process another thirty-six times, the paper will be more than one billion (10^9) times as thick as the original unfolded piece. Because our brain is not optimized to recognize quickly and accurately the implications of a causal process in which variables interact over multiple periods, this is precisely where mathematical models that strip down a complex reality to key causal variables come in very handy; they offer a powerful tool for checking whether the logic of a verbal causal account implies plausible results. In formulating a verbal causal explanation, for example, for the German dominance in the synthetic dye industry, the temptation is very high to make definitive statements about why a particular outcome was observed. A mathematical model makes it possible to check the logical consistency and plausibility of one's causal explanations. Mathematical models can be used in a second powerful way. By varying slightly one's initial assumptions in a mathematical model, one can also test how robust the outcomes of the model are. If minor changes in initial values of the relevant variables lead to very different results in the model, one has good reason to be skeptical about the universality of one's verbal theory. This second use of models makes it possible to specify more accurately the boundary conditions of one's theory.[278]

Evolutionary economists have made significant use of mathematical models and simulation technologies to advance their research programs. They typically use assumptions in their mathematical models that are close to an empirical reality and then use simulation runs to recreate how an industry or an economy actually works. Nelson and Winter (1982), for example, have formulated simulation models of aggregate economic output that contain much more realistic behavioral assumptions about the way economic agents make decisions than traditional mathematical models. More recently evolutionary economists have also developed history-friendly models to test whether the existing verbal accounts about the dynamics in the U.S. computer industry, for instance, can be translated into a mathematical simulation that could recreate the development path of the industries' organization (Malerba, Nelson, Orsenigo, and Winter, 1999).

The next logical step on my research agenda then is to examine whether a simulation model of the coevolutionary causal accounts I have put forward as an explanation for why Germany came to dominate the synthetic dye industry before 1914 can generate the historical path that we have observed. Without having first done the detailed and time-consuming empirical work on the synthetic dye industry, nobody could try to offer even a semiconvincing model of the dye industry's development. On reading an early manuscript of this study, James March penetratingly asked me (personal communication, 1998), "If we restarted history 100 times, what fraction of the restarts would lead to the same outcome?" Technological evolution contains a significant random component. It was not necessary, therefore, that synthetic dyes were discovered exactly in 1856. This event could have happened at least twenty years earlier; but it could also have happened significantly later. Many other elements in the history of the synthetic dye industry have to be interpreted as the result not of a deterministic but of a probabilistic process (McKelvey, 1997). If my analysis of the observed history of the synthetic dye industry is correct, the fact that Germany had a much larger number of organic chemists in 1856 than Britain and the United States and the fact that Germany, in contrast to Britain and the United States, did not have any meaningful patent protection at the time were decisive in giving German firms a dominant position for more than four decades. We would have much greater confidence that the logic of the coevolutionary analysis is correct, if 80 of 100 runs in a simulation would show Germany with a dominant market share. But we can use simulations to subject the explanations that I have offered to an even more severe test. If we assign every country the same number of organic chemists, we should see in many fewer simulation runs that Germany acquired a dominant position. Similarly, by assigning to each country in the simulation the same patent regulations, German dominance should appear much less frequently if the theory I have developed in this chapter is correct.

Business and economic historians play an important role in creating the empirical knowledge about an industry that is required to create such "history-friendly" models for a sector of the economy. Business and economic historians can also benefit

---

[278] Of course another task in developing the scope conditions of the theory (Ocasio, 1999) is to examine variables that may mediate between the coevolutionary processes.

from history-friendly models because they allow the historian to probe more deeply into the empirical record of an industry. To the extent to which history-friendly models contain random components, the historian may be sensitized to examine more critically the accounts that place all causal power in the intentions of agents.[279] State lotteries produce few millionaires, some people who win small sums, and a large number of people who lose the money they paid for a ticket. It is very useful to remember that these dramatic performance differences of individual players have nothing to do with differences in strategies or capabilities. We know that a random process generates the lottery outcomes and that attempts to locate the explanation for performance differences in the intentions of the agents would simply be false. Having in the back of one's mind the alternative hypotheses that the differences in the performance of firms or national industries were generated by a random process disciplines one's thinking; it also has the beneficial consequence that one develops a much sharper eye for diagnosing when intentional actions on the part of managers or public policy makers really did make a difference and when they were mere causal mirages. Managers all too often are in the situation of the captain at the helm of a large boat, who erroneously believes that he or she is steering the vessel when in reality the ship has been put on autopilot. Understanding the limits of managerial action will allow managers to focus their energies on those areas where they can make a difference.

Similarly, scholarship in management informed by evolutionary theory places a much higher burden of proof not only on those analysts who want to credit individual managers for extraordinary performance of their organizations but also on those who want to blame individual managers for spectacular failures. With the benefit of hindsight it is easy to have perfect vision. To subject one's scholarly convictions about good managerial practice to a more rigorous test, one should pick a set of firms that display the apparently successful practice and a control group of firms that do not. If it turns out that these convictions lead to genuine foresight into which firms will perform better, one has a scientific basis for recommending those practices to managers. Otherwise, one should be wary about preaching good managerial practice to managers who know much more about the empirical details of their situation. Recognizing that in a very complex industrial landscape much of the success of individual firms is based on luck, management scholarship needs to find which examples of good and bad performance are not based on a lucky draw. In addition, much more detailed descriptions are needed of how managers build into their complex organizations both experimentation with novel things and retention of existing good practice, because the only way to avoid being selected out by a radically changing environment is to adapt to the new conditions.

In his recent analysis of the economic policies of the International Monetary Fund (IMF), Nobel Laureate Joseph Stiglitz (2002) argues that the IMF is in large measure to blame for the lack of economic progress of many nations because the IMF pursued policies that make sense for advanced market economies but are devastating for developing countries, which do not possess the institutional infrastructure that has developed over long periods of time in the leading industrial nations. Stiglitz faults IMF officials for deliberately ignoring the "facts on the ground" in the countries to

---

[279] See Gaddis (2002) for an excellent overview of what historians and social scientists can learn from each other.

which they were offering recommendations. The strength of Stiglitz's critique derives from his detailed knowledge of the policy issues and their empirical context, first as a member and later as chairman of the U.S. Council of Economic Advisers (1993 to 1997), and then, from 1997 to 2000, as chief economist and senior vice president of development economics at the World Bank. My point here is not to evaluate whether Stiglitz is fair and correct in his indictment of the IMF but simply to amplify Friedman's (2002) assessment that the only person who can provide a convincing refutation of Stiglitz's account will be someone who, in addition to knowing economic theory, is very familiar with the empirical reality of developing economies and the policies applied to them by the IMF. Economic analysis and policy making without detailed engagement with empirical reality is prone to go wrong. Joseph Schumpeter, of course, saw this very clearly after a lifetime of work on economic development. He opened our inquiry in this book and so it is only fitting to return to him at the end. On page 11 of his 1,260-page *History of Economic Analysis*, Schumpeter leaves little doubt about what he regards as the most important tool for building a compelling theory of economic development:

> *I wish to state right now that if, starting my work in economics afresh, I were told that I could only study one of the three [economic history, statistics, theory] but could have my choice, it would be economic history that I would choose.*

I A Technological History of Dyes

The purpose of this short technological history is to provide an overview of the technological developments that made the synthetic dye industry such a dynamic arena in the period before 1914. To understand the timing of particular dye innovations and the resulting industrial dynamics, it is useful to have a sense of the new knowledge that had to be created to develop innovative dyes. Knowing something about the technological underpinnings of new dyes helps us to understand why Perkin was able to develop the first synthetic dye all by himself, whereas synthetic indigo required large R&D laboratories and many years of systematic development. Because these differences in knowledge and technological requirements had profound effects on the industrial organization of the industry, a technological overview can facilitate a greater understanding of the technical changes surrounding dyes until 1914.

The commercial challenges faced by synthetic dye firms cannot be properly appreciated without some knowledge of how dyers and printers attached dyes to different kind of fabrics. It is absolutely essential to understand the basic steps of coloring different fabrics to appreciate that successful dye firms did not sell a commodity but rather a quite elaborate piece of technological know-how. Similarly, one cannot understand which firms were able to come up with new dyes without knowing something about the chain of chemical reactions that led from basic organic and inorganic chemicals by way of an often large number of intermediate chemicals to the dyes that were purchased by dyers and printers. I will begin by discussing the most important performance dimensions of dyes. This will set the stage for a discussion of natural dyes, the crafts of dyeing and printing, and finally the innovations in synthetic dyes until World War I.

Uses of Dyes

Although most dyes before 1914 were used for the dyeing and printing of textiles, small quantities were also used for the coloring of leather, and making printing inks, and paint pigments. When the first synthetic dye appeared on the market in 1857, it was traded at the price of platinum. By 1914 the price of synthetic dyes had fallen dramatically, and dyes represented only about 1.5 percent of the cost of a particular piece of clothing (Hardie and Pratt, 1966, p. 69). Because the textile industry was very large, however, dyes were nonetheless a sizable industry. Following the "standard invention strategies" of the time, people simply tried out the new synthetic dyestuffs in all sorts of different contexts. Food coloration was one of them; another, with dramatic consequences, led to an entire new branch of industry, synthetic pharmaceuticals. In the 1880s, scientists who colored germs with synthetic dyes found that some dyes were often lethal to these germs. Various synthetic chemicals associated with dye production proved to have several different therapeutic effects. Thus dye firms such as Bayer and Hoechst could diversify into pharmaceuticals on the basis of their accumulated know-how in dye chemistry. Today most dyestuffs are still consumed by the textile industry, but the leather, paper, food, and cosmetics industries are also important users.

Performance Dimensions of Dyes

Dyes have eight critical performance dimensions that determine quality and cost.

1. Shading. The human eye can discriminate between many different shades of color. The ability of a dye molecule to create a specific color shade desired by users is an important factor in determining the utility of a dye.
2. Brilliance. Some dyestuffs create only diffuse, dull coloration; others are able to confer a brilliant quality to the colored material. Given that light is composed of electromagnetic waves of different wavelengths, brilliance is a function of how narrowly the electromagnetic waves are focused around a particular wavelength. As a simple rule, dyes become more brilliant as they radiate light with decreasing bandwidth. Because brilliant colors are often preferred by the human eye, brilliance is an important factor in the performance of dyes.
3. Rubfastness. Any contact between a dyed fabric and a solid surface leads to rubbing. The more a dyed fabric can withstand this strain, the longer the fabric will maintain its color. To illustrate, the color of blue jeans comes off as a pair of jeans is worn precisely because the dye used is not rubfast. Although coloring blue jeans with dyes that would be very rubfast is clearly possible, manufacturers have no incentive to do so because in this case fashion has turned a technical defect into a highly prized virtue.
4. Washfastness. Moisture and contact with other chemicals can destroy the color of a dyed fabric. In washing a fabric its colors are put under severe strain. High-quality dyes can withstand washing much better than low-quality dyes. Because washfast colors last longer, they can reduce the overall cost of using a particular dye.
5. Sunlight fastness. A dye may confer a beautiful hue on a fabric after the initial dyeing process. Yet when the dyed fabric is exposed to sunlight, the color may fade away rapidly. The longer the color can withstand exposure to sunlight, the higher the performance of a particular dye.
6. Color range. Because all colors visible to the human eye can be created by mixing the three primary colors – red, blue, and green – a particular dyestuff molecule can often give rise to several different colors, depending on the dyeing process used, the substance to be dyed, and the molecular structure of the other dyestuffs used for mixing. If a particular dyestuff can lead to many different colors, producers and users can often realize significant cost advantages.
7. Fabric versatility. Different fibers do not all absorb dye molecules to the same degree. Thus a dye may, for instance, work with silk but not with cotton and wool. When a particular dye can be used on many different fibers, producers and users of dyes may reap important cost benefits.
8. Cost. The effective price of a dye is the sum of how much it costs to produce the dye and how much it costs to put the dye on a specific fabric. A particular dye

may be superior either because it has lower production costs, or because dyers and printers can apply the dye in more efficient ways, or both.

Mother Nature and, much later, chemists have been the source of many different molecules that give rise to a particular color shade. As shown in *The Color Index*, edited by the Society of Dyers and Colorists and the American Association of Textile Chemists and Colorists (3rd edition, 1972–92), many different molecules that all create a specific shade continue to be marketed, in large part because they differ along these eight performance dimensions and offer advantages to particular market segments.

Natural Dyes and the Craft of Dyeing and Printing
Natural Dyes
Evidence for the use of colors goes back to 9000 BC. For at least 2,000 years, human cultures all over the world have used naturally occurring coloring materials to dye fabrics, to paint, and to create other works of art. Natural dyes were derived mainly from plants but also from animals. Hundreds of dyes from nature have been documented as sources of color, but only about twenty-four dyes became commercially important (Knaggs, 1956). These dyes were traded for the past 4,000 years because their superior quality put them in demand in many parts of the world. The most extensively used of these twenty-four natural dyes were cochineal (bright red), Tyrian purple (purple), madder (mainly red), indigo (blue), saffron (bright yellow), safflower (red to yellow), woad (blue), and logwood (violet, purple, black). Tyrian purple was not only the most famous purple dye but also the most expensive of the natural dyes. Its source is a small amount of color in a tiny gland of the body of a mollusk, 12,000 animals being required to make one gram of Tyrian purple. Not surprisingly, only kings and high nobility could afford cloth dyed with this expensive material (Seefelder, 1994, pp. 78–85). Because the climate of Europe was hospitable to it, madder, a dye in the red to yellow range extracted from the roots of the madder plant, was also among these eight "market leaders." Indigo, a dye in the blue to purple range extracted from a tropical plant, had become in the Middle Ages the "king" of all dyestuffs. Nature produced many different extractable colors in the red and yellow color spectrum but very few in the blue range (Seefelder, 1994, pp. 12, 54). Indigo, therefore, was a highly valued dyestuff because it delivered a bright blue dye that was very fast to sunlight. Indigo was imported into the textile centers of Europe and America mainly from India but also from other tropical and subtropical climates since the sixteenth century, when a competing color native to Europe, woad, was no longer protected by high tariffs on indigo.

Before the revolution in textile manufacturing, much dyeing was carried out by individual households rather than professional dyers. It is estimated that in 1774 each family in the United States consumed one pound of indigo every year (Haynes, 1945, vol. 1, p. 47). When the textile industry became able to provide cheap clothing in the early nineteenth century, household dyeing became less prevalent and dyeing tended to concentrate in the hands of professional dyers and printers.

The Craft of Dyeing and Printing
There are two ways in which finished textiles can receive coloration – dyeing and printing. In dyeing, a piece of fabric receives one particular color by immersion in a solution of that dye. In printing, many different dyes can be pressed onto the

same piece of fabric. Thus, whereas dyeing gives only one color, printing makes it possible to confer a very elaborate design to a piece of fabric. To create colored fabrics, dyeing and printing methods are sometimes combined. Printing was becoming more important in the course of the nineteenth century because advances in machinery and rising demand for cotton-based textiles made it possible to deliver high-quality printed fabric at lower cost.

Most fabrics can be dyed at any stage in the conversion of raw textile fibers to finished goods. Quality woolen textiles, for example, are often dyed in the form of loose fiber. At the other end of the textile production process, some manufacturers stock white goods and dye them only when a particular color is ordered, to reduce the risk of producing finished products whose colors fall out of fashion.

Dyeing has been a craft for thousands of years. Local dye traditions developed both because the climates around the world call for different clothing and because regions differ in their natural endowment of fabrics. These local traditions were maintained because dyers and printers, like so many other crafts, tried to protect their competitive position by keeping their dyeing practices as secret as possible. In Europe wool was the most widely used fabric in the Middle Ages because it was available locally. Silk was traded for many centuries as a luxury good, and with the establishment of cotton plantations in the United States and the advent of cheap transportation in the nineteenth century, cotton also became an important raw fiber for textiles.

As noted earlier, because different fabrics do not have the same dye-absorbing quality, a particular dye may work very well with silk, but not with wool and cotton. Often, so-called mordants, chemical substances (inorganic salts) that bind the dye and the textile together, had to be developed. When applied with different mordants, natural dyes often give different colorations, as in the case of madder. When cotton fibers are pretreated with different mordants, for example, madder produces the following colors: red with aluminum hydroxide, violet with magnesium mordants, purple-red with calcium, blue with barium, and black-violet with ferrous mordants. What mordant to use and how to apply the mordant during the different stages of dyeing and printing were among the trade secrets dyers and printers were often eager to keep to prevent entry by others and competition in their trade.

Dyeing Techniques
Before 1914 dyers developed three general kinds of dyeing processes to attach dyes to fabric. The most simple process is direct dyeing. Here the fabric is simply immersed in a solution known as the dye or liquor bath. During the dyeing process, the dye molecules attach themselves to pores in the fiber surface. Heat is applied to transfer the dye from the solution to the surface of the fiber. In mordant dyeing, the fabric is pretreated with inorganic salts that make the surface of the fabric more susceptible for the attachment of dye molecules; after this the fabric is immersed in a dye bath. Finally, to deal with dye molecules that are not soluble in water, dyers had already devised in ancient times a technique called vat dyeing, in which an insoluble dye molecule is reacted with a chemical that makes the resulting compound soluble and the fabric is then immersed in a bath of a solution carrying the transformed dyestuff. (Traditionally this took place in big vats, hence the name.) The desired coloration is achieved only through oxidation once the dye fabric is exposed to air. Natural indigo, for instance, was applied through such vat-dyeing techniques.

One of the great challenges in dyeing lies in getting the color to spread uniformly across the fabric. This is where a great deal of handicraft skill makes the difference between high-quality and low-quality dyeing. Dyeing with madder, for example, often required more than twenty operations to give a bright, fast red (Travis, 1993, p. 13).

Printing Techniques

In printing, the challenge is of a different kind. The printer's task is to concentrate a dye on a particular location on the fabric and prevent it from diffusing to its surroundings. The differentiating feature of printing lies in the method of application. All printing techniques use pressure to apply the mordant or dyestuff onto the fabric. Among the different printing techniques developed and used before 1914, the oldest is block printing. Typically, the blocks are made of wood and the design is carved to stand above the block surface. (An office stamp that prints a name and address works according to the same principle.) Only one color at a time can be put on the surface of the block. To print in multiple colors, different blocks must be used in sequence, making block printing relatively expensive. Hence its use became restricted to high-end products such as heavy linen for upholstery and pure silks for dress goods.

In roller printing, first invented in 1763 by Thomas Bell, colored paste is injected into the engraved areas of a smooth copper roll. A design is printed by bringing the roll in contact with the cloth, which then absorbs the paste from the copper roll. Multicolor prints are created by using a machine having a number of rolls, each of which prints a particular color on the textile. Advances in mechanization made this process the most widely used method for large-scale textile printing.

Finally there is the copperplate printing method, which shares one key technological principle with roller printing. Designs are engraved on a copper plate and transferred onto the cloth by bringing the cloth and plate into contact under pressure. Copperplate printing enjoyed popularity from the time it was developed in the middle of the eighteenth century because it could print much finer lines than in block printing. Nonetheless, block printing and copperplate printing developed side by side. After 1820, however, roller printing become more and more the leading printing technique because its greater mechanization potential allowed printers to reduce dramatically its cost over time.[280]

Sometimes printing and dyeing techniques are combined. By printing a mordant on cloth and then immersing the cloth in a dye bath, only those areas covered with the particular mordant will absorb the dye and the others will remain uncolored. When different mordants are printed next to one another on the same cloth, multicolor patterns can be created.

With the rise of the textile industry in the eighteenth century, the demand for natural dyes surged dramatically, increasing the prices for natural dyes. This increased the incentives to find more cost-efficient dyes. And here begins the story of synthetic dyes.

[280] I have not found data that would tell us the market share of the different printing techniques in 1914. However, the *Encyclopedia Britannica* reports that since the middle of the twentieth century the greatest percentage of cloth has been printed with the roller method. I suspect that roller printing had become the dominant method in the industrialized world by 1914. Ernst Homburg (personal communication) confirms this estimate.

Figure 10. **Chemical Pathway to First Synthetic Dye.**

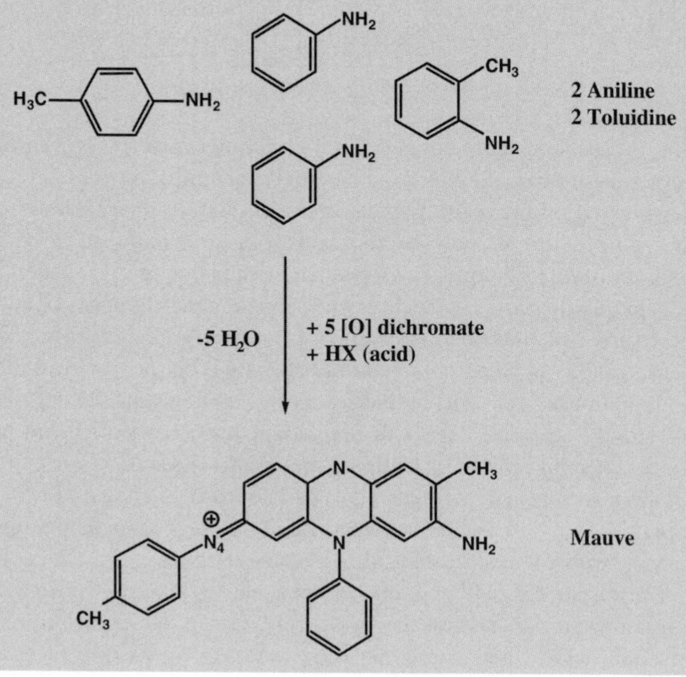

2 Aniline
2 Toluidine

-5 H$_2$O   + 5 [O] dichromate
             + HX (acid)

Mauve

The First Synthetic Dyes

Chemists had long dreamed of making synthetic dyes. Justus von Liebig, one of the most important organic chemists in the nineteenth century, articulated long before the first synthetic dye was invented the vision that chemists would be able to outdo nature by creating cheap and brilliant dyes (one of his predictions is quoted at the beginning of Chapter 2).

The beginning of the synthetic dye industry can be dated very precisely, unlike that of many other trades. After creating aniline purple (mauveine or mauve) in his laboratory in 1856, William H. Perkin had a commercial plant running near London by 1857 and sold aniline purple to dyers in Britain and continental Europe. The fast commercialization of synthetic dyes was made possible because the dyeing and printing trades were already experiencing a wave of innovations in the decades before the first synthetic dye appeared (Homburg, 1983). From the 1830s onward, chemical knowledge was increasingly imported into the printing branch of the coloring trade. To develop dyes and mordants that would work with mechanized printing machines running at ever faster speeds, printers hired highly skilled colorists who had acquired substantial chemical knowledge (Figure 10). The period until 1856 was marked by a proliferation of natural dyes and mordants, particularly in the printing side of the coloring trade. Advances in chemistry led these colorists to experiment with new ways to treat and process traditional natural dyes. This widespread experimentation, for instance, led to the preparation of murexide, which is, properly speaking, a semisynthetic dye because it involves both the traditional extraction of coloring matter as well as synthetic chemical procedures in manufacture and application. The rapid commercial success

Figure 11. **Chemical Pathway to Aniline Red (Fuchsine) Dye.**

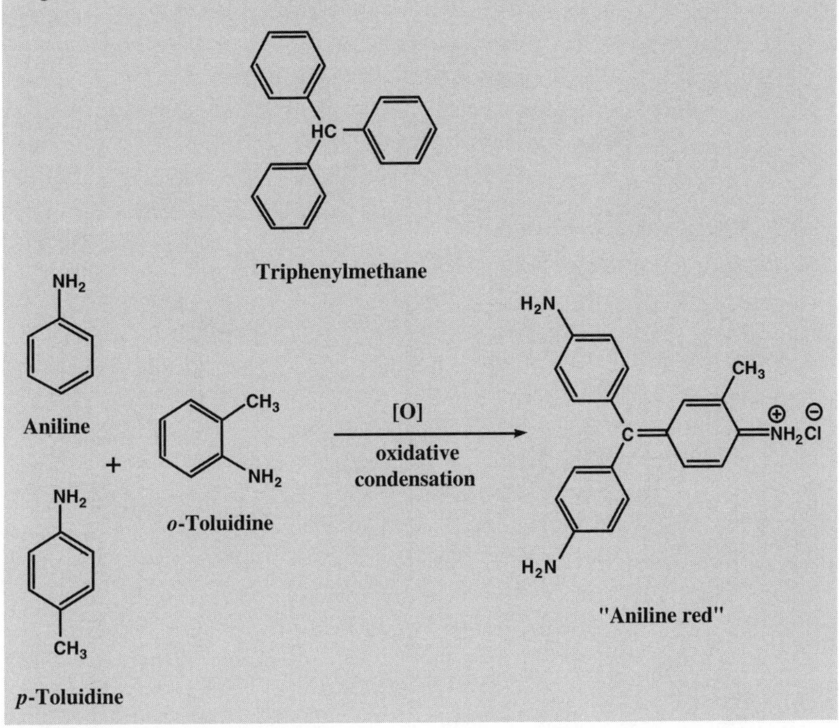

Triphenylmethane

Aniline

+

o-Toluidine

$\xrightarrow{[O]}$ oxidative condensation

"Aniline red"

p-Toluidine

of aniline dyes was made possible because chemical knowledge had already become important in the printing trade, and the leading dyeing and printing houses were ready to absorb the first synthetic dye that was prepared in a radically different way (Homburg, 1983).

Aniline purple swept away many natural purple dyes, but it did not have a very long commercial life itself. Soon other synthetic dyes appeared that surpassed aniline purple and launched the synthetic dye industry on a strong growth trajectory. For example, the second synthetic dye (also derived from aniline) became quickly more successful than mauveine because it gave fabric a red color. Given that red was a color in high demand, many firms sprang up to get into the business of making aniline red (which is also known in the literature as fuchsine or magenta) (Figure 11).

What made the first synthetic dyes so popular from the very beginning was their brilliance and fastness compared to the existing natural dyes. Another advantage of synthetic dyes was that dye-makers could guarantee dyers and printers a dyestuff that would always have the same shade, whereas the hue of natural dyes would vary from season to season.

Synthetic dyes were manufactured in a long series of chemical and mechanical operations, processes that were often based on different technological principles. Commercial production of synthetic dyes from coal tar required several basic raw materials: coal, salt, nitrates (saltpeter), and sulfur. These raw materials were processed to create basic organic and inorganic chemicals, which in turn were processed many times to produce various intermediate organic chemicals before, in the final

Figure 12. **Relations between Early Synthetic Dyes.**

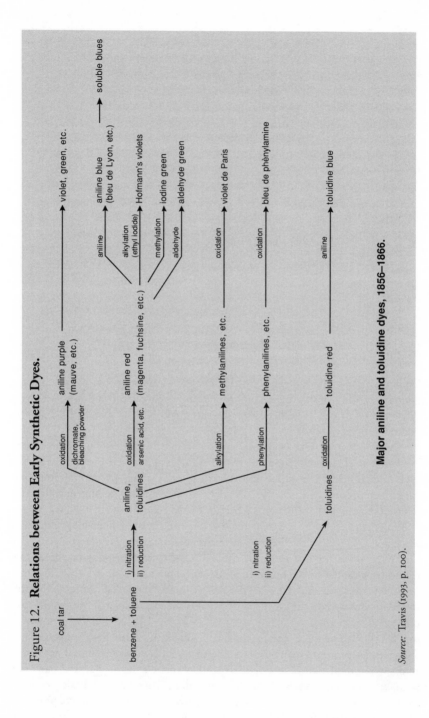

Major aniline and toluidine dyes, 1856–1866.

Source: Travis (1993, p. 100).

steps, dyes emerged that could be applied to fabrics (Figure 12). Many of the early production steps were not carried out by makers of synthetic dye firms but rather by coal-tar distillers and makers of heavy chemicals (Murmann and Homburg, 2001). Because a market already existed for coal tar and heavy chemicals, many entrepreneurs could enter the dye industry by focusing on the later stages of dye production. Also, given that making dyes consumed large amounts of acids (sulfuric, hydrochloric, and nitric) as well as alkalis, some dye companies integrated back into the production of such basic chemicals. From its inception in 1865, the German firm BASF, for example, was designed as an integrated company that made acids, alkalis, dye intermediates, and finished dyes within the firm.

Innovations in Synthetic Dyes until 1914
A Quantitative Overview

Potential for innovation existed along all the points in the production chain from basic raw materials to the finished dyes. There were innumerable innovations in dyes and dye production until the First World War. Although I focus here mainly on chemical product innovations, it is important to realize that advances in steam engines and metallurgy also made possible a large number of equipment innovations that automatized many steps in the dye production process and reduced the production cost of dyes. If one were to walk into a dye plant of the 1860s and then into a dye plant of 1914, one would find the production facilities dramatically changed. The early dye plants would look more or less like scaled-up chemical laboratories. By 1914, however, plants had become real factories with specialized machinery and equipment (for innovations in plants and equipment, see Travis, 1993, pp. 88–104, and Hornix, 1992).

Given continuous innovations in dyes and dye intermediates, many dyes had a short life span. Hesse reports that the coal-tar dye industry in 1912 consisted of 921 distinct and different chemical substances made from 270 intermediates (themselves not dyes) that, in turn, were made from 9 products obtained or obtainable from coal tar by distillation, refrigeration, expression, or the like (Hesse, 1914, p. 1013). Redlich, one of the most reliable scholars of the synthetic dye industry before World War I, found two somewhat higher figures. His first source counted around 1,200 and his second source 2,000 dyes on the market by 1913 (Redlich, 1914, pp. 11, 44). However, Redlich seems to give more credence to the 1,200 figure because that is the figure he refers to more often.

The discrepancy among the various estimates can come from at least two distinct sources. Hesse seems to have relied on the 1912 edition of dye tables, the information of which would reflect that market in 1911. This could explain the difference between 921 and Redlich's later 1,200 estimate. For the Redlich figure of 2,000 dyes, another reason may be involved. Given that a particular dye molecule can be sold under several different trade names, it simply may have been difficult to count the number of chemically distinct dyes.[281] Hesse says that already in 1897 the existing dye molecules were sold under 8,000 different trade names. By 1913 many, many more would have appeared. When it is reported that Hoechst (German firm) sold 10,000 different

---

[281] It is also possible that Hesse's calculations refer to the American market, where some of the dyes sold in other markets were not present. I do not give much credence to this explanation because Hesse seems to rely on the Schulz dye tables published in Germany.

trade names in 1913 and when the 50th Anniversary Chronicle of Germany's Bayer (Farbenfabriken-Bayer, 1918) states that Bayer sold 1,800 dyestuffs in 1911, a possible confusion between counting trade names as opposed to distinct chemical molecules becomes obvious. The two firms had roughly the same output of dyes and are likely to have made roughly same number of distinct dyes.

Estimating the exact number of dyes that appeared between 1857 and 1914 is a somewhat difficult undertaking, and not just because the same dye molecules were often marketed under different names. A further complication is that the number of dyes synthesized in the new R&D laboratories would run to the tens of thousands but most would never reach the market. After some dye firms began to create units whose sole function was to search for new dyes, chemists combed systematically through thousands of molecules, looking for the few that would make superior dyes. Figures from Bayer (as reported in Meyer-Thurow, 1982) illustrate how many molecules had to be synthesized to find a few commercially competitive dyes. In 1906, for example, the Bayer laboratories synthesized 2,656 new dyestuff compounds. After the first screening, only sixty were tested on a larger scale. Thirty-six dyes were marketed in that year, some of which were not even among the sixty tested dyes because they were only new mixtures of old dyes or dyes of competitors that had come off patent protection. In theory, millions of different dye molecules are possible! Hesse reports that the 8,000 different German dye patents before 1913 embraced many thousand of millions of theoretically possible dyestuffs wholly distinct from each other. But he adds that only 400 individual dyes from these patents had survived the rigors of the marketplace. Similarly, he relates that before 1914 there were about 2,000 different intermediate dye chemicals possible but only 270 had been found useful (Hesse, 1914, p. 1018).

To give a sense of the magnitude of dyes produced in 1914, let us compare the 1914 figure to later market offerings. By 1925, 3,500 chemically distinct dyestuffs were on the market in Germany (Flechtner, 1959, p. 50). The number was rising into the 1930s, but such a great variety proved not to be economical and could not be sustained in the marketplace. The rationalization efforts during the Great Depression were massive. In 1927–1928, the German dye cartel, I. G. Farben, sold 33,000 mixtures of dyes[282] under 50,000 different brand names. By 1932, I. G. Farben offered only 6,000 dyes (Marsch, 1994, p. 47). According to the *Encyclopedia Britannica* (1997 World Wide Web edition), some 8,000 colorants (colorants are defined as dyes and pigments) with more than 40,000 trade names are in use today.

In summary, it is safe to assume that at least a couple of thousand dyes appeared on the market from 1857 until 1914. Dyers and printers could choose from at least 900 different dyes as World War I broke out, a variety that was never available before the advent of synthetic dyes. This large number helps to explain why managerial hierarchies, not family-controlled firms, came to dominate the dye industry. If a firm wanted to offer the full spectrum of dyes, it had to develop a large administrative apparatus for processing information about user preferences and for selling an extensive portfolio in the market. Furthermore, unless a dye firm wanted to serve niche markets, it also had to develop the ability to develop new dyes on a systematic basis to keep up

---

[282] At this point, around 4,000 distinct dye molecules probably have formed the basis of the 33,000 different dyes.

with competitors. The process of creative destruction that made natural dyes obsolete was continued among the ranks of synthetic dyes such that the early pioneers – aniline purple and the like – were swept away as a new generations of dyes appeared, offering superior performance.

Radical Innovations

In my attempt to portray the changing knowledge requirements for creating new dyes, I will focus on the most important innovations because they had the greatest impact on changes in the competitive position of individual firms. I will discuss the development of synthetic alizarin, the new class of azo dyes, and synthetic indigo. Synthetic alizarin and indigo are very important because they replaced natural dyes of great economic significance. In both cases, the synthetic dyestuff industry ruined the fortunes of madder and indigo farmers throughout the world, who could not compete with the cheaper synthetic products. Particularly important also was the class of direct azo dyes; by not requiring a mordant to attach the dye to cotton textiles, they offered substantial cost advantages.

Synthetic Alizarin

I mentioned earlier that madder was one of the most important natural dyestuffs. Given the size of the market for madder, it is not surprising that the early pioneers of the dye industry had their minds set on finding a synthetic route to alizarin – the most important colorant present in madder – that would be cheaper than the natural product. This took, nonetheless, another ten years after the discovery of the first synthetic dyestuff, mauveine, and more than thirty years from the first experiments to find a chemical path to artificial alizarin. When Graebe and Liebermann synthesized alizarin in 1869 and swiftly filed for a patent, it was the first time that chemists had been able to recreate a natural dyestuff synthetically. The synthetic product was not only cheaper but also purer than the natural one. Within little more than a decade, madder plantations were forced to give up operations and disappeared.

Alizarin could not be made from benzene (the coal-tar crude from which the early aniline colors were derived). Graebe and Liebermann derived it from anthracene, another one of the nine useful coal-tar crudes. Because the existing dye intermediates also were not suitable for producing artificial alizarin, new chemical intermediates had to be synthesized to develop the synthetic dye. Anthracene was first converted into the intermediate anthraquinone, which in turn was converted into anthraquinone monosulfonic acid before the finished dye was produced (Figure 13).

As is often the case with new chemical inventions, Graebe and Liebermann's laboratory process did not work on a commercial scale. Only in alliance with BASF (a German firm) and its technical director, Heinrich Caro, did Graebe and Liebermann managed to design a process that would provide sufficient yields of the key intermediates. The big challenge was to derive as much anthracene in as pure a form as possible and to devise chemical pathways that would increase the yield of the intermediates. This was no small problem because the existing equipment was inadequate for such procedures. New boilers that could carry out the reaction at higher temperatures and pressures had to be constructed. Hence the development of the new dye required not only chemical innovations but also new production technology. Substantial empirical work had to be done at BASF to get the process under control.

Figure 13. Graebe and Liebermann's Laboratory Pathway to Alizarin.

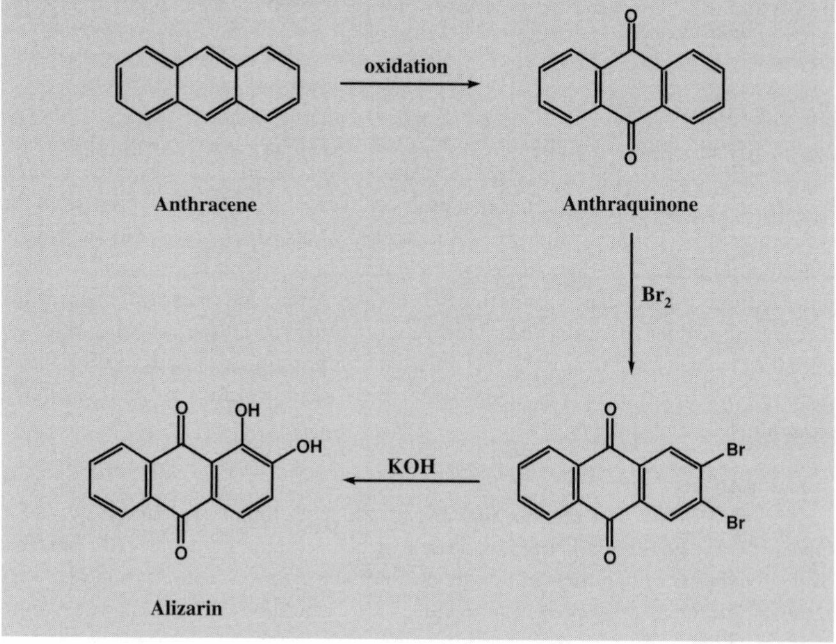

Anthracene

oxidation

Anthraquinone

Br₂

KOH

Alizarin

Because Graebe and Liebermann had disclosed the synthesis of alizarin in a German academic journal (see Figure 14), firms set out right away to find a suitable production process. Perkin, the inventor of the first synthetic dye, worked out a production process that gave much better economic results. He filed for a patent in Britain one day after BASF, with Graebe and Liebermann, filed their revised process patent in Britain. Perkin and BASF agreed to divide up the market instead of battling in court over who had priority and what rights. But this agreement did not work because Hoechst had also found a process for alizarin two months before the British patent filings (Bayer, 1963, p. 8). Bayer also entered into the market, given that BASF was denied a patent for Prussia. The ensuing competition forced all firms to focus on developing superior production processes. When BASF's process could not match the

Figure 14. Industrial Process for Alizarin Manufacture.

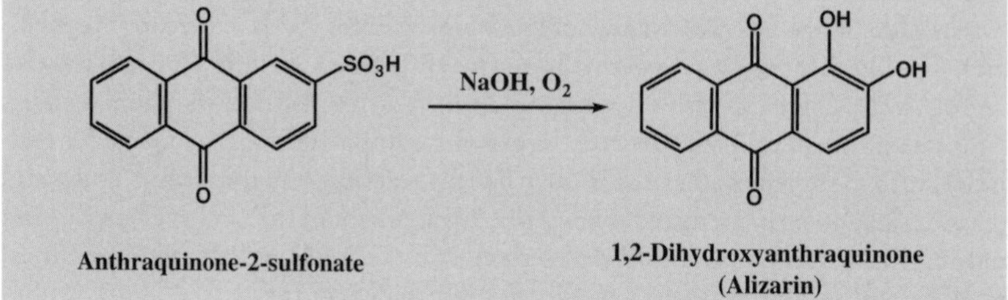

Anthraquinone-2-sulfonate

NaOH, O₂

1,2-Dihydroxyanthraquinone
(Alizarin)

performance of that of Perkin & Sons, the latter firm provided substantial technical help to BASF to get its plants running. This was the last time that a British firm was ahead of the German competitors in the exploitation of a major innovation.

Just as with the red aniline dye (fuchsine), synthetic alizarin was the source of more dyes. Later chemists learned how to transform the dye to make orange-yellow and blue colors. By systematically exploring the addition of new functional groups to the anthraquinone intermediate, it was possible to create a large number of new dyes from this original invention. The class of anthraquinone dyes, of which alizarin was, so to speak, a "founding member," was still an important product in 1912, representing 116 of the 921 dyes Hesse counted on the market.

Azo Dyes

Hesse's calculations reveal that of the 921 different dyes on the market in 1912, 462 fell into the class of azo dyes. Already in 1858 Peter Griess, a German chemist who later emigrated to Great Britain, had discovered a very powerful reaction that could create organic compounds fused together by double nitrogen bonds. The importance of this discovery lay in its ability to provide a general mechanism for coupling organic molecules. Because the discovery literally opened up the possibility of synthesizing millions of different dyes, it represents one of the great breakthroughs in dye chemistry. But it took almost three decades before the full potential of this class of compounds was realized.[283]

Azo dyes had a relatively slow start. Although several dyes appeared in the 1860s, the exact chemical composition of these azo dyes, as was often the case in the dye industry, was not certain for a long time. At that time, dye firms had no inkling of the versatile reactivity of a double nitrogen group attached to a benzene ring. This started to change when Kekulé's work illuminated the structure of the benzene ring, the basic building block of all coal-tar chemicals. After publication of Kekulé's benzene ring theory in 1865, chemists had a much more useful model for determining the structure of dye molecules. The development of the full potential of this dye class, then, required both theoretical and empirical advances in the science of chemistry. As was often the case with synthetic dyes, the ability to make a particular dye often outstripped the actual understanding of the molecule and the reaction that gave rise to the compound.

Millions of dyes: The coupling reaction. Azo dyes are the most important example of the general pattern that chemists in many cases were able to shed light on the structure and the chemical reactions leading to a particular dyestuff only after long, painstaking experiments. It took almost twenty years after Griess had first documented a chemical reaction with a double nitrogen (diazo) group for chemists to harness the full potential of this reaction as a general tool for synthesizing many new dyes. But when this versatile mechanism for coupling benzene rings was more fully understood, chemists had a powerful instrument to synthesize novel compounds from existing molecules. It took twenty years because only by the mid-1870s had Kekulé, Baeyer, Griess, and Witt, among others, understood well enough the composition of the azo dye molecules to facilitate a wave of new research into the dyestuffs with the azo group.

---

[283] This section on azo dyes relies principally on Caro (1892), Hesse (1914), Bayer (1963), Verg et al. (1988), and Travis (1993).

At this point, companies were able to utilize the reaction to create numerous new dyestuffs by purposeful search. Witt's British employer at the time – Williams, Thomas & Dower – put the so-called London orange on the market. In 1876, BASF commercialized Caro's yellow and orange azo dyestuff, Bayer came out with orange dyestuff, and Hoechst offered a family of red azo dyes. Levinstein (a British firm) also was soon on the market with an orange dye. No leading dye firm wanted to be left out of this bonanza. They entered the race and assigned chemists to develop azo dyestuffs, hoping to hit on a new dye that would bring riches.

This diazo coupling technology provided a big stimulus for creating R&D laboratories. Given the great potential of coupling molecules, R&D laboratories delivered the organizational tool for combing through these millions of possible dye combinations. Heinrich Caro, the long-term research director of BASF, remarked that azo dyes transformed the search for new dyes to an "endless combinatorial game" (as quoted in van den Belt and Rip, 1987, p. 151). And Carl Duisberg, one of the first research chemists and later CEO of Bayer, characterized the development of new azo dyes with the words, "Nowhere any trace of a flash of genius" (as quoted in van den Belt and Rip, 1987, p. 155).

Just as with alizarin, new chemical intermediates (e.g., naphtholdisulfonic acid) had to be developed to manufacture azo dyes (Figure 15). Once again, firms experienced difficulties with getting sufficient yields, and a substantial amount of process development work had to be done to achieve more efficient processes. This was as important as ever because many firms entered this new class of dyes, and price competition was a key factor in market success.

A radical innovation: Congo Red. The first patent for a direct azo dye (one that would not require a mordant to dye cotton) was issued to Peter Griess in 1883. He had continued to research the diazo reaction since his original discovery in 1858. Griess showed his direct cotton dyes to Bayer and the firm began working on an economical process. But another Bayer chemist, Paul Böttiger, left the firm and filed a patent in 1884 on his own behalf for a beautiful red color. He offered the patent to Bayer, BASF, and Hoechst, all of which rejected the dye because it would turn into blue when coming in contact with acid. All three firms misjudged the market badly. AGFA (German) bought the patent on the advice of a colorist and, immediately after the firm put Congo Red on the market, the dye became a stellar success. Congo Red was a blockbuster innovation because it allowed dyers for the first time to dispense with mordants in cotton dyeing and printing. This made dyeing much simpler and required dyers who were less skilled than those in charge of previous operations. The dramatic cost reductions and the attractive color of Congo Red stimulated dye firms to search for similar dyes. After going down a few dead alleys (the old problem of not being able to make the intermediate for a promising dye at sufficient yields again haunted the efforts), one of Bayer's newly-hired chemists, Carl Duisberg, synthesized Benzopurpurin 4B, which was not only fast against acid but also more brilliant than Congo Red (Figure 16). Because the chemical structure between the two dyes differed only slightly, AGFA felt that its patent was infringed and launched one of the most important German patent fights, as is described in detail in the main body of this book.

Figure 15. **Examples of Dyes Based on Diazo Reactions.**

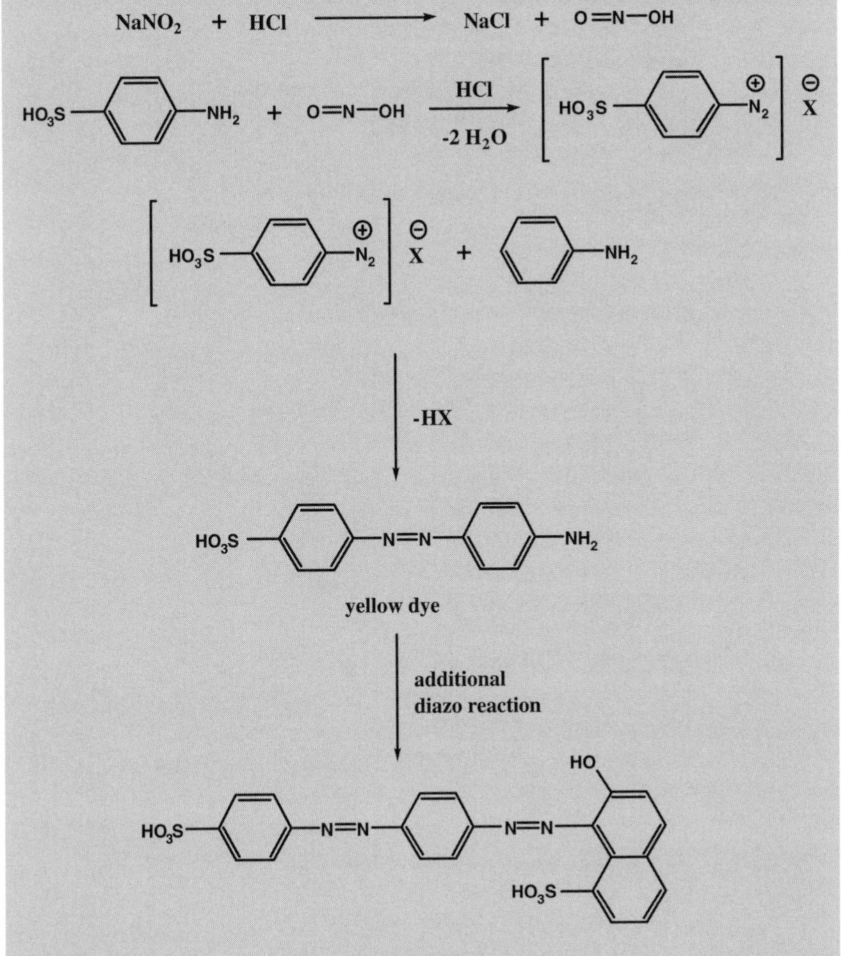

yellow dye

additional
diazo reaction

Crocein Scarlet 3B

Synthetic Indigo

From the very beginning of the synthetic dye era, chemists tried to synthesize a dyestuff that could rival the excellent dyeing properties of natural indigo. Although thousands of dye molecules had been synthesized, a real competitor for indigo remained elusive. Just as had happened earlier with natural dyes, the color palette was rich in red and yellows but there was a gap where blue should be (Seefelder, 1994, p. 54). After trying for fifteen years, Adolf Baeyer, professor of chemistry at the Gewerbeschule (Technical College) in Berlin and later at the University of Munich, was finally able to synthesize indigo from phenylacetic acid. His synthetic route, however, was too expensive to be commercially viable in direct competition with natural indigo. When BASF and Hoechst signed an agreement with Baeyer to develop the latter's indigo patent commercially, none of the participants had an inkling that it would take another

Figure 16. **Chemical Differences between Congo Red, Benzopurpurin 1B, and Benzopurpurin 4B.**

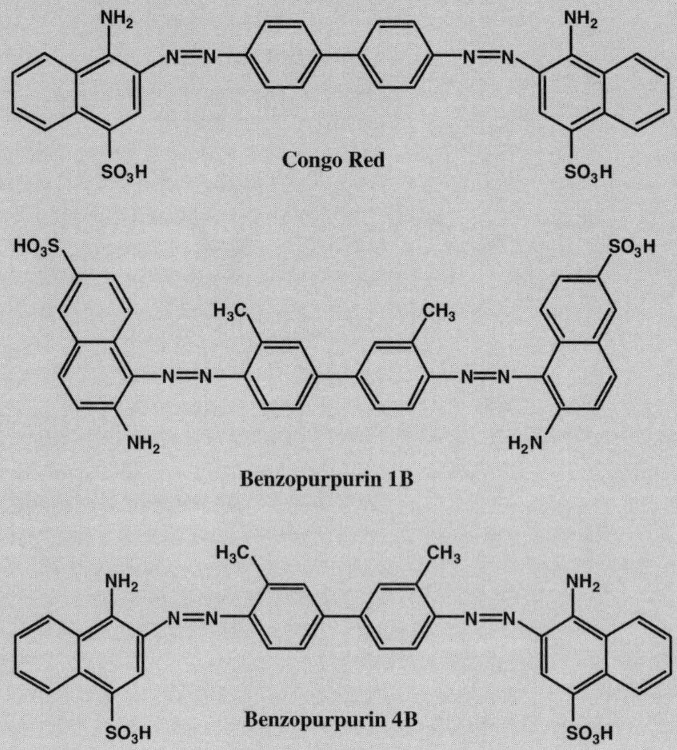

Congo Red

Benzopurpurin 1B

Benzopurpurin 4B

seventeen years and many dead alleys before BASF would have the first commercially viable process ready.

Many innovations had to be made to achieve a process that could rival natural indigo. The key problem was to produce the precursor indoxyl in high yields, starting with raw materials that were cheap. Different intermediate routes had to be explored and a wide variety of different starting materials were used, such as nitrocinnamic acid, naphthalene, and aniline derived from benzene. The cognitive breakthrough occurred when Heumann, a German working at the Federal Polytechnic in Zurich, freed himself of Baeyer's laboratory method of creating in the indoxyl precursor the five-membered ring that contained the nitrogen. He instead closed the five-membered ring at two carbon atoms, as illustrated in Figure 17. Heumann started with cheap raw materials: aniline, acetic acid, chlorine, and alkali. Having recognized the break-through of Heumann, Hoechst and BASF both acquired the rights to his invention.

During the seventeen years of intermittently working on the indigo problem, BASF realized that a synthetic indigo process with a competitive cost structure required several dramatic complementary innovations. The sulfuric acid traditionally used in dye manufacture was not strong enough for indigo production. BASF hired Rudolph

Figure 17. **Two Ring-Closure Possibilities for Indigo Synthesis.**

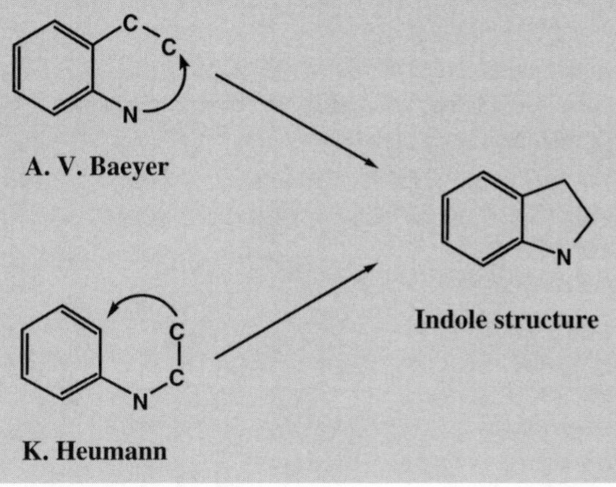

A. V. Baeyer

Indole structure

K. Heumann

Knietsch, who worked out the ideas of Winkler and created the so-called contact process for sulfuric acid manufacture, which delivered high-concentration sulfuric acid. To meet the need for huge quantities of cheap chlorine required for the alkali fusion production step, BASF bought a license for the electrolytic chlorine process and built a plant based on the new technology.

When synthetic indigo first appeared on the market, it was a bit more expensive then natural indigo. Yet from the beginning it had the advantage of providing a more brilliant hue and being easier to handle; moreover, it could be sold to dyers and printers with unchanging performance characteristics from one shipment to the next. In the first couple of years of production, the synthetic process was made dramatically more efficient, which proved to be the "kiss of death" for indigo farmers around the world. By 1901 four different commercial routes to synthetic indigo were in use. The one developed by Pfleger, a scientist at Degussa, delivered an even cheaper route than the one originally worked out by the BASF engineers and scientists. BASF and Hoechst shared this new process and then formed a convention to control the indigo market (Figure 18).

But BASF's indigo efforts were challenged by more than a cheaper process developed by a competitor. In BASF's own laboratories René Bohn developed a blue dye he called Indanthrone, based on 2-aminoanthraquinone, which like alizarin is derived from the anthracene crude. Indanthrone was much superior to indigo because it possessed a similar hue and light fastness; unlike indigo, however, it stuck to the fiber like glue. In the same year another competing dye was discovered, Hydron Blue, a member of the inexpensive class of sulfur dyes. The technical realization of synthetic indigo and its swift technical obsolescence shows how inherently unpredictable these innovations were. Only the conservativeness of dyers around the world assured that synthetic indigo was nonetheless a commercial success.[284] But over time, synthetic

---

[284] In many areas of the world, craft-based dyers and printers were very resistant to change from natural dyes to synthetic dyes. Not surprisingly, in many areas of the world, selling synthetic dyes was a formidable marketing challenge.

Figure 18. **Industrial Indigo Synthesis by Degussa/Hoechst.**

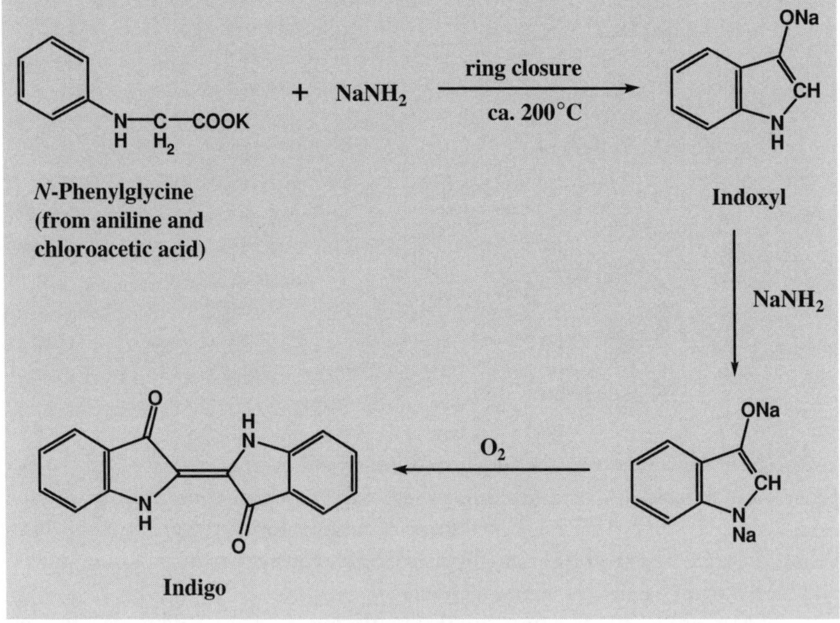

ONa
N—C—COOK
H H2
+ NaNH2
ring closure
ca. 200°C
CH
N
H
N-Phenylglycine
(from aniline and
chloroacetic acid)
Indoxyl
NaNH2
O
H
N
O2
ONa
CH
N
Na
N
H
O
Indigo

indigo was pushed into very small niche markets. At BASF the color survived only because it could be used as a intermediate for others dyes. In the 1960s, then, the worldwide blue jeans fashion gave the former "king" of all dyestuffs a new lease on life, albeit now not as the color of royalty but of the people.

What is the significance of this synthetic indigo episode? Developing a commercial process posed great technical obstacles that only a firm with enormous development capabilities could overcome. Single individuals, as in the case of Perkin and the first synthetic dye, could not have developed a commercially viable process that could compete with the natural indigo. BASF spent 18 million gold marks (more than the entire stock capital of the firm) until it had a commercially viable process. The time of the lone innovator was clearly long gone. Indigo set the trend for the chemical developments in the twentieth century, which were for the most part achieved by large teams. When even BASF's existing staff was not adequate, the firm recruited outside talent (Heumann and Knietsch are important examples), either bringing them inside the organization or retaining them as technical advisors. The industrial R&D laboratory had became an indispensable tool for pushing the envelope of dye chemistry forward. The dye industry was the first one to experience this shift in how innovations were achieved. Once the R&D laboratories proved to be a viable organizational form for developing new dyes, small firms lost their ability to compete in the center of the dye market. The dye industry played a pioneering role in the industrialization of innovation in the form of R&D laboratories that diffused to many other sectors of the economy of the twentieth century.

Table 11. Indian Exports and Price of Natural Indigo

Year	Exports (tons × 10³)	Price (£/ton)
1877	5,000	400
1887	6,900	360
1897	8,500	350
1903	3,250	230
1913	550	260
1914	900	710
1917	1,700	830
1918	1,550	500
1921	500	550
1922	200	540

Source: Park and Shore (1999, p. 159).

Economic Consequences of Synthetic Dyes

Until 1895–1900, natural dyes were still used in considerable quantities (Pfitzner, 1916, p. 54). But by 1914, synthetic dyes had reduced natural dyes to economic insignificance. Hesse (1914, p. 1018) reports that 95 percent of world indigo consumption was produced by Germany. Only the disruption of World War I led to a temporary resurgence of indigo plantations in India. Table 11, reporting Indian exports of natural indigo and its prices, quantifies this replacement dynamic. The value of Indian indigo exports fell from £3,570,00 in 1896 to £225,000 in 1911.[285] In the same period German indigo exports rose from 3,520 tons to 22,970 tons (Alter, 1987, p. 110, footnote 106). Today only one natural dye, logwood, is still in use, though only to a small degree, to dye silk, leather, and nylon black.

Looking Ahead: More Innovations to Come

One of the leaders of the German dye industry, Carl Duisberg, predicted in 1907 that all dyes had been pretty much discovered, thanks to the systematic search of the German R&D laboratories. He was wrong. Since 1914, a substantial number of dyes have been developed. The rise of synthetic fibers in the twentieth century provided a great stimulus for continued research in the chemistry of coloring materials. For example, in 1956, ICI, the successor firm of Levinstein and Read Holliday, developed so-called reactive dyes, which delivered an unprecedented degree of fastness. By no means was the technological history of dyes completed in 1914. I plan to examine in a future work the innovations in dyes after the outbreak of the First World War. This next study will cover the industrial dynamics in the synthetic dye industry up to present times.

---

[285] Redlich (1914, p. 50) reports that in 1896–97 a total of 1,583,808 acres in India with indigo were planted. Note that the figures from the different sources are not fully consistent.

II Short Description of Databases on Firms and Plants

To be able to compare firms along a variety of dimensions, the present study has drawn on a database that I have put together with Professor Ernst Homburg of the University of Maastricht, The Netherlands. We have made a systematic effort to identify all the dye firms and their plants that existed in the world from 1850 until 1914. Virtually all of the firms come from European countries and the United States. The database appears to be unique because it goes further back in time than any previous attempt to study the process of industry evolution in a systematic way.

The database comprises four levels. The fundamental unit of observation is a plant, a firm, or a country in a given year. If a firm or plant existed for the entire period from 1850 to 1914, there would be sixty-five records for the firm or plant in the database. If a firm existed for only two years, there would be two records for the firm in the database. Besides enumerating at the plant and firm levels, the database also surveys each national dye industry as a whole on a yearly basis. Finally, to facilitate cross-country comparisons, the national data are pulled together on a global record for a given year. The four levels of the database design and the variables they track are displayed below. The database is created with FileMaker Pro, a relational database software that has a very user-friendly interface and is fully portable across Macintosh and Windows (PC) computing platforms.

FileMaker Pro does not have the advanced data manipulation capabilities of the program SAS. To probe more deeply into the industrial dynamics of the early dye industry, the data were also converted into SAS datafile formats. We plan to make the synthetic dye industry database available over the Internet sometime in the future. Because we identify all our sources for a particular firm or plant record, researchers will be able return to the original data. For more information on the databases, visit the website of the synthetic dye industry project: <http://johann-peter.murmann.name/dye-project.htm>.

Overview of Databases

The numbers displayed in the accompanying forms are based on more firms than reported in the numbers presented throughout the manuscript because at the beginning of this project we coded a new firm each time the firm changed its legal status. For the present analysis, however, I counted only truly new economic ventures.

Firm ID # 171   Corporate ID # 171   **Dubious Firm**

Firm Name **Actien Gesellschaft für Anilinfabrikation**
(AGFA)

Year 1873

Firm Year Code 1711873   **Investigate**

Country Germany

Country Year ID# 21873

Legal Status AG

Ownership

Town Berlin

Location

Predecessors Dr. M. Jordan
Gesellschaft für Anilinfabrikation

Successors IG Farben AG (not in database)

Founding Date 15-08-1873

End Date 1925

Total Workforce ——————— Number of Workers ————

Number of Chemists 3   Total Staff ————

No Direct Sales to Endusers 1   Predominantly Trader ———   1 **Firm Entry Year**

Sales Offices Töpke & Leidloff, Magdeburg   — **Firm Exit Year**

Company Capital ——————— Sales Mininum   Sales Maximum

Sales ——————— ————— —————

Profits ———————

Firm Year Code Copy 1711873

Dividends ————

Director Dr. Carl Alexander Martius, Dr. Paul Mendelsohn Bartholdy & E. W.
Hallensleben.

Previous Activities: **Specification**

Trading of Dyes ——————   ————————————

Trading of Other Products ——————   ————————————

Dyeing Works ——————   ————————————

Print Works ——————   ————————————

Natural Dye Works ——————   ————————————

Fine Chemicals ——————   ————————————

Tar Destillation ——————   ————————————

Pharmacy ——————   ————————————

Other Previous Activity 1_____   Aniline production_____

Double Count Firms 1_____

References | Homburg, 1986

Notes

_____

_____

_____

_____

_____

_____

_____

_____

_____

_____

_____

_____

done by   Marjan van de Goor_____   1711873_____

corrected by ——————————————————

Plants Directly Owned / Firm's Domestic Product Portfolio

ID#	Town	ND	FC	IBC	OBC	Int	AnD	F	AzD	Ali	Ind	Res	Nap	PhD	Sul	M	Pha	Pho
147	Rummelsburg, near	—	—	—	—	1	—	—	—	—	—	—	—	—	—	—	—	—
148	Berlin	—	—	—	—	—	1	1	—	—	—	—	—	—	—	—	—	—

Plants Indirectly Owned / Firm's Foreign Portfolio

ID#	Town	ND	FC	IBC	OBC	Int	AnD	F	AzD	Ali	Ind	Res	Nap	PhD	Sul	M	Pha	Pho

# of Plants for	Domestic	Foreign	World
Natural Dyes			
Fine Chemicals			
Inorganic Basic Chemical			
Organic Basic Chemicals			
Intermediates	1		1
Aniline Dyes	1		1
Fuchsine	1		1
Azo Dyes			
Alizarine Dyes			

Plants Directly Owned / Firm's Domestic Product Portfolio

ID#	Town	ND	FC	IBC	OBC	Int	AnD	F	AzD	Ali	Ind	Res	Nap	PhD	Sul	M	Pha	Pho
147	Rummelsburg, near	—	—	—	—	1	—	—	—	—	—	—	—	—	—	—	—	—
148	Berlin	—	—	—	—	—	1	1	1	—	—	1	—	—	—	—	—	—

Plants Indirectly Owned / Firm's Foreign Portfolio

ID#	Town	ND	FC	IBC	OBC	Int	AnD	F	AzD	Ali	Ind	Res	Nap	PhD	Sul	M	Pha	Pho
64	Pantin (Seine)	—	—	—	—	1	—	—	—	—	—	—	—	—	—	—	—	—
167	Moscow	—	—	—	—	—	—	—	1	—	—	—	—	—	—	—	—	—
169	Frankfurt am Main	—	—	—	—	1	—	—	1	—	—	—	—	—	—	—	—	—

# of Plants for	Domestic	Foreign	World
Natural Dyes			
Fine Chemicals			
Inorganic Basic Chemical			
Organic Basic Chemicals			
Intermediates	1	1	2
Aniline Dyes	1	1	2
Fuchsine	1		1
Azo Dyes	1	1	2
Alizarine Dyes		1	1

FIRM LEVEL DATABASE

Indigo	_____	_____	_____
Resorcine	_____	_____	_____
Naphtaline	_____	_____	_____
Phenol	_____	_____	_____
Sulphur	_____	_____	_____
Murexide	_____	_____	_____
Pharmaceuticals	_____	_____	_____
Photochemicals	_____	_____	_____

Intermediates only	0
Aniline Dyes only	0
Alizarine only	0
Intermediates and Aniline Dyes	1
Intermediates and Aniline Dyes	0
Aniline Dyes and Alizarine	0
Intermediates and Aniline Dyes and Alizarine	0
Synthetic Dye Firm	1
Dye Firm integrated Back to Organic Basic Chemicals	0
Dye Firm integrated Back to Organic Basic Chemical	0
Dye Firm integrated Forward to Pharmaceuticals and Photochemicals	0
Fully Integrated Firm from IBC to Photo	0

Plant ID# 147   Corporate ID# 1   **Dubious Plant**

Firm ID# 171   **Actien Gesellschaft für Anilinfabrikation (AGFA)**

Country Germany   **Investigate**

Town Rummelsburg, near Berlijn

Location

Name

Year 1873

Firm Year Code 1711873   — **Plant Entry Year**

Country Year ID# 21873   — **Plant Exit Year**

	Yes/No	Tons	Value
Natural Dyes			
Fine Chemicals			
Inorganic Basic Chemicals			
Organic Basic Chemicals			
Intermediates	1		
Aniline Dyes			
Fuchsine			
Azo Dyes			
Alizarine Dyes			
Indigo			
Resorsine Dyes			
Naphtaline Dyes			
Phenol Dyes			
Sulphur Dyes			
Murexide			
Pharmaceuticals			
Photochemicals			

Director Paul Mendelssohn-Bartholdy

Number of workers

Double Count Plants

done by Marjan van de Goor

corrected by

Notes

References Homburg, 1986

		Number of Records	1
Country	Germany	Number of Firms	43
Year	1873	Number of Plants	56
Country Year ID#	21873	Total Country Workforce	
Notes			
References			

Number of Natural Dye Plants	9	Number of Former Dye Trading Firms	3
Number of Fine Chemical Plants	7	Number of Former "Other" Trading Firms	
Number of Inorganic Basic Chemicals Plants	6		
Number of Organic Basic Chemicals Plants	4	Number of Former Dyeing Works	
Number of Intermediates Plants	15	Number of Former Printing Works	
Number of Aniline Dye Plants	30	Number of Former Natural Dye Works	6
Number of Fuchsine Dye Plants	13	Number of Former Fine Chemicals Works	5
Number of Azo Dye Plants	1	Number of Former Tar Destillers	4
Number of Alizarine Dye Plants	14	Number of Former Pharmacists	
Number of Indigo Dye Plants		Number of Former "Other Activity" Shops	3
Number of Resorsine Dye Plants	2		
Number of Naphtaline Dye Plants	2		
Number of Phenol Dyes Plants	7		
Number of Sulfur Dye Plants			
Number of Murexide Plants	1		
Number of Pharamaceutical Plants			
Number of Photochemicals Plants			

Firms Active in Country

Firm Name	Founding	End	Number of Employees
BASF (Badische	1865	1925	
Cl. Courtois et Cie	b. 1863	1883	
Fabrique des	1-4-1872	1883	
H. Siegle	b. 1848	1873	
R.E. Knosp,	1845	1873	

Number of Firm Entries	9
Number of Firm Exists	7

Product Portfolio of National Firms (only domestic plants)

Number of Intermediates only Firms	5
Number of Aniline Dyes only Firms	16
Number of Alizarine Dyes only Firms	7
Number of Intermediates as well as Aniline Dyes Firms	6
Number of Intermediates as well as Alizarine Dye Firms	4
Number of Aniline as well as Alizarine Dyes Firms	4
Number of Int Aniline Alizarine Dyes Firms	2
Number of Synthetic Dye Firms	33
Number of Dye Firm Integrated back to OBC	1
Number of Dye Firm Integrated back to IBC	0
Number of Dye Firm Integrated Forward to Pho	0
Number of Fully Integrated Firms from IBC to Photo	0

Year   1873

Country	# of ND Pl	# of FC Pl	# of IBC Pl	# of OBC Pl	# of Int Pl	# of AnD Pl	# of F Pl	# of AzD Pl	# of Ali Pl	# of Ind Pl	# of PhD Pl	# of M Pl	# of Pha Pl	# of Pho Pl
France	2	3	1	3	8	7	1		2		6			
Great Britain	2	5		6	6	12	6	2	2		4			
Germany	9	7	6	4	15	30	13	1	14		7	1		
United States					1	2	2							
Russia														
Austrian Empire	1	2	1		1	1			1		1			
Netherlands														
Belgium		1			2	4								
Italy														
Switzerland	1				3	6	3		3					

Country	# of For DTF	# of For OTF	# of For DW	# of For PW	# of For NDW	# of For FCW	# of For TD	# of For Phar	# of For OAc
France	1	1	2		2	2	2	1	2
Great Britain	1				1		1		
Germany	3				6	5	4		3
United States									
Russia									
Austrian Empire						1			
Netherlands									
Belgium									
Italy									
Switzerland	1							1	1

Country	# of Firms	# of Plants	Total Country Workforce
France	18	17	
Great Britain	16	20	
Germany	43	56	
United States	2	2	
Russia			
Austrian Empire	3	3	
Netherlands			
Belgium	6	5	
Italy			
Switzerland	7	7	126

Country Germany

Year	All Firms	All Plants	Syn Dye Firms	Int only Firms	Ani only Firms	Ali only Firms	Int & Ani Firms	Int & Ali Firms	Int, Ani & Ali Firms	Dye to OBC Firms	Dye to IBC Firms	Dye to Pho Firms	Fully Integr Firms
1848			0	0	0	0	0	0	0	0	0	0	0
1849			0	0	0	0	0	0	0	0	0	0	0
1850			0	0	0	0	0	0	0	0	0	0	0
1851	1	1	0	0	0	0	0	0	0	0	0	0	0
1852	2	2	0	0	0	0	0	0	0	0	0	0	0
1853	1	1	0	0	0	0	0	0	0	0	0	0	0
1854	1	1	0	0	0	0	0	0	0	0	0	0	0
1855	3	3	0	1	0	0	0	0	0	0	0	0	0
1856	2	2	0	1	0	0	0	0	0	0	0	0	0
1857	2	2	0	1	0	0	0	0	0	0	0	0	0
1858	4	5	2	1	2	0	0	0	0	0	0	0	0
1859	8	9	3	3	3	0	0	0	0	0	0	0	0
1860	12	13	6	3	5	1	0	0	1	0	0	0	0
1861	18	19	10	5	7	0	3	0	0	1	0	0	0
1862	24	25	18	4	14	0	4	0	0	2	0	0	0
1863	27	31	22	3	18	0	4	0	0	2	0	0	0
1864	27	31	24	1	20	0	4	0	0	2	0	0	0
1865	28	32	23	1	19	0	4	0	0	2	0	0	0
1866	28	36	24	1	20	0	4	0	0	2	0	0	0
1867	34	43	26	3	22	0	4	0	0	1	0	0	0
1868	31	40	24	3	21	0	3	0	0	1	0	0	0
1869	31	42	23	4	19	0	4	1	1	1	0	0	0
1870	31	42	25	3	18	1	4	2	1	1	0	0	0
1871	36	45	27	5	20	1	4	2	1	1	0	0	0
1872	38	48	28	6	19	3	4	2	1	1	0	0	0
1873	43	56	33	5	16	7	6	4	2	1	0	0	0
1874	43	55	28	10	13	7	5	4	3	1	0	0	0
1875	42	54	26	10	11	6	4	4	3	1	0	0	0
1876	44	56	24	13	11	5	5	4	3	1	0	0	0
1877	43	57	24	12	11	5	6	5	3	1	0	0	0
1878	45	57	25	13	12	5	7	4	3	1	0	0	0
1879	49	62	29	11	17	4	7	4	3	1	0	0	0
1880	48	62	29	11	16	4	8	5	4	1	0	0	0
1881	59	75	31	14	17	4	8	4	3	1	0	0	0
1882	59	72	35	14	20	4	9	3	2	1	0	0	0
1883	52	64	30	13	15	5	8	3	2	1	0	0	0
1884	55	69	30	16	16	4	8	3	2	1	0	0	0
1885	57	71	32	15	18	4	8	3	2	1	0	0	0
1886	57	71	32	16	18	4	8	3	2	1	0	0	0
1887	64	77	34	18	18	4	10	3	2	1	0	0	0
1888	66	86	37	19	22	4	10	5	4	1	0	0	0
1889	61	81	34	20	22	3	9	4	4	1	0	0	0
1890	62	80	34	20	22	3	9	4	4	1	0	0	0
1891	67	85	35	24	22	4	9	4	4	1	0	0	0
1892	74	95	37	28	22	3	11	4	4	3	1	0	0
1893	66	84	37	23	24	3	9	3	3	2	1	0	0
1894	67	84	37	24	24	3	9	3	3	2	1	0	0
1895	66	85	37	24	24	3	9	3	3	2	1	0	0
1896	65	88	38	24	24	3	10	3	3	3	2	0	0
1897	71	93	37	31	25	2	9	3	3	3	2	0	0
1898	82	102	43	36	26	0	14	3	3	5	4	0	0
1899	59	80	36	20	23	2	10	4	3	3	2	0	0
1900	59	83	37	20	23	3	10	4	3	3	2	1	0
1901	59	84	35	21	22	2	10	4	3	3	2	0	0
1902	54	77	33	18	22	0	10	4	3	3	2	0	0
1903	49	69	31	15	21	0	9	4	3	2	1	0	0
1904	49	68	32	14	22	0	9	4	3	2	1	0	0
1905	48	69	32	13	21	0	10	4	3	3	2	0	0
1906	48	70	34	11	20	0	11	4	3	4	4	1	0
1907	38	62	28	9	13	1	11	4	3	4	4	1	0
1908	39	63	29	9	14	1	11	4	3	4	4	1	0
1909	39	63	28	8	12	0	10	5	4	4	4	1	0
1910	38	62	28	8	12	1	10	5	4	4	4	0	0
1911	47	61	28	8	12	1	10	5	4	4	4	0	0
1912	41	63	31	8	15	1	10	5	4	4	4	0	0
1913	38	59	26	9	8	1	12	7	6	4	4	0	0
1914	38	60	26	10	9	1	12	8	7	5	5	1	1

Bibliography

Abbe, Ernst (1896). Statut der Carl Zeiss – Stiftung zu Jena. Reprinted (1989) in *Gesammelte Abhandlungen. Bd. III: Vorträge, Reden und Schriften sozialpolitischen und verwandten Inhalts.* Hildesheim: Olms, pp. 262–329.

Abbott, Andrew (1998). Causal devolution. *Sociological Methods & Research* 27(2): 148–81.

Aitken, Hugh G. J. (1976). *Syntony and Spark: The Origins of Radio.* New York: John Wiley & Sons.

Aldrich, Howard (1999). *Organizations Evolving.* London: SAGE Publications.

Allen, R. C. (1983). Collective invention. *Journal of Economic Behavior and Organization* 4: 1–24.

Alter, Peter (1987). *The Reluctant Patron: Science and the State in Great Britain, 1850–1920.* New York: Berg (distributed in the United States by St. Martin's Press).

Amstrong, Henry E. (1893). The appreciation of science by German manufacturers. *Nature* 48: 29–34.

Anderson, Philip, and Michael L. Tushman (1990). Technological discontinuities and dominant design: A cyclical model of technological change. *Administrative Science Quarterly* 35(December): 604–33.

Anonymous (1895). Vorgeschichte der Farbenfabriken vormals Friedrich Bayer & Co., 1860 bis 1881. Leverkusen: Bayer Archive 7/B. I.

Aoki, Masahiko (2001). *Toward a Comparative Institutional Analysis.* Cambridge, MA: MIT Press.

Aoki, Masahiko, and Ronald Dore, eds. (1994). *The Japanese Main Firm: Sources of Competitive Strength.* New York: Oxford University Press.

Arora, Ashish, Ralph Landau, and Nathan Rosenberg, eds. (1998). *Chemicals and Long-Term Economic Growth: Insights from the Chemical Industry.* New York: John Wiley & Sons, Inc.

Arthur, W. Brian (1994). *Increasing Returns and Path Dependence in the Economy.* Ann Arbor, MI: University of Michigan Press.

Aunger, Robert (2000). *Darwinizing Culture: The Status of Memetics as a Science.* New York: Oxford University Press.

Aunger, Robert (2002). *The Electric Meme: A New Theory of How We Think.* New York: Free Press.

Barnett, W. P., and G. R. Carroll (1987). Competition and mutualism among early telephone companies. *Administrative Science Quarterly* 30: 400–21.

Barnett, William P., and Glenn R. Carroll (1995). Modeling internal organizational change. *Annual Review of Sociology* 21: 217–36.

Barnett, William P., and Morten T. Hansen (1996). The Red Queen in organizational evolution. *Strategic Management Journal* 17(Special Issue): 139–57.

Barney, J. B. (1991). Firm resources and sustained competitive advantage. *Journal of Management* 17(1): 99–120.

Basalla, George (1988). *The Evolution of Technology.* New York: Cambridge University Press.

Baum, Joel A. C., and Bill McKelvey, eds. (1999). *Variations in Organization Science: In Honor of Donald T. Campbell.* Thousand Oaks, CA: SAGE Publications.

Baum, Joel A. C., and Jitendra V. Singh, eds. (1994). *The Evolutionary Dynamics of Organizations.* New York: Oxford University Press.

Bäumler, Ernst (1988). *Die Rotfabriker: Familiengeschichte eines Weltunternehmens.* Munich: R. Piper GmbH & Co.

Baumol, William J. (1993). *Entrepreneurship, Management, and the Structure of Payoffs.* Cambridge, MA: MIT Press.

Bayer AG, ed. (1963). *Beiträge zur hundertjährigen Firmengeschichte 1863–1865.* Leverkusen: Bayer AG.

Beer, J. H. (1959). *The Emergence of the German Dye Industry.* Urbana, IL: University of Illinois Press.

Ben-David, Joseph (1971). *The Scientist's Role in Society.* Chicago: University of Chicago Press, 1984 edition.

Ben-David, Joseph (1977). *Centers of Learning: Britain, France, Germany, United States.* New York: McGraw-Hill Book Co.

Berghoff, H., and R. Möller (1994). Tired pioneers and dynamic newcomers? A comparative essay on English and German entrepreneurial history, 1870–1914. *Economic History Review* 47(2): 262–87.

Best, Michael (1990). *The New Competition: Institutions of Industrial Restructuring.* Cambridge, MA: Harvard University Press.

Biernacki, Richard (1995). *The Fabrication of Labor: Germany and Britain, 1640–1914.* Berkeley, CA: University of California Press.

Bijker, Wiebe E., Thomas P. Hughes, and Trevor Pinch, eds. (1987). *The Social Construction of Technological Systems: New Directions in the Sociology and History of Technology.* Cambridge, MA: MIT Press.

Bijker, Wiebe E., and John Law, eds. (1992). *Shaping Technology/Building Society.* Cambridge, MA: MIT Press.

Blackmore, Susan J. (1999). *The Meme Machine.* New York: Oxford University Press.

Bloede, Victor G. (1924). Some early attempts to establish the aniline industry in the United States. *Industrial and Engineering Chemistry* 16(4): 409–11.

Blute, Marion (1997). History versus science: The evolutionary solution. *Canadian Journal of Sociology/ Cahiers Canadiens de Sociologie* 22(3): 345–64.

Boig, Fletcher S., and Paul W. Howerton (1952). History and development of organic chemistry: 1877–1949. *Science* 115: 25–31.

Borges, Jorge Luis (2000). *Selected Non-Fictions.* New York: Penguin.

Borscheid, Peter (1976). *Naturwissenschaft, Staat und Industrie in Baden (1848–1914).* Stuttgart: Klett.

Bourgeois, L. J., and Kathleen M. Eisenhardt (1988). Strategic decision processes in high velocity environments: Four cases in the microcomputer industry. *Management Science* 34(7): 816–35.

Boyd, Robert, and Peter J. Richerson (1985). *Culture and the Evolutionary Process.* Chicago: University of Chicago Press.

Broadberry, S. N. (1997). *The Productivity Race: British Manufacturing in International Perspective 1850–1990.* New York: Cambridge University Press.

Brocke, Bernhard vom (1980). Hochschul- und Wissenschaftspolitik in Preußen und im Deutschen Kaiserreich 1882–1907: Das "System Althoff." In *Bildungspolitik in Preußen zur Zeit des Kaiserreichs.* Peter Baumgart, ed. Stuttgart: Klett-Cotta, pp. 9–118.

Brockway, Lucile H. (1979). *Science and Colonial Expansion: The Role of the British Royal Botanic Gardens.* New York: Academic Press.

Brubacher, John S., and Willis Rudy (1958). *Higher Education in Transition: A History of American Colleges and Universities.* Republished in 1997; New Brunswick, NJ: Transaction Publishers.

Buchholz, Klaus (1979). Verfahrenstechnik (chemical engineering) – Its development, present state and structure. *Social Studies of Science* 9: 33–62.

Bud, Robert, and Gerrylynn K. Roberts (1984). *Science versus Practise: Chemistry in Victorian Britain.* Manchester, U.K.: Manchester University Press.

Burchardt, Lothar (1992). Wissenschaft, Industrie und Kultur zur Zeit August Wilhelm Hofmanns. In *Die Allianz von Wissenschaft und Industrie: August Wilhelm Hofmann (1818–1892).* Christoph Meinel and Hartmut Scholz, eds. Weinheim & New York: VCH Publishers, pp. 7–26.

Burgelman, Robert A. (1991). Intraorganizational ecology of strategy making and organizational adaptation: Theory and field research. *Organization Science* 2(3): 239–62.

Burt, Ronald S. (1992). *Structural Holes: The Social Social Structure of Competition.* Cambridge, MA: Harvard University Press.

Campbell, Donald T. (1960). Blind variation and selective retention in creative thought as in other thought processes. *Psychological Review* 67: 380–400.

Campbell, Donald T. (1969). Variation and selective retention in socio-cultural evolution. *General Systems* 14: 69–85.

Campbell, Donald T. (1974). Evolutionary epistemology. In *The Philosophy of Karl Popper.* P. A. Schilpp, ed. La Salle, IL: Open Court, pp. 413–63.

Cardwell, D. S. L. (1957). *The Organisation of Science in England: A Retrospect.* London: Heinemann.

Carl, R. W. (1926). *Carl Jäger, G.M.B.H, Anilinfarbenfabrik, 1823–1926.* Düsseldorf: Kunstdruckerei Linder & Longuich.

Caro, Heinrich (1892). Über die Entwicklung der Theerfarben-Industrie. *Berichte der deutschen chemischen Gesellschaft* 25(3): 955–1105.

Caro, Heinrich (1904). Über die Entwicklung der chemischen Industrie von Mannheim-Ludwigshafen am Rhein. Vortrag, Gehalten auf der Hauptversammlung deutscher Chemiker in Mannheim, 25.–28. Mai 1904. *Zeitschrift für Angewandte Chemie* 7(37): 1343–62.

Carroll, G. R., and A. Swaminathan (1991). Density dependent organizational evolution in the American brewing industry from 1633 to 1988. *Acta Sociologica* 34: 155–75.

Carroll, Glenn R., Lyda S. Bigelow, Marc-David L. Seidel, and Lucia B. Tsai (1996). The fates of de novo and de alio producers in the American automobile industry 1885–1981. *Strategic Management Journal* 17: 117–37.

Carroll, Glenn R., and Jacques Delacroix (1982). Organizational mortality in the newspaper industries of Argentina and Ireland: An ecological approach. *Administrative Science Quarterly* 27: 169–98.

Carroll, Glenn R., and Michael T. Hannan (1995a). Automobile manufacturers. In *Organizations in Industry: Strategy, Structure, and Selection*. Glenn R. Carroll and Michael T. Hannan, eds. New York: Oxford University Press, pp. 195–214.

Carroll, Glenn R., and Michael T. Hannan, eds. (1995b). *Organizations in Industry: Strategy, Structure, and Selection*. New York: Oxford University Press.

Carroll, Glenn R., and Michael T. Hannan (2000). *The Demography of Corporations and Industries*. Princeton, NJ: Princeton University Press.

Chandler, Alfred D. (1962). *Strategy and Structure: Concepts in the History of American Industrial Enterprise*. Cambridge, MA: MIT Press.

Chandler, Alfred D. (1977). *The Visible Hand*. Cambridge, MA: Belknap Press of Harvard University Press.

Chandler, Alfred D. (1990). *Scale and Scope: The Dynamics of Industrial Capitalism*. Cambridge, MA: Harvard University Press.

Chandler, Alfred Dupont, Franco Amatori, and Takashi Hikino, eds. (1997). *Big Business and the Wealth of Nations*. New York: Cambridge University Press.

Child, John (1972). Organization structure, environment, and performance – The role of strategic choice. *Sociology* 6(1): 1–22.

Christensen, Clayton M., and Richard S. Rosenbloom (1995). Explaining the attacker's advantage: Technological paradigms, organizational dynamics, and the value network. *Research Policy* 24: 233–57.

Clark, Kim B., W. Bruce Chew, and Takahiro Fujimoto (1987). Product development in the world auto industry. *Brookings Papers on Economic Activity* 3: 729–71.

Cobban, Alan B. (1975). *The Medieval Universities: Their Development and Organization*. London: Methuen.

Cocks, Geoffrey, and Konrad Hugo Jarausch (1990). *German Professions, 1800–1950*. New York: Oxford University Press.

Cohen, Michael D., Roger Burkhart, Giovanni Dosi, Massimo Edigi, Luigi Marengo, Massimo Warglien, and Sidney Winter (1996). Routines and other recurring action patterns of organizations: Contemporary research issues. *Industrial and Corporate Change* 5(3): 653–98.

Conner, K. R. (1991). A historical comparison of resource-based theory and five schools of thought within industrial organization economics: Do we have a new theory of the firm? *Journal of Management* 17: 121–54.

Conner, Kathleen R., and C. K. Prahalad (1996). A resource-based theory of the firm: Knowledge versus opportunism. *Organization Science* 7(5): 477–501.

Coriat, Benjamin, and Giovanni Dosi (1998). Learning how to govern and learning how to solve problems: On the co-evolution of competences, conflicts and organizational routines. In *The Dynamic Firm: The Role of Technology, Strategy, Organization and Regions*. Alfred Dupont Chandler, Peter Hagström, and Örjan Sölvell, eds. New York: Oxford University Press, pp. 103–33.

Croft, William (2000). *Explaining Language Change: An Evolutionary Approach*. Harlow, Essex: Longman.

Cyert, Richard M., and James G. March (1963). *A Behavioral Theory of the Firm*. Cambridge, MA: Blackwell Publishers, 1992 edition.

Daniel, Edward Morton (1884). *A Complete Treatise upon the New Law of Patents, Designs and Trade Marks Act 1883*. London: Steven and Haynes.

Da Rin, Marco (1998). Finance and the chemical industry. In *Chemicals and Long-Term Economic Growth: Insights from the Chemical Industry*. Ashish Arora, Ralph Landau, and Nathan Rosenberg, eds. New York: John Wiley & Sons, Inc., pp. 307–40.

Darwin, Charles (1964). *On the Origin of Species. A Facsimile of the First [1859] Edition*. Cambridge, MA: Harvard University Press.

Davis, Gerald F., and Tracy A. Thompson (1994). A social movement perspective on corporate control. *Administrative Science Quarterly* 39(March): 141–73.

Dawkins, Richard (1976). *The Selfish Gene.* New York: Oxford University Press.

Dennett, Daniel C. (1995). *Darwin's Dangerous Idea: Evolution and the Meanings of Life.* New York: Simon & Schuster.

Derrick, C. G. (1927). Twenty-five years of the American dye industry. *Chemical and Metallurgical Engineering* 34: 248–50.

Dierickx, Ingemar, and Karel Cool (1989). Asset stock accumulation and sustainability of competitive advantage. *Management Science* 35(12): 1504–11.

DiMaggio, Paul J. (1994). The challenge of community evolution. In *The Evolutionary Dynamics of Organizations.* Jitendra Singh and Joel Baum, eds. New York: Oxford University Press, pp. 444–50.

Dobbin, Frank (1994). *Forging Industrial Policy: The United States, Britain, and France in the Railway Age.* New York: Cambridge University Press.

Dobbin, Frank, and Timothy J. Dowd (2000). The market that antitrust built: Public policy, private coercion, and railroad acquisitions, 1825 to 1922. *American Sociological Review* 65(6): 631–57.

Donnelly, James Francis (1987). Chemical education and the chemical industry in England from the mid-nineteenth to the early twentieth century. Doctoral Dissertation, University of Leeds School of Education. Leeds, U.K.: University of Leeds, 446p.

Dosi, Giovanni (1984). *Technical Change and Industrial Transformation.* New York: St. Martin's Press.

Dosi, Giovanni (2000). *Innovation, Organization and Economic Dynamics: Selected Essays.* Northampton, MA: Edward Elgar Publishing.

Dosi, Giovanni, Richard R. Nelson, and Sidney G. Winter (2000). *The Nature and Dynamics of Organizational Capabilities.* New York: Oxford University Press.

Duisberg, Carl (1923). *Abhandlungen, Vorträge und Reden aus den Jahren 1882–1921.* Berlin: Verlag Chemie.

Duisberg, Carl (1933). *Meine Lebenserinnerungen (My Life).* Leipzig: P. Reclam.

Durham, William H. (1991). *Coevolution: Genes, Culture, and Human Diversity.* Stanford, CA: Stanford University Press.

Eichengreen, Barry (1998). Monetary, fiscal, and trade policies in the development of the chemical industry. In *Chemicals and Long-Term Economic Growth: Insights from the Chemical Industry.* Ashish Arora, Ralph Landau, and Nathan Rosenberg, eds. New York: John Wiley & Sons, pp. 265–306.

Eisenhardt, K. M., and L. J. Bourgeois (1988). Politics of strategic decision making in high-velocity environments: Toward a midrange theory. *Academy of Management Journal* 31(4): 737–70.

Eisenhardt, Kathleen M. (1989a). Building theories from case study research. *Academy of Management Review* 14(4): 532–50.

Eisenhardt, Kathleen M. (1989b). Making fast strategic decisions in high velocity environments. *Academy of Management Journal* 32(3): 543–76.

Eisenhardt, Kathleen M., and D. Charles Galunic (2000). Coevolving: At last, a way to make synergies work. *Harvard Business Review* 78(1): 91–101.

Elbaum, Bernard, and William Lazonick, eds. (1987). *The Decline of the British Economy.* Oxford: Clarendon Press.

Eldredge, Niles (1985). *Unfinished Synthesis: Biological Hierarchies and Modern Evolutionary Thought.* New York: Oxford University Press.

Elliot, E. Donald (1985). The evolutionary tradition in jurisprudence. *Columbia Law Review* 85(January): 38–94.

Eulenberg, Franz (1904). Die Frequenz der Deutschen Universitäten. *Abhandlungen der Königlichen Sächsischen Gesellschaft der Wissenschaften: Philologisch-historische Klasse* 24(2): 1–323.

Farbenfabriken-Bayer (1918). *Geschichte und Entwicklung der Farbenfabriken vormals Friedrich Bayer in Elberfeld in den ersten Fünfzig Jahren (also known as Böttingerschrift).* Leverkusen: Bayer.

Federico, Giovanni (1997). *An Economic History of the Silk Industry, 1830–1930.* New York: Cambridge University Press.

Fell, Ulrike (1998). The chemistry profession in France: The Société Chimique de Paris/de France 1870–1914. In *The Making of the Chemist: The Social History of Chemistry in Europe, 1789–1914.* David Knight and Helge Kragh, eds. Cambridge: Cambridge University Press, pp. 15–38.

Ferguson, Adam (1767). *An Essay on the History of the Civil Society.* New Brunswick, NJ: Transaction Books, 1980 edition.

Ferleger, Louis, and William Lazonick (1994). Higher education for an innovative economy: Land-grant colleges and the managerial revolution in America. *Business and Economic History* 23(Fall): 116–28.

Fischer, Wolfram, and Peter Lundgreen (1975). The recruitment of administrative and technical personnel. In *The Formation of National States in Europe*. Charles Tilly, ed. Princeton, NJ: Princeton University Press, vol. 8, pp. 456–561.

Flechtner, H. J. (1963). Die Elberfelder Farbenfabriken. In *Beiträge zur hundertjährigen Firmengeschichte 1863–1865*. Bayer Management Board, eds. Leverkusen: Bayer AG, pp. 5–20.

Flechtner, Hans-Joachim (1959). *Carl Duisberg: Vom Chemiker zum Wirschaftsführer (From a Chemist to an Industrial Leader)*. Düsseldorf: ECON Verlag GmbH.

Fleischer, Arndt (1984). *Patentgesetzgebung und Chemisch-Pharmazeutische Industrie im Deutschen Kaiserreich (1871–1918)*. Stuttgart: Deutscher Apotheker Verlag.

Flexner, Abraham (1930). *Universities: American, English, German*. New York: Oxford University Press.

Fligstein, Neil (1990). *The Transformation of Corporate Control*. Cambridge, MA: Harvard University Press.

Foss, Nicolai J. (1997). *Resources, Firms, and Strategies: A Reader in the Resource-Based Perspective*. Oxford and New York: Oxford University Press.

Fox, Maurice R. (1987). *Dye-Makers of Great Britain, 1856–1976*. Manchester, U.K.: Imperial Chemical Industries PLC.

Freeman, Christopher (1982). *The Economics of Industrial Innovation*. Cambridge, MA: MIT Press.

Freeman, Christopher, and Francisco Louçã (2001). *As Time Goes By: From the Industrial Revolution to the Informaton Revolution*. Oxford: Oxford University Press.

Frenken, Koen (2000). A complexity approach to innovation networks. The case of the aircraft industry (1909–1997). *Research Policy* 29(2): 257–72.

Frenken, Koen, and Loet Leydesdorff (2000). Scaling trajectories in civil aircraft (1913–1997). *Research Policy* 29(3): 331–48.

Frenken, Koen, Paolo P. Saviotti, and Michel Trommetter (1999). Variety and niche creation in aircraft, helicopters, motorcycles and microcomputers. *Research Policy* 28(5): 469–88.

Friedman, Benjamin M. (2002). Globalization: Stiglitz's case. A review of *Globalization and Its Discontents* by Joseph E. Stiglitz. *New York Review of Books* 49(August 15): 13.

Fruin, W. M. (1992). *The Japanese Enterprise System: Competitive Strategies and Cooperative Structures*. Oxford: Oxford University Press.

Fruton, Joseph S. (1988). The Liebig research group – A reappraisal. *Proceedings of the American Philosophical Society* 132(1): 1–66.

Furter, William F., ed. (1980). *History of Chemical Engineering*. Advances in Chemistry Series. Washington, DC: American Chemical Society.

Furter, William F., ed. (1982). *A Century of Chemical Engineering*. New York: Plenum Press.

Futuyma, Douglas J., and Montgomery Slatkin, eds. (1983). *Coevolution*. Sunderland, MA: Sinauer Associates.

Gaddis, John Lewis (2002). *The Landscape of History: How Historians Map the Past*. New York: Oxford University Press.

Galambos, Louis (1966). *Competition & Cooperation: The Emergence of a National Trade Association*. Baltimore: Johns Hopkins University Press.

Galambos, Louis, and Jane Eliot Sewell (1995). *Networks of Innovation: Vaccine Development at Merck, Sharp & Dohme, and Mulford, 1895–1995*. New York: Cambridge University Press.

Gardner, Walter M., ed. (1915). *The British Coal-Tar Industry: Its Origins, Development and Decline*. London: Williams and Norgate.

Garfield, Simon (2001). *Mauve: How One Man Invented a Color That Changed the World*. New York: W. W. Norton & Co.

Geertz, Clifford (1973). *The Interpretation of Cultures*. New York: Basic Books.

Gerlach, Michael (1992). *Alliance Capitalism: The Social Organization of Japanese Business*. Berkeley, CA: University of California Press.

Gerschenkron, A. (1962). *Economic Backwardness in Historical Perspective*. Cambridge, MA: Harvard University Press.

Gispen, Kees (1989). *New Profession, Old Order: Engineers and German Society, 1815–1914*. New York: Cambridge University Press.

Glaser, Barney G., and Anselm L. Strauss (1967). *The Discovery of Grounded Theory: Strategies for Qualitative Research*. Chicago: Aldine Publishing Co.

Gort, Michael, and Steven Klepper (1982). Time paths in the diffusion of product innovations. *Economic Journal* 92(367): 630–61.

Granovetter, M. (1985). Economic action and social structure: The problem of embeddedness. *Social Structure and Network Analysis* 91: 481–510.

Guillén, Mauro (1991). *States, Professions, and Organizational Paradigms: German Scientific Management, Human Relations, and Structural Analysis in Comparative Perspective*. Madrid: Centro de Estudios Avanzados en Ciencias Sociales Instituto Juan March de Estudios e Investigaciones.

Guillén, Mauro F. (1994). *Models of Management: Work, Authority, and Organization in a Comparative Perspective*. Chicago: University of Chicago Press.

Guillén, Mauro F. (2001). *The Limits of Convergence: Globalization and Organizational Change in Argentina, South Korea, and Spain*. Princeton, NJ: Princeton University Press.

Gulati, Ranjay (1998). Alliances and networks. *Strategic Management Journal* 19(4; Special Issue Supplement): 293–317.

Haber, L. F. (1958). *The Chemical Industry during the Nineteenth Century*. Oxford: Oxford University Press.

Haber, L. F. (1971). *The Chemical Industry, 1900–1930*. Oxford: Clarendon Press.

Hagen, Antje (1999). Export versus direct investment in the German optical industry: Carl Zeiss, Jena, and Glaswerk Schott & Gen. in the UK, from the beginning to 1933. *Business History* 38(4): 1–20.

Hall, Bronwyn H., and Rosemarie Ham Ziedonis (2001). The patent paradox revisited: An empirical study of patenting in the U.S. semiconductor industry, 1979–1995. *Rand Journal of Economics* 32(1): 101–28.

Hall, Peter A., and David W. Soskice eds. (2001). *Varieties of Capitalism: The Institutional Foundations of Comparative Advantage*. New York: Oxford University Press.

Haller, Albin (1903). *Les Industries Chimique et Pharmaceutiques. Exposition de Paris 1900. Classe 87: Arts Chimique et Pharmaceutique. Rapport du Jury International.* Paris: Gauthier-Villars.

Hambrick, D. C., and P. A. Mason (1984). Upper echelons: The organization as a reflection of its top managers. *Academy of Management Review* 9: 193–200.

Hannan, Michael T., and John H. Freeman (1977). The population ecology of organizations. *American Journal of Sociology* 82: 929–64.

Hannan, Michael T., and John H. Freeman (1984). Structural inertia and organizational change. *American Sociological Review* 49: 149–64.

Hannan, Michael T., and John H. Freeman (1989). *Organizational Ecology*. Cambridge, MA: Harvard University Press.

Hardie, D. W. F., and J. Pratt (1966). *A History of the Modern British Chemical Industry*. Oxford: Pergamon Press.

Harrison, Tony (1992). *Square Rounds*. London: Faber and Faber.

Haveman, Heather A. (1993). Organizational size and change: Diversification in the savings and loan industry after deregulation. *Administrative Science Quarterly* 38(1): 20–50.

Haveman, Heather A., and Hayagreeva Rao (1997). Structuring a theory of moral sentiments: Institutional and organizational coevolution in the early thrift industry. *American Journal of Sociology* 102: 1606–51.

Hayek, Friedrich A. (1973). *Law, Legislation and Liberty, Volume I: Rules and Order*. Chicago: University of Chicago Press.

Hayek, Friedrich A. (1989). *The Fatal Conceit: The Errors of Socialism*. Chicago: University of Chicago Press.

Haynes, Williams (1945–1954). *American Chemical Industry*, vols. 1–6. New York: D. Van Nostrand Co., Inc.

Haynes, Williams (1954). *American Chemical Industry: Background and Beginnings*. New York: D. Van Nostrand Co., Inc.

Heggen, Alfred (1975). *Erfindungsschutz und Industrialisierung in Preussen: 1793–1877*. Gottingen: Vandenhoeck und Ruprecht.

Helfat, Constance E., ed. (2000). The evolution of firm capabilities. *Strategic Management Journal.* 21: 10–11.

Henderson, Rebecca M., and Kim B. Clark (1990). Architectural innovation: The reconfiguration of existing product technologies and the failure of established firms. *Administrative Science Quarterly* 35: 9–30.

Hendrick, Ellwood (1924). Record of the coal-tar color industry at Albany. *Industrial and Engineering Chemistry* 16(4): 411–13.

Henneking, Ralf (1994). *Chemische Industrie und Umwelt: Konflikte um Umweltbelastungen durch die chemische Industrie am Beispiel der Schwerchemischen, Farben, und Düngemittelindustrie der Rheinprovinz (ca. 1800–1914)*. Stuttgart: Franz Steiner Verlag.

Herrigel, Gary (1996). *Industrial Constructions: The Sources of German Industrial Power*. New York: Cambridge University Press.

Hesse, Bernard C. (1914). The industry of the coal tar-dyes: An outline sketch. *Journal of Industrial and Engineering Chemistry* 6(December): 1013–27.

Hesse, Bernard C. (1915). Lest we forget! Who killed Cock Robin? The U.S. tariff-history of coal-tar dyes. *Journal of Industrial and Engineering Chemistry* 7(August): 694–709.

Hirsch, Paul M. (1975). Organizational effectiveness and the institutional environment. *Administrative Science Quarterly* 20(September): 327–44.

Hirschman, Albert O. (1977). *The Passions and the Interests: Political Arguments for Capitalism before Its Triumph*. Princeton, NJ: Princeton University Press, 1997 edition.

Hodgson, Geoffrey M. (2001). *How Economics Forgot History: The Problem of Historical Specificity in the Social Sciences*. New York: Routledge.

Hodgson, Geoffrey Martin (1998). *The Foundations of Evolutionary Economics, 1890–1973*. Northampton, MA: Edward Elgar Publishing, Inc.

Hofmann, A. W. (1863). *Colouring Derivatives of Organic Matter, Recent and Fossilized*. International Exhibition 1862. Report by the juries on the subjects in the thirty-six classes into which the exhibition was divided, Class II – Section A (Chemical and Pharmaceutical Products and Processes). London.

Hofmann, A. W. (1877). Noch ein Wort über das Chrysoïdin. *Berichte der Deutschen Chemischen Gesellschaft* 10: 388–91.

Hollingsworth, J. Rogers, and Robert Boyer (1997). *Contemporary Capitalism: The Embeddedness of Institutions*. Cambridge: Cambridge University Press.

Holm, Peter (1995). The dynamics of institutionalization: Transformation in processes in Norwegian fisheries. *Administrative Science Quarterly* 40(3): 398–423.

Holmes, Lawrence (1989). The complementarity of research and teaching at Liebig's laboratory. *Osiris* 5(2nd series): 121–64.

Homburg, Ernst (1983). The influence of demand on the emergence of the dye industry. The roles of chemists and colourists. *Journal of the Society of Dyers and Colourists* 99(November): 325–33.

Homburg, Ernst (1992). The emergence of research laboratories in the dyestuffs industry, 1870–1900. *British Journal for the History of Science* 25: 91–111.

Homburg, Ernst (1993). *"Chemiker" by Occupation: The Rise of the Industrial Chemist and Polytechnic Education in Germany, 1790–1850*. Delft, The Netherlands: Delftse Universitaire Pers (in Dutch).

Homburg, Ernst (1998). Two factions, one profession: The chemical profession in German society 1780–1870. *The Making of the Chemist: The Social History of Chemistry in Europe, 1789–1914*. David Knight and Helge Kragh, eds. Cambridge: Cambridge University Press, pp. 39–76.

Hornix, Willem J. (1992). From process to plant: Innovation in the early artificial dye industry. *British Journal for the History of Science* 25: 65–90.

Hounshell, David A. (1984). *From the American System to Mass Production*. Baltimore: Johns Hopkins University Press.

Hückstädt, Harald (1967). Carl Rumpf und Carl Duisberg. *Unser Werk: Werkzeitschrift der farbenfabriken Bayer Aktiengesellschaft* 18(12): 385–95.

Hughes, Thomas Parke (1989). *American Genesis: A Century of Invention and Technological Enthusiasm, 1870–1970*. New York: Viking.

Hull, David (1995). La filiation en biologie de l'évolution et dans l'histoire des langues. In *Le Paradigme de la Filiation*. Jean Gayon and Jean-Jacques Wunenburger, eds. Paris: Éditions L'Harmattan, pp. 99–119.

Hull, David L. (1988). *Science as a Process: An Evolutionary Account of the Social and Conceptual Development of Science*. Chicago: University of Chicago Press.

Hull, David L. (1989a). *The Metaphysics of Evolution*. Albany, NY: State University of New York Press.

Hull, David L. (1989b). The ontological status of species as evolutionary units. In *The Metaphysics of Evolution*. Albany, NY: State University of New York Press, pp. 79–88.

Hull, David L. (1989c). Individuality and selection. In *The Metaphysics of Evolution*. Albany, NY: State University of New York Press, pp. 89–109.

Hull, David L., Rodney E. Langman, and Sigrid S. Glenn (2001). A general account of selection: Biology, immunology and behavior. *Behavioral and Brain Sciences* 24: 511–73.

Hume, David (1741). *Essays, Moral, Political, and Literary*. Indianapolis: Liberty Classics, 1987 edition.

Ingram, Paul, and Joel A. C. Baum (1997). Chain affiliation and the failure of Manhattan hotels, 1898–1980. *Administrative Science Quarterly* 42(1): 68–102.

Ingram, Paul, and Crist Inman (1996). Institutions, intergroup competition, and the evolution of hotel populations around Niagara Falls. *Administrative Science Quarterly* 41(4): 629–58.

Jarausch, Konrad Hugo (1990). *The Unfree Professions: German Lawyers, Teachers, and Engineers, 1900–1950.* New York: Oxford University Press.

John, Richard R. (1997). Elaborations, revisions, dissents: Alfred D. Chandler, Jr.'s "The Visible Hand" after twenty years. *Business History Review,* 71(Summer): 151–206.

Johnson, J. A. (1990). *The Kaiser's Chemists.* Chapel Hill, NC: University of North Carolina Press.

Johnson, Jeffrey A. (1985). Academic chemistry in imperial Germany. *Isis* 76: 500–24.

Johnson, Jeffrey A. (1992). Hofmann's role in reshaping the academic–industrial alliance in German chemistry. *Die Allianz von Wissenschaft und Industrie: August Wilhelm Hofmann (1818–1892).* Christoph Meinel and Hartmut Scholz, eds. Weinheim & New York: VCH Publishers.

Johnson, Jeffrey A. (1998). German women in chemistry, 1895–1925 (Part I). *International Journal of History and Ethics of Natural Sciences, Technology, and Medicine* 6: 1–21.

Jones, Geoffrey (1996). *The Evolution of International Business: An Introduction.* New York: Routledge.

Jones, Geoffrey (1997). Great Britain: Big business, management and competitiveness in twentieth-century Britain. In *Big Business and the Wealth of Nations.* Alfred Dupont Chandler, Franco Amatori, and Takashi Hikino, eds. New York: Cambridge University Press, pp. 102–38.

Jones, Geoffrey (2000). *Merchants to Multinationals: British Trading Companies in the Nineteenth and Twentieth Centuries.* New York: Oxford University Press.

Kauffman, Stuart (1995). *At Home in the Universe: The Search for Laws of Self-Organization and Complexity.* New York: Oxford University Press.

Kauffman, Stuart A. (1993). *The Origins of Order: Self-Organization and Selection in Evolution.* New York: Oxford University Press.

Kennedy, Paul M. (1980). *The Rise of the Anglo–German Antagonism, 1860–1914.* Atlantic Highlands, NJ: Ashfield Press.

Keynes, John Maynard (1933). *The Collected Writings of John Maynard Keynes (X): Essays in Biography.* London and New York: Macmillan and St. Martin's Press for Royal Economic Society, 1971 edition.

Kieser, Alfred (1989). Organizational, institutional, and societal evolution: Medieval craft guilds and the genesis of formal organizations. *Administrative Science Quarterly* 34(4): 540–64.

Kieser, Alfred (1994). Why organization theory needs historical analyses – and how this should be performed. *Organization Science* 5(4): 609–23.

Klepper, Steven (1996). Entry, exit, growth, and innovation over the product cycle. *American Economic Review* 86(3): 562–83.

Klepper, Steven (1997). Industry life cycles. *Industrial and Corporate Change* 6(1): 145–82.

Klepper, Steven (2001). Employee startups in high-tech industries. *Industrial and Corporate Change* 10(3): 639–74.

Klepper, Steven (2002). Firm survival and the evolution of oligopoly. *Rand Journal of Economics* 33(1): 37–61.

Klepper, Steven, and Elizabeth Graddy (1990). The evolution of new industries and the determinants of market structure. *Rand Journal of Economics* 21(1): 27–42.

Klepper, Steven, and Kenneth L. Simons (1996). Innovation and industry shakeouts. *Business & Economic History* 25(1): 81–9.

Klepper, Steven, and Kenneth L. Simons (1997). Technological extinctions of industrial firms: An inquiry into their nature and causes. *Industrial and Corporate Change* 1997(2): 379–460.

Klepper, Steven, and Kenneth L. Simons (2000a). Dominance by birthright: Entry of prior radio producers and competitive ramifications in the U.S. television receiver industry. *Strategic Management Journal* 21(10/11): 997–1016.

Klepper, Steven, and Kenneth L. Simons (2000b). The making of an oligopoly: Firm survival and technological change in the evolution of the U.S. tire industry. *Journal of Political Economy* 108(4): 728–60.

Klevorick, Alvin K., Richard C. Levin, Richard R. Nelson, and Sidney G. Winter (1995). On the sources and significance of interindustry differences in technological opportunities. *Research Policy* 24(2): 185–205.

Knaggs, Nelson S. (1956). Dyestuffs of the ancients. Republished in 1992 in *American Dyestuff Reporter* 75(11; Aniversary Jubiliee Issue): 109–11.

Kogut, Bruce, ed. (1993). *Country Competitiveness: Technology and the Organization of Work.* New York: Oxford University Press.

Kogut, Bruce, and Andrew Spicer (2002). Capital market development and mass privatization are logical contradictions: Lessons from Russia and the Czech Republic. *Industrial and Corporate Change* 11(1): 1–37.

Kogut, Bruce, and Udo Zander (1992). Knowledge of the firm, combinative capabilities, and the replication of technology. *Organization Science* 3: 383–97.

Kogut, Bruce, and Udo Zander (1996). What firms do? Coordination, identity and learning. *Organization Science* 7(5): 502–18.

Kogut, Bruce, and Udo Zander (2000). Did socialism fail to innovate? A natural experiment of the two Zeiss companies. *American Sociological Review* 65(2): 169–90.

Koza, Mitchell P., and Arie Y. Lewin (1998). The co-evolution of strategic alliances. *Organization Science* 9(3): 255–64.

Kraatz, Matt, and Edward Zajac (2001). How organizational resources affect strategic change and performance in turbulent environments: Theory and evidence. *Organization Science* 12: 632–57.

Krugman, Paul (1991). *Geography and Trade*. Cambridge, MA: MIT Press.

Krugman, Paul, and Maurice Obstfeld (1997). *International Economics: Theory and Policy*. New York: Harper Collins College Publishers.

Lamoreaux, Naomi R., Daniel M.G. Raff, and Peter Temin, eds. (1995). *Coordination and Information: Historical Perspectives on the Organization of Enterprise*. Chicago: University of Chicago Press.

Lamoreaux, Naomi R., Daniel M.G. Raff, and Peter Temin, eds. (1999). *Learning by Doing in Markets, Firms, and Countries*. Chicago: University of Chicago Press.

Lamoreaux, Naomi R., and Kenneth L. Sokoloff (2000). The geography of invention in the American glass industry, 1870–1925. *Journal of Economic History* 60(3): 700–29.

Lamoreaux, Naomi R., and Kenneth L. Sokoloff (2001). Market trade in patents and the rise of a class of specialized inventors in the 19th-century United States. *American Economic Review* 91(2): 39–44.

Landau, Ralph (1997). Education: Moving from chemistry to chemical engineering and beyond. *Chemical Engineering Progress* 93(January): 52–65.

Landes, David S. (1969). *The Unbound Prometheus: Technological Change and Industrial Development in Western Europe from 1750 to the Present*. New York: Cambridge University Press.

Landes, David S. (1998). *The Wealth and Poverty of Nations: Why Some Are So Rich and Some Are So Poor*. New York: W. W. Norton.

Langlois, Richard N. (1992). External economies and economic progress: The case of the microcomputer industry. *Business History Review* 66: 1–50.

Langlois, Richard N., and Paul L. Robertson (1995). *Firms, Markets, and Economic Change: A Dynamic Theory of Business Institutions*. New York: Routledge.

Langton, John (1984). The ecological theory of bureaucracy: The case of Josiah Wedgwood and the British pottery industry. *Administrative Science Quarterly* 29(3): 330–54.

Lazonick, William (1990). *Competitive Advantage on the Shop Floor*. Cambridge, MA: Harvard University Press.

Lazonick, William (1991). *Business Organization and the Myth of the Market Economy*. New York: Cambridge University Press.

Lazonick, William (1992). *Organization and Technology in Capitalist Development*. Brookfield, VT: Edward Elgar.

Lazonick, William (2002). Innovative enterprise and historical transformation. *Enterprise and Society* 3(1): 3–47.

Lazonick, William, and Mary O'Sullivan (1997a). Finance and industrial development. Part I: The United States and the United Kingdom. *Financial History Review* 4(1): 7–29.

Lazonick, William, and Mary O'Sullivan (1997b). Finance and industrial development: Evolution to market control. Part II: Japan and Germany. *Financial History Review* 4(2): 117–38.

Lepsius, B. (1918). Festschrift zur Feier des 50 Jährigen Bestehens der Deutschen Chemischen Gesellschaft und 100. Geburtstags ihres Begründers August Wilhelm von Hofmann. *Berichte der Deutschen Chemischen Gesellschaft* 51 (Sonderheft): 88–99.

Levin, Richard C., Alvin K. Klevorick, Richard R. Nelson, and Sidney G. Winter (1987). Appropriating the returns from industrial research and development. *Brookings Papers on Economic Activity* 3(Special Issue on Microeconomics): 783–820.

Levinstein, Ivan (1886). Observations and suggestions on the present position of the British chemical industry, with special reference to coal-tar derivatives. *Journal of the Society of Chemical Industry* 5: 351–9.

Levinthal, Dan, and J. Myatt (1995). Co-evolution of capabilities and industry: The evolution of mutual fund processing. *Strategic Management Journal* 15: 45–62.

Levinthal, Daniel A., and James G. March (1993). The myopia of learning. *Strategic Management Journal* 14(Special Issue): 95–112.

Lewin, Arie Y., Chris P. Long, and Timothy N. Carroll (1999). The coevolution of new organizational forms. *Organization Science* 10(5): 535–50.

Lewin, Arie Y., and Henk W. Volberda (1999). Prolegomena on coevolution: A framework for research on strategy and new organizational forms. *Organization Science* 10(5): 519–34.

Lewontin, Richard C. (1974). *The Genetic Basis of Evolutionary Change*. New York: Columbia University Press.

Liebenau, Jonathan (1988). Patents and the chemical industry: Tools of business strategy. In *The Challenge of New Technology: Innovation in British Business since 1850*. Jonathan Liebenau, ed. Brookfield, VT: Gower, pp. 135–50.

Liebowitz, Stanley J., and Stephen E. Margolis (1999). *Winners, Losers & Microsoft: Competition and Antitrust in High Technology*. Oakland, CA: Independent Institute.

Lipartito, Kenneth (1995). Culture and the practice of business history. *Business and Economic History* 24(2): 1–41.

Little, Arthur D. (1915). The dyestuffs situation and its lessons. *The Journal of Industrial and Engineering Chemistry* 7(3): 237–9.

Loasby, Brian J. (1998). The organisation of capabilities. *Journal of Economic Behavior and Organization* 35(2): 139–60.

Loasby, Brian J. (2001). Time, knowledge and evolutionary dynamics: Why connections matter. *Journal of Evolutionary Economics* 11(4): 393–412.

Locke, Robert R. (1984). *The End of Practical Man: Higher Education and the Institutionalization of Entrepreneurial Performance in Germany, France and Great Britain, 1880–1940*. Greenwich, CT: JAI Press.

Lumsden, Charles J., and Edward Osborne Wilson (1981). *Genes, Mind, and Culture: The Coevolutionary Process*. Cambridge, MA: Harvard University Press.

Lundgreen, Peter (1990). Engineering education in Europe and the U.S.A., 1750–1930: The rise to dominance of school culture and the engineering professions. *Annals of Science* 47: 33–75.

Machlup, Fritz (1958). *Economic Review of the Patent System*. Washington, DC: U.S. Government Printing Office.

Maddison, Angnus (1991). *Dynamic Forces in Capitalist Development*. New York: Oxford University Press.

Magee, Gary Bryan (1997). *Productivity and Performance in the Paper Industry: Labour, Capital, and Technology in Britain and America, 1860–1914*. New York: Cambridge University Press.

Maine, Henry Sumner (1861). *Ancient Law: Its Connection with the Early History of Society, and Its Relation to Modern Ideas*. London: J. Murray.

Malerba, Franco, Richard Nelson, Luigi Orsenigo, and Sidney Winter (1999). "History-friendly" models of industry evolution: The computer industry. *Industrial and Corporate Change* 8(1): 3–40.

Mandeville, Bernard (1715). *The Fable of the Bees, or, Private Vices, Publick Benefits*. Indianapolis: Liberty Classics, 1988 edition.

March, James G. (1994). The evolution of evolution. In *The Evolutionary Dynamics of Organizations*. Jitendra Singh and Joel Baum, eds. New York: Oxford University Press, pp. 39–49.

March, James G. (1999). *The Pursuit of Organizational Intelligence*. Walden, MA: Blackwell Business.

March, James G., Martin Schulz, and Hsüeh-kuang Chou (2000). *The Dynamics of Rules: Change in Written Organizational Codes*. Stanford, CA: Stanford University Press.

March, James G., and Herbert A. Simon (1958). *Organizations*. New York: Wiley.

Marsch, Ulrich (1994). Strategies for success: Research organization in German chemical companies and IG Farben until 1936. *History and Technology* 12: 23–77.

Marshall, Alfred (1890). *Principles of Economics*. Amherst, NY: Prometheus Books, 1997 edition.

Marshall, Alfred (1923). *Industry and Trade: A Study of Industrial Technique and Business Organization and of Their Influences on the Conditions of Various Classes and Nations*. London: Macmillan.

Marshall, Gloria J. (1995). The survival of colleges in America: A census of four-year colleges 1636–1973. Doctoral Dissertation in the School of Education, Stanford University, UMI Publication Number: 9535631.

Martius, Carl Alexander (1918). August Wilhelm Hofmann: Chemische Erinnerungen an die Berliner Vergangenheit. Berlin: Deutsche chemische Gesellschaft. 17p.

McAdam, Doug, John D. McCarthy, and Mayer N. Zald, eds. (1996). *Comparative Perspectives on Social Movements: Political Opportunities, Mobilizing Structures, and Cultural Framings*. New York: Cambridge University Press.

McCraw, Thomas K. (1997a). American capitalism. In *Creating Modern Capitalism: How Entrepreneurs, Companies, and Countries Triumphed in Three Industrial Revolutions*. Thomas K. McCraw, ed. Cambridge, MA: Harvard University Press, pp. 301–48.

McCraw, Thomas K., ed. (1997b). *Creating Modern Capitalism: How Entrepreneurs, Companies, and Countries Triumphed in Three Industrial Revolutions*. Cambridge, MA: Harvard University Press.

McGrath, Rita Gunther, Ian C. MacMillan, and S. Venkataraman (1995). Defining and developing competence: A strategic process paradigm. *Strategic Management Journal* 16: 251–75.

McKelvey, Bill (1997). Quasi-natural organization science. *Organization Science* 8(4): 352–80.

McKelvey, Bill (1999). Avoiding complexity catastrophe in coevolutionary pockets: Strategies for rugged landscapes. *Organization Science* 10(3): 294–321.

Meinel, Christoph (1988). Artibus Academicis Inserenda: Chemistry's place in eighteenth and early nineteenth century universities. *History of Universities* 8: 89–115.

Meinel, Christoph (1992). August Wilhelm Hofmann – "Regierender Oberchemiker." In *Die Allianz von Wissenschaft und Industrie: August Wilhelm Hofmann (1818–1892)*. Christoph Meinel and Hartmut Scholz, eds. Weinheim & New York: VCH Publishers, pp. 27–64.

Meinel, Christoph, and Hartmut Scholz, eds. (1992). *Die Allianz von Wissenschaft und Industrie: August Wilhelm Hofmann (1818–1892) [the Alliance of Science and Industry: August Wilhelm Hofmann (1818–1892)]*. Weinheim & New York: VCH Publishers.

Meldola, Raphael (1910). Tinctorial chemistry, ancient and modern. *Journal of the Society of Dyers and Colourists*: 103p. Republished in Gardner (1915, 259–68).

Menger, Carl (1871). *Principles of Economics*. New York: New York University Press, 1981 edition.

Merz, August (1944). Early American coal tar dye industry. *Chemical and Engineering News* 22(15): 1275–80.

Metcalfe, J. Stanley (1998). *Evolutionary Economics and Creative Destruction*. London & New York: Routledge.

Metcalfe, Stanley, and Michael Gibbons (1989). Technology, variety, and organization: A systematic perspective on the competitive process. *Research on Technological Innovations, Management and Policy* 59: 153–93.

Meyer, John W., and Brian Rowan (1977). Institutionalized organizations: Formal structure as myth and ceremony. *American Journal of Sociology* 83(September): 340–63.

Meyer-Thurow, Georg (1982). The industrialization of invention: A case study from the German chemical industry. *Isis* 73: 363–81.

Miall, Stephen (1931). *A History of the British Chemical Industry*. New York: Chemical Publishing Company.

Mitchell, Will, and Kulwant Singh (1996). Survival of businesses using collaborative relationships to commercialize complex goods. *Strategic Management Journal* 17(3): 169–95.

Mokyr, Joel (1990). *The Lever of Riches: Technological Creativity and Economic Progress*. New York: Oxford University Press.

Mokyr, Joel (1999). Science, technology, and knowledge: What historians can learn from an evolutionary approach. Working paper. Department of Economics. Northwestern University, Evanston, IL.

Mokyr, Joel (2002). *The Gifts of Athena: Historical Origins of the Knowledge Economy*. Princeton, NJ: Princeton University Press.

Moore, Tom Sidney, and James Charles Philip (1947). *The Chemical Society, 1841–1941: A Historical Review*. London: Chemical Society.

Morrell, J. B. (1972). The chemist breeders: The research schools of Liebig and Thomas Thomson. *Ambix* 19: 1–46.

Morrell, Jack (1993). W. H. Perkin, Jr., at Manchester and Oxford. *Osiris* 8(Second Series): 104–26.

Morris, Peter J. T., and Anthony S. Travis (1992). A history of the international dyestuff industry. *American Dyestuff Reporter* 81(11[75 Anniversary Jubilee Issue]): 59–100, 192–95.

Mowery, David C. (1984). Firm structure, government policy, and the organization of industrial research: Great Britain and the United States, 1900–1950. *Business History Review* 58(4): 504–31.

Mowery, David C. (1996). *The Interntional Computer Software Industry: A Comparative Study of Industry Evolution and Structure*. New York: Oxford University Press.

Mowery, David C., and Richard R. Nelson, eds. (1999). *Sources of Industrial Leadership: Studies of Seven Industries*. New York: Cambridge University Press.

Mühlfriedel, Wolfgang, Edith Hellmuth, and Walter Rolf (1996). *Carl Zeiss: Die Geschichte eines Unternehmens*. Weimer: Böhlau.

Müller, Max (1870). Review of August Schleicher's "Darwinism tested by the science of language"; translated from German by Alex. V. W. Bikkers. *Nature* Jan. 6: 256–9.

Munroe, Charles E., and Aida M. Doyle (1924). Washington's relation to the dye industry prior to 1914. *Industrial and Engineering Chemistry* 16(4): 417–9.

Murmann, Johann Peter, Howard Aldrich, Daniel Levinthal, and Sidney Winter (2003). Evolutionary thought in management and organization theory at the beginning of the new millennium: A symposium on the state of the art and opportunities for future research. *Journal of Management Inquiry* 12(1): 22–40.

Murmann, Johann Peter, and Ernst Homburg (2001). Comparing evolutionary dynamics across different national settings: The case of the synthetic dye industry, 1857–1914. *Journal of Evolutionary Economics* 11: 177–205.

Murmann, Johann Peter, and Ralph Landau (1998). On the making of competitive advantage: The development of the chemical industries in Britain and Germany since 1850. In *Chemicals and Long-Term Economic Growth: Insights from the Chemical Industry*. Ashish Arora, Ralph Landau, and Nathan Rosenberg, eds. New York: John Wiley & Sons, Inc., pp. 27–70.

Murmann, Johann Peter, and Michael L. Tushman (2001). From the technology cycle to the entrepreneurship dynamic: The social context of entrepreneurial innovation. In *The Entrepreneurial Dynamic: Origins of Entrepreneurship and Its Role in Industry Evolution*. Elaine Romanelli and Claudia Schoonhoven, eds. Palo Alto, CA: Stanford University Press, pp. 178–206.

Murtha, Thomas P., Jennifer W. Spencer, and Stephanie Ann Lenway (1996). Moving targets: National industrial strategies and embedded innovation in the global flat panel display industry. *Advances in Strategic Management* 13: 247–81.

Nadler, David, and Michael Tushman (1988). *Strategic Organization Design*. New York: Harper Collins.

Nadler, David, Michael Tushman, and Mark B. Nadler (1997). *Competing by Design: The Power of Organizational Architecture*. New York: Oxford University Press.

Nakagawa, Keiichir (1975). *Strategy and Structure of Big Business: Proceedings of the First Fuji Conference*. Tokyo: University of Tokyo Press.

Naumann, Bernd, Frans Plank, and Gottfried Hofbauer (1992). *Language and Earth: Effective Affinities between the Emerging Sciences of Linguistics and Geology*. Philadelphia: J. Benjamins.

Nelson, Richard R., ed. (1962). *The Rate and Direction of Inventive Activity: Economic and Social Factors*. NBER Special Conference Series. Princeton, NJ: Princeton University Press.

Nelson, Richard R. (1990). Capitalism as an engine of progress. *Research Policy* 19(3): 193–214.

Nelson, Richard R. (1991). Why do firms differ, and how does it matter? *Strategic Management Journal* 12: 61–74.

Nelson, Richard R. (1995a). Co-evolution of industry structure, technology and supporting institutions, and the making of comparative advantage. *International Journal of the Economics of Business* 2(2): 171–84.

Nelson, Richard R. (1995b). Recent evolutionary theorizing about economic change. *Journal of Economic Literature* 33(March): 48–90.

Nelson, Richard R. (1995c). Why should managers be thinking about technology policy? *Strategic Management Journal* 16: 581–8.

Nelson, Richard R. (1996a). The evolution of competitive or comparative advantage: A preliminary report on a study. *Industrial and Corporate Change* 5(2): 597–618.

Nelson, Richard R. (1996b). *The Sources of Economic Growth*. Cambridge, MA: Harvard University Press.

Nelson, Richard R., and Bhaven N. Sampat (2001). Making sense of institutions as a factor shaping economic performance. *Journal of Economic Behavior and Organization* 44(1): 31–54.

Nelson, Richard R., and Sidney G. Winter (1982). *An Evolutionary Theory of Economic Change*. Cambridge, MA: The Belknap Press of Harvard University Press.

Nelson, Richard R., and Gavin Wright (1994). The erosion of U.S. technological leadership as a factor in the postwar economic convergence. In *Convergence of Productivity: Cross-National Studies and Historical Evidence*. William J. Baumol, Richard R. Nelson, and Edward N. Wolff, eds. New York: Oxford University Press, pp. 129–63.

Nitecki, Matthew H., ed. (1983). *Coevolution*. Chicago: University of Chicago Press.

Noble, David F. (1977). *America by Design: Science, Technology, and the Rise of Corporate Capitalism*. New York: Alfred A. Knopf.

North, Douglass (1990). *Institutions, Institutional Change, and Economic Performance*. New York: Cambridge University Press.

Nye, Mary Jo (1993). National styles? French and English chemistry in the nineteenth and early twentieth century. *Osiris* 8(Second Series): 30–52.

Ocasio, William (1999). Institutionalized action and corporate governance: The reliance on rules of CEO succession. *Administrative Science Quarterly* 44(2): 384–416.

O'Sullivan, Mary (2000). *Contests for Corporate Control: Corporate Governance and Economic Performance in the United States and Germany*. New York: Oxford University Press.

Park, James, and John Shore (1999). Dye and fibre discoveries of the twentieth century. Part 1: From the magic of the electric light to the nightmare of world war. *Journal of the Society of Dyers and Colourists* 115(May–June): 157–67.

Parsons, Talcot (1966). *Societies: Evolutionary and Comparative Perspectives*. Englewood Cliffs, NJ: Prentice-Hall.

Paulsen, Friedrich (1906). *The German Universities and University Study*. New York: Charles Scribner's Sons.

Penrose, Edith T. (1951). *The Economics of the International Patent System*. Baltimore: Johns Hopkins University Press.

Penrose, Edith T. (1959). *The Theory of Growth of the Firm*. New York: John Wiley.

Perkin, W. H. (1868). The aniline or coal-tar colours (Cantor Lectures). *Journal of the Society of Arts*. Republished in Gardner (1915, 1–45).

Perkin, W. H. (1885). The colouring matters produced from coal-tar. *Journal of the Society for Chemical Industry*. Republished in Gardner (1915, pp. 75–105).

Perkin, W. H. (1896). The origins of the coal-tar color industry, and the contributions of Hofmann and his pupils (Hofmann Memorial Lecture). *Journal of the Chemical Society*. Republished in Gardner (1915, pp. 141–87).

Petroski, H. (1992). *The Evolution of Useful Things*. New York: Alfred Knopf.

Pfeffer, Jeffrey (1983). Organizational demography. *Research in Organizational Behavior* 5: 299–357.

Pfeffer, Jeffrey, and Gerald R. Salancik (1978). *The External Control of Organizations*. New York: Harper & Row.

Pfitzner, Johannes (1916). *Beiträge zur Lage der Chemischen, Insbesondere der Farbstoffindustrie in den Vereinigten Staaten von Amerika*. Jena: Gustav Fischer.

Playfair, Lyon (1868). Minutes of evidence. In *Select Committee on the Provisions for Giving Instruction in Theoretical and Applied Science to the Industrial Classes* vol. 1 Shannon: Irish University Press, pp. 101–12, 334–40.

Plumpe, Gottfried (1990). *Die I. G. Farbenindustrie AG: Wirtschaft, Technik und Politik 1904–1945 (I. G. Farbenindustrie AG: Economics, Technology, and Politics 1904–1945)*. Berlin: Duncker & Humblot.

Porter, Michael E. (1980). *Competitive Strategy*. New York: Free Press.

Porter, Michael E. (1990). *Competitive Advantage of Nations*. New York: Free Press.

Porter, Michael E. (1991). Towards a dynamic theory of strategy. *Strategic Management Journal* 12: 95–117.

Potts, Jason D. (2000). *The New Evolutionary Microeconomics: Complexity, Competence, and Adaptive Behaviour*. Northampton, MA: Edward Elgar.

Powell, Walter W., and Paul J. DiMaggio, eds. (1991). *The New Institutionalism in Organizational Analysis*. Chicago: University of Chicago Press.

Prochazka, George A. (1924). American dyestuffs: Reminiscently, autobiographically, and otherwise. *Industrial Engineering and Engineering Chemistry* 16(4): 413–17.

Ragin, Charles C. (1987). *The Comparative Method: Moving beyond Qualitative and Quantitative Strategies*. Berkeley, CA: University of California Press.

Ranger-Moore, James, Jane Banaszak-Holl, and Michael T. Hannan (1991). Density dependence in regulated industries: Founding rates of banks and life insurance companies. *Administrative Science Quarterly* 36: 36–65.

Rao, Hayagreeva, and Eric H. Neilsen (1992). An ecology of agency arrangements: Mortality of savings and loan associations, 1960–1987. *Administrative Science Quarterly* 37(3): 448–70.

Rao, Hayagreeva, and Jitendra V. Singh (1999). Types of variation in organizational populations: The speciation of new organizational forms. In *Variations in Organization Science: In Honor of Donald T. Campbell*. Joel A. C. Baum and Bill McKelvey, eds. Thousand Oaks, CA: SAGE Publications, pp. 63–78.

Rashdall, Hastings, Alfred Brotherston Emden, and Frederick Maurice Powicke (1936). *The Universities of Europe in the Middle Ages*. Oxford: The Clarendon Press of Oxford University Press.

Reader, W. J. (1970). *Imperial Chemical Industries: A History.* Vol. I. London: Oxford University Press.

Redlich, Fritz (1914). *Die volkwirtschaftliche Bedeutung der Deutschen Teerfarbenindustrie.* München–Leipzig: Duncker & Humblot.

Reichspatentamt (1927). *Das Reichspatentamt 1877–1927: Rückblick auf sein Werden und Wirken.* Berlin: Carl Sehmanns Verlag.

Reimer, Thomas M. (1996). Bayer & Company in the United States: German Dyes, Drugs, and Cartels in the Progressive Era. Doctoral Dissertation. Syracuse, NY: Syracuse University.

Reinhardt, Carsten (1997). *Forschung in der chemischen Industrie: Die Entwicklung synthetischer Farbstoffe bei BASF und Hoechst, 1863 bis 1914.* Freiberg: Technische Universität Bergakademie Freiberg.

Ricardo, David (1817). *The Principles of Political Economy and Taxation.* Republished in 1911; London: Everyman's Library.

Richardson, H. W. (1962). The development of the British dyestuffs industry before 1939. *Scottish Journal of Political Economy* 9(2): 110–29.

Roberts, Gerrylynn Kuszen (1992). Bridging the gap between science and practice: The English years of August Wilhelm Hofmann, 1845–1865. In *Die Allianz von Wissenschaft und Industrie: August Wilhelm Hofmann (1818–1892).* Christoph Meinel and Hartmut Scholz, eds. Weinheim & New York: VCH Publishers, pp. 89–99.

Rocke, Alan J. (1985). Hypothesis and experiment in the early development of Kekule's benzene theory. *Annals of Science* 42: 355–81.

Roggersdorf, Wilhelm (1965). *Im Reiche der Chemie: 100 Jahre BASF.* Düsseldorf: ECON-Verlag GmbH.

Rose, Mary B. (2000). *Firms, Networks, and Business Values: The British and American Cotton Industries since 1750.* New York: Cambridge University Press.

Rosenberg, Nathan (1982). *Inside the Black Box.* New York: Cambridge University Press.

Rosenberg, Nathan (1992). Economic experiments. *Industrial and Corporate Change* 1(1): 181–203.

Rosenberg, Nathan (1998). Technological change in chemicals: The role of the university–industry interface. In *Chemicals and Long-Term Economic Growth: Insights from the Chemical Industry.* Ashish Arora, Ralph Landau, and Nathan Rosenberg, eds. New York: John Wiley & Sons, Inc, pp. 193–230.

Rosenberg, Nathan, and Richard R. Nelson (1994). American universities and technical advance in industry. *Research Policy* 23(3): 323–48.

Rosenbloom, Richard S., and Clayton M. Christensen (1994). Technological discontinuities, organizational capabilities, and strategic commitments. *Industrial and Corporate Change* 3(3): 655–85.

Rossiter, Margaret W. (1975). *The Emergence of Agricultural Science: Justus Von Liebig and the Americans, 1840–1880.* New Haven, CT: Yale University Press.

Roy, William G. (1997). *Socializing Capital: The Rise of the Large Industrial Corporation in America.* Princeton, NJ: Princeton University Press.

Ruhlen, Merritt (1994). *The Origin of Language: Tracing the Evolution of the Mother Tongue.* New York: Wiley.

Russell, Colin A. (1992). August Wilhelm Hofmann – Cosmopolitan chemist. In *Die Allianz von Wissenschaft und Industrie: August Wilhelm Hofmann (1818–1892).* Christoph Meinel and Hartmut Scholz, eds. Weinheim & New York: VCH Publishers, pp. 65–75.

Samuels, M. L. (1972). *Linguistic Evolution.* Cambridge: Cambridge University Press.

Sanderson, Michael (1972). *The Universities and British Industry 1850–1970.* London: Routledge & Kegan Paul.

Saviotti, Paolo, and J. Stanley Metcalfe (1991). *Evolutionary Theories of Economic and Technical Change.* Reading, MA: Academic Publishers.

Scheinert, Wolfgang (1988). Joseph Wilhelm Weiler, Julius Weiler und das Anilin: Zur Entwicklungsgeschichte der deutschen Teerfarbenindustrie und der chemischen Technik vor dem ersten Weltkrieg. *Zeitschrift für Unternehmensgeschichte* 33: 217–31.

Schelling, Thomas C. (1978). *Micromotives and Macrobehavior.* New York: Norton.

Scherer, Federic M. (1996). *Industry Structure, Strategy, and Public Policy.* New York: HarperCollins College Publishers.

Schleicher, August (1850). *Die Sprachen Europas in systematischer Übersicht: Linguistische Untersuchungen.* Philadelphia: John Benjamins Publishing Co., 1983 edition.

Schmeiser, Martin (1994). *Akademischer Harsard: Das Berufsschicksal des Professors und das Schicksal der deutschen Universität 1870–1920.* Stuttgart: Klett-Cotta.

Schmookler, J. (1965). Catastrophe and utilitarianism in the development of science. In *Economics of Research and Development*. Richard A. Tybout, ed. Columbus, OH: Ohio State University, pp. 19–33.

Schnabel, Franz (1934). *Deutsche Geschichte im Neunzehnten Jahrhundert: Erfahrungswissenschaften und Technik*. Freiburg im Breisgau: Herder.

Schnabel, Franz (1937). *Deutsche Geschichte im Neunzehnten Jahrhundert: Die Grundlagen*. Freiburg im Breisgau: Herder.

Scholz, Hartmut (1992). Reform der Chemikerausbildung. In *Die Allianz von Wissenschaft und Industrie: August Wilhelm Hofmann (1818–1892)*. Christoph Meinel and Hartmut Scholz, eds. Weinheim & New York: VCH Publishers, pp. 221–33.

Schröter, Hans (1991). *Friedrich Engelhorn*. Landau/Pfalz: Pfälzische Verlagsanstalt.

Schumpeter, Joseph (1934). *The Theory of Economic Development*. Cambridge, MA: Harvard University Press.

Schumpeter, Joseph A. (1942). *Capitalism, Socialism and Democracy*. New York: Harper & Row, 1950 edition.

Schumpeter, Joseph Alois, and Elizabeth Boody Schumpeter (1954). *History of Economic Analysis*. New York: Oxford University Press, 1986 edition.

Scott, W. Richard (1995). *Institutions and Organizations*. Thousand Oaks, CA: SAGE Publications.

Seefelder, Matthias (1994). *Indigo in Culture, Science and Technology*. Landsberg, Germany: Ecomed.

Servos, John W. (1980). The industrial relations of science: Chemical engineering at MIT, 1900–1939. *Isis* 71: 531–49.

Simon, Herbert A. (1981). *The Sciences of the Artificial*. Cambridge, MA: MIT Press.

Simpson, Renate (1983). *How the PhD Came to Britain: A Century of Struggle for Postgraduate Education*. Guildford, Surrey: Society for Research into Higher Education.

Skocpol, Theda (1984). *Vision and Method in Historical Sociology*. New York: Cambridge University Press.

Skolnik, Herman, and Kenneth M. Reese, eds. (1976). *A Century of Chemistry: The Role of Chemists and the American Chemical Society*. Washington, DC: American Chemical Society.

Smith, Adam (1761). *The Theory of Moral Sentiments*. London: Printed for A. Millar, A. Kincaid, and J. Bell in Edinburgh.

Smith, Adam (1776). *The Wealth of Nations*. New York: Random House, 1937 edition.

Sober, Elliott (1984). *The Nature of Selection: Evolutionary Theory in Philosophical Focus*. Cambridge, MA: MIT Press.

Sober, Elliott, and David Sloan Wilson (1998). *Unto Others: The Evolution and Psychology of Unselfish Behavior*. Cambridge, MA: Harvard University Press.

Society of Dyers and Colorists and American Association of Textile Chemists and Colorists. *Color Index* (1971–1996). Bradford, U.K.

Steen, Kathryn (1995). Wartime Catalyst and Postwar Reaction: The Making of the U.S. Synthetic Organic Chemicals Industry, 1910–1930. Doctoral dissertation, University of Delaware.

Stern, Fritz (1977). *Gold and Iron: Bismarck, Bleichröder and the Building of the German Empire*. New York: Alfred A. Knopf.

Stern, Fritz (1987). Americans and the German past: A century of American scholarship. In *Dreams and Delusions: National Socialism in the Drama of the German Past*. New York: Vintage Books, pp. 243–73.

Stigler, George (1963). *The Organization of Industry*. Chicago: University of Chicago Press.

Stiglitz, Joseph E. (2002). *Globalization and Its Discontents*. New York: W. W. Norton.

Stinchcombe, Arthur (2000). Review of *Organizations Evolving* by Howard Aldrich. *Evolutionary Theories in the Social Scienes*. www.etss.net (January 14): http://etss.net/reviews/organizations_evolving_stinch.htm.

Stinchcombe, Arthur L. (1965). Social structure and organizations. In *Handbook of Organizations*. James G. March, ed. Chicago: Rand McNally, pp. 142–93.

Stinchcombe, Arthur L. (1968). *Constructing Social Theories*. Chicago: University of Chicago Press.

Storper, Michael (1996). Innovations as collective action: Conventions, products, and technologies. *Industrial and Corporate Change* 5(2): 761–90.

Taylor, Frederick W. (1903). Shop management. In *Scientific Management*. Frederick W. Taylor. London: Harper and Row, 1964 edition.

Teece, David J. (1986). Profiting from technological innovation: Implications for integration, collaboration, licensing and public policy. *Research Policy* 15: 285–305.

Teece, David J., and Gary Pisano (1994). The dynamic capabilities of firms: An introduction. *Industrial and Corporate Change* 3(3): 537–56.

Teece, David J., Gary Pisano, and Amy Shuen (1997). Dynamic capabilities and strategic management. *Strategic Management Journal* 18(7): 509–33.

Teece, David J., Richard Rumelt, Giovanni Dosi, and Sidney Winter (1994). Understanding corporate coherence: Theory and evidence. *Journal of Economic Behavior and Organization* 23: 1–30.

Temin, Peter, ed. (1991). *Inside the Business Enterprise: Historical Perspectives on the Use of Information.* Chicago: University of Chicago Press.

Teubner, Gunther (2002). Idiosyncratic production regimes: Co-evolution of economic and legal institutions in the varieties of capitalism. In *The Evolution of Cultural Entities.* Michael Wheeler, John Ziman, and Margaret A. Boden, eds. New York: Oxford University Press, pp. 161–81.

Thackray, Arnold, Jeffrey L. Sturchio, P. Thomas Carroll, and Robert F. Bud (1985). *Chemistry in Amerika, 1876–1976.* Dordrecht: Reidel.

Thelen, Kathleen (1999). Historical institutionalism in comprative politics. *Annual Review of Political Science* 2: 369–404.

Thissen, F. (1922). Die Stellung der deutschen Teerfarbenindustrie in der Weltwirtschaft (Vor, in, und nach dem Kriege), Doctoral Dissertation, University of Giessen.

Thomas, L. G. (2001). *The Japanese Pharmaceutical Industry: The New Drug Lag and the Failure of Industrial Policy.* Cheltenham, U.K.: Edward Elgar.

Thompson, E. P. (1963). *The Making of the English Working Class.* New York: Vintage Books.

Thompson, James D. (1967). *Organizations in Action.* New York: McGraw-Hill Publishing Co.

Thompson, John N. (1994). *The Coevolutionary Process.* Chicago: University of Chicago Press.

Thomson, Ross, and Richard R. Nelson (1997). The internationalization of technology, 1874–1929: Evidence from the U.S., British and German patent experience. Working Paper. Department of Economics, University of Vermont.

Tilly, Charles (1978). *From Mobilization to Revolution.* Reading, MA: Addison-Wesley.

Tilly, Charles (1995). *Popular Contention in Great Britain, 1758–1834.* Cambridge, MA: Harvard University Press.

Tilly, Charles (1997). *Roads from Past to Future (with a Review Essay by Arthur Stinchcombe).* Lanham, Maryland, Rowman & Littlefield.

Tilly, Charles (1998). *Durable Inequality.* Berkeley, CA: University of California Press.

Titze, H. (1987). *Das Hochschulstudium in Preussen und Deutschland 1820–1944 (Higher Education in Prussia and Germany 1820–1944).* Goettingen: Vandenhoek & Ruprecht.

Tocqueville, Alexis de (1898). *Democracy in America.* New York, Century Company.

Travis, A. S. (1992). Colour makers and consumers: Heinrich Caro's British network. *Journal of the Society of Dyers and Colourists* 108(July/August): 311–16.

Travis, Anthony S. (1993). *The Rainbow Makers: The Origins of the Synthetic Dyestuffs Industry in Western Europe.* Bethlehem, PA: Lehigh University Press.

Turner, R. Steven (1989). Commentary: Science in Germany. In "Science in Germany: The Intersection of Institutional and Intellectual Issues," Kathryn M. Olesko, ed. *Osiris* (Second Series) 5: 296–304.

Tushman, Michael, and Philip Anderson (1997). *Managing Strategic Innovation and Change: A Collection of Readings.* New York: Oxford University Press.

Tushman, Michael, and Charles A. O'Reilly (1997). *Winning through Innovation: A Practical Guide to Leading Organizational Change and Renewal.* Boston, MA: Harvard Business School Press.

Tushman, Michael L., and Philip Anderson (1986). Technological discontinuities and organizational environments. *Administrative Science Quarterly* 31: 439–65.

Tushman, Michael L., and Johann Peter Murmann (1998). Dominant designs, technology cycles and organizational outcomes. *Research in Organizational Behavior* 20: 231–66.

Tushman, Michael L., and Elaine Romanelli (1985). Organizational evolution: A metamorphosis model of convergence and reorientation. *Research in Organizational Behavior* 7: 171–222.

Tushman, Michael L., and Lori Rosenkopf (1992). On the organizational determinants of technological change: Towards a sociology of technological evolution. *Research in Organizational Behavior.* B. Staw and L. Cummings, eds. Greenwich, CT, JAI Press, pp. 311–347.

Ungewitter, C. (1927). *Ausgewählte Kapitel aus der chemisch–industriellen Wirtschaftspolitik, 1877–1917.* Berlin: Verein zur Wahrung der Interessen der Chemischen Industrie Deutschlands e. V.

Usher, Abbott P. (1954). *History of Mechanical Invention.* Cambridge, MA: Harvard University Press.

Utterback, James M. (1994). *Mastering the Dynamics of Innovation: How Companies Can Seize Opportunities in the Face of Technological Change.* Boston: Harvard Business School Press.

Uzzi, Brian (1997). Social structure and competition in interfirm networks: The paradox of embeddedness. *Administrative Science Quarterly* 42(1): 35–67.

van den Belt, H., B. Gremmen, E. Homburg, and W. Hornix (1984). *De Ontwikkeling van de Kleurstofindustrie (The Development of the Synthetic Dye Industry)*. Nijmegen, The Netherlands: Faculteit der Wiskunde en Naturwetenschappen, University of Nijmegen (final report of research project).

van den Belt, Henk, and Arie Rip (1987). The Nelson–Winter–Dosi model and synthetic dye chemistry. In *The Social Construction of Technological Systems: New Directions in the Sociology and History of Technology.* Wiebe E. Bijker, Thomas P. Hughes, and Trevor Pinch, eds. Cambridge, MA: MIT Press, pp. 135–58.

Van De Ven, Andrew, and David N. Grazman (1999). Evolution in a nested hierarchy: A genealogy of Twin Cities health care organizations, 1853–1995. In *Variations in Organization Science: In Honor of Donald T. Campbell.* Joel A. C. Baum and Bill McKelvey, eds. Thousand Oaks, CA: Sage Publications, pp. 185–209.

Vaupel, Elisabeth Christine (1992). Chemie auf den Weltausstellungen. In *Die Allianz von Wissenschaft und Industrie: August Wilhelm Hofmann (1818–1892).* Christoph Meinel and Hartmut Scholz, eds. Weinheim & New York: VCH Publishers, pp. 183–209.

Veblen, Thorstein (1899). *The Theory of the Leisure Class: An Economic Study in the Evolution of Institutions.* New York: MacMillan.

Veblen, Thorstein (1915). *Imperial Germany and the Industrial Revolution.* New Brunswick, NJ: Transaction Publishers, 1990 edition.

Verg, Erik, Gottfried Plumpe, and Heinz Schultheis (1988). *Meilensteine: 125 Jahre Bayer, 1863–1988.* Leverkusen: Bayer AG.

Vincenti, Walter (1990). *What Engineers Know and How They Know It.* Baltimore: Johns Hopkins University Press.

Vincenti, Walter G. (1991). The scope for social impact in engineering outcomes: A diagrammatic aid to analysis. *Social Studies of Science* 21: 761–7.

von Savigny, Friedrich Karl (1831). *Of the Vocation of Our Age for Legislation and Jurisprudence, Translated from the German of Frederick Charles von Savigny by Abraham Hayward.* London: Littlewood & Co.

Vrba, Elisabeth, and Niles Eldredge (1984). Individuals, hierarchies, and processes: Towards a more complete evolutionary theory. *Paleobiology* 10: 146–71.

Vromen, Jack J. (1995). *Economic Evolution: An Enquiry into the Foundations of New Institutional Economics.* London and New York: Routledge.

Wade, James (1995). Dynamics of organizational communities and technological bandwagons: An empirical investigation of community evolution in the microprocessor market. *Strategic Management Journal* 16: 113–33.

Webb, R. K. (1980). *Modern England: From the Eighteenth Century to the Present.* New York: Harper Collins Publishers.

Weick, Karl E. (1979). *The Social Psychology of Organizing.* Reading, MA: Addison-Wesley Publishing Co.

Wernerfeld, Birger (1984). A resource-based view of the firm. *Strategic Management Journal* 5: 171–80.

Wertheimer, Herbert F. (1912). The German patent system. *Journal of Industrial and Engineering Chemistry* 4(June): 464–5.

Wetzel, Walter (1991). *Naturwissenschaften und chemische Industrie in Deutschland: Voraussetzungen und Mechanism ihres Aufstiegs im 19. Jahrhundert (Science and Chemical Industry in Germany: Conditions and Mechanisms of Its Rise in the 19th Century).* Stuttgart: F. Steiner.

Whittaker, C. M. (1956). Some early stages in the renaissance of the British dyemaking industry 1899–1920. *Journal of the Society of Dyers and Colourists* 73: 560–1.

Wilcox, David N. (1966). Kekulé and the dye industry. In *Kekulé Centennial.* O. Theodor Benfey, ed. Washington, DC: American Chemical Society, pp. 24–71.

Wilkins, Mira (1970). *The Emergence of Multinational Enterprise: American Business Abroad from the Colonial Era to 1914.* Cambridge, MA: Harvard University Press.

Wilkins, Mira (1974). *The Maturing of Multinational Enterprise: American Business Abroad from 1914 to 1970.* Cambridge, MA: Harvard University Press.

Wilkins, Mira (1989). *The History of Foreign Investment in the United States to 1914.* Cambridge, MA: Harvard University Press.

Wilkins, Mira, and Harm G. Schröter (1998). *The Free-Standing Company in the World Economy, 1830–1996.* New York: Oxford University Press.

Williamson, Oliver E. (2000). The new institutional economics: Taking stock, looking ahead. *Journal of Economic Literature* 38(3): 595–613.

Winter, Sidney (1995). Four Rs of profitability: Rents, resources, routines and replication. In *Resource-Based and Evolutionary Theories of the Firm: Towards a Synthesis*. Cynthia A. Montgomery, ed. Boston: Kluwer Academic Publishers, pp. 147–78.

Winter, Sidney, and Gabriel Szulanski (2001). Replication as strategy. *Organization Science* 12(6): 730–43.

Winter, Sidney G. (1990). Survival, selection, and inheritance in evolutionary theories of organization. In *Organizational Evolution: New Directions*. Jintendra V. Singh, ed. Newbury Park, CA: SAGE Publications, pp. 269–97.

Witt, Otto N. (1876). Zur Kenntniss des Baues und der Bildung färbender Kohlenstoffverbindungen. *Berichte der deutschen chemischen Gesellschaft* 9: 324ff.

Witt, Otto N. (1894). *Die Chemische Industrie auf der Columbischen Weltaustellung zu Chicago und in den Vereinigten Staaten von Nord-Amerika im Jahre 1893*. Berlin: R. Gaertner's Verlagsbuchhandlung, Hermann Heyfelder.

Witt, Ulrich (1992). *Evolutionary Economics*. London: Edgar Elgar.

Witt, Ulrich (1998). Imagination and leadership: The neglected dimension of an evolutionary theory of the firm. *Journal of Economic Behavior and Organization* 35(2): 161–77.

Witt, Ulrich (2000). Changing cognitive frames – Changing organizational forms: An entrepreneurial theory of organizational development. *Industrial and Corporate Change* 9(4): 733–55.

Woodruff, David (1992). Where employees are management: Commitment equals empowerment at Saturn. *Business Week* (August 17): 66.

Wright, Sewall (1931). Evolution in Mendelian populations. *Genetics* 16: 97–159.

Wright, Sewall (1932). The roles of mutation, inbreeding, crossbreeding and selection in evolution. *Proceedings of the Sixth International Congress on Genetics* 16: 356–66.

Wrigley, Julia (1987). Technical education and industry in the nineteenth century. In *The Decline of the British Economy*. Oxford: Clarendon Press, pp. 162–88.

Yates, JoAnne (1993). Co-evolution of information processing technology and use: Interaction between the life insurance and tabulating industries. *Business History Review* 67(1): 1–51.

Young, A. (1928). Increasing returns and economic progress. *Economic Journal* 38(152): 527–42.

Zander, Udo, and Bruce Kogut (1995). Knowledge and the speed of the transfer and imitation of organizational capabilities: An empirical test. *Organization Science* 6(1): 1–17.

Ziman, John M. (1999). The marriage of design and selection in the evolution of cultural artefacts. *Interdisciplinary Science Review* 24(2): 139–54.

Ziman, John M., ed. (2000). *Technological Innovation as an Evolutionary Process*. Cambridge: Cambridge University Press.

Zimmermann, Paul A. (1965). *Patentwesen in der Chemie: Ursprünge, Anfänge, Entwicklung (Patents in Chemistry: Origins, Beginnings, Development)*. Ludwigshafen: BASF AG.

Zukin, Sharon, and Paul DiMaggio (1990). *Structures of Capital: The Social Organization of the Economy*. New York: Cambridge University Press.

Index

Note: Page numbers in italics point to figures or tables.

competitive implications of, 89–92
German
  British and American versus, 87–8
  dye-industry-relevant, 89, 181
  entities protected by, 133
  inception of, 179–83
  industry's role in amending, 185
individuals among, 20
industry influences on
  British, 185–92
  German, 179–85
populations of, 20
working clauses, 88, 187–91
patents
  as success co-factor, 86
  criteria for award of, 88
  fuchsine, litigation over, 117–18, 119
  German requirements for, 87
  judicial bodies over, 87
  litigation over, 90
  movement to eliminate, 180n.216
  number reaching term, 85–6
  ownership by country, 38–41
  protection of
    British, 29
    effectiveness of, 85
    German, 29
    timing of, 29
Paulsen, Friedrich, 58n.58
Perkin & Sons
  alizarin production, 127
  beginning of, 32
  ingredient acquisition by, 106–7
  marketing by, 109–10, 114–15, 129
  mauve licensing, 119
  mauve patent and, 117
  sale to BS&S, 127–8
Perkin, Dix, 101
Perkin, William Henry
  alizarin production and, 127
  BASF and, 250–1
  choice to leave industry, 218–19
  marketing by, 109–10, 114–15, 129
  on start in industry, 94–5
  pioneering work, 2
  reputation, 35
  retirement, 103n.119, 127
Playfair, Lyon, 56
price-fixing, 161
printing techniques, 243
professional organizations, 63–5
public policy, 16

'raw capabilities,' 7, 198, 219
Read Holliday
  chemist compensation, 153n.185

expansion abroad, 36, 115
  market share, 42
  number of dyes produced, 140
  success strategy of, 120
red azo dye, 132
replicators, 11, 14
Reports of the German Chemical Society,
    67
research, 115–17, 131–3, 150–2
Roccelline, 135–6
Roscoe, Henry E., 57n.55, 173–4, 175
routines, 14, 15–16, 233–5
Royal College of Chemistry, 54–5, 62, 173
Rudolf Knosp, 114
Rumpf, Carl
  business sense of, 98, 126
  career, 130, 155n.188
  initiative of, 123, 131, 163

sales agents, 128–9
Sampat, Bhaven N., 219n.268
Schoellkopf Aniline & Chemical Company
  acid production by, 141
  Bayer, relationship with, 159n.192
  black convention and, 161
  black dyes from, 141
  chemist recruitment, 152
  intermediates acquisition by, 141
  market share, 42–3
  overview of, 103–4
  patenting by, 159
  U.S. market entry, 120
  workforce, 146
Schoellkopf, Jacob. F., 121, 123
schools. *See* universities and colleges
Schuman, Frank, 125
Schumpeter, Joseph A., 1, 238
selection, 11–14
silk consumption, 104
Simpson, Maule, & Nicholson
  licenses obtained by, 117
  litigation over fuchsine, 117–18, 119
  nitrobenzene and, 107
  productions techniques and, 108, 109
  status of, 103
SM&N. *See* Simpson, Maule, & Nicholson
smuggling fuchsine, 118
social Darwinism, 9
social environments, 4–5
societies, 224
Society of Chemical Industry, 57, 65, 66
Society of Dyers and Colourists, 66
Stinchcombe, Arthur, 16n.19
strategic trade theory, 197
sulfuric acid plants, 141
synthetic dye industry. *See* dye industry